Modeling Dyadic and Interdependent Data in the Developmental and Behavioral Sciences

Modeling Dyadic and Interdependent Data in the Developmental and Behavioral Sciences

edited by

Noel A. Card
Universiy of Arizona

James P. Selig
Universiy of Kansas

Todd D. Little
Universiy of Kansas

Routledge
Taylor & Francis Group
New York   London

Cover design by Kathryn Houghtaling

Cover graphics by Donald A. Gay and Todd D. Little

The final camera copy for this book was prepared by the author and therefore the publisher takes no responsibility for consistency or correctness of typographical style.

Routledge
Taylor & Francis Group
270 Madison Avenue
New York, NY 10016

Routledge
Taylor & Francis Group
2 Park Square
Milton Park, Abingdon
Oxon OX14 4RN

© 2008 by Taylor & Francis Group, LLC
Routledge is an imprint of Taylor & Francis Group, an Informa business

Printed in the United States of America on acid-free paper
10 9 8 7 6 5 4 3 2 1

International Standard Book Number-13: 978-0-8058-5973-7 (Softcover) 978-0-8058-5972-0 (Hardcover)

Library of Congress Cataloging-in-Publication Data

Modeling dyadic and interdependent data in the developmental and behavioral sciences / edited by Noel A. Card, James P. Selig, Todd D. Little.
    p. cm.
Includes indexes.
ISBN 978-0-8058-5973-7 (softcover) -- ISBN 978-0-8058-5972-0 (hardcover)
    1. Psychology--Research--Methodology. 2. Interpersonal relations. I. Card, Noel A. II. Selig, James P. III. Little, Todd D.

BF39.M595 2008
150.72--dc22   2008013699

Visit the Taylor & Francis Web site at
http://www.taylorandfrancis.com

and the Psychology Press Web site at
http://www.psypress.com

Contents

Preface

Children and adolescents develop within a context largely defined by interpersonal relationships with others. These relationships include those with parents, siblings, peers, and other family members. Many of these relationships can be characterized as friendships, antipathies, and cliques involving dyads, triads, and larger group associations. Unfortunately, using analytic techniques that appropriately model such dyadic and group interdependencies has not yet taken root in developmental research. Similarly, recent quantitative efforts to develop models for interdependent data have rarely considered the unique challenges of developmental research designs (e.g., use of longitudinal data).

We believe that both developmental and quantitative researchers can benefit from dialogue across these two disciplines. To prompt such dialogue, we received funds from the National Science Foundation and the Society of Multivariate Experimental Psychology to hold a conference at the University of Kansas, attended by the authors of chapters in this book. We selected both developmental and quantitative researchers to come together to discuss the unique opportunities and challenges of modeling interdependent developmental data. The first goal of this book is to share the product of that discussion. As we hope you agree, this dialogue between developmental and quantitative experts has resulted in substantial advances for each discipline and in identifying much common interests, both of which are represented in the chapters of this book.

The second goal of this book is to describe techniques for analyzing interdependent developmental data. The chapters of this book provide clear descriptions of various techniques for analyzing data from dyads and small groups, including the actor-partner interdependence model, the mutual influence model, dyadic models of co-occurring change, triadic models, the social relations model, and various aspects of social network analysis. The analytic approaches being developed in these areas involve many topics of active quantitative research, making it difficult for most of us to keep abreast of current best practices. We are pleased that many of the originators and most active innovators of these techniques have provided clear and comprehensive descriptions of the methods, opportunities, and limitations of these techniques in the chapters that follow.

The third goal is to demonstrate the substantive opportunities of sophisticated techniques of interdependent data analysis. In other words, we did not want to only describe the various techniques of analyzing interdependent data; instead, we challenged the authors to lead by example, and to show the unique developmental questions that can be answered using these techniques. The content focus of these chapters is broad, including both family and peer relations, as well as topics involving adult romantic relationships, individuals initially meeting, and ecological models. This breadth is intentional, with the hopeful result that researchers will see opportunities for applying these models to answer a broad range of questions.

Although we hope this book goes far in advancing techniques of modeling interdependent developmental data, we do not view this book as the final word. As such, our fourth and final goal of this book is to prompt future work by developmental and quantitative researchers to extend what is presented here. Although the authors have clearly described the analytic approaches and how they can be applied in developmental research, we believe that the true value of this book will be in prompting further advancement and applications of these techniques.

Given these goals, we believe that this book will be of interest to both individuals engaged in developmental (e.g., developmental psychologists and child developmentalists from other disciplines) and quantitative (e.g., quantitative psychologists) research. We believe that clinical psychologists, family studies researchers, social psychologists, sociologists, and educational researchers also will find this book valuable. Given the didactic coverage of sophisticated techniques, we believe that this book is appropriate to individuals at various stages of their careers; advanced undergraduate and graduate students will find the book accessible, and more seasoned researchers should find applications within their ongoing research.

A project such as the conference and this resulting book is certainly not due to our efforts alone, and we wish to acknowledge those who have been most helpful in this project. First, we are deeply grateful to the authors who attended the conference and contributed to this book. We have asked them to write about difficult topics, and they have responded by providing insightful and innovative chapters. Second, we wish to thank the reviewers of this book, Daniel Bauer (University of North Carolina at Chapel Hill) and Theresa A. Thorkildsen (University of Illinois at Chicago). Third, we are indebted to Debra Riegert, Rebecca Larson, Kurt Roediger and the helpful staff at Lawrence Erlbaum Associates, Routledge, and Taylor & Francis Group for their help in publishing this book. Fourth, we are grateful to Donald Gay for his tireless and conscientious efforts in preparing the camera-ready copies and creating the cover design. Fifth, we are extremely grateful for the financial support for this project provided by the National Science Foundation and by the Society for Multivariate Experimental Psychology. Finally, we want to thank you, the readers, in advance for applying and extending these models in your own research.

—Noel A. Card
Tucson, Arizona

—James P. Selig
Lawrence, Kansas

—Todd D. Little
Lawrence, Kansas

CHAPTER ONE

Modeling Dyadic and Interdependent Data in Developmental Research: An Introduction

Noel A. Card

University of Arizona

Todd D. Little
James P. Selig

University of Kansas

Relationships with others play a critical role in child and adolescent development. Unfortunately, the use of analytic techniques that appropriately model dyadic and group interdependencies has not yet taken root in developmental research. Whereas we view these interdependencies as valuable information and an important focus for research, most researchers, unfortunately, often ignore or attempt to avoid interdependencies in their data. In our introduction to this volume, we emphasize the importance of interdependence in developmental science, highlight the need for specific analytic approaches for modeling interdependent data, and present the goals of this book.

Interdependence in Developmental Science

Psychology and many related fields have traditionally focused on individual differences. This focus has been useful in various ways, such as in helping to understand why some children are aggressive whereas others are not, why some adolescents are popular whereas others are unpopular, and why some adults exhibit certain personality traits whereas others exhibit quite different traits. Recently, however, there has been a shift in thinking beyond the individual to considering the relationship contexts in which much

1

of human behavior occurs. For example, personality theorists (e.g., Cervone, 2004; Mischel & Shoda, 1995) have argued for moving away from the view of personality as a global set of qualities to viewing personality as a pattern of behaviors in different contexts, including different relationship contexts. Similarly, research on childhood aggression—traditionally considered in terms of individual differences in the amount of aggression enacted—can be better understood as a dyadic relationship between aggressors and victims (Card & Hodges, 2006; Pierce & Cohen, 1995). Even sexual orientation, which has long been considered as a quality of an individual, has been shown to exhibit fluidity across romantic relationships during emerging adulthood (Diamond, 2003).

Although consideration of the role of relationships in many fields is quite recent, developmental science can be applauded for its long-standing recognition of the interdependent nature of child and adolescent development. We know, for example, that development within the family context is a product of overall family environment, parent–child relationships, and sibling relationships. With age, children increasingly interact with peers. As a result, sociometric position, group norms for various behaviors, and dyadic relationships (both friendship and antipathetic) all have substantial influences on development. In short, developmental researchers have long recognized the importance of relationships, within both the family and the peer group, for understanding developmental processes.

To illustrate this research activity, we performed a search of select descriptors of works indexed in PsycINFO. Although such a search is far from complete, we used the number of records in each year to provide a rough index of research activity on several topics in child and adolescent development. As shown in Figure 1.1, there has been an increasing amount of research on family relations, parent–child relationships, peer relations, friendships, and sibling relationships. It can also be seen that parent–child relationships and peer relations are highly active foci of research, with current rates between 300 and 800 reports per year. Studies on family relations, sibling relationships, and friendships are less common, but still represent active areas of research with approximately 50 to 150 reports published per year.

Although these topics represent only some of the relevant areas of study, these findings indicate the widespread—and increasing—interest of developmental researchers in aspects of development that are inherently interdependent in nature. In both the home and peer context, researchers have considered both group- and dyadic-level interdependencies. Specifically, various aspects of family systems (e.g., family conflict, negativity, support) can be analyzed in terms of interdependencies among different members of the family group (e.g., which family members are supportive of which other family

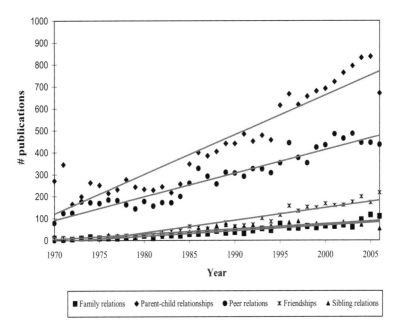

Figure 1.1. Research activity on some aspects of interdependence in child and adolescent development.

members). Consideration of the family context at the level of the dyad leads to consideration of marital, parent–child, and sibling relationships (as well as a range of other relationships, such as with extended family members). Similarly, the peer context can be considered at both the group (e.g., popularity and rejection, classroom norms) and dyadic (e.g., friendships, antipathetic relationships, romantic relationships) levels. Clearly, in both the family and peer context, when the level of analysis is either the group or the dyad, the interdependencies that exist among individuals provide valuable information and are thus important foci for research.

The Need for Analytic Approaches to Studying Interdependence

We have seen that developmental science has, as a field, long recognized the interdependent nature of child and adolescent development. Recognition of this importance has not, however, been matched by use of appropriate strategies for modeling these interdependencies. Traditionally, developmental science has relied on statistical techniques that assume independence of observations. If a researcher is studying individual characteristics of the child and samples a random group of children, then the use of traditional methods of analysis is perfectly acceptable because each observation is independent of one another—a key assumption of the traditional analytic methods. However, if a researcher is interested in friendships (for example), and some of these children in the sample are friends with one another, then traditional analytic methods are not appropriate because each observation (i.e., child) is not independent of other observations (i.e., peers) within the sample. Instead, the friendship child A has with child B makes these two children interdependent, both conceptually and statistically. In this instance, special data analytic techniques are needed.

Unfortunately, appropriate techniques for modeling these interdependent data have emerged slowly. Equally unfortunate is the fact that developmental researchers have been slow to employ the techniques that have been put forth. Two outcomes have resulted from this slow progress. First, developmental researchers too often rely on inappropriate analytic techniques that are likely to provide inaccurate answers, such as analyzing data from a sample of children as if they were independent cases (i.e., ignoring interdependence). Alternatively, researchers have attempted countless means to remove interdependence from their data, such as randomly selecting one member of a friendship pair for analysis (i.e., avoiding interdependence). The problem with either ignoring or avoiding interdependence is that it treats this interdependence as a nuisance. As outlined above, however, family relations, parent–child relationships, childhood friendships, and similar interdependencies are not nuisances to be avoided, but rather are critically important phenomena for investigation. The use of appropriate statistical models for interdependent developmental data will allow us to study these phenomena, as well as reveal novel questions that we have failed to see within our traditional analytic framework.

Why has this disconnect between data analyses (which assume independence) and foci of developmental research (which often assume interdependence) emerged? There are likely multiple causes, but we consider three interrelated possibilities here. First, the quantitative techniques of analyzing interdependent data have only slowly emerged. Although some brave quantitative researchers have ventured into this area, it is only in the last couple of decades (relatively short in the history of quantitative analysis) that systematic methods have been developed and evaluated (for a thorough overview, see Kenny, Kashy, & Cook, 2006). Second, the data analytic techniques that have been developed are not necessarily best suited to the needs of developmental research. One notable example of this point is that most techniques of interdependent data analysis have not been extended to incorporate longitudinal data. Third, we suspect that the increasing specialization of researchers in both quantitative and developmental sciences has resulted in a situation in which there is generally little communication across these areas. In other words, developmental researchers may not be aware of the techniques emerging from quantitative research, and quantitative researchers may not be aware of the unique opportunities and challenges of developmental applications of these techniques.

Goals of This Book

We believe that both developmental and quantitative researchers can benefit from dialogue across these two disciplines. To prompt such dialogue, we received funds from the National Science Foundation and the Society of Multivariate Experimental Psychology to hold a conference at the University of Kansas, attended by the authors of chapters in this book. We selected both developmental and quantitative researchers to come together to discuss the unique opportunities and challenges of modeling interdependent developmental data. The first goal of the current book is to share the product of this discussion. As we hope you agree, this dialogue between developmental and quantitative experts has resulted in substantial advances for each discipline and in identifying much common interest, both of which are represented in the chapters of this book.

The second goal of this book is to describe techniques for analyzing interdependent developmental data. The chapters of this book provide clear descriptions of various techniques for analyzing data from dyads and small groups, including the actor–partner interdependence model (Laursen, Popp, Burk, Kerr, & Stattin, chapter 2), the mutual influence model (Sadler & Woody, chapter 7), dyadic models of co-occurring change (Ferrer & Widaman, chapter 6; Kashy & Donnellan, chapter 8; Ram & Pedersen, chapter 5; Selig, McNamara, Card, & Little, chapter 9), triadic models (Bond & Cross, chapter 16), the social relations model (Branje, Finkenauer, & Meeus, chapter 12; Card, Little, & Selig, chapter 11; Cook, chapter 3; Malloy & Cillessen, chapter 10), and various aspects of social network analysis (Cillessen & Borch, chapter 4; Kindermann, chapter 14; Laursen, Popp, Burk, Kerr, & Stattin, chapter 2; Templin, chapter 13; Zijlstra, Veenstra, & Van Duijn, chapter 15). The analytic approaches being developed in these areas involve many topics of active quantitative research, making it difficult for most of us to keep abreast of current best practices. We are pleased that many of the originators and most active innovators of these techniques have provided clear and comprehensive descriptions of the methods, opportunities, and limitations of these techniques in the chapters that follow (see especially the concluding chapter by Kenny, chapter 17).

The third goal is to demonstrate the substantive opportunities of sophisticated techniques of interdependent data analysis. In other words, we did not want to only describe the various techniques of analyzing interdependent data; instead, we challenged the authors to lead by example, and to show the unique developmental questions that can be answered using these techniques. The content focus of these chapters is broad, including both family (Branje et al., chapter 12; Cook, chapter 3; Kashy & Donnellan, chapter 8) and peer relations (Bond & Cross, chapter 16; Card et al., chapter 11; Cillessen & Borch, chapter 4; Kindermann, chapter 14; Laursen et al., chapter 2; Malloy & Cillessen, chapter 10; Selig et al., chapter 9; Templin, chapter 13; Zijlstra et al., chapter 15), as well as various topics including adult romantic relationships (Ferrer & Widaman, chapter 6), individuals initially meeting (Sadler & Woody, chapter 7), and ecological models (Ram & Pedersen, chapter 5). This breadth is intentional, with the hopeful result that researchers will see opportunities for applying these models to answer a broad range of questions.

We do not view this book as the final word on modeling interdependent developmental data. As such, our fourth and final goal of this book is to prompt future work by developmental and quantitative researchers to extend what is presented here. Although the authors have done a wonderful job in laying out the analytic approaches and how they can be applied in developmental research, we believe that the true value of this book will be in prompting further advancement and applications of these techniques. The concluding chapter of this book (Kenny, chapter 17) summarizes what is known and not yet known about interdependent models of development.

REFERENCES

Bond, C. F., Jr., & Cross, D. (chapter 16). Beyond the dyad: Prospects for social development. In N. A. Card, J. P. Selig, & T. D. Little (Eds.), *Modeling dyadic and interdependent data in the developmental and behavioral sciences.* New York, NY: Routledge/Taylor & Francis Group.

Branje, S. J. T., Finkenauer, C., & Meeus, W. H. J. (chapter 12). Modeling interdependence using the Social Relations Model: The investment model in family relationships. In N. A. Card, J. P. Selig, & T. D. Little (Eds.), *Modeling dyadic and interdependent data in the developmental and behavioral sciences.* New York, NY: Routledge/Taylor & Francis Group.

Card, N. A., & Hodges, E. V. E. (2006). Shared targets for aggression by early adolescent friends. *Developmental Psychology, 42,* 1327-1338.

Card, N. A., Little, T. D., & Selig, J. P. (chapter 11). Using the bivariate Social Relations Model to study dyadic relationships: Early adolescents' perceptions of friends' aggression and prosocial behavior. In N. A. Card, J. P. Selig, & T. D. Little (Eds.), *Modeling dyadic and interdependent data in the developmental and behavioral sciences.* New York, NY: Routledge/Taylor & Francis Group.

Cervone, D. (2004). The architecture of personality. *Psychological Review, 111,* 183-204.

Cillessen, A. H. N., & Borch, C. (chapter 4). Analyzing nested structures of social networks in adolescence. In N. A. Card, J. P. Selig, & T. D. Little (Eds.), *Modeling Dyadic and Interdependent Data in the Developmental and Behavioral Sciences.* New York, NY: Routledge/Taylor & Francis Group.

Cook, W. L. (chapter 3). Application of the Social Relations Model formulas to developmental research. In N. A. Card, J. P. Selig, & T. D. Little (Eds.), *Modeling Dyadic and Interdependent Data in the Developmental and Behavioral Sciences.* New York, NY: Routledge/Taylor & Francis Group.

Diamond, L. M. (2003). Was it a phase? Young women's relinquishment of lesbian/bisexual identities over a 5-year period. *Journal of Personality and Social Psychology, 84,* 352-364.

Ferrer, E., & Widaman, K. F. (chapter 6). Dynamic factor analysis of dyadic affective processes with inter-group differences. In N. A. Card, J. P. Selig, & T. D. Little (Eds.), *Modeling dyadic and interdependent data in the developmental and behavioral sciences.* New York, NY: Routledge/Taylor & Francis Group.

Kashy, D. A., & Donnellan, M. B. (chapter 8). Comparing MLM and SEM approaches to analyzing developmental dyadic data: Growth curve models of hostility in families. In N. A. Card, J. P. Selig, & T. D. Little (Eds.), *Modeling dyadic and interdependent data in the developmental and behavioral sciences.* New York, NY: Routledge/Taylor & Francis Group.

Kenny, D. A. (chapter 17). Thinking about the developmental course of relationships. In N. A. Card, J. P. Selig, & T. D. Little (Eds.), *Modeling dyadic and interdependent data in the developmental and behavioral sciences.* New York, NY: Routledge/Taylor & Francis Group.

Kenny, D. A., Kashy, D. A., & Cook, W. L. (2006). *Dyadic data analysis.* New York: Guilford Press.

Kindermann, T. A. (chapter 14). Can we make causal inferences about the influence of children's naturally-existing social networks on their school motivation? In N. A. Card, J. P. Selig, & T. D. Little (Eds.), *Modeling dyadic and interdependent data in the developmental and behavioral sciences.* New York, NY: Routledge/Taylor & Francis Group.

Laursen, B., Popp, D., Burk, W. J., Kerr, M., & Stattin, H. (chapter 2). Incorporating interdependence into developmental research: Examples from the study of homophily and homogeneity. In N. A. Card, J. P. Selig, & T. D. Little (Eds.), *Modeling dyadic and interdependent data in the developmental and behavioral sciences.* New York, NY: Routledge/Taylor & Francis Group.

Malloy, T. E., & Cillessen, A. H. N. (chapter 10). Variance component analysis of generalized and dyadic peer perceptions in adolescence. In N. A. Card, J. P. Selig, & T. D. Little (Eds.), *Modeling dyadic and interdependent data in the developmental and behavioral sciences.* New York, NY: Routledge/Taylor & Francis Group.

Mischel, W., & Shoda, Y. (1995). A cognitive-affective system theory of personality: Reconceptualizing situations, dispositions, dynamics, and invariance in personality structure. *Psychological Review, 102,* 246-268.

Pierce, K. A., & Cohen, R. (1995). Aggressors and their victims: Toward a contextual framework for understanding children's aggressor-victim relationships. *Developmental Review, 15,* 292-310.

Ram, N., & Pedersen, A. B. (chapter 5). Dyadic models emerging from the longitudinal structural equation modeling tradition: Parallels with ecological models of interspecific interactions. In N. A. Card, J. P. Selig, & T. D. Little (Eds.), *Modeling dyadic and interdependent data in the developmental and behavioral sciences.* New York, NY: Routledge/Taylor & Francis Group.

Sadler, P., & Woody, E. (chapter 7). It takes two: A dyadic, SEM-based perspective on personality development. In N. A. Card, J. P. Selig, & T. D. Little (Eds.), *Modeling dyadic and interdependent data in the developmental and behavioral sciences.* New York, NY: Routledge/Taylor & Francis Group.

Selig, J. P., McNamara, K. A., Card, N. A., & Little, T. D. (chapter 9). Techniques for modeling dependency in interchangeable dyads. In N. A. Card, J. P. Selig, & T. D. Little (Eds.), *Modeling dyadic and interdependent data in the developmental and behavioral sciences.* New York, NY: Routledge/Taylor & Francis Group.

Templin, J. (chapter 13). Methods for detecting subgroups in social networks. In N. A. Card, J. P. Selig, & T. D. Little (Eds.), *Modeling dyadic and interdependent data in the developmental and behavioral sciences.* New York, NY: Routledge/Taylor & Francis Group.

Zijlstra, B. J. H., Veenstra, R., & Van Duijn, M. A. J. (chapter 15). An application of the multilevel p_2 model for binary network data on bully-victim relationships. In N. A. Card, J. P. Selig, & T. D. Little (Eds.), *Modeling dyadic and interdependent data in the developmental and behavioral sciences.* New York, NY: Routledge/Taylor & Francis Group.

CHAPTER TWO

Incorporating Interdependence Into Developmental Research: Examples From the Study of Homophily and Homogeneity

Brett Laursen
Danielle Popp
Florida Atlantic University

William J. Burk
Margaret Kerr
Håkan Stattin
Örebro University

Interdependence is a central feature of close relationships. One widely accepted definition holds that close relationships are characterized by interdependent social exchanges, which are manifest in frequent, strong, and diverse interconnections that are maintained over an extended period of time (Kelly et al., 1983). This definition emphasizes objective assessments of interdependence, identifying readily measured and observable features that signal closeness on the part of both participants (Berscheid, 1999). The metric has more than face validity. Participants in relationships that are typically defined as close, such as those between family members, friends, and romantic partners, are more apt to be interdependent than participants in other relationships (Laursen & Bukowski, 1997).

The statistical implications of relationship interdependence are not widely appreciated. If we start from the premise that two individuals have interdependent thoughts, feelings, and behaviors, then it follows that data describing

11

these thoughts, feelings, and behaviors must necessarily be interdependent. Simply put, relationship interdependence begets statistical interdependence (Kenny, 1996). Statistical interdependence refers to the correlated or reciprocally dependent nature of data collected from or about participants in a close relationship. Statistical interdependence is not a methodological artifact; nonindependence characterizes observational and self-report data alike. On most topics that concern close relationships, pervasive mutual influence gives rise to shared variance (Laursen, 2005). As a consequence, there is a growing recognition that statistical interdependence must be built into models of close relationships, rather than treating it as a measurement error or an unfortunate obstacle to be overcome.

To acknowledge interdependence is to acknowledge the need for analytic techniques that are not compromised by data that lack statistical independence. Social psychologists have devoted considerable effort to this task and their efforts are beginning to bear fruit. Several methods have been developed that disentangle variance shared across participants from variance unique to specific participants (Kashy & Kenny, 2000). Dyadic methods focus exclusively on relationships between two individuals, where the goal is to separate variance shared across participants from variance unique to specific participants. Network methods involve groups in which each member participates in multiple dyads, where the goal is to separate variance shared by groups from variance shared by dyads from variance unique to individuals. Each of these approaches will be illustrated in this chapter.

Developmental scholars have been slow to recognize the statistical limitations imposed by interdependence. To be sure, close relationships have long been understood to be an important context for development (Hartup & Laursen, 1999). Family and peer relationships have been characterized as the fundamental building blocks of human culture and the primary vehicle through which lessons about survival and well-being are transmitted within and across generations (Reis, Collins, & Berscheid, 2000). Interdependence is considered so essential to human survival that it has been postulated to be part of an innate need for belonging (Baumeister & Leary, 1995), which serves as the foundation for the creation of a distinct set of relationship categories that facilitate functioning in different social domains (Bugenthal, 2000). Unfortunately, widespread acceptance by developmental scholars of the significance of relationship interdependence has not translated into widespread acceptance of analytic techniques designed for use with nonindependent data. Developmental science has suffered as a consequence.

Our chapter is divided into three sections. The first section includes an overview of developmental approaches to interdependent data. The limitations of previous analytic strategies will be considered, followed by a discussion of procedures that address these limitations. Although these points apply to research on all close relationships, we will limit our examples to research on peers. Our particular focus is peer similarity, which encompasses selection and socialization influences. The second section describes a novel adaptation of the Actor–Partner Interdependence Model (APIM; Kashy & Kenny, 2000; Kenny & Cook, 1999) to longitudinal data on friendship homophily. Conventional APIM procedures are well suited to describe concurrent patterns of association; our modified structural equation modeling approach utilizes multiple group analyses with indistinguishable dyads to shed light on socialization and selection effects across time. The third section describes a new statistical application designed to estimate peer group homogeneity from longitudinal data. The SIENA statistical software package (Snijders, Pattison, Robins, & Handcock, 2006) simultaneously models selection and socialization effects over time, we describe how to partition variance into parameters that ascribe similarity to networks, dyads, and individuals. We close with a call for developmental scholars to take seriously the need to incorporate interdependence into the design of new research.

Our analytic examples describe data drawn from Kerr and Stattin's *10 to 18 Study*, a longitudinal study of all children between the ages of ten and eighteen attending school in a small city in central Sweden (Kerr, Stattin, & Kiesner, 2007). The study utilizes a cohort sequential design. A new group of 10-year-olds joins the study every year to replace 18-year-olds who graduate from high school. Every year each participant identifies three important peers, nonadults who occupy a special place in the youth's life. Each participant also identifies up to 10 peers with whom they spend time in school and up to 10 peers with whom they spend time out of school. All together, participants annually nominate as many as 23 different peer affiliates. Standardized measures of delinquency are available for participants ages 12 and older. The sample for our analytic examples includes participants for whom two successive waves of peer nomination and delinquency data are available.

The Developmental Study of Interdependence

Developmental scholars have long appreciated that the dyadic properties of a relationship are key to understanding the significance of a relationship. Robert Sears (1951) famously made this point in his presidential address to the American Psychological Association: "A dyadic unit is essential if there is to be a conceptualization of the relationships between people, as in the parent-child, teacher-pupil, husband-wife, or leader-follower instances. To have a science of interactive events, one must have variables and units of action that refer to such events" (p. 479). Sears proposed a model in which relationships are conceptualized in terms of behavioral interdependencies, wherein changes in one individual's cognitions, emotions, and actions effect changes in the other individual. Influential examples followed, most notably Bell's (1968) quantification of the ways in which infants are both the recipients of socialization efforts as well as socialization agents in their own right. Objective measures of interdependence gained prominence, particularly observations of social interactions and self-reports gathered from or about both participants in a relationship.

The tradition of collecting data concerning both participants in a relationship had an unfortunate corollary: Few developmental scholars knew how to best utilize these data. Most developmental models are about processes that underlie behavior change in individuals rather than in dyads or groups, even though many models purportedly addressed transactional processes (Hartup & Laursen, 1999). Relationship constructs have been difficult to accommodate within conceptual and analytic frameworks designed to account for individual development. Statistical procedures adapted to examine change over time cannot easily accommodate data from multiple interdependent sources. As a consequence, most conventional statistical techniques adopted in developmental research failed to capture the richness or the significance of relationship experiences.

One common solution to the problem of dyadic data is to sum or average scores across participants in a relationship; difference or residual scores are used to similar effect. This solution has the advantage of reducing multiple data points to a single score, but it does so by eliminating variation that might be attributed to the individual. No evidence remains of heterogeneity among dyads with the same composite score. Friends who report similar moderate levels of relationship satisfaction are indistinguishable from dyads that consist of one satisfied and one dissatisfied friend. A variant of this approach involves separately analyzing data for each participant in a relationship. No small amount of confusion can be traced to the contradictory findings that have emerged from this strategy.

Another common approach is to treat interdependent data in the same manner that one treats independent data. This strategy provides results that describe individual contributions to relationships, but these conclusions are apt to be inaccurate because conventional parametric statistics are built upon the assumption that cases (i.e., scores for participants within dyads) are uncorrelated. Violation of the independence assumption introduces systematic bias into significance tests (Kenny, 1995). The type of error depends on the direction of the correlation. Type II error is inflated when scores from two sources are positively correlated. Type I error increases when scores from different sources are negatively correlated.

Fifty years ago, the implications of interdependence were unsettling for early scholars interested in the development of close relationships. Bidirectional models that featured reciprocal effects were eventually crafted to replace outmoded unidirectional constructs (Hinde, 1997). The implications of statistical interdependence may prove to be equally unsettling to developmental scientists because most of what we know about relationships is predicated on research employing inadequate designs and inappropriate statistics. The fact that robust effects are immune to all but the most egregious violations of independence is likely to be small comfort because the magnitude of these effects will inevitably decline as new techniques are adopted that apportion variance among different sources and improve statistical power to detect higher order interactions (Laursen, 2005).

Some developmental scholars anticipated this trend. The earliest modifications of the Social Relations Model (SRM: Kenny & La Voie, 1984) enabled developmental scholars to explore interactions between family members (Cook & Dreyer, 1984). The technique has proven especially useful in the field of peer relations, where it was initially applied to interactions between playmates (Ross & Lollis, 1989), and then extended to perceptions of classmates (Malloy, Sugarman, Montvilo, & Ben-Zeev, 1995), aggressive behavior towards peers (Coie et al., 1999), social information processing deficits (Hubbard, Dodge, Cillessen, Coie, & Schwartz, 2001), the quality of friend and nonfriend play (Simpkins & Parke, 2002), and peer social status (Card, Hodges, Little, & Hawley, 2005). More recently, the APIM was adopted by developmental scholars to describe characteristics of adolescent friendships (Burk & Laursen, 2005; Cillessen, Jian, West, & Laszkowski, 2005). The application of these variance partitioning models (and other similar strategies, e.g., Gonzalez & Griffin, 1999) represents an important step forward for the field, because it enables developmental scholars to distinguish group and relationship effects, which describe variance shared by participants, from individual effects, which describe variance unique to particular participants.

It is important to note, however, that there have been few truly developmental applications of these techniques. The hallmark of developmental research is the identification of age related trends or, preferably, changes over time. Yet, with two recent exceptions, developmental studies of interdependence have examined concurrent effects only. The exceptions explored developmental processes using APIM analyses to address the stability of mother-child attachment-related views (Cook & Kenny, 2005) and the stability of aggression among children with reciprocated and unreciprocated friends (Adams, Bukowski, & Bagwell, 2005). The dearth of research on developmental processes is understandable; although it should be possible to treat age or time as a moderator in multiple group comparisons of associations within age groups or time periods, most statistical procedures are not well suited for the analysis of change. We turn our attention to this issue next.

Interdependence and Peer Similarity

Few areas of developmental research illustrate the importance of interdependence as well as the study of peer similarity. It is well known that individuals who affiliate with one another tend to be similar on key behaviors, traits, and attributes (Lazarsfeld & Merton, 1954). The question arising from this observation is tantalizingly simple. What is the origin of this similarity? Two forms of similarity have been identified. *Homophily* describes similarity at the level of the dyad, typically between friends (Kandel, 1978). Individuals who identify each other as friends tend to resemble one another on a variety of attributes. *Homogeneity* describes similarity at the level of the group, typically among members of the same clique (Cohen, 1977). Members of the same peer group tend to resemble one another on key attributes.

Two processes explain similarities between friends and among groups. *Selection* emphasizes prior similarities. Because children are attracted to similar others, friendships grow out of acquaintanceships that are established on the basis of similarities. Interconnections among friends who share similar attributes form the basis for the establishment of cliques and groups. *Socialization* emphasizes acquired similarities. Because affiliation promotes similarity, mutual influence processes should gradually heighten similarities between friends. As new friends are incorporated into the group, these individuals must change in ways that increase their value to the group. A third process, *selective elimination*, describes instances when the individual fails to become more similar to the group and is eventually excluded as a consequence, thereby increasing the level of similarity among the remaining group members. Selective elimination is a phenomenon unique to groups. Selection and socialization apply equally to dyads and groups and will be the focus of our chapter.

There is no question that selection and socialization contribute to peer similarity. The relative importance of each, however, remains poorly understood. Interest in this issue is more than academic. During adolescence and young adulthood, delinquent and antisocial activities are often perpetuated in the presence of peers (Cairns & Cairns, 1994). Efforts to prevent the establishment of antisocial relationships and to intervene in those that have already formed are likely to emphasize different strategies depending on whether similarity is primarily a product of selection or socialization. Failure to anticipate these processes has undermined many intervention efforts (Dishion, McCord, & Poulin, 1999). To illustrate selection and socialization processes as they apply to homophily and homogeneity, we will selectively review a few representative studies of each.

Friendship Homophily

The first (and perhaps best known) study of homophily concerned self-reports of similarity among adolescent friendship dyads (Kandel, 1978). During the fall and the subsequent spring of a single academic year, students from five high schools were asked to identify one best friend from school. Unilateral nominations characterized 60% of the friends and reciprocal nominations characterized the remaining dyads. Friends were divided into three groups. Stable friends were friends at both time points. Unstable friends were friends at time one only. Future friends were friends at time two only. Across the two time points, there were increases in the similarity of stable friends on marijuana use, educational aspirations, political orientation, and minor delinquency, suggesting socialization effects. At both time points, future friends were somewhat more similar than unstable friends on marijuana use and minor delinquency, suggesting selection effects.

More recently, three similar longitudinal studies examined friendship socialization using statistical controls to partial out the effects of friendship selection. The first study involved 7th and 8th graders from three schools who completed inventories twice during the course of a school year describing their behavior in school and their friendships (Berndt & Keefe, 1995). Stable friends became more similar over time in terms of self- (but not teacher) rated disruption, teacher (but not self-) rated school involvement, and school grades. The second study involved 6th, 8th, and 10th graders from four schools who completed questionnaires describing friendships and cigarette and alcohol use at the beginning and end of the school year (Urberg, Değirmencioğlu, & Pilgrim, 1997). Youth with stable friends were more likely to experiment with cigarettes and alcohol if their friends had previously done so and they were more likely to drink alcohol and get drunk regularly if their friends previously did so. The third study involved 7th through 11th graders from a large representative sample of U.S. students who completed questionnaires describing levels of alcohol consumption and the initiation of sexual activity at one year intervals (Jaccard, Blanton, & Dodge, 2005). Youth with stable friends were slightly more likely to become sexually active and to engage in binge drinking if their friends reportedly began the same activities during this time period.

These studies are important because each demonstrated that friends socialize one another across time, over and above initial selection effects. But methodological concerns limit confidence in this conclusion. To avoid problems with nonindependent data, children in each study were permitted only one mutual friendship and nominations were limited to children who attended the same school. Berndt and Keefe (1995) conducted supplemental analyses that included all friendship dyads, permitting unequal contributions from individuals and thus violating assumptions of independence; most of their statistically significant findings emerged from these analyses. Only Jaccard and colleagues (2005) examined baseline levels of similarity among nonfriends, determining that changes in similarity among peers did not account for changes in similarity between friends. Kandel (1978) conducted separate analyses for stable and unstable friendships, conflating characteristics of individuals with characteristics of the different friendship groups; the other studies were limited to children with stable friends, excluding those who changed friends or who did not have friends. Finally, only one study attempted to estimate selection effects. Kandel (1978) concluded that selection rivaled socialization in terms of its contribution to homophily, a claim made in the absence of straightforward statistical contrasts. This conclusion is controversial because selection and socialization processes cannot be readily disentangled with two waves of data unless children who are new friends at the outset of the study are separated from children who were friends prior to beginning of the study.

Peer Group Homogeneity

The earliest study of homogeneity involved Cohen's (1977) reanalysis of data from Coleman's (1961) classic study, *The Adolescent Society*. Adolescents in a large high school completed surveys during the fall and spring of a single academic year describing their attitudes, behaviors, and same-sex associates. Estimates of change in within-group variance contrasting clique and nonclique associates revealed moderate socialization effects on a small number of questionnaire items. Selection effects were described in terms of decreasing variance attributed to the addition of new members to existing cliques during the second wave of data collection. Moderate selection effects were evident in an equally small number of items. A final set of analyses estimated selection effects in cliques that emerged during the second wave of data collection, comparing the similarity of future clique members during the first wave of data collection with random pairings of nonclique members. These analyses suggested large initial selection effects on most items.

Three other longitudinal studies adopted different approaches to estimate peer group homogeneity. In the first study, adolescents from nine high schools identified their closest friends in school and completed self-reports of internalizing problems during two successive school years (Hogue & Steinberg, 1995). Evidence for selection effects was mixed: Initial adolescent internalizing predicted subsequent internalizing in the peer group when controlling for subsequent adolescent internalizing but not when controlling for initial peer group internalizing. There was no evidence of socialization effects among girls, but boys' initial peer group internalizing predicted subsequent adolescent internalizing when controlling for initial adolescent internalizing. In the second study, adolescents from five high schools identified their best friends and described whether and how often they smoked cigarettes at the beginning of the 9th grade and at the beginning of the 10th grade (Ennett & Bauman, 1994). Analyses of selection effects, limited to a very small group of adolescents who changed cliques, indicated that smokers disproportionately joined smoking cliques and nonsmokers disproportionately joined nonsmoking cliques. Analyses of socialization effects, limited to nonsmokers during the first wave of data collection, indicated that those who belonged to smoking cliques at both time periods were somewhat more likely to become smokers when compared with nonsmokers who belonged to nonsmoking cliques at both time periods. Both of these studies concluded that socialization and selection contributed about equally to peer group homogeneity, although neither provided a clear empirical basis for this claim. In the third study, estimates of friendship selection for cigarette and alcohol consumption (described above) were supplemented with estimates of group selection effects for the same variables (Urberg et al., 1997). These results indicated that youth were not more likely to experiment with cigarettes and alcohol if members of their peer group did but they were more likely to smoke cigarettes regularly and get drunk.

These studies are important because they indicate that selection and socialization contribute to peer group homogeneity, but effects were small and inconsistent. Estimates of selection and socialization were drawn from different samples, which varied dramatically in terms of the number and characteristics of participants; the lone exception to this rule (Hogue & Steinberg, 1995) neither validated self-reports of group membership with reports from other group members nor restricted analyses to groups that were stable over time. In most cases, nominations were limited to peers who attended the same school or were in the same grade. Only Cohen (1977) contrasted homogeneity within peer groups to that among randomly selected peers, determining that the overall tendency toward similarity among youth in the same school attenuated but did not eliminate effects for increased homogeneity within groups. Finally, analogous to studies of friendship homophily, all comparisons of selection and socialization effects are suspect because no distinctions were made between groups that were formed during the initial wave of data collection and groups that existed prior to the initial wave of data collection.

Advances in the Study of Friendship Homophily

In this section we describe recent advances in the study of homophily
between friends. In its simplest form, homophily represents concurrent similarities between friends, which can be determined by intraclass correlations.
Matters quickly get complicated, however, when the goal is to identify changes
in homophily over time, which necessitates separating selection effects from
socialization effects. In the section that follows, we outline procedures for
examining changes in homophily with techniques designed specifically for use
with interdependent data.

Describing APIM. The Actor–Partner Interdependence Model (APIM:
Kenny & Cook, 1999; Kashy & Kenny, 2000) is a data analytic approach
that simultaneously estimates the effect that an individual's predictor variable
has on his or her own outcome variable (the actor effect) and on his or her
partner's outcome variable (the partner effect), partialling out variance shared
across participants in the predictor variable and in the outcome variable.
The APIM, and related interdependent dyadic data analytic procedures (e.g.,
Campbell & Kashy, 2002; Gonzalez & Griffin, 1999), were initially designed
to model concurrent effects. Recent advances extending these techniques to
longitudinal data serve as the starting point for our discussion.

The longitudinal application of the APIM requires that data be collected
from the same dyads at two different time points. Different variables may
be included at different time points, although this strategy precludes conclusions about change in the outcome variable over time, so it is not generally
recommended.

Figure 2.1 describes a study in which identical forms of data are collected
at two time points, such that the predictor variable and the outcome variable represent different assessments of the same construct. For purposes of
illustration, assume that both participants provide self-report data on their
relationship at each time point. Effects are modeled simultaneously, partialling out each of the other effects. Actor effects (paths $a1$ and $a2$) describe
the extent to which each participant's reports of the relationship are stable
over time. Partner effects (paths $p1$ and $p2$) describe the extent to which one
partner's reports of the relationship at Time 1 predict the other partner's
reports of the relationship at Time 2. Within dyads, reports provided by
the two participants are presumed to be interdependent at each time point.
Levels of concurrent interdependence are separately estimated, so as not to
inflate actor effects and partner effects. Thus, interdependence at the outset
of the study reflects the association between participant reports of the relationship at Time 1 ($c1$). Actor and partner effects rarely explain all of the
variance in outcome variables; interdependence at the conclusion of the stu-

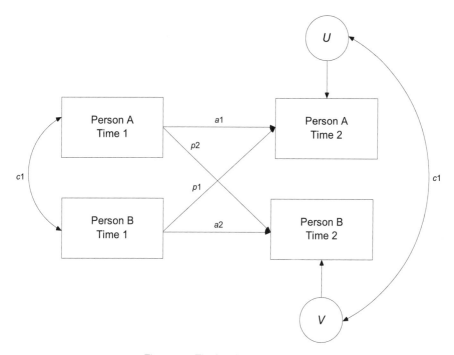

Figure 2.1. The longitudinal APIM.

Note. $a1$ = Person A's actor or stability effect. $a2$ = Person B's actor or stability effect. $p1$ = Person A's partner effect. $p2$ = Person B's partner effect. $c1$ = correlation between Person A and Person B at Time 1. U = residual variance in Person A's outcome variable at Time 2. V = residual variance in Person's B outcome variable at Time 2. $c2$ = correlation between Person A's residual (U) and Person B's residual (V) at Time 2.

dy is gauged with a correlation ($c2$) between the residuals of participant reports of the relationship at Time 2 (U and V). The latter represents the correlation between the variance left over in the outcome variable. In APIM analyses with concurrent data, $c2$ is often disregarded, but in longitudinal analyses the correlation holds special significance because it describes increases or decreases in similarity from the first to the second measurement point. Put simply, $c2$ captures changes in dyadic similarity.

One of the first longitudinal applications of APIM procedures involved mother and adolescent child reports of attachment security (Cook & Kenny, 2005). The mother–child relationship represents a prototypically distinguishable dyad, because the participants can be readily classified into discrete roles. Procedures for analyzing data from distinguishable dyads are relatively straightforward (Gonzalez & Griffin, 1999; Kashy & Kenny, 2000). Other types of dyads, such as same-sex friends, lack features that distinguish between participants. These indistinguishable dyads—also known as exchangeable or interchangeable dyads—are not amenable to conventional interdependent data procedures. As a consequence, APIM procedures have been modified for use with indistinguishable dyads (Olsen & Kenny, 2006; Woody & Sadler, 2005); one of the first developmental applications of this new technique involved an examination of concurrent associations between characteristics of same-sex friends (Cillessen et al., 2005). Structural equation modeling is recommended when analyzing data from indistinguishable dyads, because the estimation of actor and partner effects requires equality constraints on several parameters, including the variance and mean for the predictor variables, actor paths, partner paths, intercepts, and the mean and the variance of disturbances.

Applying APIM. In our recent work, we have modified approaches for longitudinal APIM analyses with indistinguishable dyads to examine homophily between friends. We illustrate with three waves of data from the *10 to 18 Project* (Kerr, Stattin, & Kiesner, 2007). The sample included 676 adolescents from 50 classrooms in 11 different schools. Friendship, the focus of our inquiry, was defined as dyads consisting of individuals who reciprocally nominated one another as important peers. A total of 602 adolescents were involved in at least one reciprocated friendship with another member of the study during at least one of the three time periods ($N = 301$ dyads). Seventy-four participants were not involved in any reciprocated friendships. Some participants were involved in more than one friendship at a time and some had different friends at different times; to simplify matters, analyses focused on the highest ranked reciprocal friends. As a consequence, each participant belonged to one and only one dyad. It is possible to conduct analyses with all possible friendship dyads, treating each dyad as if it contained participants who were not members of other dyads, but this introduces the potential for bias due to unequal contributions by individuals.

Friends were classified into one of seven groups according to the status of their friendship over time. Four groups involved stable dyads that were friends during more than one time period: (a) *enduring friends* were friends at three consecutive time points, (b) *waning friends* were friends at Times 1 and 2 but not at Time 3, (c) *new friends* were friends at Times 2 and 3 but not at Time 1, and (d) *intermittent friends* were friends at Times 1 and 3 but not at Time 2. Three groups of unstable dyads were friends at one time period only: (a) *Time 1 friends*, (b) *Time 2 friends*, and (c) *Time 3 friends*. In addition, two comparison groups were created to gauge baseline levels of similarity. The *friendless* group involved the 74 adolescents who were not involved in any reciprocated friendships at any time; these individuals were paired with a randomly selected same-age, same gender participant. The *friended* group involved the 602 adolescents with friends; these individuals were paired with a randomly selected same-age, same-gender participant. Neither member of these dyads ever nominated their partner as a friend.

A multiple groups structural equation modeling procedure has been devised to compare actor and partner effects across different types of dyads (Neyer, 2002). We adapted this approach for use with our longitudinal APIM design, contrasting patterns of results across the different friendship groups in multiple group analyses using AMOS 6.0 (Arbuckle, 2003). Socialization effects cannot be disentangled from selection effects during the first wave of data collection, because it is impossible to distinguish friendships that were recently established from friendships that were longer lived. For this reason the first wave of data was only used to classify participants into friendship groups. Longitudinal APIM analyses focused on reports of delinquency during the second and third waves of data collection. Figure 2.2 depicts a structural equation model with longitudinal data on delinquency from Time 2 to Time 3. Note the constraints necessary for APIM analyses involving indistinguishable dyads of same-sex friends (Cillessen et al., 2005; Olsen & Kenny, 2006).

The effects are modeled simultaneously, partialling out each of the other effects. The *stability of individual behavior* is estimated across two time points (a). Concurrent associations at time two ($c1$) represent an estimate of *initial dyadic similarity*. Associations at time three ($c2$) represent an estimate of subsequent *change in dyadic similarity* that reflect increases or decreases in similarity. Residual correlations are often treated as error in APIM analyses of concurrent data, but they hold special significance in longitudinal analyses because they capture changes in dyadic similarity. Technically, changes in similarity ($c2$) represent correlations between residual scores, but these residual associations differ little from those involving partial correlations between raw scores. Cross-lagged effects (p), which are given special emphasis in APIM analyses of concurrent data, must be treated as error in longitudinal analyses of same-sex friends because estimates of over-time dyadic similarity cannot quantify the magnitude or direction of longitudinal change in the behavior of a partner when the participants are indistinguishable. Although the partner effects for over-time dyadic similarity are uninterpretable, the paths are retained in the model because they would otherwise inflate estimates of change in concurrent dyadic similarity. Similarity coefficients are akin to intraclass correlations that approximate the total variance estimated from concurrent associations.

Recent advances in structural equation modeling give rise to a multiple groups APIM procedure that contrasts specific paths within and between subgroups with indistinguishable dyads (Neyer, 2002). This application is well-suited for an examination of homophily because it is necessary to examine patterns of similarity in friendships that begin and end at different time

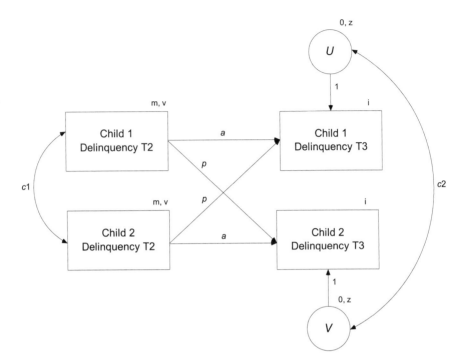

Figure 2.2. The longitudinal APIM applied to the second and third waves of delinquency data from indistinguishable friendship dyads.

Note. a = actor or stability effects. p = partner effects. $c1$ = correlation between Child 1 delinquency and Child 2 delinquency at Time 2. U = residual variance in Child 1's delinquency at Time 3. V = residual variance in Child 2's delinquency at Time 3. $c2$ = correlation between Child 1's delinquency residual (U) and Child 2's delinquency residual (V) at Time 3.
m = predictor means. v = predictor variances. i = outcome intercepts. z = residual variances.

points in order to disentangle selection effects from socialization effects. To isolate selection effects, similarity needs to be estimated prior to the establishment of a friendship. To isolate socialization effects, changes in similarity need to be estimated after the friendship was established. When three data points are available, selection effects and socialization effects can be estimated. Consider Time 3 friends by way of example. Selection effects are operationalized in terms of concurrent associations between two individuals during the time preceding the establishment of the friendship. Socialization effects are operationalized in terms of changes in similarity subsequent to the establishment of the friendship. Time 3 estimates of similarity reflect increases in similarity, over and above those attributed to Time 2 estimates of stability and to actor and partner effects. Thus, for Time 3 friends (i.e.,

TABLE 2.1
Deliquency Selection and Socialization: Standardized Parameter Estimates of Concurrent Similarity From Unconstrained Longitudinal Actor–Partner Interdependence Models With Multiple Friendship Groups

Friendship Group	Time 2	Time 3	n of dyads
Socialization Only			
Enduring (Time 1, 2, & 3)	.37	.12	68
Nascent (Time 2 & 3)	.24	.12	39
Selection and Socialization			
Time 3 only	.14	.39	23
Comparison			
Friended	.02	-.03	301
Friendless	-.03	-.07	74
Time 1 only	.02	-.01	99

Note. Time 2 column describes unique correlations ($c1$) between Child 1's delinquency and Child 2's delinquency. Time 3 column describes unique correlations ($c2$) between Child 1's delinquency residual (U) and Child 2's delinquency residual (V). Selection effects are estimated at Time 2 for Time 3 only friends. Socialization effects are estimated at Time 3 for Time 3 only friends and at Times 2 and 3 for enduring friends and for nascent friends.

those who were not friends at Times 1 and Time 2 but were friends at Time 3), Time 2 similarity describes selection effects, and Time 3 similarity describes socialization effects.

Three groups of children provide a baseline measure of similarity in delinquency scores. Results for the friendless and nonfriend groups track changes in delinquency that may be a product of normative experimentation among a large proportion of youth during a similar developmental period (i.e., adolescence-limited antisocial behavior: Moffitt, 1993); results for Time 1 friends track effects among dyads that presumably share more central traits than random pairings of youth.

Table 2.1 describes the results. The best test of selection effects comes from estimates of similarity among Time 3 friends at Time 2, before they nominated each other as friends at Time 3. Time 3 friends demonstrated modest levels of similarity at Time 2, indicating that youth who are about to become friends were somewhat similar in terms of delinquency. The best test of socialization effects comes from estimates of similarity among Time 3 friends at Time 3, after controlling for socialization effects at Time 2. Time 3 friends demonstrated moderate levels of similarity at Time 3, indicating that youth become more similar in delinquent behavior after becoming friends. Socialization effects were also evident among enduring friends and nascent friends at Time 2 and at Time 3, which suggests that socialization continues beyond the initial phases of friendship formation. Estimates for nascent friends and enduring friends do not control for the contribution of selection, but the magnitude of these socialization effects resembles that of socialization effects for Time 3 friends, where selection effects were discounted.

Associations among youth in comparison groups did not differ from zero, ruling out the possibility that age-related increases in delinquent behavior are responsible for heightened similarity among friends. Associations between Time 1 friends resemble those of randomly paired youth from the friendless and nonfriend groups, indicating that the null findings of comparison groups are not an artifact of the random pairings. We conclude that in this sample of Swedish youth, socialization effects for delinquency are stronger than selection effects.

Advances in the Study of Peer Group Homogeneity

We turn our attention next to recent advances in the study of peer group homogeneity. Previous studies have made inroads into parsing selection effects from socialization effects, but interdependencies due to structural effects of social networks and dependencies between network characteristics and individual behavior have proven to be formidable obstacles. Recent advances in social network analyses, however, offer new approaches to surmounting these obstacles (Carrington, Scott, & Wasserman, 2005). In this section we describe models of network-behavioral dynamics using the Simulation Investigation for Empirical Network Analyses (SIENA: Snijders, 2005; Snijders, Steglich, & Schweinberger, 2007) a software package that delineates selection and socialization processes by simultaneously modeling changes in social networks and changes in individual behaviors.

Static Approaches to Social Networks

Most previous efforts to separate selection and socialization collapse network data (i.e., peer nominations) into individual-level variables (e.g., sociometric position) or dyad-level variables (e.g., behavioral similarity). These are then incorporated into conventional data analytic techniques as outcome variables to estimate selection effects and as predictor variables to estimate socialization effects. There are several limitations to this approach. One potential problem arises from the fact that data from members of the same group are interdependent, which violates the statistical assumption of independent observations. Another drawback is that individual variables and dyad-level variables do not fully account for transitivity in the network structure, wherein youth nominate the friends of their friends as friends (Davis, 1979). Neither individual variables nor dyad-level variables can adequately capture the centrality of an individual's position in the network, their involvement in cohesive subgroups, or their exclusive access to other individuals (Wasserman & Faust, 1994). A final concern involves the fact that the dynamics of individuals and networks cannot be accurately estimated because of changes occurring between observation points. To model continuous change between discrete time points, network analysts utilize continuous-time Markov chains using a probabilistic or stochastic process. Within a social network context, a Markov process indicates that the conditional probability distribution of the changes in network ties at any moment depend on the current network configuration, not on previous configurations (Leenders, 1995).

Another approach involves the identification of social networks with procedures that specify subgroups within networks and categorize individuals into network positions (e.g., isolate, liaison, peripheral, and popular). Examples of social network programs used for this purpose include NEGOPY (Richards & Rice, 1981) and SCM (Cairns & Cairns, 1994). Similar network approaches make use of information concerning network or subgroup density and individual network or subgroup centrality to examine network and individual attributes. Examples of social network programs used for this purpose include Multinet (Richards & Seary, 2003), and NetMiner II (Cyram, 2004). Other network modeling approaches, such as exponential random graph models (p^*: Snijders, Pattison, Robins, & Handcock, 2006), also include estimates of reciprocity, transitivity, and popularity for nonlongitudinal data. There are advantages and disadvantages to these approaches. The primary advantage of these network approaches is their ability to represent various aspects of network structure that account for interdependence. Disadvantages include the fact that selection effects cannot be distinguished from socialization effects because changes in network and individual dynamics cannot be accurately estimated. For instance, an individual's sociometric position may change or the identities of fellow peer group members may change but these changes cannot be incorporated into statistical analyses assessing dynamic network and behavioral characteristics.

Dynamic Approaches to Social Networks

New techniques have been developed that overcome limitations with static network approaches. Actor-oriented models of network evolution (Snijders, 1996, 2001) and actor-oriented models of network-behavioral co-evolution (Snijders, 2005; Snijders et al., 2007) incorporate dynamic principles into models of network and individual behavioral change. The models reflect the assumption that actors make decisions about their own network ties and their own behaviors. That is, actors are presumed to make decisions intended to optimize their position in the network according to short-term preferences and constraints. These decisions prompt changes in network ties (i.e., selection effects) and changes in behaviors (i.e., socialization effects).

The evolution of social networks and individual behaviors are separately estimated using transition probabilities associated with all possible combinations of changes in network ties and individual behaviors, respectively. The number of possible transitions is large, so to limit the number, modeling procedures adopt three key assumptions. First, changes between measurement points are assumed to be part of a continuous time Markov chain process in which the first measurement point represents the starting value for the model. This means that to obtain parameter estimates, the model imputes likely developmental trajectories between observations moments; these changes are assumed to depend only on the current state of affairs, not on the past. Second, actors may only change one network tie (a network microstep) or one increment of behavior (a behavior microstep) at a time, although it is assumed that many changes will take place between observations. This eliminates large simultaneous changes, which are instead modeled as the cumulative result of a series of smaller changes over time. Third, individuals react to changes that other individuals make in their network ties and behavior, but they do not negotiate or enact joint changes. These assumptions simplify the dynamic process and reduce the modeling procedures to two smaller tasks: (a) modeling the preferences and other tendencies guiding the types of specific changes in network or behavioral microsteps, referred to as *objective functions*, and (b) modeling the frequencies of network and behavioral microsteps, referred to as *rate functions*. The total observed change between measurement points is decomposed into sequences of many small changes. The estimated model parameters indicate which of these sequences is most probable, given the observed data.

The two separate functions describing network evolution and behavior evolution models are integrated because the current state of the continuously changing network operates as a constraint on changes in behavior, and the current state of the continuously changing behavior operates as a constraint on changes in the network. The complexity of the resulting model does not allow for its properties to be explicitly calculated, but the model may be implemented as a computer simulation model and parameter estimates can be estimated from iterative simulations with a Markov Chain Monte Carlo approach.

Describing SIENA. SIENA (Snijders, Pattison, et al., 2006) is one of the statistical modules of StOCNET (Boer et al., 2006), a family of statistical programs for social network analysis. The programs and user manuals are free to all users (http://stat.gamma .rug.nl/stocnet/). The SIENA homepage (http://stat.gamma .rug.nl/snijders/siena.html) provides links to many of the references cited in this chapter, as well as technical reports and articles in which SIENA is applied to empirical data. SIENA holds several advantages over previous attempts to apportion network homogeneity, including the capability to (a) model structural components of social networks, (b) simultaneously consider social network and individual behavior dynamics, and (c) utilize Markov processes to model network and behavioral changes within a continuous time framework. A brief overview of SIENA parameter estimates and model specification procedures follows, using the original program variable labels for ease of reference.

SIENA estimates parameters corresponding to network rate and objective functions and to behavioral rate and objective functions. The parameters described here include some but not all of the possible network and behavioral effects (see Snijders, Steglich, Schweinberger, & Huisman, 2006, for a more complete listing). Typically, the network and behavior rate functions are either held constant or permitted to vary only as a function of the attributes of network actors. The network objective function includes structural network effects, as well as effects involving individual and dyadic covariates. Network effects include three sources of network influence. *Density* describes the tendency of actors to nominate individuals with whom one associates. The density parameter is usually negative, which indicates that nominations are selective rather than arbitrary and that ties are unlikely without being embedded within a network. *Reciprocity* describes the tendency for actors to reciprocate nominations, which is a marker of friendship. The reciprocity parameter is usually positive, indicating that reciprocated nominations are more prevalent than unreciprocated nominations. *Transitive triplets* describe the tendency for actors to nominate the same individuals that their friends nominate. The transitive triplets parameter is usually positive, indicating that friends of friends often become friends in their own right.

Individual and dyadic attributes may be included in the model as covariates. Each individual-level covariate may include three parameters. *Attribute ego* describes the effect of the actor's attributes on the nomination of associates. *Attribute alter* describes the effect of the group's attributes on the nomination of associates. *Attribute similarity* describes the tendency of actors to nominate associates with similar characteristics. Using delinquent behavior as an example, a positive attribute ego effect indicates that those with higher scores on delinquency make more friendship nominations. A positive attribute alter effect indicates that those with higher scores on delinquency receive more friendship nominations. A positive attribute similarity effect indicates that adolescents tend to nominate others with similar delinquency scores. Dyad-level covariates describe effects specific to pairings of individuals such that each dyad-level covariate constitutes a separate network. *Dyadic similarity* describes the tendency to select friends and other associates who have connections to the dyadic-level network and the larger peer network. For example, a positive dyadic classroom similarity effect indicates a tendency to nominate affiliates who are in the same class. Dyad-level covariates may be specified as constant or changing over time. Interactions between individuals and dyadic attributes and structural network effects may also be considered.

The behavioral objective function encompasses at least two parameters. *Behavioral tendency* describes individual scores on a behavioral variable, with positive scores indicating high levels of an attribute and negative scores indicating low levels of an attribute. *Behavioral similarity* describes the tendency of actors to adopt the behavior of associates with whom they are tied, with positive scores indicating that associates become more similar over time and negative scores indicating that associates become less similar over time. Interactions between behavioral parameters and structural network effects may also be considered.

Applying SIENA. Technical details on SIENA model fitting procedures are described elsewhere (Burk, Steglich, & Snijders, 2007; Snijders, 2005; Snijders et al., 2007). We present a nontechnical overview. In the first step, a dyadic independence model is tested to determine whether dyads within a network are independent. A statistically significant transitive triplets score signals network interdependence beyond that associated with dyadic interdependence, which suggests that the model should include additional network structuring variables. The second step determines the independence of the network evolution and behavioral evolution functions. A statistically significant test of network effects on behavior and behavior effects on network structure indicates interdependence, which is required for the final stage of model fitting. The third step involves fitting an interdependence model to the data. This final model includes the network and behavioral parameters of interest, providing an estimate of the relative strength of components that represent selection and socialization effects.

By way of example, we present results on peer group homogeneity for a subsample of youth drawn from the first four annual waves of data from the *10 to 18 Study* (Kerr et al., 2007). The target sample included 152 13 and 14 year-old youth with at least two consecutive waves of data. The participants represented a majority of the 8th grade students in two schools. Also included were all of the friends that the target participants nominated as important peers and associates. Thus, network analyses included 160 girls and 199 boys, ranging in age from 10 to 18 years (M = 14.1 years) from 49 classrooms in 9 different schools. Only parameter estimates associated with network structure, selection, and socialization are described here. Extensive SIENA results from a similar subsample of participants are described elsewhere (Burk et al., 2007).

Table 2.2 presents parameter estimates for the final model. The model included density, reciprocity, and transitive triplets parameters to estimate structural characteristics of the network. All three effects were significant, indicating that participants nominated peers (a) in a selective, rather than random fashion; (b) who returned their nominations; and (c) who were nominated as associates of those they nominated. The model also included a changing dyadic-level covariate, classroom, based on classroom membership at each measurement point. This dyadic parameter accounts for affiliation tendencies arising from increased opportunities for interaction that might otherwise be attributed to different forms of selection. The class effect was positive, indicating that participants tended to nominate their classmates.

Four parameters estimating selection effects based on individual attributes were included in the model. Strong effects emerged for age and gender, indicating that participants tended to nominate same age, same-sex peers as associates. Selection effects for delinquency and for the delinquency by reciprocity interaction were positive but failed to reach statistical significance. The model included two behavioral evolution effects that describe socialization. The significant main effect for delinquency similarity and the significant interaction between delinquency similarity and reciprocity indicated that youth tended not to adopt the delinquent behaviors of those they nominated as associates unless these nominations were reciprocated.

Taken together, the results suggest that adolescents selectively nominate (a) peer affiliates who returned their nomination and who were associates of those who were nominated and (b) same-age, same-sex classmates. Selection effects failed to reach statistical significance, but strong socialization effects emerged such that youth tended to adopt the delinquent behaviors of peers who reciprocated their nomination. Thus, we conclude that these peer networks formed on the basis of similarities in age, sex, and classroom but not delinquency, and that mutual friends in these networks grow more similar

TABLE 2.2
Parameter Estimates of the Final SIENA Model

Parameter	Estimate	Standard Error	t-ratio
Network Dynamics			
Rate period 1	14.795	1.795	
Rate period 2	24.384	3.812	
Rate period 3	16.699	2.027	
Density	-3.288	0.105	-31.40**
Reciprocity	2.188	0.180	12.17**
Transitive triplets	0.281	0.006	46.82**
Classroom	0.492	0.005	10.25**
Age similarity (selection)	2.289	0.222	10.29**
Gender similarity (selection)	0..832	0.048	17.33**
Delinquent similarity (selection)	0.467	0.554	0.84
Delinquent similarity (selection) by reciprocity	0.013	1.378	0.01
Behavior Dynamics			
Rate period 1	78.324	12.235	
Rate period 2	42.637	7.567	
Rate period 3	37.503	10.214	
Delinquency tendency	-0.369	0.054	-6.85**
Delinquent similarity (influence)	-18.520	4.723	-3.92**
Delinquent similarity (influence) by reciprocity	11.460	2.379	4.82**
Delinquency by gender	-0.068	0.032	-2.12*

Note. The *t*-ratio is defined as the parameter estimate divided by standard error.
$*p < .05.$ $**p < .01.$

over time in terms of delinquent behavior. As was the case in our APIM analyses, we found that in this network of Swedish youth, socialization effects for delinquency were stronger than selection effects.

CONCLUSION

Incorporating interdependent data into the design and analysis of longitudinal research is one of the greatest challenges facing contemporary developmental scholars. Nowhere is this challenge more pressing than in the developmental study of close relationships, which requires prospective data concerning both participants in a relationship. A review of the literature suggests that interdependent data are often underutilized because of a perceived lack of appropriate analytic tools. This chapter describes examples of recent statistical advances designed to address this problem. Two of these techniques were applied to three waves of longitudinal data on friendship homophily and to four waves of longitudinal data on peer group homogeneity in an effort to disentangle delinquency selection effects from delinquency socialization effects. Both procedures indicated that the latter was stronger than the former.

Few topics in relationship research are as complex as the origins of similarity between friends and among members of the same peer group. It is no surprise, therefore, that few topics in relationship research have yielded such murky results. We selected this seemingly intractable problem to demonstrate that tools are available to help scholars who are struggling to parse variance on interdependent relationships using interdependent data. Developmental scholars who ignore interdependence do so at the risk of jeopardizing the validity of their research efforts. Fortunately, new tools have been developed that make it possible for the first time to incorporate interdependence in developmental research. The chapters that follow provide indispensable guidance for the expert and novice alike as they seek to embrace interdependence.

ACKNOWLEDGMENTS

Support for the preparation of this chapter was provided to Brett Laursen by the U.S. National Institute of Mental Health (MH058116). During the preparation of this chapter, William J. Burk was supported by the Swedish Research Council. Support for the *10 to 18 Project* was provided to Margaret Kerr and Håkan Stattin by the Swedish Research Council.

REFERENCES

Adams, R. E., Bukowski, W. M., & Bagwell, C. (2005). Stability of aggression during early adolescence as moderated by reciprocated friendship status and friend's aggression. *International Journal of Behavioral Development, 29*, 139-145.

Arbuckle, J. L. (2003). *Amos 5.0.* Chicago: Smallwaters.

Batagelj, V., & Mrvar, A. (2004). *Pajek: Package for large networks. Version 0.98.* Ljubljana, Slovenia: University of Ljubljana.

Baumeister, R. F., & Leary, M. R. (1995). The need to belong: Desire for interpersonal attachments as a fundamental human motivation. *Psychological Bulletin, 117*, 497-529.

Bell, R. (1968). A reinterpretation of the direction of effect in studies of socialization. *Psychological Review, 75*, 81-95.

Berndt, T. J., & Keefe, K. (1995). Friends' influence on adolescents' adjustment to school. *Child Development, 66*, 1312-1329.

Berscheid, E. (1999). The greening of relationship science. *American Psychologist, 54*, 260-266.

Boer, P., Huisman, M., Snijders, T. A. B., Steglich, C. E. G., Wichers, L. H. Y., & Zeggelink, E. P. H. (2006). *StOCNET: An open software system for the advanced statistical analysis of social networks. Version 1.7.* Groningen: ICS/Science Plus.

Bugenthal, D. B. (2000). Acquisition of the algorithms of social life: A domain-based approach. *Psychological Bulletin, 126*, 187-219.

Burk, W. J., & Laursen, B. (2005). Adolescent perceptions of friendship and their associations with individual adjustment. *International Journal of Behavioral Development, 29*, 156-164.

Burk, W. J., Steglich, C. E. G., & Snijders, T. A. B. (2007). Beyond dyadic interdependence: Actor-oriented models for co-evolving social networks and individual behaviors. *International Journal of Behavioral Development, 31*, 397-404.

Cairns, R. B., & Cairns, B. D. (1994). *Lifelines and risks: Pathways of youth in our time.* New York: Cambridge University Press.

Campbell, L. J., & Kashy, D. A. (2002). Estimating actor, partner, and interaction effects for dyadic data using PROC MIXED and HLM5: A user-friendly guide. *Personal Relationships, 9*, 327-342.

Card, N. A., Hodges, E. V. E., Little, T. D., & Hawley, P. H. (2005). Gender effects in peer nominations for aggression and social status. *International Journal of Behavioral Development, 29*, 146-155.

Carrington, P., Scott, J., & Wasserman, S. (2005). *Models and methods in social network analysis.* New York: Cambridge University Press.

Cillessen, A. H. N., Jiang, X. L., West, T. V., & Laszkowski, D. K. (2005). Predictors of dyadic friendship quality in adolescence. *International Journal of Behavioral Development, 29*, 165-172.

Cohen, J. M. (1977). Sources of peer group homophily. *Sociology of Education, 50,* 227-241.

Coie, J. D., Cillessen, A. H. N., Dodge, K. A., Hubbard, J. A., Schwartz, D., Lemerise, E. A., et al. (1999). It takes two to fight: A test of relational factors and a method for assessing aggressive dyads. *Developmental Psychologyy, 35,* 1179-1188.

Coleman, J. (1961). *The adolescent society.* Glencoe, IL: Free Press.

Cook, W. L., & Dreyer, A. (1984). A Social Relations Model: A new approach to analysis of family-dyadic interaction. *Journal of Marriage and the Family, 46,* 679-687.

Cook, W. L., & Kenny, D. A. (2005). The Actor-Partner Interdependence Model: A model of bidirectional effects in developmental studies. *International Journal of Behavioral Development, 29,* 101-109.

Cyram. (2004). *Cyram NetMiner II. Version 2.4.0.* Seoul, Korea: Cyram Co.

Davis, J. A. (1979). The Davis-Holland-Leinhardt studies: An overview. In P. W. Holland & S. Leinhardt (Eds.), *Perspectives on social network research.* New York: Academic Press.

Dishion, T. J., McCord, J., & Poulin, F. (1999). When interventions harm: Peer groups and problem behavior. *American Psychologist, 54,* 1-10.

Ennett, S. T., & Bauman, K. E. (1994). The contribution of influence and selection to adolescent peer group homogeneity: The case of adolescent cigarette smoking. *Journal of Personality & Social Psychology, 67,* 653-663.

Gonzalez, R., & Griffin, D. W. (1999). The correlational analysis of dyad-level data in the distinguishable case. *Personal Relationships, 6,* 449-469.

Griffin, D. W., & Gonzalez, R. (1995). Correlational analysis of dyad-level data in the exchangeable case. *Psychological Bulletin, 118,* 430-439.

Hartup, W. W., & Laursen, B. (1999). Relationships as developmental contexts: Retrospective themes and contemporary issues. In W. A. Collins & B. Laursen (Eds.), *The Minnesota Symposia on Child Psychology: Vol. 30. Relationships as developmental contexts* (pp. 13-35). Mahwah, NJ: Erlbaum.

Hinde, R. A. (1997). *Relationships: A dialectical perspective.* Hove, England: Psychology Press.

Hogue, A., & Steinberg, L. (1995). Homophily of internalized distress in adolescent peer groups. *Developmental Psychology, 31,* 897-906.

Hubbard, J. A., Dodge, K. A., Cillessen, A. H. N., Coie, J. D., & Schwartz, D. (2001). The dyadic nature of social information processing in boys' reactive and proactive aggression. *Journal of Personality and Social Psychology, 76,* 677-685.

Jaccard, J., Blanton, H., & Dodge, T. (2005). Peer influences on risky behavior: An analysis of the effects of a close friend. *Developmental Psychology, 41,* 135-147.

Kandel, D. B. (1978). Homophily, selection, and socialization in adolescent friendships. *American Journal of Sociology, 84,* 427-436.

Kashy, D. A., & Kenny, D. A. (2000). The analysis of data from dyads and groups. In H. T. Reis & C. M. Judd (Eds.), *Handbook of research methods in social and personality psychology* (pp. 451-477). New York: Cambridge University Press.

Kelly, H. H., Berscheid, E., Christensen, A., Harvey, J. H., Huston, T. L., Levinger, G., et al. (1983). *Close relationships*. New York: Freeman.

Kenny, D. A. (1995). The effect of nonindependence on significance testing in dyadic research. *Personal Relationships, 2,* 65-75.

Kenny, D. A. (1996). Models of non-independence in dyadic research. *Journal of Social and Personal Relationships, 13,* 279-294.

Kenny, D. A., & Cook, W. (1999). Partner effects in relationship research: Conceptual issues, analytic difficulties, and illustrations. *Personal Relationships, 6,* 433-448.

Kenny, D. A., & La Voie, L. (1984). The Social Relations Model. In L. Berkowitz (Ed.), *Advances in experimental social psychology. Vol. 18* (pp. 141-182). Orlando, FL: Academic Press.

Kerr, M., Stattin, H., & Kiesner, J. (2007). Peers and problem behavior: Have we missed something? In R. C. M. E. Engles, M. Kerr, & H. Stattin (Eds.), *Friends, lovers, and groups: Key relationships in adolescence* (pp. 125-153). Chichester, England: John Wiley & Sons.

Laursen, B. (2005). Dyadic and group perspectives on close relationships. *International Journal of Behavioral Development, 29,* 97-100.

Laursen, B., & Bukowski, W. M. (1997). A developmental guide to the organisation of close relationships. *International Journal of Behavioral Development, 21,* 747-770.

Lazarsfeld, P. F., & Merton, R. K. (1954). Friendship as a social process. In M. Berger, T. Abel, & C. H. Page (Eds.), *Freedom and control in modern society* (pp. 18-66). Princeton: Van Nostrand.

Leenders, R. T. A. J. (1995). Models for network dynamics: A markovian framework. *Journal of Mathematical Sociology, 20,* 1-21.

Malloy, T. E., Sugarman, D. B., Montvilo, R. K., & Ben-Zeev, T. (1995). Children's interpersonal perceptions: A social relations analysis of perceiver and target effects. *Journal of Personality and Social Psychology, 68,* 418-426.

Moffitt, T. E. (1993). Adolescence-limited and life-course-persistent antisocial behavior: A developmental taxonomy. *Psychological Review, 100,* 674-701.

Neyer, F. J. (2002). The dyadic interdependence of attachment security and dependency: A conceptual replication across older twin pairs and younger couples. *Journal of Social and Personal Relationships, 19,* 483-503.

Olsen, J. A., & Kenny, D. A. (2006). Structural equation modeling with interchangeable dyads. *Psychological Methods, 11,* 1-15.

Reis, H. T., Collins, W. A., & Berscheid, E. (2000). The relationship context of human behavior and development. *Psychological Bulletin, 126,* 844-872.

Richards, W. D., & Rice, R. E. (1981). The NEGOPY network analysis program. *Social Networks, 3,* 215-223.

Richards, W. D., & Seary, A. J. (2003). *Multinet. Version 4.38 for Windows.* Burnaby: Simon Fraser University.

Ross, H. S., & Lollis, S. P. (1989). A social relations analysis of toddler peer relations. *Child Development, 60,* 1082-1091.

Sears, R. R. (1951). A theoretical framework for personality and social behavior. *American Psychologist, 6,* 476-483.

Simpkins, S. D., & Parke, R. D. (2002). Do friends and nonfriends behave differently? A social relations analysis of children's behavior. *Merrill-Palmer Quarterly, 48,* 263-283.

Snijders, T. A. B. (1996). Stochastic actor-oriented models for network change. *Journal of Mathematical Sociology, 21,* 149-172.

Snijders, T. A. B. (2001). The statistical evaluation of social network dynamics. *Sociological Methodology, 31,* 361-395.

Snijders, T. A. B. (2005). Models for longitudinal network data. In P. Carrington, J. Scott, & S. Wasserman (Eds.), *Models and methods in social network analysis* (pp. 215-247). New York: Cambridge University Press.

Snijders, T. A. B., Pattison, P. E., Robins, L., G., & Handcock, M. S. (2006). New specifications for exponential random graph models. *Sociological Methodology, 36,* 99-153.

Snijders, T. A. B., Steglich, C. E. G., & Schweinberger, M. (2007). Modeling the co-evolution of networks and behavior. In K. van Montfort, H. Oud, & A. Satorra (Eds.), *Longitudinal models in the behavioral and related sciences* (pp. 41-71). Mahwah, NJ: Erlbaum.

Snijders, T. A. B., Steglich, C. E. G., Schweinberger, M., & Huisman, M. (2006). *Manual for SIENA, version 3.* University of Groningen.

Urberg, K. A., Değirmencioğlu, S. M., & Pilgrim, C. (1997). Close friend and group influence on adolescent cigarette smoking and alcohol use. *Developmental Psychology, 33,* 834-844.

Wasserman, S., & Faust, K. (1994). *Social network analyses. Methods and applications.* Cambridge: Cambridge University Press.

Woody, E., & Sadler, P. (Eds.). (2005). Structural equation models for interchangeable dyads: Being the same makes a difference. *Psychological Methods, 10,* 139-158.

CHAPTER THREE

Application of the Social Relations Model Formulas to Developmental Research

William L. Cook

Maine Medical Center

A key challenge for the study of development is to understand interdependence between the individual and the environment. In terms of human social development, we need to observe the individual embedded within his or her social context as both change over time to assess how much each influences the other. The family system is one of the most important contexts for human development and for observing processes of interdependence. As noted by Baumrind (1980), "Within a reciprocal and interacting system such as the family, individuals produce by their actions the environmental conditions that affect their own as well as others' behavior. One person's behavior is simultaneously a response to environmental stimuli and a stimulus to others' response within the interactive system of social exchange" (p. 640). The focus of this chapter is the measurement of interdependence between the individual and the family environment, the goal being to address questions of how the organization of individual behavior can develop and be maintained through processes of interpersonal influence. To accomplish this, components of the Social Relations Model (SRM: Kenny & La Voie, 1984) are treated as scores in longitudinal analyses. Following a description of the SRM, the formulas for calculating the SRM effects are described and explained. Three analyses are then presented to illustrate the versatility of the approach: (1) a model that simultaneously tests temporal stability in SRM components measured at the family, individual and dyadic levels of analysis, (2) a hybrid SRM-APIM (Actor–Partner Interdependence Model), and (3) a model testing the stability of actor–partner reciprocity.

The Social Relations Model

The SRM was originally developed by David Kenny and his colleagues for the analysis of round-robin designs (Kenny & La Voie, 1984; Warner, Kenny, & Stoto, 1979). A round-robin design is one in which each member of a group has a relationship with each of the other members. A family group is a naturally occurring round-robin design, so it was natural that it would be applied to family data (Cook & Dreyer, 1984). The family SRM provides key information on the dynamics of the family system (Cook, 1994). Recent studies have applied the family SRM to the study of attachment security in families (Buist, Dekovic, Meeus, & van Aken, 2004; Cook, 2000), relational support in families (Branje, van Aken, & van Leishout, 2002), the prediction of adolescent problem behavior (Delsing, van Aken, Oud, De Bruyn, & Scholte, 2005), the affective quality of family relationships (Ross, Stein, Trabasso, Woody, & Ross, 2005), and the clinical assessment of families (Cook, 2005; Cook & Kenny, 2004; Manders, Cook, Scholte, Janssens, & De Bruyn, 2007). Many other studies have applied the SRM effectively to non-family data, including studies of aggressive behavior (Coie et al., 1999) and perceptions of status and aggression among school children (Card, Hodges, Little, & Hawley, 2005).

Although the complete SRM is too complex to be illustrated well using a single path model, Figure 3.1 presents a path model of SRM components affecting just the two variables of mother and child attachment security. Note that the complete model could not be estimated by just these two variables. According to the family version of the SRM, the relationship of one family member to another is a function of four systematic sources of variance: a family factor, an actor factor, a partner factor, and a relationship factor. This is illustrated in Figure 3.1. There are two observed variables represented by the rectangles in the model. On the left side of the figure is the observed score for the child's attachment security in relationship to the mother, and on the right side is the observed score for the mother's attachment security in relationship to the child. Focusing first on the child's attachment security in relationship to the mother, it is reasonable to expect that some children will be more secure than others. Consequently, within a sample of families there will be variance in this measure. The causal arrows directed at the rectangle for the child to mother attachment stem from the four systematic sources of variance in this measure. Child attachment to mother is a function of the family factor, the child actor factor, the mother partner factor, and the child–mother relationship factor. Variance in the measure that is not explained by these systematic sources of variance is attributed to errors of measurement (e_1). Similarly, the mother's attachment to the child is predicted by the family

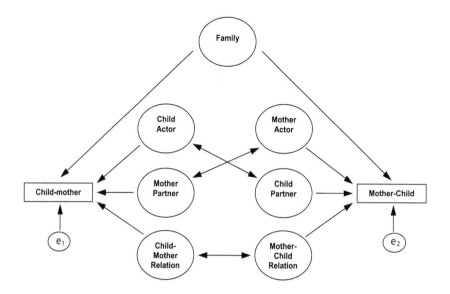

Figure 3.1. The SRM components for the mother-child dyad.

factor, the mother actor factor, the child partner factor, and the mother–child relationship factor. The residual variance is labeled e_2.

Family Effects

The family factor measures variance across families in the family effect. The family effect is the score representing the average person in the family, the family mean. As such, it will reflect a group-level trait to the extent that most people in the group have the trait or are affected by it. The family factor will be statistically significant if there is some degree of similarity among members of a family and if there are between-family differences in the level of the variable on which they are similar. In other words, it measures similarity at the group level. For example, to the extent that negativity is contagious, some families will be higher in negativity than other families even after controlling for the tendency of some individuals to bring negativity to the group or to elicit it from the group (i.e., actor and partner effects). In SRM research with families, variance in the family–group effect tends to be small (e.g., Cook, 2000). Perhaps this is because family members often compensate for each others' behavior. So if someone is overly negative, someone else may compensate by being unusually positive. Such patterns make family members dissimilar and therefore diminish family-level effects. Despite its small variance, a family–group effect can be a powerful predictor of individual outcomes (Delsing, van Aken, Oud, De Bruyn, & Scholte, 2005). Note in Figure 3.1 that both the mother's attachment to the child and the child's attachment to the mother are affected by the family factor.

Actor Effects

The actor factor measures variance across families in an actor effect. The actor effect reflects characteristics of the person who provides the measure, whether by self-report or, indirectly, via a knowledgeable informant or trained observer. If the actor is reporting about an interpersonal perception (e.g., another family member's responsiveness), the actor effect would be called a perceiver effect. The actor or perceiver effect is not based on the measure of a single relationship. Rather, it reflects the person's general behavior or perspective measured across multiple relationships in which the actor participates; for example, ratings of the child's security in relationship to mother, father, and sibling. It therefore measures a kind of cross-situational consistency, much like a personality trait (Malloy & Kenny, 1986). In this case, however, the different situations are actually the different partners, not different physical settings. Actor factors are estimated for each role in the family and the key statistical question is whether there is reliable variance in the actor effect within the sample of families. In a sample of two-parent two-child families, four actor factors would be estimated; mother, father, older sibling, and younger sibling. Only the mother and child actor factors are presented in Figure 3.1.

Partner Effects

The partner factor measures variance in a partner effect. A partner effect reflects characteristics of the person who is the object of the relationship. For example, a child's attachment security in relationship to mother may be determined by the mother's characteristic level of responsiveness. Because the child's score is explained by the mother's characteristics, there is a partner effect. If the measure involved interpersonal perceptions (e.g., if the child were rating mother's responsiveness), the partner effect would be called a target effect. Like the actor effect, the partner effect is not based on the measurement of one person's relationship to mother; it is based on the experience of multiple people (e.g., father, child, and sibling) in relationship to mother. It reflects cross-situational consistency in how others experience the partner. Because they are based on consistencies across multiple relationships, actor and partner effects are presumed to measure individual differences. Like actor factors, a partner factor is estimated for each role in the family group. Because the family effect is one of the variables predicting each observed score, variance explained by the actor and partner effects is independent of the family effect. Only the mother and child partner factors are presented in Figure 3.1.

Relationship Effects

A relationship factor measures variance in a relationship effect. Relationship effects reflect the unique adjustment of the actor to the partner, independent of characteristics of the group, the actor, and the partner. A relationship effect is comparable to an interaction effect in the ANOVA model (Warner, Kenny, & Stoto, 1979). In the case of the child's attachment security in relationship to the mother, the relationship effect reflects a crossing of the child's actor effect with the mother's partner effect. The child–mother relationship effect is not caused by an actor effect because it is not the child's general state, and it is not due to a partner effect because not everyone feels so secure with the mother. It is measured at the dyadic level of analysis. Note the similarity between relationship effects in the SRM, Sameroff's (1975) interactional model, and the notion of "goodness of fit" in developmental psychology (Lerner, 1993; Thomas & Chess, 1977). The idea is that the crossing of traits from two people may produce an outcome that is not due to either person's trait alone (i.e, a main effect) but rather to the unique way the two people fit together (i.e., an interaction effect). It should be noted, however, that SRM relationship effects are directional. That the child has a uniquely secure relationship to the mother does not imply that the mother is uniquely secure in relationship to the child. In a two-parent two-child family, there will be 12 relationship factors. Only the child–mother and mother–child relationship factors are presented in Figure 3.1.

Reciprocity: Individual and Dyadic

Family and partner effects are two important sources of interdependence in family relationships. The family effect represents the overall context or micro-culture in which much of individual development takes place. The partner effect represents the ability of other people to elicit uncharacteristic thoughts, feelings, and behavior from an actor. From the view of family systems theory, however, the SRM reciprocity correlations are the most important sources of interdependence. The reciprocity correlations measure the positive and negative feedback loops that give family systems their self-organizing capacity. The SRM provides estimates of reciprocity at both the individual and dyadic levels of analysis. Individual level or generalized reciprocity is represented in

Figure 3.1 by the double-headed arrow connecting the child actor factor with the child partner factor (i.e., the child's actor–partner reciprocity correlation), and again by the double-headed arrow connecting the mother actor factor and the mother partner factor (i.e., the mother's actor–partner reciprocity correlation). Actor–partner reciprocity is usually estimated separately for each participating family member. An actor–partner correlation will be positive if there is a positive feedback loop (i.e., the person usually gets what he or she gives). The actor–partner correlation will be negative if there is a negative feedback loop (i.e., a compensatory process is operating). A dyadic reciprocity correlation is represented in Figure 3.1 by the double-headed arrow connecting the child–mother relationship factor with the mother–child relationship factor. Like the individual level reciprocity correlation, dyadic reciprocity correlations can be positive or negative, depending upon whether they are measuring reciprocal or compensatory feedback processes. In the case of dyadic reciprocity, however, the feedback process is restricted to a particular dyad (e.g., mother–child), whereas individual-level reciprocity involves all the individual's relationships within the group.

Cook (2000) tested the SRM effects for attachment security (relationship-specific comfort depending on the partner) in a sample of 208 families consisting of an adolescent, an older sibling, and two parents. There was a small, statistically nonsignificant family factor, indicating that family members are not generally similar in their level of comfort depending on other family members. The mother and child actor factors were both significant, indicating individual differences for both mothers and adolescents in attachment security. The mother and the adolescent partner factors were also significant, indicating that families differ in the degree to which the mother and the child serve as a secure base to others in the family. Finally, the mother–adolescent relationship factor and the adolescent–mother relationship factor were significant, indicating that across families, there are differences in how much mothers' and adolescents' attachments to each other reflect unique, dyadic adjustments. In terms of reciprocity of attachment security, adolescents generally get what they give (i.e., the correlation between actor and partner effects for adolescents was statistically significant). However, the generalized reciprocity correlation for mother and the dyadic reciprocity correlation for mothers and adolescents were not statistically significant.

The SRM provides a great deal of information about interdependence in family relationships. For this reason, it is desirable to study change in the SRM effects over the course of development. However, the SRM is difficult to study longitudinally. If one uses structural equation modeling to estimate the SRM for a two-parent two-child family (mother, father, older child, younger child), there will be 12 observed variables (mother–father, father–older child, younger child–mother, etc), 4 latent variables for the actors, 4 latent variables for the partners, 12 residual variables that contain unique relationship variance, and a family/group factor. Four actor–partner reciprocity correlations and six dyadic reciprocity correlations must also be specified. The study of change in the family SRM factors would require replication of the full model at Wave 2, plus paths to test the temporal stability of each component in the model, plus any causal paths that might be of interest. Thus, longitudinal analysis of the SRM is at best unwieldy.

The primary reason for testing the SRM in a structural equation model is to determine via confirmatory factor analysis which factors in the model have reliable variance. It is not necessary or desirable, however, to include all the SRM components in longitudinal models. Rather, there are formulas for calculating the SRM effects that can be used to generate only those components needed for a particular analysis. These formulas were presented in the very first publication about the SRM (Warner, Kenny, & Stoto, 1979), and subsequently in the first application of the SRM to family data (Cook & Dreyer, 1984). They can now be located in other sources as well (Cook & Kenny, 2004; Kenny, Kashy, & Cook, 2006).[1]

Formulas for Calculating the SRM Effects

We will focus here on calculating the SRM effects for data from four-person families, but the formulas can be used with family groups of three or larger. The procedure begins with the calculation of the family mean. The family mean is the mean of the 12 observed scores (mother–father, mother–older sibling (mother–OS), mother–younger sibling (mother–YS), father–mother, father–older sibling (father–OS), father–younger sibling (father–YS), OS–mother, OS–father, OS–YS, YS–mother, YS–father, YS–OS). For relationship specific attachment security, the family effect is the average of the 12 measures of relationship-specific comfort depending on the partner. Note that such a measure has much in common with ratings of whole family functioning (Manders et al., 2007) such as the Family Environment Scale (Moos & Moos, 1981) and the Family Adaptability and Cohesion Scales (Olson, Portner, & Lavee, 1985). The calculation of actor, partner, and relationship effects all depend on the measure of the family mean. An actor effect reflects an individual's average relationship based on the person's scores with multiple partners. However, to be an unbiased measure, the mean score for

---

[1]When working with the formula-based components, one should exclude from study any components that have not been shown via confirmatory factor analysis to have reliable variance.

a particular actor must be adjusted. The first adjustment is to subtract the family mean from the actor's mean score. This will reveal how the person differs from the average family member. If the family mean were not subtracted out, group-level effects would confound the measure of the actor effect. The actor effect must also be adjusted for the person's characteristics as a partner to remove "missing partner" bias in the data (Warner, Kenny, & Stoto, 1979). Missing partner bias occurs because the person does not have him- or herself as a partner. For example, the person in the family who is most negative does not have the most negative person as a partner, so his or her actor effect (e.g., perceptions of negativity from others) will tend to be smaller than those of other family members. The adjustment for the family effect and the missing partner bias can be seen in the equation for actor effects.

$$
\begin{aligned}
actor\ effect_i \ = \ & actor\ mean_i\ (n-1)^2/[n(n-2)] \\
& + partner\ mean_i\ (n-1)/[n(n-2)] \\
& - family\ mean\ (n-1)/(n-2)
\end{aligned} \tag{1}
$$

There are three steps in computing an actor effect. First, for any given family member i, the actor mean is computed as the weighted average of the person's scores in relation to each of the $n-1$ other family members. It is then adjusted by the person's partner mean (i.e., weighted average of the $n-1$ other family members' scores with that person as the partner) to remove the bias due to the missing partner score. As the third step, the weighted mean for the family is subtracted out. Actor effects can be either positive or negative. If the person is generally the source of scores that are greater than the family mean, the actor effect will be positive. If the person is the source of scores that are less than the average score in the family, the actor effect will be negative. In other words, actor effects are relative to the average score for all relationships within the family. They reflect deviations around the family mean. Note that for a four-person family, the weighting of the actor mean will be $(4-1)^2/[4(4-2)]$ or 9/8, plus the weighting for the partner mean, $(4-1)/[4(4-2)]$ or 3/8, minus the weighting for the family mean, $(4-1)/(4-2)$ or 1.5, which equals zero. That the actor effects sum to zero simply reflects the standard ANOVA constraints. Thus for a four-person family there will be three degrees of freedom (i.e., three unique pieces of information) for actor effects. The fourth actor effect can always be calculated as the difference between the sum of the other three and zero. More generally, there are $n-1$ degrees of freedom for actor effects, where n = the number of family members in the group.

The parallel formula for the partner effect is based on the partner mean for each person in the same way the actor effect is based on the actor mean.

$$partner\ effect_i\ =\ partner\ mean_i\ (n-1)^2/[n(n-2)] \quad (2)$$
$$+\ actor\ mean_i\ (n-1)/[n(n-2)]$$
$$-\ family\ mean\ (n-1)/(n-2)$$

Because the partner mean does not include scores reflecting the person as an actor, it is adjusted by the actor mean. This adjustment is the complement to the adjustment for the missing partner bias when calculating actor effects. The family mean is then subtracted from the adjusted partner mean. If the person is generally on the receiving end of scores that exceed the family mean, the partner effect will be positive. If the person is generally on the receiving end of scores that are less than the family mean, the partner effect will be negative. Thus, like the actor effects, the size of the partner effects is relative to the average family relationship; they reflect deviations from the family mean. The ANOVA constraints apply to partner effects, just as they do to actor effects. For a given family they will sum to zero. Consequently, for a four-person family, there are three degrees of freedom for partner effects. Relationship effects measure the unique adjustment of an actor to a partner, controlling for family, actor, and partner effects. Consequently, for an actor with just two partners (e.g., in a three-person family), there is only one relationship effect. This makes sense because relationship effect reflects a person's unique adjustment to a particular partner. When one has only two partners, a unique adjustment to one implies a unique adjustment to the other:

$$relationship\ effect_{i,j}\ =\ X_{i,j}\ -\ actor\ effect_i \quad (3)$$
$$-\ partner\ effect_j$$
$$-\ family\ mean$$

In this equation the actor effect for person i, the partner effect for person j, and the family mean are subtracted from the raw score for a particular actor in relationship to a particular partner ($X_{i,j}$). If a score is not due to the family as a group, the actor, or the partner, that only leaves the relationship and errors of measurement as its source. The formula for degrees of freedom for relationship effects is [(the number of actors minus 1) multiplied by (the number of partners minus 1)] minus the number of empty diagonal cells (i.e., the cell where the actor is also the partner, which is equal to the number of participants). For a four-person family this will equal $(4-1)$ times $(4-1)$ $= 9$, minus 4 empty diagonal cells for a total of 5. Thus, there are 5 degrees of freedom for unique relationship effects in a four-person family. Note that by this formula there is a total of only one degree of freedom for relationship effects in a three-person family.

There are numerous situations in which the use of these formulas may facilitate the study of interdependence in developmental studies. For example, Branje et al. (2005) simply wanted to correlate the SRM factors for perceived support with the SRM factors for agreeableness, to determine if agreeable people are supportive. This required a structural equation model with an extremely large number of parameters, because all the SRM components for both variables had to be specified in the model. An attempt to include even one additional construct (e.g., responsiveness) would surely be overwhelming. Moreover, developmental theories tend to focus on the growth and change of particular individuals within the family. As noted elsewhere, the necessity of estimating the SRM effects for all the roles in the family makes it difficult to maintain a focus of the outcomes of a particular family member (Cook, 2003). By using the SRM formulas, interdependence in the relationships of specific individuals (e.g., adolescents) may be studied over time in abstraction from the rest of the family system without the loss of contextualization.

ILLUSTRATIONS

Participants

These analyses involved 123 two-parent two-child families, a subgroup of the samples used in previous studies (Cook, 2000; Cook & Kenny, 2005). This subsample is smaller than the other samples because of missing data at Wave 2 and should not be considered representative of U.S. families. As noted elsewhere (Cook, 2000), the sample is predominantly White and in the middle to upper-middle SES group. Family groups included 57 adolescent males and 64 adolescent females. At Wave 1, the mothers averaged 45.9 years old (sd = 4.13), the fathers averaged 48.5 years old (sd = 5.83), the older siblings (56 men and 67 women) averaged 19.8 years old (sd = 2.20) and the adolescents (60 boys and 63 girls) averaged 16.0 years old (sd = 2.19).

Illustration 1: Temporal Stability at Three Levels of Analysis

This first illustration simply tests the over-time correlations for attachment security at the family, individual, and dyadic levels of analysis. This model illustrates the ability to isolate particular SRM components and estimate their relations with other variables. Specifically, the correlations between Wave 1 and Wave 2 data for the family effect, the adolescent actor effect, and the adolescent–mother relationship effect are estimated. Because of the way these variables are computed, they are uncorrelated with each other.

By three standard indicators of model fit, the fit of this model is excellent, $\chi^2(df = 12, N = 123) = 13.574$, $p = .33$, Comparative Fit Index (CFI) = .99, Root Mean Square Error of Approximation (RMSEA) = .033. All three stability correlations are statistically significant. Perhaps due to the effect of aggregation (i.e., collection of systematic variance due to summing over multiple variables), stability is greatest at the family level ($r = .808, p < .001$), second at the individual level ($r = .653, p < .001$), and least at the relationship level of analysis ($r = .364, p < .001$).

Whether the differences in stability are, in fact, due to differences in reliability accruing with aggregation across relationships could be tested using latent variable measures of the SRM effects. The relationship-specific scale scores could be split into two scores (i.e., item parcels) and each would be subjected separately to the SRM formulas. This would produce two indicators of each SRM effect. These indicators could then be used to specify the latent variable measure of each effect. The latent variable measures of the SRM effects would be, in principle, error free (i.e., perfectly reliable). Thus, any remaining differences in their stability over time would have to be due to other factors. Item parcels could be used to create latent variable measures of the SRM effects in the next two models as well.

Illustration 2: A Hybrid SRM-APIM Model

The Actor–Partner Interdependence Model (APIM) tests whether a person's outcome is affected by one's own and one's partner's characteristics. For example, Cook and Kenny (2005) tested whether a mother's and adolescent's attachment security scores at one point in time predicted their own and each other's attachment security one year later. However, SRM analysis reveals that measures of dyadic relationships, such as these attachment security scores, consist of multiple systematic factors. Adolescent–mother attachment security could be due to family characteristics, the adolescent's characteristics as an actor, the mother's characteristics as a partner, and unique characteristics of the adolescent–mother relationship. Any or all of these components may predict the Wave 2 observed score for adolescent–mother attachment security. Similarly, mother–adolescent attachment security could be due to family characteristics, the mother's characteristics as an actor, the adolescent's characteristics as a partner, and unique characteristics of the mother–adolescent relationship. Thus, by having the SRM components as the Time 1 predictors rather than the observed adolescent–mother and mother–

50   COOK

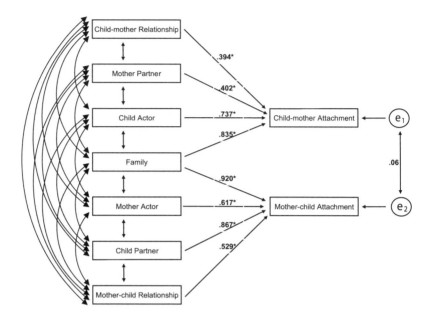

Figure 3.2. Hybrid of the SRM and APIM Models.

Note. Parameter estimates are unstandardized regression coefficients.
*p < .01.

adolescent attachment security scores, a more informative model of change in
each person's attachment security can be obtained. This model is depicted
in Figure 3.2.

In this model, the six SRM components relevant to adolescent–mother
and mother–adolescent attachment security—measured at Wave 1—serve as
predictors of adolescent–mother and mother–adolescent attachment security
at Wave 2. Specifically, the adolescents security in relationship to mother is
predicted by the family group effect, the adolescent actor effect, the mother
partner effect, and the adolescent–mother relationship effect. The mother's
security in relationship to the adolescent is predicted by the family group
effect, the mother actor effect, the adolescent partner effect, and the mother–
adolescent relationship effect.[2] Whereas these components of the SRM were
selected as predictor variables based on the measurement model specified by
the SRM, a particular theory probably would have specified only one or two
of these components as predictors. For example, a personality oriented theory

---

[2] If analyzing data from a three-person family, the value of the adolescent–mother relationship effect will be the same as the mother–adolescent relationship effect except that
the sign is reversed (see Cook & Kenny, 2004; Kenny, Kashy, & Cook, 2006).

may predict only actor effects. Knowledge of the SRM measurement model may therefore be the basis for a more elaborate model, one that is informed by a more sophisticated theory of measurement in social relationships. In any case, a theoretical rationale (based either on measurement theory or substantive theory) should guide the selection of predictors.

Generally in longitudinal models, the dependent variables (i.e., those measured at Wave 2) are predicted controlling for their values as measured at Wave 1. This insures that the effects of the predictor variables reflect change in the dependent variable and are not simply spurious correlations with the Wave 1 measures. However, in this model, the SRM effects encompass all the variance in the adolescent–mother and mother–adolescent attachment security scores measured at Wave 1. Consequently, the raw score measures should not be included as additional predictors at Wave 1. Note, however, that all of the SRM effects from Wave 1 are allowed to correlate. This specification would not be necessary if the SRM components had been estimated using confirmatory factor analysis because the components would be estimated controlling for each other.[3]

Note also that the only variable predicted to affect both mother–child and child–mother attachment security is the family effect. Implicit in this specification is the fact that the partner effects in the APIM may be spuriously due to the family effect. If this is true, however, the APIM partner effects should have the same sign and be approximately equal (Kenny & Cook, 1999). The APIM correlation between the observed scores at Wave 1 will usually provide sufficient control for this effect.

Results. The fit of the model is excellent, $\chi^2(6, N = 121) = 5.254, p = .51$, CFI $= 1.00$, and RMSEA $= .000$. The unstandardized regression coefficients indicate that the family effect is a significant longitudinal predictor of both child–mother attachment security ($B = .835, p < .001$) and mother–child attachment security ($B = .920, p < .001$). Each observed score is also predicted by the respective actor effect for the person from whom the score was taken. Adolescent–mother attachment security is significantly predicted by the adolescent actor effect ($B = .737, p < .001$) and mother–adolescent attachment security is predicted by the mother actor effect ($B = .616, p < .001$). Thus, the SRM actor effects are significant actor effects in the APIM sense of the term. Note that there is no path from the adolescent SRM partner effect to adolescent–mother attachment security or from the mother SRM partner ef-

---

[3]Unless specified otherwise, the actor effects for a given family are assumed to be independent of each other, as are partner effects and each of the relationship effects for a given actor (or partner). In some cases (e.g., Cook, 2001) specific actor or partner effects are allowed to correlate with each other; for example, to test whether parental partner effects for influenceability reflect a compensatory pattern.

fect to mother–adolescent attachment security. These would both have tested APIM actor effects had they been specified in the model.

In the APIM, interdependence is determined by whether characteristics of a partner predict a person's thoughts, feelings, or behavior. In this model we test whether SRM partner effects (how much attachment security the partner affords others in general) determines the actor's attachment security. In other words, the SRM partner effects are the predictors in the tests of APIM partner effects. Even after controlling for family effects, the adolescent SRM partner effect was a significant predictor of mother–adolescent attachment security ($B = .867, p < .001$) and the mother SRM partner effect was a significant predictor of adolescent–mother attachment security ($B = .402, p < .005$). Note that there is no path from the mother SRM actor effect to adolescent–mother attachment security or from the adolescent SRM actor effect to mother–adolescent attachment security. These paths would also have tested APIM partner effects at the individual level of analysis had they been included in the model.

It is sometimes assumed that when testing the APIM, one is testing relationship specific effects. As the preceding analyses indicate, other more general characteristics of the dyad members (i.e., SRM family, actor, and partner effects), all of which are embedded within the observed scores, contribute significantly to each person's relationship outcome. The paths from the SRM relationship effects to the respective attachment security outcomes tests whether the unique adjustment a person makes to a partner is stable over time, controlling for the other variables in the model. Thus, the SRM relationship effects are used to test APIM actor effects. Both effects are significant ($B = .394, p < .01$ for adolescent–mother and $B = .529, p < .001$ for mother–adolescent). Note that the path from the SRM adolescent–mother relationship effect to mother–adolescent attachment security is not included in the model, nor is the path from the SRM mother–adolescent relationship effect to adolescent–mother attachment security. These paths would have tested APIM partner effects at the dyadic level of analysis. It is interesting that, controlling for partner effects at the individual level of analysis, partner effects at the dyadic level of analysis (i.e., based on SRM relationship effects) are not needed in the model. Thus, the APIM partner effects in the standard APIM may actually reflect broader individual traits of the partner rather than relationship specific traits.

Illustration 3: Stability of Reciprocity

Two theories for the stability of adult attachment styles have been proposed in the literature. By far the dominant view is that adult attachment styles are stable because the individual experiences are filtered through internal working models of relationships and are largely forced to accommodate to these schemas. Thus someone with an insecure attachment style remains insecure because they interpret the behavior of others in a way that is consistent with this style. A more dynamic, interpersonal model proposes that individuals with particular attachment styles behave in ways that elicit the behavior from others that is consistent with the internal working model (Cook, 2000; Kobak & Hazan, 1991). Thus, the social perceptions are not so much forced to accommodate to the individual's internal working model of relationships as the individual's social behavior produces observable behavior in others that is consistent with the attachment-based expectations; a form of self-fulfilling prophecy. Large SRM actor–partner correlations ($r = .67$) have been reported in support of the "reciprocity model" of attachment security for adolescents (Cook, 2000). The actor–partner reciprocity correlation measures whether a person generally gets what they generally give, so this correlation indicates that insecure adolescents elicit insecurity from those with whom they interact (in this case, family members). However, this correlation is based on cross-sectional data. If the theory is correct, then this process of reciprocity must persist over time. This is tested by the model in Figure 3.3.[4] In this model, adolescent actor and partner effects for attachment security, calculated using the formulas, serve as indicators of latent-variable measures of actor–partner reciprocity at Wave 1 and Wave 2. The path from the latent variable at Wave 1 to the latent variable at Wave 2 tests whether there is stability of reciprocity of attachment security over the course of one year. Adolescent age and gender also serve as predictors of actor–partner reciprocity. And finally, the stability of the actor and partner effects themselves are tested.

The fit of this model was excellent, $\chi^2(df = 5, N = 123) = 1.359, p = .93$; CFI $= 1.00$, and $RMSEA = .000$. The results indicate that there is considerable stability in the actor–partner reciprocity factor for attachment security ($B = .330, p < .03$), independent of the stability of the actor and partner effects themselves. These stabilities, however, were also statistically significant. Independent of processes of reciprocal influence, there is stability in the tendency of adolescents to perceive their relationships as secure ($B = .511, p < .001$) and for others to experience their relationship with the adolescent as secure ($B = .615, p < .001$). Thus, the results of this analysis

---

[4]One might choose to specify correlated errors for residuals for the latent variables of the actor effects, and also for the residuals of the partner effects, rather than specifying that the observed effects at Wave 1 "cause" the observed effect at Wave 2. The model as specified would not be identified were it not for the fact that age and gender are correlated with the latent variable at Wave 1.

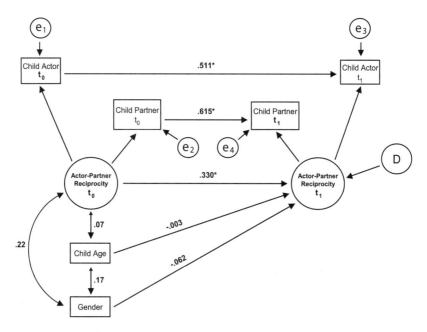

Figure 3.3. Stability of the adolescent actor–partner reciprocity correlation.

Note. Causal paths are unstandardized regression coefficients.
$*p < .01$.

support both theories of stability in attachment security. Age and gender did not have statistically significant effects on reciprocity of attachment security.

DISCUSSION

In this chapter I have presented the formulas for computing the family, actor, partner, and relationship effects from the SRM. Although these formulas have been presented elsewhere, they have not been presented specifically in the developmental psychology literature, and they remain unfamiliar to most developmental researchers. The purpose of this chapter has been to demonstrate how these formulas can facilitate developmental research that uses the SRM components. The SRM is a complex model with many parameters, especially when applied to family groups where there are separate actor and partner effects for each role, and two relationship effects for every dyad observed. The use of structural equation modeling or multilevel modeling approaches to estimate the SRM components, and the relationship of these components to the corresponding SRM components of other constructs, quickly becomes forbiddingly difficult.

The formulas provide a means of computing and using only the SRM components one needs to test a specific hypothesis. This not only simplifies the analysis of the developmental hypothesis, it simplifies the conceptualization of the hypothesis by helping the investigator focus on only those variables that are needed and at the level of analysis that is appropriate. The first illustration, for example, evaluated the temporal stability of attachment security at three levels of analysis, family, individual, and dyadic. However, does attachment theory specify that factors at all three levels are important to a child's development? If not, should it? The ability to abstract the components of the model from the model as a whole helps one maintain a focus on the factors expected to affect the dependent variable and not get lost in irrelevant complexities of the larger system.

The purpose of the second illustration was to clarify the similarities and differences between the APIM and the SRM. Rather than using the observed scores of the independent variables in this APIM analysis, I used the SRM components that account for those observed scores. This provided a more fine-grained analysis of the interdependence in mother and child relationship outcomes. For both mother and child, it was the way the partner is generally experienced by others (i.e., the SRM partner effect) that accounted for relationship-specific attachment security a year later, an APIM partner effect. In contrast, neither mother nor child relationship-specific attachment security was predicted by the other's general level of attachment security (i.e., the SRM actor effect) in the preceding year. The model fit very well without specifying either partner's SRM actor effect as a predictor of attachment security outcomes. The unique adjustment of the partner to the actor (i.e., the partner's relationship effect) was also excluded from the analysis without consequence. For example, the mother–child relationship effect at Wave 1 was not a predictor of the child to mother attachment security at Wave 2.

Positive and negative feedback processes are fundamental to a dynamic systems view of interpersonal relationships. Most of the research supporting such a view has used sequential analysis or similar procedures to measure reciprocity in particular dyads (Gottman, 1979; Patterson, 1982). However, feedback loops that affect an individual's development may involve his or her relationships with more than one other person. The actor–partner reciprocity correlation captures this notion; that is, the individual may *generally* get what he or she *generally* gives, or in terms of compensatory processes, the individual *generally* gets less the more he or she *generally* gives. Such feedback processes are one way of defining subsystems within the family, in contrast to the more common and arbitrary specification based on role relationships (e.g., the marital subsystem). The third illustration demonstrates how the SRM formulas can be used to construct the indicators of actor–partner reciprocity, and thus enable the study of such family subsystems (dynamically defined) over time. This relatively simple model evaluated the degree of temporal stability in adolescents' actor–partner reciprocity for attachment security over one year, and whether the development of actor–partner reciprocity is affected by the gender or age of the adolescent. The results indicate (a) that an adolescent's comfort depending on other family members is strongly related to other family members' comfort depending on the adolescent; (b) that there is temporal stability in the process, confirming that the process is self-maintaining; and (c) that gender and age are only weakly related to this process, if at all.

As these illustrations demonstrate, SRM effects calculated by means of the formulas can be used to address interesting and important questions related to social development. Moreover, in contrast to using confirmatory factor analysis to estimate the SRM effects, using the formulas allows one to test predictive models that include only those variables of theoretical interest. However, there are a number of considerations that should be taken into account. First, although the formulas make it easier to test developmental hypotheses using SRM effects, the formulas do not make it any easier to collect the round-robin family data. This study used data from the 123 families that provided complete data at Wave 2. The sample size is seriously diminished from the N of 208 complete families that participated in Wave 1. To some extent the effect of missing data might be minimized by using missing data replacement techniques and multilevel modeling procedures to estimate the models. However, it is still unlikely that the assumption that the missing data is "missing at random" required by these procedures could be justified given such a large loss of data. In this regard, the present analysis should be viewed as primarily for purposes of demonstration, and theory construction based on these results should be entertained very cautiously. Clearly, developmental researchers will need to pay special attention to psychological and social factors facilitating and inhibiting family members' participation in such studies across multiple waves of data collection. However, it can be done, and it is worth it.

A second issue concerns the determination of reliability and validity for the SRM components. When estimated via confirmatory factor analysis, the validity of the SRM components is based on a *priori* hypotheses regarding their operationalization, and their reliabilities are tested by whether the components have significant variance. The actual degree of reliability for each component can also be calculated from the output of the CFA. This suggests that one should first conduct a standard SEM or multilevel analysis for each construct on which SRM components will be calculated prior to using the formula-based components in other analyses. If the parameter in the model that one wants to use outside the CFA model (e.g., an actor effect or an actor–partner reciprocity correlation) is not significant within the CFA, it probably should not be used. For example, the family factor for attachment security in the second illustration was not significant in the CFA of the Wave 1 data (Cook, 2000). Because its reliability and validity have not been supported, it probably should not have been included in the analysis. That it was a significant predictor of child–mother and mother–child attachments at Wave 2 is a complicating factor, but should not mitigate the application of the most rigorous standards.

Along similar lines, the SRM components calculated by the formulas may not produce the best estimates in models such as those presented above. The reason is that the SRM components calculated using the formulas contain errors of measurement. Latent variables do not have errors of measurement, at least in principle. The effect of errors of measurement (i.e., noise) is to reduce the size of correlations involving the variable (Judd & Kenny, 1981). This has important effects on regression models, which are based on correlations. For example, the size of a regression coefficient relating a predictor variable to an outcome variable may be too small because the predictor variable has a lot of measurement error (i.e., noise). On the other hand, the size of this regression coefficient may be too large because it was estimated controlling for another variable that was also measured imperfectly. Because the effect of this other variable on the outcome variable is underestimated, the effect of the first variable on the outcome has not controlled for the other variable perfectly. It may therefore be overestimated.

As noted elsewhere, to estimate all the components of the SRM family model requires data contributed by at least four family members (Kashy & Kenny, 1990; Cook, Kenny, & Goldstein, 1991). Alternative CFA models have been proposed for three-person families (Kenny, Kashy, & Cook, 2006). The most common solution is to leave the family factor out of the model. In this case one would substitute the overall grand mean for the family mean in the formulas. Because this value will be a constant, it would essentially serve as a placeholder that enables the other components to be calculated.

Finally, unless otherwise specified (see Kenny, Kashy, & Cook, 2006), the SRM assumes there is no correlation between the actor effects for different family members, or between their partner effects, or between the relationship effects for a particular person (or role). If this assumption is seriously flawed, the results of the CFA will indicate that the model does not fit the data. However, even if these assumptions are supported in the CFA, components that are not supposed to be correlated may in fact be correlated when they are based on the formulas. This occurs because the CFA provides statistical control for associations that are not controlled when the formulas are used. For this reason, there should be strong theoretical grounds for inclusion of the formula-based components in further analyses. It may also be wise to test for spuriousness by using a step-wise regression procedure subsequent to testing the theory-driven model. If a key theoretical variable were unexpectedly replaced by another SRM factor, it may suggest an alternative theoretical view of the phenomenon to be tested. Because group and family processes are so complex, and because application of the SRM in evaluating these systems is still so new, such possibilities merit serious consideration.

CONCLUSION

The SRM was introduced almost three decades ago (Warner, Kenny, & Stoto, 1979), and we have barely scratched the surface of what can be learned using this powerful method. Its role in the study of group processes is comparable to the role of the microscope in the study of things small. For the first time, group, individual, and relationship processes can be simultaneously evaluated for their influence on social and developmental outcomes. Processes of reciprocity and compensation can be identified at both the individual and dyadic levels of analysis, and the distinction in the meaning of group and system can finally be resolved. The group effect is just one component in a system that includes actors, partners, and unique relationships, and the positive and negative feedback processes that modulate them. It is quite possible that the group effect is itself an emergent property of these lower-order processes.

If this were the field of physics or microbiology and a tool as important as the SRM was introduced, there would be a rush to master and utilize it in research. Not so in the social sciences. When I was planning my study of attachment security in family relationships, I was discouraged from doing so by a senior investigator. I was told that the method was too complicated and graduate students would not want to study attachment theory if they thought they had to use such techniques. The method is difficult to master, but not too difficult for graduate students in most disciplines. Perhaps the ability to use the formulas for the SRM components to test important hypotheses in social development will motivate researchers to accept the challenge of studying complex social processes using methods designed to address complexity. And perhaps the attitudes of the "old guard" will inhibit only their own research and not the advances that bright students using the SRM will inevitably make.

REFERENCES

Baumrind, D. (1980). New directions in socialization research. *American Psychologist, 35*, 639-652.

Branje, S. J. T., van Aken, M. A. G., & van Leishout, C. F. M. (2002). Relational support in families with adolescents. *Journal of Family Psychology, 16*, 351-362.

Branje, S. J. T., van Lieshout, C. F. M., & van Aken, M. A. G. (2005). Relations between agreeableness and perceived support in family relationships: Why nice people are not always supportive. *International Journal of Behavioral Development, 29*, 120-128.

Buist, K. L., Dekovic, M., Meeus, W. H. J., & van Aken, M. A. G. (2004). Attachment in adolescence: A Social Relations Model analysis. *Journal of Adolescent Research, 19*, 826-850.

Card, N. A., Hodges, E. V. E., Little, T. D., & Hawley, P. H. (2005). Gender effects in peer nominations for aggression and social status. *International Journal of Behavioral Development, 29*, 146-155.

Coie, J. D., Cillessen, A. H. N., Dodge, K. A., Hubbard, J. A., Schwartz, D., Lemerise, E. A., et al. (1999). It takes two to fight: A test of relational factors and a method for assessing aggressive dyads. *Developmental Psychology, 35*, 1179-1188.

Cook, W. L. (1994). A structural equation model of dyadic relationships within the family system. *Journal of Consulting and Clinical Psychology, 62*, 500-509.

Cook, W. L. (2000). Understanding attachment in family context. *Journal of Personality and Social Psychology, 78*, 285-294.

Cook, W. L. (2001). Interpersonal influence in family systems: A Social Relations Model analysis. *Child Development, 72*, 1179-1197.

Cook, W. L. (2003). Quantitative methods for deductive (theory testing) research on parent-child dynamics. In L. Kuczynski (Ed.), *Handbook of dynamics in parent-child relations* (pp. 347-372). Thousand Oaks, CA: Sage Publications.

Cook, W. L. (2005). The SRM approach to family assessment: An introduction and case example. *European Journal of Psychological Assessment, 21*, 216-225.

Cook, W. L., & Dreyer, A. S. (1984). The Social Relations Model: A new approach to the analysis of family-dyadic interaction. *Journal of Marriage and the Family, 46*, 679-687.

Cook, W. L., Kenny, D. A., & Goldstein, M. (1991). Parental affective style risk and the family system: A Social Relations Model analysis. *Journal of Abnormal Psychology, 100*, 492-501.

Cook, W. L., & Kenny, D. A. (2004). Application of the Social Relations Model to family assessment. *Journal of Family Psychology, 18*, 361-371.

Cook, W. L., & Kenny, D. A. (2005). An examination of self-report assessments of family functioning: A question of the level of analysis. *Journal of Family Psychology, 20*, 209-216.

Delsing, M. J. M. H., van Aken, M. A. G., Oud, J. H. L., De Bruyn, E. E. J., &
Scholte, R. H. J. (2005). Family loyalty and adolescent problem behavior:
The validity of the family group effect. *Journal of Research on Adolescence,*
15, 127-150.

Gottman, J. M. (1979). *Marital interaction: Experimental investigations.* New
York: Academic Press.

Judd, C. M., & Kenny, D. A. (1981). *Estimating the effects of social interventions.*
New York: Cambridge University Press.

Kashy, D. A., & Kenny, D. A. (1990). Analysis of family research designs: A model
of interdependence. *Communication Research, 17,* 462-482.

Kenny, D. A., & Cook, W. (1999). Partner effects in relationship research: Conceptual issues, analytic difficulties, and illustrations. *Personal Relationships,*
6, 433-488.

Kenny, D. A., Kashy, D. A., & Cook, W. L. (2006). *Dyadic data analysis.* New
York: Guilford Press.

Kenny, D. A., & La Voie, L. (1984). The Social Relations Model. In L. Berkowitz
(Ed.), *Advances in experimental social psychology: Vol. 18.* (pp. 141-182).
San Diego: Academic Press.

Kobak, R. R., & Hazan, C. (1991). Attachment in marriage: Effects of security and
accuracy of working models. *Journal of Personality and Social Psychology,*
60, 861-869.

Lerner, J. V. (1993). The influence of child temperamental characteristics on
parent behaviors. In T. Luster & L. Okagaki (Eds.), *Parenting: An ecological*
perspective (pp. 101-120) Hillsdale, NJ: Lawrence Erlbaum Associates.

Malloy, T. E., & Kenny, D. A. (1986). The Social Relations Model: An integrative
method for personality research. *Journal of Personality, 54,* 199-225.

Manders, W. A., Cook, W. L., Oud, J. H. L., Scholte, R. H. J., Janssens, J. M.
A. M., & De Bruyn, E. E. J. (2007). Level validity of self-report whole family
measures. *Journal of Family Psychology, 21,* 605-613.

Moos, R. H., & Moos, B. S. (1981). *Family Environment Scale Manual.* Palo Alto,
CA: Consulting Psychologists Press.

Olson, D. H., Portner, J., & Lavee, Y. (1985). *FACES III.* St. Paul, MN: Family
Social Science, University of Minnesota.

Patterson, G. R. (1982). *Coercive Family Processes.* Eugene, OR: Castalia.

Ross, H. S., Stein, N., Trabasso, T., Woody, E., & Ross, M. (2005). The quality of
family relationships within and across generations: A social relations analysis.
International Journal of Behavioral Development, 29, 110-119.

Sameroff, A. J. (1975). Early influence on development: Fact or fancy. *Merrill-*
Palmer Quarterly, 21, 267-294.

Thomas, A., & Chess, S. (1977). *Temperament and development.* New York:
Bruner-Mazel.

Warner, R. M., Kenny, D. A., & Stoto, M. (1979). A new round-robin analysis
of variance for social interaction data. *Journal of Personality and Social*
Psychology, 37, 1742-1757.

CHAPTER FOUR

Analyzing Social Networks in Adolescence

Antonius H. N. Cillessen

Radboud Universiteit Nijmegen and University of Connecticut

Casey Borch

University of Alabama at Birmingham

OVERVIEW

This chapter focuses on the problem of nesting of persons in social networks or cliques, and the analyses of such data over time. The study of social networks and cliques is an important topic in the social development literature. This chapter begins with a brief description of the history of this research and its position in the broader context of research on peer relations. Some of the unique measurement and scoring challenges that define social networks research with children or adolescents will then be presented. Next, results will be presented of the analysis of longitudinal patterns of various aspects of social clique membership, using data from a larger longitudinal study on the academic and social development of children and youth. Finally, theoretical and methodological implications of these findings will be discussed.

Levels of Analysis

Peer relations researchers typically distinguish three levels of analysis in the study of peer relations (Rubin, Bukowski, & Parker, 1998). At the level of the individual are peer status and social roles, characteristics that can be ascribed to the individual child or adolescent. At the level of the dyad, various relationships are found. A large portion of this research has focused on friendships (see, Bukowski, Newcomb, & Hartup, 1996), but other types of dyads are increasingly investigated, such as enemies (e.g., Hartup & Abecassis, 2002), bully-victim pairs (e.g., Hawkins, Pepler, & Craig, 2001), mutually aggressive dyads (e.g., Coie, Cillessen, Dodge, Hubbard, Schwartz, Lemerise, & Bateman, 1999), and romantic relationships (see Furman, Brown, & Feiring, 1999). Specific statistical methods are needed when dyads are the unit of analysis (see Kenny, Kashy, & Cook, 2006).

At the third level of analysis are social networks, social groups, cliques, and crowds (see, e.g., Brown, 1990; Kindermann, chapter 14, Rodkin & Hanish, 2007). The terms social networks and social cliques are used the most frequently and are often used interchangeably. At this level of analysis, neither individuals nor dyads are the unit of analysis. Analyses focus either on individuals nested in groups, or directly on the groups themselves. In past research, the fact that children are nested in groups was often overlooked in the peer relations literature.

The conceptual distinction between the individual, dyadic, and group levels of analysis has been a useful framework to guide theory and research, and studies of peer relations often focus their analyses primarily on one of these three levels. This limited focus does not do full justice to the complexity of children and adolescents' peer relations. First, the three levels are nested within one another and this needs to be accounted for rather than treating each in isolation. Second, the nesting is not necessarily "clear"—individuals are members of multiple dyads and multiple groups, dyad members may not be in the same groups. Third, there are developmental changes in the importance or weight of each level of analysis. Individual status, dyadic relationships, and social cliques and networks may be differentially important at different developmental stages. This differential importance may be due to developmental factors, such as the emergence of friendships in early childhood, the growth of peer groups in middle childhood, and the emergence of romantic relations in early adolescence, but it may also be due to structural changes such as school transitions that have nothing to do with development but are correlated with it. These complexities have been recognized in research on the social context at large (e.g., Bronfenbrenner & Morris, 1998; Levitt, Guacci-Franco, & Levitt, 1993). The ideas from this research could also be applied to understanding how individual peer status, dyadic relationships, and social networks interact to influence social development. Dynamic systems theory provides a useful tool toward this effort (see e.g., Granic & Dishion, 2003; Granic & Patterson, 2006).

Social Network Level

In comparison to the individual and dyadic levels of analyses, the social network (group) level has been studied the least often. There is now a large database of literature on individual sociometric status (see, e.g., Cillessen & Mayeux, 2004; Newcomb, Bukowski, & Pattee, 1993). There is also a large literature on friendship dyads (e.g., Bukowski et al., 1996; Newcomb & Bagwell, 1995) and an emerging literature on other dyad types (see, e.g., Hodges & Card, 2003). The social networks literature has been smaller perhaps because the computation of social networks is more difficult than the determination of individual status or dyadic relationships. There are various reasons for this difficulty. First, the definition of what a social network is, and when someone is or is not in a network, is less clear-cut than the definition of individual peer status or a dyadic relationship (see Templin, chapter 13). Second, there are also various methods to collect the data to identify social networks, and these methods have different advantages and disadvantages. Third, the methods for the assessment of social networks tend to be labor intensive and complex, both in data collection and data manipulation. Fourth, while much progress has been made in the statistical analysis of dyads (cf. Kenny et al., 2006), similar guidelines are not yet available for the analysis of social networks in the developmental literature.

In the peer relations field, three methods for the identification of social networks have commonly been used. The text below presents a brief description of these methods. The first two have their roots in developmental psychology, whereas the third originates from sociology.

Social-Cognitive Maps

An influential approach for measuring social networks in childhood or adolescence is the Social-Cognitive Map (SCM) method developed by Cairns and colleagues (Cairns et al., 1985, 1988). In this method, participants are asked to think about their classroom or grade, and are then asked to indicate if there are "any groups of kids who hang out together a lot." By examining the consensus among the groups identified by different respondents, a picture of the group's social structure is created.

This method has been used in a large number of studies with preadolescent and adolescent groups ranging from 4th to 12th grade, and has yielded important results (e.g., Cairns et al., 1985, 1988; Cairns, Leung, Buchanan, & Cairns, 1995; Farmer & Rodkin, 1996; Kindermann, 1993, 1996, 1998; Neckerman, 1992, 1996). For example, this research has supported the homophily principle that social networks tend to consist of members who are similar to one another (Kandel, 1978). For example, Cairns et al. (1988) identified cliques of aggressive peers among fourth-grade boys and seventh-grade boys and girls. Kindermann (1993) found evidence for self-selection and socialization in cliques. At the beginning of the school year, students self-selected into groups that were homogeneous in school motivation, and membership in those groups predicted change in school engagement across the school year.

The SCM approach has several strengths. First, social groups are derived directly from the actual affiliations observed by participants in the larger peer system. Second, this method allows students to belong to multiple groups, which is important from the perspective of ecological validity. Third, this method can be used with young samples, and thus has added to our understanding of social networks in early adolescent peer groups. Based on these strengths, this method has made important contributions to the study of social networks in peer relations.

Peer Nomination Method

Another method of identification of social cliques is based on peer nominations (Bagwell, Coie, Terry, & Lochman, 2000; Coie, Terry, & Christopoulos, 1991; Coie, Terry, Zakriski, & Lochman, 1995; Terry, 1989). In this method, children are asked to name the peers in their grade whom they "hang around with." An unlimited nomination procedure is used, allowing same-gender and other-gender choices. Nominations are arranged into a voter by votee matrix, with rows representing voters and columns representing votees. Person-centered factor analysis is then used to identify social groups.

The data needed for this method are relatively easy to obtain when sociometric data are already collected, as it requires the addition of one peer nomination to the sociometric instrument ("who do you hang around with?"). The method provides both categorical and continuous measures of group membership, and allows for simultaneous membership in multiple groups. This method seems to be well suited for the study of social networks in large samples, such as an entire school grade, when it is difficult to collect individual interviews, but peer nominations can be collected relatively efficiently.

Block Modeling Procedure

The block modeling procedure has its origins in sociology (see Wasserman & Faust, 1994). The basics of this method are simple. Participants are asked to identify who their friends are in the social network that is being examined. This is the equivalent of a "friend" or "best friend" peer nomination in a sociometric study. In most applications, reciprocal friendship nominations are called "ties" and are the building blocks to determine cliques. For example, if persons A, B, and C all name each other as friends, they will form a three-person clique.

Although the basics are simple, the field of social network analysis has a long history during which many advanced methods and measures were developed. For example, in addition to identifying the cliques in a social network and the persons that are in them, it is also possible to assess continuous-type information, such as the centrality or prominence of each person in the social network. Being in a prominent position depends on the sociometric choices made and received by the individual, as well as on the connections between the peers one is indirectly associated with. At the network level, it is possible to compute measures that capture the dispersion or inequality of roles in the network. Wasserman and Faust (1994) provide an in-depth overview of social network analysis methods. Because the block modeling procedure was used to identify social cliques and network centrality in this paper, some details of the unique language and concepts of social network analysis are provided below.

Basic Concepts

The social network refers to the larger social system that is being analyzed; cliques are the subgroups that exist within it. The persons in the social network are called *actors*. There are two types of relations between actors. A *directional* relation is called an *arc* and has an origin (actor) and a destination (actor). It is the equivalent of a unilateral peer nomination where one person names another as a friend but the other does not reciprocate it. Two actors are *adjacent* when there is an arc in either direction between them. A *nondirectional* relation is called an *edge* or a *tie* and is the equivalent of a reciprocal peer nomination. The proportion of actual ties relative to the maximum number of possible ties is called the *density* of a social network. The density is 1 if all actors reciprocally named one another.

A network can be represented by a graph or a matrix. In a graph, each actor is a *node*, the arcs are arrows pointing from one node to another, and the ties are lines without arrowheads between two nodes. In a matrix, each actor has a row and a column. To record a tie between actors A and B, a 1 is placed in cells (A, B) and (B, A). An arc from A to B is represented by a 1 in cell (A, B) and a 0 in cell (B, A). If A and B are not connected, a 0 is placed in both cells.

The number of arcs beginning at a node is called the *outdegree* of the node. It is the same as the number of friendship nominations given by the actor, or the row sum in the network matrix. The number of arcs ending at a node is called the *indegree* of the node. It is the same as the number of nominations received by the actor, or the column sum for that actor in the matrix.

An actor is *connected* when there is at least one arc from the actor to another actor. Actors can be directly related or *adjacent* (there is one step between them) or indirectly related (more than one step apart). An actor can be a *transmitter* (has at least one arc going out but none coming in), a *receiver* (has at least one arc coming in but none going out), a *carrier* (has at least one arc coming and going out), or *isolated* (has no arcs coming in or going out). Thus, a node is a transmitter if its indegree is zero and its outdegree is non-zero. A node is a receiver if its indegree is non-zero and its outdegree is zero, and it is *isolated* if both indegree and outdegree are zero (Wasserman & Faust, 1994).

Centrality or Prominence

Actors who are central or prominent in a network are frequently involved in relationships with others. Centrality is a measure of the amount of access a person has to others or the influence she has over them. A central actor occupies a position in the network through which much information passes or where other valuable resources are exchanged. In contrast, peripheral actors are located at the margins of the network. There are at least five measures of prominence: *local centrality, local prestige, closeness, betweenness*, and *degree centrality*.

Local centrality is the same as the outdegree, and local prestige is the same as the indegree for a person. The computations of closeness and betweenness make use of the *geodesic distance*, the length of the shortest path between two nodes (Wasserman & Faust, 1994). The closeness of an actor is the inverse of the distance between this actor and all other actors. Thus, it measures how close an actor is on average to all other persons in the network. The betweenness of an actor measures how often the shortest path between other actors goes through this person. Thus, it measures how often a person is an intermediary on the shortest way from each person in the network to each other person.

Degree centrality is an actor's number of connections in a graph of non-directional relations, or in a graph of directional relations is the number of nominations. Degree centrality is a good proxy for perceived popularity because more popular people generally have more ties. The degree centrality index can be standardized by dividing it by the maximum number of possible connections (number of actors minus 1). The resulting proportion scores can be compared between networks of different sizes.

Bonacich (1987) proposed a modification of this measure (see Hanneman & Riddle, 2005). Degree centrality as described above depends only on the number of connections an actor has. Bonacich argued that centrality should not only be a function of the number of peers one is connected to, but also of their level of connectedness. For example, a person is more influential when connected to others who are also more influential. Bonacich argued that being connected to well-connected others makes an actor more central. Thus, Bonacich proposed that centrality is a function of the connections of the actors in one's neighborhood. This is the index of centrality that was used in the analyses of this paper (see below).

Cliques

A clique is a subgroup of members of the network who all chose each other on the sociometric criterion. Thus, the density within the clique is 1. Theoretically, cliques are assumed to serve important functions that may serve prosocial as well as antisocial goals. Clique members share information, create solidarity, and act collectively (Wasserman & Faust, 1994). Because they interact frequently with each other, and infrequently with other members of the social network outside of their clique, cliques may become increasingly homogeneous in thought, identity, and behavior (Wasserman & Faust, 1994). In a developmental perspective, clique membership is a source of social support for adolescents (Cairns et al., 1988), but cliques are also homogeneous in aggression, at least partly due to aggressive socialization within cliques (Farmer & Rodkin, 1996).

Formally, a clique is a subgroup of at least three nodes, which excludes dyads. Several software packages are available that do social network analysis. It is common to set the minimum clique size to three, but it is possible to set this to a higher number which will obviously lead to the identification of fewer cliques. It is important that social network programs allow persons to be members of more than one clique. The requirement that all clique members reciprocally choose each another on the sociometric criterion (friendship) is the purest but also strictest operational definition. It is possible to relax this criterion in a number of ways and identify what are sometimes called quasi-cliques such as the *n-clique*, *n-clan*, and *k-plex* (Wasserman & Faust, 1994, see also Templin, chapter 13). Using these subgroups leads to a larger number of subgroups in the network, but possibly at the expense of the validity of the clique identification. For the purpose of this study, UCINET VI was used for clique identification (see Borgatti, Everett, & Freeman, 1992). The strict criterion was used, and the minimum clique size was set at 3. The program also yields the Bonacich index of social network centrality as well as several of the other indices discussed above.

Goals of the Current Study

This study had four main goals. The first goal was to contribute to peer relations research by examining the group level of analysis, considering both continuous and categorical measures of social network involvement. The second goal was to examine these variables over time in the context of a long-term longitudinal study. The third goal was methodological and was to demonstrate how individual-level information (e.g., aggression) and group-level information (e.g., clique membership) can be integrated in one developmental analysis. The fourth and substantive goal was to predict longitudinal trajectories of clique membership in general and membership in aggressive cliques from individual-level aggression, peer status, and academic achievement. The role of gender and ethnicity as predictors and moderators of all other predictions was examined as well. These four research goals were addressed using data from a longitudinal study on the social and academic development of children and youth, in which participants had been followed yearly across a 9-year period from Grade 4 to Grade 12. Together, the goals of this study make both substantive and methodological contributions to understanding the multilayered complexity of the role of peer relations in development.

METHOD

Participants and Procedure

Data were collected yearly in the spring of grades 4-12 (1995-2004) from 1,213 participants in the public school system of a working class community in the Northeast of the United States (51% female, 66% White, 21% African American, 11% Latino). A total of 261 students (21.5%) participated in all 9 consecutive years (Grades 4-12); 709 (58.5%) participated in at least three. The participation rate was 95% or higher in each year, resulting in a cross-sectional sample size of about 500 to 600 students in each consecutive school year. At each wave, children completed group-administered peer nomination forms and self-report forms in their classrooms. At the time of testing, teachers rated children's social and school functioning on a separate instrument.

Measures

The following variables were used in the main analyses: sociometric and perceived popularity, overt and relational aggression, and academic achievement. Popularity and aggression were assessed with sociometric measures, whereas academic achievement was derived from teacher ratings.

A grade-wise sociometric procedure with unlimited nominations was used in each year of the study in which students were asked to name the peers in their grade who fit each of several criteria. Participants could name as many or as few peers as they saw fit for each question. Same-sex and other-sex nominations were allowed. The percentage of students in each grade who participated as voters in the sociometric procedure ranged from 70% to 95% over the years, with lower percentages in higher grades. A participation rate of 60% is considered the lower limit to obtain reliable sociometric scores when an unlimited procedure is used (Terry, 2000).

To assess sociometric popularity, students were asked to name the peers in their grade whom they "liked most" and "liked least." The number of liked most and liked least nominations was counted for each student and standardized within grade. A score for social preference was created by computing the difference between the standardized numbers of liked most and liked least nominations received and restandardizing the resulting difference score within grade. This score was used as the continuous measure of sociometric popularity. In addition, students named the peers in their grade who they considered "most popular" and "least popular." The numbers of most and least popular nominations received were again counted for each student and standardized within grade. A continuous score for perceived popularity was created by computing the difference between the standardized numbers of most popular and least popular votes received, and restandardizing the resulting difference score within grade.

Overt and relational aggression were assessed with two further peer nominations. Overt aggression was measured by asking participants to name the peers in their grade who start fights, say mean things, or pick on others. Relational aggression was assessed with two peer nominations that were averaged: the peers in your grade who exclude others from being in a group, and the peers in your grade who gossip and tell rumors about others. Nominations were again counted and standardized within grade. The two relational aggression items were averaged.

Finally, academic achievement was derived from teacher ratings on several items measuring school competence and academic achievement in each year. Items were derived from the T-CRS in the younger grades and the Bracken Scales in the older grades. The internal consistency of the scales ranged from

.75 to .85 across the years of the study. An average teacher rating of academic competence was computed across the items in each year.

Cliques and Centrality

As part of the sociometric procedure in each grade, students were also asked to name "the people in your grade who are your best friends." These nominations were used to identify cliques. A complete matrix of all students by all students was created for a grade that noted the presence (1) or absence (0) of a tie between each possible pair of students. A tie was defined as a reciprocal best friend nomination between two students. Cliques were then identified from this matrix of ties using UCINET VI (Borgatti et al., 1992). A clique was defined as a group of at least three students who all named each other reciprocally as best friend. This strict criterion reduces the number of cliques that are found as well as the overlap between cliques.

To determine clique aggressiveness, the standardized overt and relational aggression scores of the members of each clique were averaged to a continuous measure of clique aggression. Highly aggressive cliques were defined as cliques with an average aggression larger than 1. This categorical information was used in the descriptive analysis. The continuous scores (average clique aggressiveness) were used as outcomes in the predictive analysis.

To examine clique homogeneity, the variance among the members of each clique was computed for each measure of aggression and popularity. Across all cliques identified at any time, the average within-clique variance was .83 ($SD = 2.67$, range 0-38) for overt aggression, .96 ($SD = 2.31$, range 0-39) for relational aggression, .72 ($SD = .96$, range 0-12) for social preference, and .92 ($SD = 2.08$, range 0-31) for perceived popularity. These estimates suggest that the average within-clique variance was relatively low, with some exceptions of heterogeneous cliques for each variable. Notice that within-clique variability was lowest for social preference, and about the same for popularity and both measures of aggression.

The Bonacich (1987) centrality index was obtained for each participant as part of the UCINET VI output. This measure is a function of the participant's own degree (number of connections to others), and the degree (number of connections) of the peers to which he or she is connected. Centrality is high when a person has many connections to others who are also well-connected. The details of the computation of this index can be found in Bonacich (1987).

TABLE 4.1
Stability of Social Network Centrality Across Grades 4-12

Grade	4	5	6	7	8	9	10	11	12
4		.28	.25	.14	.14	.21	.12	.22	.28
5	.24		.35	.26	.19	.16	.05	.05	.04
6	.19	.39		.51	.37	.23	.13	.04	.01
7	.21	.36	.63		.36	.41	.22	.10	.11
8	.18	.29	.52	.43		.34	.18	.15	.01
9	.33	.25	.36	.39	.35		.41	.31	.22
10	.26	.15	.19	.20	.28	.51		.40	.27
11	.09	.15	.03	.18	.13	.41	.39		.42
12	.03	.17	.25	.26	.13	.32	.27	.42	

Note. Girls above the diagonal, boys below the diagonal. All correlations > .13 are reliably different from zero ($p < .05$). Correlations underlined are reliably different by gender.

RESULTS

Stability of Network Centrality

First, the stability of social network centrality (Bonacich index) was examined. Table 4.1 shows the correlations of this index among all years of the study, separately for boys and girls. Correlations were based on the maximum of observations per time period (for girls $235 < n < 318$; for boys $238 < n < 345$). Correlations for the overall sample were very similar to those by gender. The few significant correlations indicated relatively low stability for both sexes. Not surprisingly, correlations were higher between adjacent time periods than for periods further apart.

To test for differences by sex, Fisher Z tests for independent correlations were computed. The significant correlations by sex were underlined in Table 4.1. The results indicate that of the three stability correlations for social network centrality that differed significantly by sex all were larger for boys. These results suggest that although the constructs are relatively unstable over time, they did not differ meaningfully by sex.

TABLE 4.2
Structural Characteristics of 3-Person Cliques in Each of Nine Consecutive Grades

Grade	Number of Cliques	Average Clique Size (SD)	Maximum Clique Size	Proportion of Grade Members Belonging to at Least One Clique	Average Number of Cliques per Person (SD)	Maximum Clique Membership by Person
4	167	3.23 (0.54)	6	275/640 = 43.0	1.96 (1.70)	17
5	371	3.26 (0.54)	6	419/639 = 65.6	2.88 (2.36)	20
6	277	3.38 (0.66)	6	334/598 = 55.9	2.81 (2.40)	19
7	185	3.16 (0.39)	5	272/599 = 45.4	2.15 (1.98)	15
8	212	3.24 (0.49)	6	294/607 = 48.4	2.33 (1.88)	11
9	103	3.13 (0.39)	5	196/586 = 33.4	1.64 (1.09)	10
10	83	3.18 (0.42)	5	161/542 = 29.7	1.60 (0.84)	4
11	87	3.17 (0.46)	5	156/491 = 31.8	1.77 (0.93)	5
12	53	3.18 (0.44)	5	108/481 = 22.5	1.56 (0.86)	5

Descriptive Clique Statistics

Table 4.2 displays the structural characteristics of the cliques from grades 4-12. Across grades, there were 1,538 cliques of at least three people across all 9 grades covered by our study. The number of cliques was especially high in grades 5-8, and lower in high school. However, the average clique size remained about the same over time, about 3.2 people per clique for each year, and the maximum clique size never exceeded 6. Given that students in our study could be in multiple cliques, to count the total number of people by summing across cliques would be misleading. Therefore, we calculated the total number of unique people who were in at least one clique during grades 4-12. Across grades, we found 731 participants, or 60.3% of the total population of 1,213 students, were members of at least one clique from grades 4-12. We also found, on average, girls were members of more cliques than boys. The average number of cliques that girls belong to across all grades ($M = 7.23$, $SD = 7.13$) was marginally higher than the average for boys ($M = 6.35$, $SD = 6.19$); $t_{(729)} = 1.77$, $p < .05$, one-tailed. Concerning ethnicity across all grades, on average, White students belong to significantly more cliques than Black or Latino students. The number of cliques that White students belong to across all grades ($M = 7.45$, $SD = 6.96$) was significantly

TABLE 4.3
Gender and Ethnic Composition of 3-Person Cliques in Each of Nine Consecutive Grades

Grade	Proportion of Cliques Gender Segregated	Of the Gender Segregated Cliques: Proportion Female	Proportion of Cliques Ethnically Segregated	Of the Ethnically Segregated Cliques: Proportion White
4	68.9	68/115 = 59.1	51.5	77/86 = 80.2
5	82.5	135/306 = 44.1	64.2	173/238 = 72.6
6	86.6	153/240 = 63.8	67.5	161/187 = 86.1
7	83.8	84/155 = 54.2	78.4	123/145 = 84.8
8	83.0	96/176 = 54.5	76.4	135/162 = 83.3
9	91.3	66/94 = 70.2	82.5	78/85 = 91.8
10	81.9	41/68 = 60.3	83.1	61/68 = 89.7
11	74.7	40/65 = 61.5	85.1	65/74 = 87.8
12	79.2	23/42 = 54.8	86.8	35/46 = 76.1

higher than for Black students ($M = 5.77$, $SD = 6.49$) or Latino students ($M = 5.13$, $SD = 4.86$); $t_{(635)} = 2.57$, and $t_{(572)} = 2.85$, $p < .01$ for both. The means for Black and Latino students were not different from one another, $t_{(219)} = 0.76$.

Within grades, about 50% of all grade members were members of cliques in grades 4-8, with a high of over 65% in grade 5. In high school, the proportion of grade members belonging to cliques drops to about one-third in 9th grade and continues to fall to a low of 22.5% in 12th grade. The average number of cliques to which a person belongs follows a similar pattern. On average, students belonged to more than 2 cliques in grades 5-8, but less than 2 in high school. The maximum number of cliques to which a person belongs reached a high of 20 in grade 5 and a low of 4 in grade 10. These results suggest that clique membership is important to a child's social environment in the early grades and less so by the later grades.

Table 4.3 displays the gender and ethnic composition of the cliques by grade. The results show that a large majority of cliques are gender segregated and that gender segregation was fairly stable across grades. In fact, the proportion of all male or all female cliques hovers around 80% across all years. It is interesting to note that the grade with the highest proportion of mixed gender cliques is 4th grade. Most researchers would have argued for the opposite—that we should have seen more gender segregation in the early grades. Of the gender-segregated cliques, we found that in most grades the majority were all-female cliques. In fact, all-girl cliques outnumbered all-boy cliques in every grade except 5th grade. This finding corroborates earlier work on gender and clique membership (Bagwell et al., 2000; Ennett & Bauman, 1996; Hallinan & Smith, 1989; Henrich, Kuperminc, Sack, Blatt, & Leadbeater, 2000; Kandel, 1978; Urberg, Değirmencioğlu, Tolson, & Hallidayscher, 1995).

The proportion of cliques that were ethnically segregated shows an intriguing pattern; the proportion of ethnically diverse groups was much higher in early grades than in later ones even though the school system had become more diverse over the same time period. Given that one would expect clique membership to become more diverse as well, the opposite pattern was found. In Grade 4, nearly 50% of cliques were mixed, but by grades 9–12 only about 12–17% of cliques were ethnically diverse. Of the cliques that were ethnically homogeneous, 80–90% were White. This proportion remained fairly stable over time, suggesting that the increase in ethnic segregation occurred as Black and Latino students formed cliques with same-ethnicity peers. These findings raise important developmental questions that deserve further study (see Aboud, 2005; Schofield & Hausmann, 2004).

Table 4.4 shows the proportions of cliques that were highly aggressive by grade. Overtly aggressive cliques made up 10–15% of all cliques in each grade. This proportion was fairly stable over time. Although the proportion of overtly aggressive cliques nearly doubled to 28% by Grade 12, the total number of cliques in Grade 12 was relatively small (53). As found in previous research, the majority of adolescents in overtly aggressive cliques are male. In every grade except Grade 7, over three-fourths of all overtly aggressive cliques consisted of boys only.

The proportion of relationally aggressive cliques increased markedly over time. In Grade 5 (relational aggression was not measured in Grade 4), only 5.4% of cliques were highly relationally aggressive. By Grade 8, the proportion had tripled, and by high school over 20% of all cliques were relationally aggressive. The increase in the proportion of relationally aggressive cliques was driven mainly by boys. In the early grades, 70–80% of relationally aggressive cliques consisted of girls only. By Grade 10, this proportion was 40%. Thus, relational aggression among boys seemed to increase across the duration of the study.

Growth Curve Model Analysis

Three growth curve models were run, one to predict the number of cliques students belonged to over time (Model 1), one to predict the average overt ag-

TABLE 4.4
Aggression Characteristics of 3-Person Cliques in Each of Nine Consecutive Grades

Grade	Proportion of Highly Overtly Aggressive Cliques	Of the Highly Overtly Aggressive Cliques: Proportion All Male	Proportion of Highly Relationally Aggressive Cliques	Of the Highly Relationally Aggressive Cliques: Proportion All Female
4	17.4	22/29 = 75.9	---	---
5	10.0	33/37 = 89.2	5.4	17/20 = 85.0
6	10.5	22/29 = 75.9	12.6	25/35 = 71.4
7	13.5	12/25 = 48.0	22.2	30/41 = 73.2
8	15.6	25/33 = 75.8	18.9	23/40 = 57.5
9	13.6	11/14 = 78.6	26.2	22/27 = 81.5
10	15.7	13/13 = 100.0	26.5	9/22 = 40.9
11	14.9	11/13 = 84.6	21.8	10/19 = 52.6
12	28.3	14/15 = 93.3	35.8	9/19 = 47.4

gression of these cliques (Model 2), and one to predict their average relational aggression (Model 3). There were two time-invariant predictors, gender ($1 =$ female, $0 =$ male) and ethnicity (majority/White $= 1$, minority/non-White $= 0$), and five time-varying predictors, sociometric popularity, perceived popularity, overt aggression, relational aggression, and academic achievement. In each model, level and slope of the dependent variable were predicted by: (1) the effects of gender, ethnicity, and gender × ethnicity; (2) the main effects of the five time-varying predictors; and (3) the interactions of gender, ethnicity, and gender × ethnicity with each time-varying predictor. This last group of predictors examined whether the effects of each time-varying predictor on level and slope were moderated by gender and/or ethnicity. Time was measured as grade in school and centered at Grade 4.

Across all time points, clique membership ranged from 0–20, but lower values were more common. In Model 1, the estimated level of clique membership in Grade 4 was .31 ($p = .344$). There was no significant change in clique membership ($\gamma = -.03$, $p = .644$). Thus, clique membership remained stable, with the average adolescent participating in less than one clique. However, level and slope of clique membership were predicted in several ways.

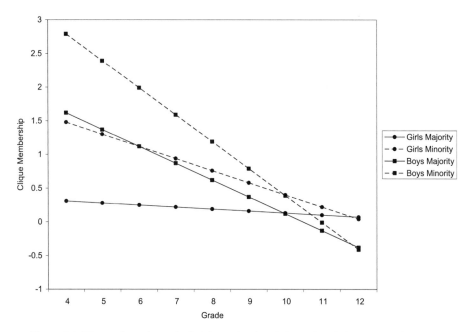

Figure 4.1. Effects of gender and ethnicity on level and slope of social clique membership.

Gender and ethnicity predicted both level and slope of clique member-ship. Girls ($\gamma = 1.32$, $p < .001$) and majority students ($\gamma = 1.17$, $p = .003$) had higher levels of clique membership than boys or minority students. In addition, girls ($\gamma = -.22$, $p < .001$) and majority students ($\gamma = -.15$, $p = .027$) had lower slopes of clique membership than boys or minority students. To understand these effects, prototypical plots (Singer & Willett, 2003) were created for clique membership by gender and ethnicity. These are presented in Figure 4.1. As can be seen, girls and majority students were more likely to be involved in cliques, but also had stronger declines, because they had higher levels of clique membership to begin with.

Sociometric popularity ($\gamma = .45$, $p = .032$) significantly and positively predicted level of clique membership. As might be expected, higher levels of sociometric popularity were associated with higher levels of clique member-ship.

Perceived popularity, overt aggression, and academic achievement pre-dicted both level and slope of clique membership. The effects on level were positive ($\gamma = .43$, $.54$, and $.25$, respectively, $p < .035$). Thus, higher levels of perceived popularity, overt aggression, and academic achievement were asso-ciated with higher levels of clique membership. The effects on the slope were negative ($\gamma = -.07$, $-.06$, and $-.03$, respectively, $p < .035$). To understand these effects, prototypical plots were created that followed an identical pat-

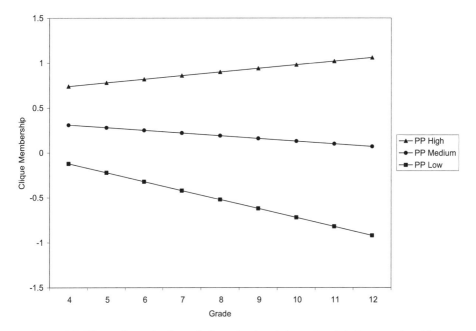

Figure 4.2. Effects of perceived popularity on level and slope of social clique membership.

tern for these three predictors. This pattern is illustrated in Figure 4.2 with the results for perceived popularity.

The effect of overt aggression on level of clique membership was further qualified by gender ($\gamma = -.92$, $p = .002$) and ethnicity ($\gamma = -.60$, $p = .008$). The incremental effect of overt aggression on level of clique membership was smaller for girls than boys and smaller for majority students than minority students. Gender also qualified the effect of overt aggression on the slope ($\gamma = .12$, $p = .021$). Because the effect for boys was $-.06$ ($p < .001$), this puts the effect for girls at .06. This pattern means that while overt aggression predicted slight decreases in clique membership for boys, it predicted slight increases in clique membership for girls.

Gender also qualified the effects of academic achievement on level ($\gamma = -.24$, $p = .004$) and slope ($\gamma = .04$, $p = .006$). The incremental effect of academic achievement on clique membership was weaker for girls than for boys. Because the slope for boys was $-.03$ ($p = .035$), this puts the slope for girls at .01. Thus, while academic achievement predicted slight decreases in clique membership for boys, it predicted no change in clique membership for girls.

In Model 2, the estimated level of clique overt aggression in Grade 4 was $-.10$ ($p = .444$). There was a significant increase in clique overt aggression over time ($\gamma = .17$, $p < .001$). Level of clique overt aggression was influenced by individual overt aggression ($\gamma = .59$, $p < .001$). Adolescents who were more overtly aggressive belonged to more overtly aggressive cliques.

The slope of clique overt aggression was influenced by several predictors. Gender ($\gamma = -.09$, $p = .022$), majority status ($\gamma = -.10$, $p = .032$), sociometric popularity ($\gamma = -.04$, $p = .027$), and overt aggression ($\gamma = -.03$, $p = .011$) negatively predicted the slope of clique overt aggression. Perceived popularity ($\gamma = .12$, $p < .001$) positively predicted the slope of clique overt aggression.

Ethnicity further qualified the effects of sociometric popularity ($\gamma = .07$, $p = .006$), perceived popularity ($\gamma = -.09$, $p = .008$), and overt aggression ($\gamma = .04$, $p = .028$) on the slope. This pattern of effects for perceived popularity is shown in Figure 4.3 and for sociometric popularity in Figure 4.4. The effect for overt aggression followed a pattern similar to the effect of sociometric popularity.

In Model 3, the estimated level of clique relational aggression in Grade 4 was .11 ($p = .446$). There was no significant change in clique relational aggression over time ($\gamma = .02$, $p = .582$). Level of clique relational aggression was influenced by individual relational aggression ($\gamma = .30$, $p < .001$). Adolescents who were more relationally aggressive were also members of more relationally aggressive cliques.

CONCLUSION

The goal of this chapter was to examine the role of social networks in peer relations, and specifically examine the interconnections between individual level and group (social network) level variables in the development of peer relations over time. The overarching goal of this paper was to contribute to an integration of the multiple levels of peer relations that have traditionally been distinguished in peer relations research.

Several sets of analyses were conducted. First, we examined the stability of social network centrality across the nine consecutive years of the longitudinal study. The stability of network centrality was low, and did not vary by gender. Jiang and Cillessen (2005) conducted a meta-analysis of the stability of social preference across 72 published peer nomination studies and found the average 1-year stability of social preference to be around .60. The stability of perceived popularity is typically even higher than the stability of social preference (Cillessen & Borch, 2006; Cillessen & Mayeux, 2004). Compared to these stabilities, the stability of network centrality is low, especially across school transitions. This finding is not surprising. Preference and popularity are general perceptions carried by the peer group at large that remain fairly constant even when the peer group changes. However, network centrality, as

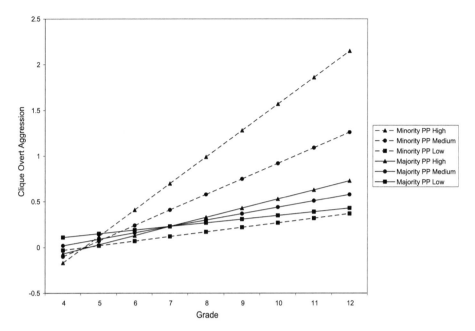

Figure 4.3. Effects of ethnicity and perceived popularity on clique overt aggression.

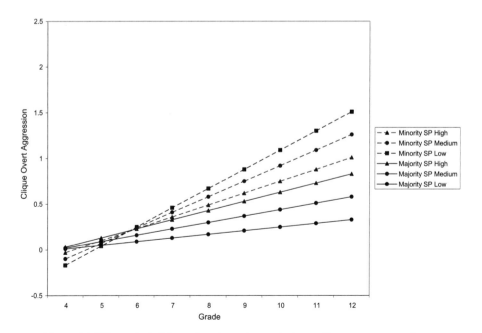

Figure 4.4. Effects of ethnicity and sociometric popularity on clique overt aggression.

determined in this study, depends on dyadic friendship ties. Thus, the stability of this measure is highly dependent upon the presence of the same persons in the network over time, whereas this network presence is less true for preference and popularity. Hence, it is not surprising that network centrality is less stable, as it is the more sensitive to changes in the composition of the peer group. The fact that network centrality is less stable across school transitions (where there are more changes in the composition of the peer group) then within school systems (when there are fewer changes) corroborates this interpretation.

Moving from continuous social network information (network centrality) to categorical clique membership, a comprehensive description was provided of the structural characteristics of cliques across the early adolescent and adolescent years. The formation of cliques seemed to peak in early adolescence, although average clique size remained constant. Girls and majority students were more involved in cliques than boys and minority students. The finding for girls matches the view that girls are more relationship oriented than are boys. The finding for majority students reflects that fact that majority students were present in larger numbers, and thus even by chance alone majority students had more opportunities to form cliques with one another. Regarding trends over time, one specific finding stood out—over the duration of the longitudinal study, the number of ethnically homogeneous cliques increased rather than decreased. Thus, it seems that with development adolescents self-selected into ethnically homogeneous subgroups, rather than into more diverse cliques. This finding was perhaps surprising, given the increasing ethnic diversity of the school system over time. On the one hand, the presence of more minority students afforded adolescents increased opportunities to form friendships with peers of their own ethnicity. On the other hand, that fact that adolescents increasingly choose to form cliques with peers of their own ethnicity, even in light of the increased overall diversity of the school population, is perhaps a reason for concern. It seems as if the increased diversity of the school system had an effect that was opposite to what it was intended to have, that is, increased contact among all students of diverse backgrounds.

The third and final part of the analysis consisted of growth curve modeling analysis in which clique membership and clique aggression were predicted from various individual-level variables. A number of findings were consistent with findings from past research. For example, the fact that overt aggression positively predicted clique membership is consistent with the literature that indicates that aggressive adolescents find each other and form cliques (e.g., Cairns et al., 1988). Although the effect of aggressive behaviors on clique formation may be discouraging, equally encouraging was the fact that academic achievement led to increased clique membership, perhaps reflecting self-selection and/or selective association of academically achieving students with one another over time. Clique overt aggression increased over time and, consistent with results from other studies, overt aggression seems to be valued less negatively across the trajectory from late elementary school through middle school and high school. Interestingly, and contrary to what might be expected, this study did not show increases in the occurrence of relationally aggressive cliques over time. In fact, clique relational aggression was predicted only by individual relational aggression.

Together, the analyses in this paper demonstrated how individual-level and group-level variables can be considered in concert in the context of a large-scale longitudinal study. This study was limited by the fact that only one method of clique identification was considered, and that only certain aspects of cliques were examined. Thus, more research is needed to make further progress in the integration of multiple levels of analysis in peer relations research.

REFERENCES

Aboud, F. E. (2005). The development of prejudice in childhood and adolescence. In J. F. Dovidio, P. Glick, & L. A. Rudman (Eds.), *On the nature of prejudice: Fifty years after Allport* (pp. 310-326). Malden, MA: Blackwell.

Bagwell, C. L., Coie, J. D., Terry, R. A., & Lochman, J. E. (2000). Peer clique participation and social status in preadolescence. *Merrill-Palmer Quarterly, 46*, 280-305.

Bonacich, P. (1987). Power and centrality: A family of measures. *American Journal of Sociology, 92*, 1170-1182.

Borgatti, S. P., Everett, M. G., & Freeman, L. (1992). *UCINET IV network analysis software: Reference manual and user's guide.* Columbia, SC: Analytic Technologies.

Bronfenbrenner, U., & Morris, P. A. (1998). The ecology of developmental processes. In W. Damon (Series Ed.) & R. M. Lerner (Vol. Ed.), *Handbook of child psychology: Vol. 1. Theoretical models of human development* (5th ed., pp. 993-1028). New York: John Wiley & Sons.

Brown, B. B. (1990). Peer groups and peer cultures. In S. S. Feldman & G. R. Elliott (Eds.), *At the threshold: The developing adolescent* (pp. 171-196). Cambridge, MA: Harvard University Press.

Brown, B. B., & Lohr, M. J. (1987). Peer-group affiliation and adolescent self-esteem: An integration of ego-identity and symbolic-interaction theories. *Journal of Personality and Social Psychology, 52*, 47-55.

Brown, B. B., Mounts, N., Lamborn, S. D., & Steinberg, L. (1993). Parenting practices and peer group affiliation in adolescence. *Child Development, 64*, 467-482.

Bukowski, W. M., Newcomb, A. F., & Hartup, W. W. (1996). *The company they keep: Friendship in childhood and adolescence.* Cambridge: Cambridge University Press.

Cairns, R. B. (1998). The popularity of friendship and the neglect of social networks: Toward a new balance. In W. M. Bukowski & A. H. N. Cillessen (Eds.), *Sociometry then and now: Building on six decades of measuring children's experiences with the peer group* (pp. 25-54). San Francisco, CA: Jossey-Bass.

Cairns, R. B., Cairns, B. D., Neckerman, H. J., Gest, S. D., & Gariépy, J.-L. (1988). Social networks and aggressive behavior: Peer support or peer rejection. *Developmental Psychology, 24*, 815-823.

Cairns, R. B., Leung, M.-C., Buchanan, L., & Cairns, B. D. (1995). Friendship and social networks in childhood and adolescence: Fluidity, reliability, and interrelations. *Child Development, 66*, 1330-1345.

Cairns, R. B., Perrin, J. E., & Cairns, B. D. (1985). Social structures and social cognitions in early adolescence: Affiliative patterns. *Journal of Early Adolescence, 5*, 339-355.

Cillessen, A. H. N., & Borch, C. (2006). Developmental trajectories of adolescent popularity: A growth curve modeling analysis. *Journal of Adolescence, 29*, 935-959.

Cillessen, A. H. N., & Mayeux, L. (2004). Sociometric status and peer group behavior: Previous findings and current directions. In J. B. Kupersmidt & K. A. Dodge (Eds.), *Children's peer relations: From development to intervention* (pp. 3-20). Washington, DC: American Psychological Association Press.

Cohen, J. M. (1977). Sources of peer group homogeneity. *Sociology of Education, 50*, 227-241.

Coie, J. D., Cillessen, A. H. N., Dodge, K. A., Hubbard, J. A., Schwartz, D., Lemerise, E. A., et al. (1999). It takes two to fight: A test of relational factors and a method for assessing aggressive dyads. *Developmental Psychology, 35*, 1179-1188.

Coie, J. D., Terry, R. A., & Christopoulos, C. (1991, April). Social networks as mediators of the relations between peer status, social behavior, and adolescent adjustment. *Paper presented at biennial meeting of the Society for Research in Child Development, Seattle, WA.*

Coie, J. D., Terry, R. A., Zakriski, A. L., & Lochman, J. E. (1995). Early adolescent social influences on delinquent behavior. In J. McCord (Ed.), *Coercion and punishment in long term perspectives* (pp. 229-244). New York: Cambridge University Press.

Ennett, S. T., & Bauman, K. E. (1996). Adolescent social networks: School, demographic and longitudinal considerations. *Journal of Adolescent Research, 11*, 194-215.

Farmer, T. W., & Rodkin, P. C. (1996). Antisocial and prosocial correlates of classroom social position: The social network centrality perspective. *Social Development, 5*, 174-188.

Furman, W., Brown, B., & Feiring, C. (Eds.). (1999). *The development of romantic relationships in adolescence.* New York: Cambridge University Press.

Granic, I., & Dishion, T. J. (2003). Deviant talk in adolescent friendships: A step toward measuring a pathogenic attractor process. *Social Development, 12*, 314-334.

Granic, I., & Patterson, G. R. (2006). Toward a comprehensive model of antisocial development: A dynamic systems approach. *Psychological Review, 113*, 101-131.

Hallinan, M. T., & Smith, S. S. (1989). Classroom characteristics and student friendship cliques. *Social Forces, 67*, 898-919.

Hanneman, R. A., & Riddle, M. (Eds.). (2005). *Introduction to social network methods.* Riverside, CA: University of California, Riverside (published in digital form at http://faculty.ucr.edu/ hanneman/).

Hartup, W. W., & Abecassis, M. (2002). Friends and enemies. In P. K. Smith & C. H. Hart (Eds.), *Blackwell handbook of childhood social development* (pp. 285-306). Oxford, UK: Blackwell.

Hawkins, D. L., Pepler, D. J., & Craig, W. M. (2001). Naturalistic observations of peer interventions in bullying. *Social Development, 10*, 512-527.

Henrich, C. H., Kuperminc, G. P., Sack, A., Blatt, S. J., & Leadbeater, B. J. (2000). Characteristics and homogeneity of early adolescent friendship groups: A comparison of male and female clique and nonclique members. *Applied Developmental Science, 4*, 15-26.

Hodges, E. V. E., & Card, N. A. (2003). Enemies and the darker side of peer relations. In *New directions for child and adolescent development*, No. 102. San Francisco: Jossey-Bass.

Jiang, X. L., & Cillessen, A. H. N. (2005). Stability of continuous measures of sociometric status: A meta-analysis. *Developmental Review, 25*, 1-25.

Kandel, D. B. (1978). Homophily, selection, and socialization in adolescent friendships. *American Journal of Sociology, 84*, 427-436.

Kenny, D. A., Kashy, D. A., & Cook, W. L. (Eds.). (2006). *Dyadic data analysis*. New York: Guilford Press.

Kindermann, T. A. (1993). Natural peer groups as contexts for individual development: The case of children's motivation in school. *Developmental Psychology, 29*, 970-977.

Kindermann, T. A. (1996). Strategies for the study of individual development within naturally-existing peer groups. *Social Development, 5*, 158-173.

Kindermann, T. A. (1998). Children's development within peer groups: Using composite social maps to identify peer networks and to study their influences. In W. M. Bukowski & A. H. N. Cillessen (Eds.), *Sociometry then and now: Building on six decades of measuring children's experiences with the peer group* (pp. 55-82). San Francisco, CA: Jossey-Bass.

Levitt, M. J., Guacci-Franco, N., & Levitt, J. L. (1993). Convoys of social support in childhood and early adolescence: Structure and function. *Developmental Psychology, 29*, 811-818.

Neckerman, H. J. (1992). *A longitudinal investigation of the stability and fluidity of social networks and peer relationships of children and adolescents*. Unpublished doctoral dissertation, University of North Carolina, Chapel Hill.

Neckerman, H. J. (1996). The stability of social groups in childhood and adolescence: The role of the classroom social environment. *Social Development, 5*, 131-145.

Newcomb, A. F., & Bagwell, C. L. (1995). Children's friendship relations: A meta-analytic review. *Psychological Bulletin, 117*, 306-347.

Newcomb, A. F., Bukowski, W. M., & Pattee, L. (1993). Children's peer relations: A meta-analytic review of popular, rejected, neglected, controversial, and average sociometric status. *Psychological Bulletin, 113*, 99-128.

Rodkin, P. C., & Hanish, L. D. (Eds.). (2007). *Social network analysis and children's peer relationships. New directions in child and adolescent development, no. 118*. San Francisco, CA: Jossey-Bass.

Rubin, K. H., Bukowski, W. M., & Parker, J. G. (1998). Peer interactions, relationships, and groups. In W. Damon (Series Ed.) & N. Eisenberg (Vol. Ed.) *Handbook of child psychology: Vol. 3. Social, emotional, and personality development* (5th ed., pp. 619-700). New York: John Wiley & Sons.

Schofield, J. W., & Hausmann, L. R. M. (2004). School desegregation and social science research. *American Psychologist, 59*, 538-546.

Singer, J. D., & Willett, J. B. (Eds.). (2003). *Applied longitudinal data analysis.* Oxford, UK: Oxford University Press.

Templin, J. (chapter 13). Methods for detecting subgroups in social networks. In N. A. Card, J. P. Selig, & T. D. Little (Eds.), *Modeling dyadic and interdependent data in the developmental and behavioral sciences.* New York, NY: Routledge/Taylor & Francis Group.

Terry, R. A. (1989, April). A psychometric approach to identifying social cliques. *Paper presented at the biennial meeting of the Society for Research in Child Development, Seattle, WA.*

Terry, R. A. (2000). Recent advances in measurement theory and the use of sociometric techniques. In A. H. N. Cillessen & W. M. Bukowski (Eds.), *Recent advances in the measurement of acceptance and rejection in the peer system. New directions for child and adolescent development, no. 88* (p. 27-53). San Francisco, CA: Jossey-Bass.

Urberg, K. A., Değirmencioğlu, S. M., Tolson, J. M., & Hallidayscher, K. (1995). The structure of adolescent peer networks. *Developmental Psychology, 31*, 450-547.

Wasserman, S., & Faust, K. (Eds.). (1994). *Social network analysis: Methods and applications.* Cambridge, UK: Cambridge University Press.

CHAPTER FIVE

Dyadic Models Emerging From the Longitudinal Structural Equation Modeling Tradition: Parallels With Ecological Models of Interspecific Interactions

Nilam Ram

Pennsylvania State University

Max Planck Institute for Human Development

Amy B. Pedersen

University of Sheffield

"Developmental psychology . . . deals with changes within and among bio-cultural ecologies and with the relationships of these changes to changes within and among individuals" (Baltes, Reese, & Nesselroade, 1977, p. 1). Both biological and developmental systems theory has long suggested that there is a "dynamic interaction" or "transaction" between an individual and his or her context or environment (including other individuals) that occurs over time (Bronfenbrenner, 1979; Ford & Lerner, 1992; Lerner, 1991; Sameroff & Chandler, 1975). As illustrated in the three following quotes, the theory underlying the study of development in an ecological context is that individuals and contexts are changing while interacting with one another:

". . . the individual is changing in a changing world" (Baltes et al., 1977, p. 1);

"Individuals are dynamically interactive with a complex and changing context" (Ford & Lerner, 1992, p. 80);

"The properties of the person and of the environment, ... and the processes taking place within and between them must be viewed as interdependent and analyzed in systems terms" (Bronfenbrenner, 1979, p. 15).

In order for models to reflect the theory of developmental contextualism, multiple change processes or interactions should be considered: including individual changes, context/environmental changes, and the reciprocal relationships among individuals and/or their environments (see Ram & Nesselroade, 2007, for further elaboration). Or, as put by Wohlwill (1991), "... what [reciprocal relationships] would call for are methodologies that allow one to model the interpatterning between two sets of processes each of which is undergoing change, in part as a function of the other" (p. 128). In sum, the predominant theoretical perspective underlying the study of human development highlights the need for models that articulate how, when, and why dynamic entities interact.

Wohlwill (1991) also suggested that, in particular, models used in the study of organisms (e.g., animals) and their environments may provide a base for inquiry. "The closest approach to this kind of modeling that is indicated for this purpose are probably some of the models from the field of ecology, and similar systems-analytical work" (p. 128). Following this suggestion, we have attempted here to examine how perspectives from the field of ecology might relate to, benefit, and expand some of the modeling procedures and methodology currently being used in lifespan developmental psychology—and in particular the study of dyads.

Almost in parallel to developmental perspectives, the theoretical core in biology and ecology underscores dynamic interactions—how one or more species grow and decline within the context of other species and the environment. Ecologists, for instance, aim to understand the distribution and abundance of species, with a particular focus on how a species' long-term dynamics are affected by interactions with the surrounding environment or other organisms. From the early 20th century, ecologists have been using a combination of theory, observational data, and experimental manipulations to understand how both intraspecific (within a species) and interspecific (between species) interactions affect a species' distribution and abundance (Begon, Harper, & Townsend, 1996). Given the underlying similarity in theoretical perspectives and modeling needs, it appears that much can be gained by exploring how each field has approached and attempted to articulate, test, and understand the mechanisms driving "reciprocal relationships" and "dyadic interactions."

Ecological Models of Interspecific Interactions

For over a century ecologists have been developing and using dynamic models to understand and articulate how species interact with one another (Morin, 1999; Townsend, Begon, & Harper, 2002). These between-species (interspecific) interactions can vary dramatically based on the direction $(+/0/-)$ and strength of the interactions, the size of the interacting species and whether the interactions are reciprocal. These interactions can range from mutualisms or commensalisms, wherein each species is either positively affected or unchanged (e.g., $+/+$, $+/0$) by the presence of another species, through neutralism, wherein two species do not compete or interact (e.g., $0/0$); to parasitism or competition, wherein one or both species is negatively affected or even killed by the other species (e.g., $+/-$, $0/-$, $-/-$). Examples include interactions where both species benefit from one another's presence, as in the case of bees and flowers, to those where both species harm each other, as in mixed forest stands of oaks and maples where individual trees compete for water, light, and nutrients (Begon et al., 1996).

Building on the work of two mathematical biologists, A. J. Lotka and V. Volterra (see Wangersky, 1978), ecologists have built a mathematical/theoretical framework for modeling and exploring the mechanisms that underlie interspecific interactions. This framework, presented originally as a pair of first order, nonlinear differential equations, has been used and expanded to describe interspecific interaction processes based on symbiosis, competition, neutralism, mutualism, amensalism, commensalism, predation, parasitism, parasitoidism, etc. (Begon et al., 1996; Gotelli & Ellison, 2004; Murray, 2002; Townsend et al., 2002). In general, the Lotka–Volterra model (for competing species) can be expressed by:

$$\text{Species X: } \frac{dN_x}{dt} = r_x N_x \left[\left(1 - \frac{N_x}{K_x} \right) \pm \left(\alpha_{xy} \frac{N_y}{K_x} \right) \right] \qquad (1a)$$

$$\text{Species Y: } \frac{dN_y}{dt} = r_y N_y \left[\left(1 - \frac{N_y}{K_y} \right) \pm \left(\alpha_{yx} \frac{N_x}{K_y} \right) \right] \qquad (1b)$$

where the subscripts denote the species (x or y), N represents the population abundance of each species, r is the per capita growth rate, K is the population carrying capacity (e.g., maximum population abundance given intraspecific constraints), and α is the "interaction coefficient" indicating the effect that the abundance that one species has on the growth or decline (i.e., change, dN/dt) of the other species (Murray, 2002). These basic equations have provided a useful framework for the study of interspecific interactions in ecology. Coupled with graphical (isocline analysis) and simulation analysis, the modeling framework has provided key predictions and knowledge about the competition, co-existence, and extinction of competing species (Begon et al., 1996; Gotelli & Ellison, 2004).

Without going into the particulars of the competition model given above, we would like to highlight three aspects of how ecologists have used the model to link theories of interspecies interactions with empirical data. Generally, we believe that the focus on change, methodological approaches, and data constraints found in the study of natural systems are similar to those faced by psychologists. We examine how the paradigms and models used to study interspecies interactions might also be applied in the study of dyadic interactions (see also Gottman et al., 2002).

A focus on change. First, we highlight an underlying perspective—that entities are dynamic and can change. The mathematics of the model above are based on nonlinear dynamical systems, wherein a system of (one or more) differential equations is used to articulate how the prior (in time) state of the system leads to the present state of the system (i.e., how entities change over time). Note that the outcome variable (dN/dt) is the first derivative of population size with respect to time—or when written in discrete terms $(\Delta N/\Delta t)$ is how much the population changed between $t - 1$ and t. Thus, explicitly, change is the dependent variable or outcome of interest. The pair of differential equations, together, provide a mathematical representation of the theoretical within-species changes occurring over time (e.g., growth rates) and between-species interactions (e.g., one species out-competing the other for shared resources). This representation is made explicit in Figure 5.1 wherein the within-entity or "intraspecific" dynamics of the model are represented by two rectangles and the between-entity or "interspecific" interactions are depicted as the connecting arrows. The model articulates the "coupling" of two sets of processes, each of which is undergoing change, in part as a function of the other (just as Wohlwill, 1991, argued).

In sum, the "theory" articulated by such models is that entities (species or individuals) change over time and are influenced by environmental forces. In other words, species or individuals are viewed as dynamic entities rather than static or "trait-like" entities that are affected by (and affect) their surroundings. The parallelism to the contextualist and lifespan theoretical approaches taken in developmental psychology is very apparent (see e.g., Baltes, Lindenberger, & Staudinger, 2006).

Methodological approaches. Second, there are multiple perspectives on how theory and empirical data are linked in order to attain insight into the how and why of intra-entity change and inter-entity interactions. Theory and data must be connected. Usually, if not always, this connection happens through a mathematical model. But, there are a number of different perspec-

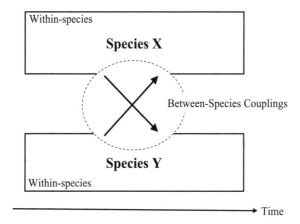

Figure 5.1. A general description of how coupled models include within-entity or "intraspecific" dynamics, the two rectangles, and between-entity or "interspecific" interactions, the connecting arrows. All three components are used to capture the change processes as they occur across time.

tives on how and in what manner the "appropriate" methodology should be selected or built in order to test theory and/or represent data (Bjørnstad & Grenfell, 2001; Hilborn & Mangel, 1997). We highlight two perspectives that are unfolding in ecology (and other fields), a mechanism-oriented approach and a data-driven approach (see also Kendall et al., 1999).

Ecologists and psychologists are interested in processes and mechanisms through which entities (e.g., species or individuals) interact with one another. Generally, the objective of the "mechanism-oriented approach" is to write out the theory of change and interaction as a set of mathematical equations, explicitly including parameters or variables that represent the specific mechanisms thought to be involved in the interaction (e.g., conversion rates, reproduction rates, etc.). Supplemented with "priors" obtained from experiments or observations (e.g., how many hares does a lynx eat in a week?) the mathematical model then is used to generate "synthetic" data (e.g., Markov Chain Monte Carlo procedures), which in turn are evaluated with respect to plausibility (e.g., is the simulated outcome possible?). In sum, the focus of the mechanistic-oriented approach is on building a theoretically sound and biologically plausible mathematical representation of the theory. Data observations are sometimes used to parameterize and evaluate the model but often play a secondary role. Thus, the mathematical model may be built "naïve," so to speak, to empirical data.

An alternative perspective is to focus on the empirical observations directly, with the intent of modeling or representing the data as accurately as possible. In the extreme case a "data-driven" approach is focused on selecting or finding the (mathematical/statistical) model that "fits" the data best. It is of secondary concern whether or not the parameters or variables in the model represent or can be directly translated to theoretical mechanisms. In other words, the model may be "naïve" to theory, yet provide a very accurate description of the current data and some ability to forecast future occurrences.

Our intent is not to make a value judgment regarding either approach, as each has strengths and weaknesses. As presented these are two rather extreme approaches, one naïve to data and the other naïve to theory. Most researchers, however, use elements of both. Within a single analysis even, theory may at certain times be used to build and judge one's models while at other times indicators of fit to the data are used. We issue a caution, though, that one should be aware of when, why, and along what criteria one's models are judged. By doing so, and as is the case in interdisciplinary research generally, the systematic "blending" of approaches should be highly productive and informative (Hilborn & Mangel, 1997).

Data constraints. Third, the data generated by or fitted to such a coupled system of differential (or discrete) equations are longitudinal time-series data—multiple observations of the same entities obtained over multiple, ordered (and usually equivalently spaced) occasions. In the study of interspecies population dynamics, accurate yearly (or monthly, etc.) estimates of population size are often difficult and laborious to obtain. Data sets are often short time-series, consisting of only 10 to 25+ repeated observations of two species (Bjørnstad & Grenfell, 2001). Comparable data in the psychological domain are often based on what is available or obtainable. For instance, in many diary studies daily observations are collected over the course of just a few weeks from a relatively small sample of couples (Bolger, Davis, & Rafaeli, 2003; Laurenceau & Bolger, 2005). Thus, it seems ecologists and psychologists are often limited to short time series. Constrained by the amount of data available to them, ecologists have often turned to modeling approaches that exploit the power of simulations in order to inform model building and theory testing. Using such techniques, even with short time-series and necessarily small N (e.g., one dyad or pair of species) ecologists have been able to obtain a rich and rather detailed picture of the different types of interspecies interactions existent in nature. Psychologists might also consider how such techniques could be used more widely in the study and examination of interpersonal processes.

Generally, ecologists have, for the greater part of a century now, maintained a theoretical focus on change and have used methodological approaches (often mechanism-oriented approaches) that are, even with relatively small amounts of empirical data, still informative to the theoretical processes underlying interspecies interactions across a wide spectrum of ecological systems (Begon et al., 1996; Bjørnstad & Grenfell, 2001; Gotelli & Ellison, 2004;Morin, 1999). We have attempted to understand and present some of the similarities between developmental contextual and ecological perspectives, modeling approaches, and data. It seems, as Wohlwill (1991) rightly pointed out, ecologists have developed a wide variety of models that may also be useful for characterizing dyadic interactions between persons and we should further explore how the paradigms and models used to study interspecies interactions might also be applied in the study of dyadic interactions (see also Gottman et al., 2002). In the following sections we examine three models developed within the longitudinal structural equation modeling tradition in psychology to see how they relate to those being used in ecology.

Developmental Methods: Recent "Dynamic" Innovations

Recently, a number of multivariate "dynamic" longitudinal models, similar to those being applied in ecology, have emerged and can be adapted and used to more clearly understand dyadic interactions and contextualist theory (Collins & Sayer, 2001). As in ecology, the aim of these models is to articulate and test specific hypotheses regarding the reciprocal influences of two or more entities over time. In particular, models based on latent difference scores (McArdle & Hamagami, 2001), coupled differential structural equation models (Boker, 2001), and dynamic factor models (Molenaar, 1985), now provide for explicit interactions of multiple dynamic entities. These reciprocal relationships or "interspecific interactions" allow us to test a variety of hypotheses about how multiple entities (species, individuals, or even domains within an individual) interact and influence each other over time (see also Ram & Nesselroade, 2007).

Latent Difference Score Models of Change. Latent growth curve modeling has become one of the main frameworks used to analyze developmental data within the longitudinal structural equation modeling tradition, allowing researchers to articulate, describe, and test hypotheses about interindividual differences in within-person change (see McArdle & Nesselroade, 2003 for an overview). Recently, the framework has been extended such that explicit renderings of the discrete changes individuals exhibit from one occasion to the next are incorporated explicitly. In particular, McArdle and Hamagami (2001) have presented a formulation of the standard latent growth curve model that is based on successive latent differences. In general form this (univariate) latent difference score model can be written as

$$X_{nt} = x_{n0} + \left(\sum_{t=2}^{t} \Delta x_{nt} \right) + e_{xnt} \qquad (2)$$

where individual n's score at time t, X_{nt}, is the sum of an initial score, x_{n0}, and all of the subsequent changes that have occurred up to that time (sum of Δx_{nt} from $t = 2$ to t). The changes, then, can be written as a function of the other variables,

$$\Delta x_{nt} = f[x, y, z]_{nt} \qquad (3)$$

In the standard growth curve modeling version of the model the function of change is given by a random slope variable (e.g., $\Delta x_{nt} = \alpha_x S_{xn}$, where α_x is a constant and S_{xn} is an individual n's overall rate of change across all t, on variable x; see Ferrer, Hamagami, & McArdle, 2004 for further elaboration of the equivalence between standard growth curve models and latent difference score renditions). More generally, however, the key innovation of this model is that the discrete changes, which accumulate over time to produce an individual's long-term trajectory, become the focal point of inquiry. Within this framework, then, the occasion-to-occasion changes, Δx_{nt}, or the "outcome" variable can be related to any "internal" and/or "external" factors or processes (e.g., x, y, z). Thus, the model opens up a number of new possibilities for examining how processes are linked together or interact over time.

Note that this framework is, in essence, the same as that outlined by the ecological model given above (Eqs. 1a and 1b). Change, Δx (or dx/dt in continuous form) is the outcome variable. Similarly, the factors driving the change can be expressed as a set of variables and parameters that model the internal (within-person or "intraspecific") or external (between-person or "interspecific) factors affecting change. Thus, in parallel to the coupled differential equations of the ecological model, we can also couple together two univariate latent difference score models (e.g., one for each member, x and y of a dyad). A model for these two "coupled" sets of changes might take this form:

$$\text{Person X: } \Delta x_{nt} = \alpha_x S_{xn} + \beta_x(x_{n(t-1)}) + \gamma_x(y_{n(t-1)}) \qquad (4a)$$

$$\text{Person Y: } \Delta y_{nt} = \alpha_y S_{yn} + \beta_y(y_{n(t-1)}) + \gamma_y(x_{n(t-1)}) \qquad (4b)$$

where n subscripts identify a particular dyad and x and y subscripts denote particular members of each dyad (e.g., mothers and children). A graphical representation is given in Figure 5.2. The changes in each variable (or person), Δx_{nt} and Δy_{nt}, are written as a function of overall within-person rates of change (given by $a_x S_{xn}$ or $a_y S_{yn}$), each member's prior state (given

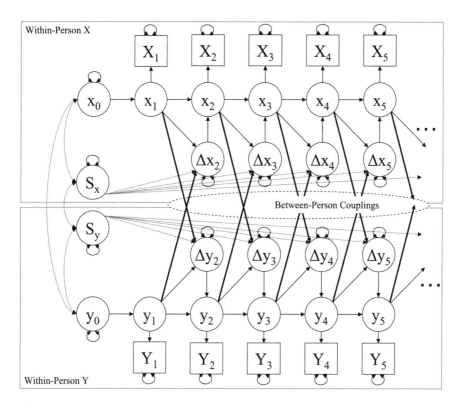

Figure 5.2. A coupled latent difference score model wherein the upper portion of the model is used to represent the within-person changes for Person X and the lower portion to represent within-person changes for Person Y. "Dynamic interactions" or between-person couplings are represented by the arrows spanning between the upper and lower portions.

by $\beta_x(x_{n(t-1)})$ or $\beta_y(y_{n(t-1)})$), and the other member's prior state (given by $\gamma_x(y_{n(t-1)})$ or $\gamma_y(x_{n(t-1)})$). The γ_x and γ_y terms serve as "interaction coefficients," indicating how one member of the dyad "influences" the subsequent changes of the other member. These interaction coefficients parallel the competition coefficients that are used to express the competitive effects of one species on another species in the Lotka-Volterra competition model (Eqs. 1a and 1b). For completeness, and as was the case for the changes in x, the changes in y are also embedded within a "measurement model" and connected to the observed scores,

$$Y_{nt} = y_{n0} + \left(\sum_{t=2}^{t} \Delta y_{nt} \right) + e_{ynt} \tag{5}$$

The coupled latent difference score model (McArdle & Hamagami, 2001) has proven applicable for modeling co-occurring within-person developmental changes in multiple domains and obtaining information about how one domain may lead or lag the other (see McArdle & Nesselroade, 2003). Initial application in the study of dyads has also begun. For example, McArdle and colleagues (McArdle, Hamagami, Kaldec, & Fisher, 2007, in preparation) have used the model to examine how, within a large sample of married couples, one member's level of depression affected subsequent changes in the others' (e.g., husband's depression affecting wife's change). Given the usefulness of this model in examining within-person couplings, and its similarity to the models used to study interspecifc interactions in ecology, we see the coupled latent difference score model (or adaptations of it) as having strong potential for use in the study of dyadic and between-person interactions. We would encourage researchers to further explore the possibilities for application.[1]

Coupled Latent Differential Equations. In addition to allowing discrete changes to be explicit through latent differences, longitudinal structural equation models have also begun articulating continuous change (and acceleration) through latent differential equation models (Boker, 2001; Boker & Graham, 1998; Boker & Bisconti, 2006). In addition to the conceptual advances obtained by rendering change explicit and modeling it as continuous in time, the innovation of such models also has practical advantages, namely that a set of differential equations can be fitted to data within the manifest and latent variable framework of "off-the-shelf" SEM programs (e.g., LISREL, Mplus, Mx, etc.). A coupled linear oscillator model, one of many models in the family of coupled differential equation models, can be written as

$$\text{Person X:} \quad \left(\frac{d^2x}{dt^2}\right) = \eta_x(x)_t + \zeta_x\left(\frac{dx}{dt}\right)_t + \left[\eta_{yx}(y)_t + \zeta_{yx}\left(\frac{dy}{dt}\right)_t\right] + e_{xt} \quad (6a)$$

$$\text{Person Y:} \quad \left(\frac{d^2y}{dt^2}\right) = \eta_y(y)_t + \zeta_y\left(\frac{dy}{dt}\right)_t + \left[\eta_{xy}(x)_t + \zeta_{xy}\left(\frac{dx}{dt}\right)_t\right] + e_{yt} \quad (6b)$$

---

[1]We note that the latent difference score model has thus far been applied to long-term within-person changes that exhibit "strong shapes" and has usually been fit to panel data from multiple individuals under the assumption that individuals are in many ways replicates of one another (as is typical in growth curve modeling and other interindividual differences approaches). However, there is flexibility in how the model can be parameterized and applied. Thus, we see further extensions for the modeling of short-term interactive processes and single-dyad time-series type data (of the type that ecologists use) as within reach.

where x and y subscripts denote particular members of a dyad (e.g., wives and husbands). The general set-up of the model is similar to those described earlier in this chapter. Here, though, the rate at which a variable (or person) x is accelerating at a given point in time t (i.e., the second-derivative with respect to time), d^2x/dt^2, is articulated as a function of location (or level) of the variable, the rate at which the variable is changing (i.e., the first-derivative with respect to time), dx/dt, the location and rate of change of the other variable (i.e., the portion of equation 6a that is in square brackets), and residual, e_{xt}. A parallel function denotes the accelerations of the y variable. Without delving too far into the specifics of the model, we hope that the similarities in structure between this model and the general ecological interspecies interaction model presented earlier are clear (i.e., with Equations 1a and 1b). Both models are written in a differential equation form, and express changes (or accelerations) in couplings between variables (persons). A graphical SEM representation of the coupled latent differential model is given in Figure 5.3. We again highlight that the model includes formal representations of the intrinsic or within-person dynamics for each member of the dyad and the "dynamic couplings" between the two persons.

Boker and Laurenceau (2007, see also 2006) used a coupled linear oscillator model (Figure 5.3) to capture the systematic dynamics of spousal disclosure (of facts, information, thoughts, and feelings)—as obtained via daily diaries over 42 days (6 weeks). Given that married couples exhibit interdependent behaviors, model parameters suggested, on average (across 96 dyads), a significant coupling between dyad members. More specifically, in the prototypical couple, wives were more affected by how far away their husband was from his equilibrium level of disclosure than by how rapidly he was changing. In contrast, husbands were more affected by how quickly their wife's level of disclosure was changing than by how far away she was from equilibrium. This complex pattern of results illustrates how such models can be used to extract and test specific hypotheses about the nature of mutual influence between members of a dyad—thus paramaterizing dyadic intimacy and disclosure as a process reflecting variability, change, and fluctuation over time (Boker & Laurenceau, 2006).

Dynamic Factor Analysis. Dynamic factor models (Molenaar, 1985) emerged as a combination of P-technique factor analysis (Cattell & Scheier, 1961) and time-series methods (e.g., Shumway & Stoffer, 2006) and are used to represent multivariate, multi-occasion data obtained from a single individual (more in depth treatment is given in Ferrer & Widaman, chapter 6). In brief, the underlying notion of the basic model is that the state of the individual at any given time point, as observed via a multivariate vector of variables, X_t, is a function of the state of the organism (observed or unobserved) at both

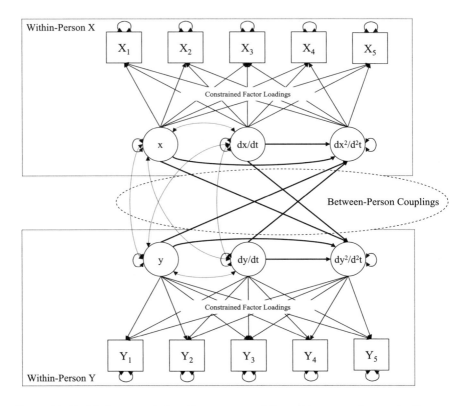

Figure 5.3. Model of two coupled oscillators, one modeling within-person changes for Person X, the other within-person changes for Person Y. Dynamic interactions between the two are represented by the between person couplings.

the current time and previous times (e.g., X_{t-1}, X_{t-2},). One general form of the model (see Browne & Nesselroade, 2005 and Ferrer & Widaman, chapter 6, for more complete descriptions and other general forms) is

$$\xi_t = [A_1\xi_{t-1} + A_2\xi_{t-2} + \ldots + A_S\xi_{t-s}] + \delta_t \qquad (7)$$

where ξ_t, the multivariate latent state of the individual at time t, is a weighted combination of his or her prior latent states, $\xi_{t-1} \ldots \xi_{t-s}$, and some residual, δ_t. Weights (autoregressive) are given by the A matrices. As can be seen, Equation 7 takes the form of a standard autoregression type model. The latent states, however, are unobserved and thus must themselves be connected to the observed variables via a "measurement" model, in this case the standard P-technique factor model

$$X_t = \Lambda_X \xi_t + u_t \qquad (8)$$

where X_t, the multivariate observed state of the individual at time t, is a weighted (by Λ_X) combination of his or her concurrent latent states, ξ_t, and a residual, u_t. Together Equations 7 and 8 can be used to represent how an individual, as a complex multivariate entity, progresses through time and are easily implemented within a structural equation modeling framework (see e.g, Nesselroade, McArdle, Aggen, & Meyers, 2002).

In the context of this chapter, our interest is in how such a model might be applied to dyadic or multi-person data. Suppose we have two individuals. We can create a "parallel" dynamic factor model for the second individual

$$\eta_t = [B_1\eta_{t-1} + B_2\eta_{t-2} + \ldots + B_s\eta_{t-s}] + \zeta_t \qquad (9)$$

$$Y_t = \Lambda_Y\eta_t + \nu_t \qquad (10)$$

where η_t and Y_t represent the multivariate latent and observed states of the second individual, the B matrices his or her autoregressive weights, and ζ_t and ν_t his or her residual scores. Thus, we have a system of equations for each individual. Expanding to the dyad, we can conceptualize "dynamic interactions," where, as the two individuals interact, each person's state is affected by the other's previous states. Within the general framework, such "reciprocal relations" are incorporated in a straightforward manner by including the appropriately weighted cross-regressions. Equations 7 and 9 become

$$
\begin{aligned}
\text{Person A: } \xi_t &= [A_1\xi_{t-1} + A_2\xi_{t-2} + \ldots + A_S\xi_{t-s}] \\
&\quad + [C_1\eta_{t-1} + C_2\eta_{t-2} + \ldots + C_s\eta_{t-s}] + \delta_t
\end{aligned}
\qquad (11a)
$$

$$
\begin{aligned}
\text{Person B: } \eta_t &= [B_1\eta_{t-1} + B_2\eta_{t-2} + \ldots + B_S\eta_{t-s}] \\
&\quad + [D_1\xi_{t-1} + D_2\xi_{t-2} + \ldots + D_s\xi_{t-s}] + \zeta_t
\end{aligned}
\qquad (11b)
$$

where the C and D matrices represent how the (past) latent states of one individual affect the latent states of the other individual, and vice versa—within dyad cross-regressions. More specifically, each individual's latent states are a function (linear combination) of his or her own previous states as well the previous states of his or her partner in the dyad. A minimalist version of the model is presented in graphical form in Figure 5.4. As with the previous models, and as is indicated in the figure, the model can be visualized as consisting of three overlapping parts: the within-person model for one member of the dyad, the within-person model for the other member of the dyad, and the "dynamic interactions" between the two. Further, although written in a

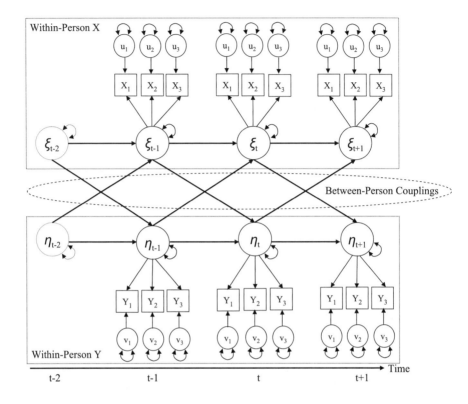

Figure 5.4. Coupled dynamic factor model depicting within-person changes for Person X, Person Y, and the bidirectional influences between X and Y as they occur over time.

different notation, the model also has strong parallels to the ecological model in Equations 1a and 1b.[2]

Ferrer and Nesselroade (2003; see also Ferrer & Widaman, chapter 6) used a dynamic factor model to capture the systematic dynamic interactions occurring between a married couple, husband and wife, over 180 days. The model was applied as indicated above, with portions of the full model representing the wife's within-person changes in mood over time, the husband's within-

---

[2]Both the ecological model given above and the dynamic factor model can be conceptualized or rewritten in the form of a state-space model (see e.g., Browne & Nesselroade, 2005; Murray, 2002). For instance, a discrete-time representation of the Lotka-Volterra competition model for Species X (Equations 1a) highlighting the within-species and between-species portions of the model is given by $N_{x(t+1)} = \left(1 + r_x - \frac{N_{x(t)}}{K_x}\right) N_{x(t)} - \left(\frac{\alpha_{xy} r_x N_{x(t)}}{K_x}\right) N_{y(t)}$. While the parameters are nonlinear, similar to the dynamic factor model, abundance of Species X at the next time point, $N_{x(t+1)}$, is "determined" by a weighted combination of Species X's abundance at the previous time point, $N_{x(t)}$, and Species Y's abundance at the previous time point, $N_{y(t)}$ (Murray, 2002).

person changes in mood, and the "dyadic interactions" occurring between the two. The model articulated how the mood of each individual "led to" or "influenced" his or her own subsequent mood and the subsequent mood of their partner. In the within-person portions of the model it was found that the wife's current mood was determined, in part, by her own mood on the previous day and that the husband's current mood was determined, in part, by his own moods from the previous two days. Additionally, in the between-person couplings portion of the model, the husband's current negative mood affected the wife's negative mood on the following day, but not vice versa. The wife's current mood did not affect the husband's future mood. In full, the model captures each partner's within-person mood process and the between-person interactive process by which the members of the dyad influence one another.

In sum, there is a growing set of tools for modeling dyadic "dynamic interactions" emerging from the longitudinal structural equation modeling tradition. We have reviewed three such innovations here, latent difference score models of change (McArdle & Hamagami, 2001), latent differential structural equation models (Boker, 2001), and dynamic factor models (Browne & Nesselroade, 2005; Molenaar, 1985). In line with theories of ecological interspecific interactions, these models (and others like them) provide for the articulation and testing of theory regarding how dyads, as an interactive system of components (e.g., equations), function over time. We are confident that such models can and will be useful in our quest to understand how, when, and why individuals affect one another.

CONCLUSION

When colleagues from different perspectives, departments, fields of study, etc. come together to explore a topic, they are often struck by differences in terminology, approach, and outlook. However, when pressed to find them, many similarities become apparent. In this chapter we have attempted to highlight how ecological theory and methods may be useful in psychology, and how some of the recently developed longitudinal structural equation models are similar to the interspecies interaction models being used in ecology. With regard to the study of dyads we highlighted a common approach that focuses on change (as an outcome or consequent) and the need for complementary use of mechanism-oriented and data-driven modeling approaches, especially when faced with data constraints.

Using a general dynamic systems framework, based in coupled differential equations, ecologists have articulated and modeled a diverse set of "transactions" or types of dyadic interaction including symbiosis, competition, neutralism, mutualism, amensalism, commensalism, predation, parasitism – all of which can and are often articulated in a manner consistent with the theoretical language of dyadic and group interactions within developmental contextualist theory (e.g., types of proximal, distal, and bidirectional influences). The methodological and computational innovations of the past decade have made it increasingly easy to incorporate dynamical systems modeling approaches, simulation studies, and the fitting of complex nonlinear models (see e.g., Gottman et al., 2002; Newell & Molenaar, 1998; Thelen & Smith, 1994; Vallacher & Nowak, 1994). As these advancements continue we encourage further consideration of how the mathematical models developed over the last century in the field of ecology might be drawn upon and extended in the study of human dyadic interaction.

REFERENCES

Baltes, P. B., Lindenberger, U., & Staudinger, U. M. (2006). Lifespan theory in developmental psychology. In W. Damon & R. M. Lerner (Eds.), *Handbook of child psychology: Vol. 1. Theoretical models of human development.* (6th ed., pp. 569-664). New York: John Wiley & Sons.

Baltes, P. B., Reese, H. W., & Nesselroade, J. R. (1977). *Life-span developmental psychology: Introduction to research methods.* Monterey, CA: Brooks/Cole.

Begon, M., Harper, J. L., & Townsend, C. R. (1996). *Ecology: Individuals, populations, and communities, 3rd edition.* Cambridge, MA: Blackwell Science Ltd.

Bjørnstad, O. N., & Grenfell, B. T. (2001). Noisy clockwork: Time series analysis of population fluctuations in animals. *Science, 293,* 638-643.

Boker, S. M. (2001). Differential structural equation modeling of intraindividual variability. In L. M. Collins & A. G. Sayer (Eds.), *New methods for the analysis of change* (pp. 5-27). Washington, DC: American Psychological Association.

Boker, S. M., & Bisconti, T. L. (2006). Dynamical systems modeling in aging research. In C. S. Bergeman & S. M. Boker (Eds.), *Quantitative methodology in aging research* (pp. 185-229). Mahwah, NJ: Lawrence Erlbaum Associates.

Boker, S. M., & Graham, J. (1998). A dynamical systems analysis of adolescence substance abuse. *Multivariate Behavioral Research, 33,* 479-507.

Boker, S. M., & Laurenceau, J. P. (2006). Dynamical systems modeling: An application to the regulation of intimacy and disclosure in marriage. In T. A. Walls & J. L. Schafer (Eds.), *Models for intensive longitudinal data* (pp. 195-218). New York: Oxford University Press.

Boker, S. M., & Laurenceau, J. P. (2007). Coupled dynamics and mutually adaptive context. In T. D. Little, J. A. Bovaird, & N. A. Card (Eds.), *Modeling contextual effects in longitudinal studies* (pp. 299-324). Mahwah, NJ: Lawrence Erlbaum.

Bolger, N., Davis, A., & Rafaeli, E. (2003). Diary methods: Capturing life as it is lived. *Annual Review of Psychology, 54,* 579-616.

Bronfenbrenner, U. (1979). *The ecology of human development: Experiments by nature and design.* Cambridge, MA: Harvard University Press.

Browne, M. W., & Nesselroade, J. R. (2005). Representing psychological processes with dynamic factor models: Some promising uses and extensions of ARMA time series models. In A. Maydeu-Olivares & J. J. McArdle (Eds.), *Contemporary psychometrics: A festschrift to Roderick P. McDonald* (pp. 415-452). Mahwah, NJ: Lawrence Erlbaum Associates.

Cattell, R. B., & Scheier, I. H. (1961). *The meaning and measurement of neuroticism and anxiety.* New York: Ronald Press.

Collins, L., & Sayer, A. (Eds.). (2001). *New methods for the analysis of change.* Washington, D.C.: American Psychological Association.

Ferrer, E., Hamagami, F., & McArdle, J. J. (2004). Modeling latent growth curves with incomplete data using different types of structural equation modeling and multilevel software. *Structural Equation Modeling, 11*, 452-483.

Ferrer, E., & Nesselroade, J. R. (2003). Modeling affective processes in dyadic relations via dynamic factor analysis. *Emotion, 3*, 344-360.

Ford, D. H., & Lerner, R. M. (1992). *Developmental systems theory: An integrative approach.* Newbury Park, CA: Sage.

Gotelli, N. J., & Ellison, A. M. (2004). *A primer of ecological statistics.* Sunderland, MA: Sinauer Associates.

Gottman, J. M., Murray, J. D., Swanson, C. C., Tyson, R., & Swanson, K. R. (2002). *The mathematics of marriage: Dynamic non-linear models.* Cambridge, MA: MIT Press.

Hilborn, R., & Mangel, M. (1997). *The ecological detective: Confronting models with data.* Princeton, NJ: Princeton University Press.

Kendall, B. E., Briggs, C. J., Murdoch, W. W., Turchin, P., Ellner, S. P., McCauley, E., et al. (1999). Why do populations cycle? A synthesis of statistical and mechanistic modeling approaches. *Ecology, 80*, 1789-1805.

Laurenceau, J. P., & Bolger, N. (2005). Using diary methods to study marital and family processes. *Journal of Family Psychology, 19*, 86-97.

Lerner, R. M. (1991). Changing organism-context relations as the basic process of development: A developmental contextual perspective. *Developmental Psychology, 27*, 27-32.

McArdle, J. J., & Hamagami, F. (2001). Latent difference score structural models for linear dynamic analysis with incomplete longitudinal data. In L. Collins & A. Sayer (Eds.), *New methods for the analysis of change* (pp. 139-175). Washington, D.C.: American Psychological Association.

McArdle, J. J., Hamagami, F., Kaldec, K., & Fisher, G. (2007, in preparation). A dynamic structural analysis of dyadic cycles of depression in the Health and Retirement study data. Unpublished manuscript, Department of Psychology, University of Southern California.

McArdle, J. J., & Nesselroade, J. R. (2003). Growth curve analysis in contemporary psychological research. In J. Shinka & W. Velicer (Eds.), *Comprehensive handbook of psychology, Volume 2: Research methods in psychology* (pp. 447-480). New York: John Wiley & Sons.

Molenaar, P. C. M. (1985). A dynamic factor model for the analysis of multivariate time series. *Psychometrika, 50*, 181-202.

Morin, P. J. (1999). *Community ecology.* Malden, MA: Blackwell Science.

Murray, J. D. (2002). *Mathematical biology: I. An introduction.* New York: Springer.

Nesselroade, J. R., McArdle, J. J., Aggen, S. H., & Meyers, J. M. (2002). Alternative dynamic factor models for multivariate time-series analyses. In D. M. Moskowitz & S. L. Hershberger (Eds.), *Modeling intraindividual variability with repeated measures data: Advances and techniques* (pp. 235-265). Mahwah, NJ: Lawrence Erlbaum Associates.

Newell, K. M., & Molenaar, P. C. M. (Eds.). (1998). *Applications of nonlinear dynamics to developmental process modeling*. Mahwah, NJ: Erlbaum.

Ram, N., & Nesselroade, J. R. (2007). Modeling intraindividual and intracontextual change: Rendering developmental contextualism operational. In T. D. Little, J. A. Bovaird, & N. A. Card (Eds.), *Modeling contextual effects in longitudinal studies* (pp. 325-342). Mahwah, NJ: Lawrence Erlbaum.

Sameroff, A. J., & Chandler, M. J. (1975). Reproductive risk and the continuum of caretaking casualty. In F. D. Horowitz, E. M. Hetherington, S. Scarr-Salapatek, & G. M. Siegel (Eds.), *Review of child development research: Vol. 4* (pp. 187-244). Chicago: University of Chicago Press.

Shumway, R. H., & Stoffer, D. S. (2006). *Time series analysis and its applications*. New York: Springer.

Thelen, E., & Smith, L. B. (1994). *A dynamic systems approach to the development of cognition and action*. Cambridge: MIT Press.

Townsend, C. R., Begon, M., & Harper, J. L. (2002). *Essentials of ecology, 2nd edition*. Malden, MA: Blackwell Sciences.

Vallacher, R. R., & Nowak, A. (1994). *Dynamical systems in social psychology*. New York: Academic Press.

Wangersky, P. (1978). Lotka-Volterra population models. *Annual Review of Ecological Systems, 9*, 189-218.

Wohlwill, J. F. (1991). Relations between method and theory in developmental research: A partial-isomorphism view. In P. van Geert & L. P. Mos (Eds.), *Annals of theoretical psychology* (Vol. 7, pp. 91-138). New York: Plenum Press.

CHAPTER SIX

Dynamic Factor Analysis of Dyadic Affective Processes With Intergroup Differences

Emilio Ferrer

Keith F. Widaman

University of California, Davis

Dynamic factor analysis (DFA) is a statistical technique used to identify lagged structure in covariance matrices. DFA was developed to overcome one of the main limitations of Cattell's P-technique factor analysis (Cattell, 1963; Cattell, Cattell, & Rhymer, 1947), which did not include the specification of any lagged relations. P-technique factor analysis, formulated by Cattell to examine within-person fluctuations in personality traits, consists of the factor analysis of multivariate time series data comprised of scores on multiple manifest variables measured on a single individual across multiple time points. Correlations or covariances are then computed among the manifest variables, so the correlations represent the degree to which manifest variables covary across time. When subjected to factor analysis, the resulting factor structure provides information about the latent dimensions that underlie intraindividual variability on the measured variables, but does not reflect any time-related dependencies among manifest or latent variables. The different techniques that are subsumed under the label of DFA were developed precisely to account for time-related dependencies among manifest and latent variables, as these time-related dependencies can be revealing of mechanisms associated with dynamic processes that underlie causal relations among variables across time.

Although initially developed to represent relations among manifest variables within an individual, DFA is a quite general set of techniques that is especially well suited to aid in the examination of dyadic interactions. In these interactions, data are measured across multiple points in time from two individuals who form a dynamic system. The analytic idea here is to represent variability on manifest variables across time for each person in terms of a set of latent variables and to identify influences among latent variables, especially between individuals, over time (Ferrer & Nesselroade, 2003; Ferrer, 2006).

Ferrer and Nesselroade (2003) outlined a series of questions involving dyadic interactions for which DFA can provide unique answers. Some dyadic interaction questions deal with structure; example questions are: Which variables are most strongly influenced by, and therefore load on, which factors? Are the factors that characterize one member of the dyad the same as those that characterize the other member? Other dyadic interaction questions focus on the dynamic temporal organization of latent variables; questions here include: What is the optimal number of lags required to represent well relations among latent variables? Are dynamic processes stable across time? Does one member of the dyad have lagged influences of larger magnitude on the other member of the dyad than vice versa? More recently, Sbarra and Ferrer (2006) extended the set of questions to include those regarding different dimensions of emotion, and their dynamics. Questions here include: Can different emotions be modeled as distinct mood states? Do these mood states influence one another across time? How is the modeling of mood states affected by an important event, say the break-up of a relationship? These are measurable dynamics for which DFA can also provide revealing answers.

Most studies using DFA have focused on analyzing data from a single person or have presented separate analyses from three or four individuals (e.g., Nesselroade et al., 2002; Shifren et al., 1997), without comparisons or information about interindividual differences. This is also true with regard to dyadic interactions, where analyses have typically focused on data from a single dyad (Ferrer & Nesselroade, 2003; Ferrer, 2006; Song & Ferrer, in press). The analysis of single units, whether these units be a person, a dyad, or another form of unit, is quite informative and legitimate. Indeed, Molenaar and colleagues (e.g., Molenaar, 2004; Nesselroade & Molenaar, 1999) demonstrated that the analysis of aggregate data cannot recover or characterize correctly information about intraindividual change over time in disaggregated data. The central problem, which is the focus of this chapter, is how to aggregate information across individuals or dyads in a way that preserves information about intraindividual or intradyad change over time, yet allows us to discuss interindividual differences in these within-individual or within-dyad change processes. Stated differently, how should we attempt to make inferences based on samples of more than one unit (i.e., person, dyad), and how do we go about making inferences that represent both the individual and the aggregate. To reconcile these competing agendas is the heart of the idiographic-nomothetic debate.

Several approaches to accurately characterizing intraindividual change over time and then aggregating information across individuals have been proposed. One approach, developed by Nesselroade and Molenaar (1999), involves the pooling of data from individuals who have similar covariance structures. If several subgroups of individuals are identified and pooled, analyses can be conducted on each pooled set of data, and the differing patterns of intraindividual change that characterize each subgroup provide descriptions of different patterns of change over time. Another approach, somewhat more radical, has been to ignore the aggregate analyses completely, analyze the data from each individual separately, and get psychological research back to origins in which it focused on the individual without any need to undertake aggregate-level analyses (Hamaker, Dolan, & Molenaar, 2005; Molenaar, 2004).

In this chapter, we present analyses that deal with this core issue, namely, generating a description that applies to both the single unit and the aggregate sample. Specifically, we present analyses in which we examine the dynamic factor structure of multivariate data for a number of dyads separately. Then, we attempt to use this "individual" or disaggregated information to generate results that represent all the dyads. We also present analyses in which we fit the same model to all dyads in a single analysis, as if they were part of a single sample. One way of construing this approach is as an indirect type of hierarchical linear dynamic factor analysis. We explain why we have chosen to proceed in this fashion and not in the framework of mixed models. We compare the results across both sets of analyses, noting the similarities and differences. After describing the ways in which our approach to analyses can be used to ask interesting developmental questions, we close by citing the next steps that must be accomplished to yield more adequate representations of dynamic relations among psychological process variables.

The Dynamic Factor Analysis Model

Several types of DFA model have been proposed, models that differ primarily in the specification of lagged relations among manifest and latent variables (Engle & Watson, 1981; Immink, 1986; McArdle, 1982; Molenaar, 1985; see Browne & Nesselroade, 2005, Nesselroade et al., 2002; and Wood & Brown, 1994, for reviews). In this paper, we focus on the so-called process factor analysis model (PFA) formulated by Browne and colleagues (Browne & Nesselroade, 2005; Browne & Zhang, 2007). In this specification, the latent variables represent unobserved constructs through which the lagged relations are structured. In its more general form, the PFA can be expressed as a function of two equations. The first equation is written as

$$y_t = \Lambda f_t + u_t \tag{1}$$

where y_t is a matrix of manifest variables measured at time t, Λ is a matrix of factor loadings that is invariant over time, f_t is a vector of common factors at time t, and u_t is a vector of unique factors at time t assuming $u_t \sim (\mathbf{0}, D_\varepsilon)$. The second equation of the model can be written as

$$f_t = \sum_{i=1}^{p} A_i f_{t-i} + \sum_{j=1}^{q} B_j z_{t-j} + z_t \tag{2}$$

where the A_i are autoregressive weight matrices, the B_j are moving average weight matrices, $z_t \sim (\mathbf{0}, \Psi)$ is a random shock vector, and other terms are as defined above.

The general model specified in Equations 1 and 2 is a variable autoregressive moving average, or VARMA model, which can be identified as a VARMA (p, q) model, where p stands for the number of autoregressive lags, and q represents the number of moving average terms in the model. Equation 1 above represents a standard factor analytic representation of a set of manifest variables in y_t as linear functions of a set of common latent variables in f_t and uncorrelated unique factors in u_t. In Equation 2, the set of latent variables at a given time, in f_t, are represented as a function of three components: (a) autoregressive or cross-lagged relations from latent variables at prior times, where regression weights associated with latent variables at prior times are contained in the A_i matrix; (b) moving average relations from random shocks at prior times, with associated regression weights in the B_j matrix; and (c) random shocks at time t, represented as z_t. When $q = 0$, the middle term on the right side of Equation 2 is omitted and this VARMA (p, q) model becomes a variable autoregressive, or VAR $(p, 0)$ PFA model, with an autoregressive lag structure with p lags.

Figure 6.1 shows a path diagram of a PFA $(2,0)$ model. Here, circles represent latent variables and squares represent observed variables. The depicted model includes two latent variables f_t, labeled as F1 and F2, at each time of measurement, and these two latent variables are measured by six manifest variables $M_1, M_2, \ldots, M_6$ at each time. The lag-2 status of the model in Figure 6.1 is embodied in the direct autoregressive paths to a given latent variable, such as F1_{t+1}, from the like-named latent variables at the prior two times of measurement, F1_t and F1_{t-1}. Cross-lagged paths of lag-1 are also shown in Figure 6.1, from one latent variable at a given time of measurement

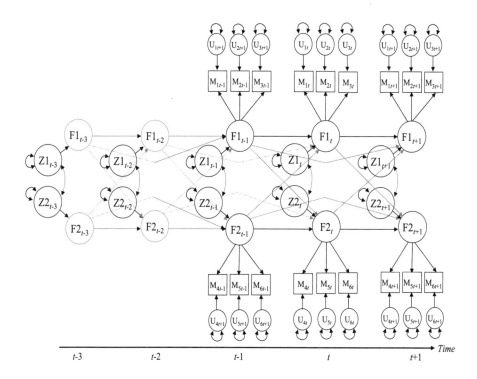

Figure 6.1. Path diagram of a lag-2 process factor analysis (2,0) model.

to the other latent variable at the next time of measurement, such as from $F1_{t-1}$ to $F2_t$ and from $F2_t$ to $F1_{t+1}$. Although not shown in Figure 6.1 to simplify the figure, lag-2 cross-lagged paths, such as from $F2_{t-1}$ to $F1_{t+1}$, were also fitted in the PFA (2,0) model. All of these autoregressive and cross-lagged path coefficients are contained in the A_i matrix in Equation 2. In addition, the factors z_t, labeled Z1 and Z2 at each time of measurement in Figure 6.1, represent unobserved exogenous forces that produce random shocks on the system.

One important feature of the model in Figure 6.1 is the inclusion of at least two latent variables, labeled as F1 and F2. If an analysis were conducted on data from a single individual and F1 and F2 represented, for example, positive and negative affect, respectively, any cross-lagged paths between F1 and F2 across time could be interpreted in terms of intraindividual dynamic processes of a psychological nature. But, if the multiple latent variables consist of one or more latent variables from each of the individuals in a dyad, then cross-lagged paths from a latent variable from one member of the dyad to one or more latent variables representing the other individual in the dyad constitute interindividual dynamic processes within the dyad. That is the ultimate goal of the current contribution: to develop ways of characterizing interdyad differences in interindividual dynamic relations between persons constituting a dyad.

METHOD

Participants

The data used in this paper are part of the Dynamics of Dyadic Interactions Project (DDIP), an ongoing project at the University of California, Davis focused on the development of models to analyze dyadic interactions. Participants in the DDIP include 235 couples (470 individuals) who, at the time of recruitment, were involved in a romantic relationship. As part of the overall project, all participants were asked to complete a daily questionnaire about their affect for 60 consecutive days. In this report we present data from a subsample of couples ($N = 82$ couples) who had at least 54 days of complete data. The age of participants ranged from 17.9 to 29.8 years ($M = 20.2$; $SD = 1.85$). The time that they had been involved in the relationship ranged from 0.04 to 5.1 years ($M = 1.35$; $SD = 1.13$). Of the 164 participants from the 82 couples, 6 reported to be "dating around," 112 were "dating exclusively," 38 were "living together," and 8 were "engaged."

Measures

General affect. The daily questionnaire was intended to examine daily fluctuations in affect and contained two sets of items. The first set was comprised of the 20 items from the Positive and Negative Affect Scale (PANAS; Watson, Clark, & Tellegen, 1988). Participants were asked to complete these items responding to the instructions "Indicate to what extent you have felt this way today." Thus, these items were intended to tap into the participants' general positive and negative affect during the day. Ten of the PANAS items represent positive affect, including the items "interested" and "excited," and the remaining 10 items reflect negative affect, including "irritable" and "hostile."

Relationship-specific affect. The second set of items was developed by the DDIP team and was comprised of 18 adjectives reflective of positive and negative emotional experiences specifically with regard to the dyadic relationship. Participants were asked to complete these items responding to the instructions "Indicate to what extent you have felt this way about your relationship today." Thus, these items were intended to tap into the participants' positive and negative affect specific to their relationship. The nine positive items included "emotionally intimate" and "trusted," whereas the nine negative mood items included "trapped" and "lonely."

For all items, participants were asked to respond using a 5-point Likert-type scale ranging from 1 (very slightly or not at all) to 5 (extremely). In prior research, the PANAS scales have demonstrated good internal consistency, reliability, and convergent and discriminant validity. In the current data, the alpha coefficients of reliability (computed using the data from all individuals at the first measurement occasion) for the PANAS scales were .88 and .91 for positive and negative affect, respectively. The alpha coefficients of reliability for the "relationship-specific" positive and negative affect scales were .93 and .92, respectively. Thus, at the scale level, both the PANAS and the relationship specific affect scales exhibited rather high levels of internal consistency reliability.

RESULTS

Descriptive Analyses of Data

Simple statistics. The means and standard deviations (SDs) for all PANAS and relationship specific affect items are shown in Table 6.1, with statistics based on the first time of measurement, t_1, shown first and then statistics based on all times of measurement, T. Several interesting trends in the descriptive statistics can be observed. First, means on positive items from both the PANAS and the relationship-specific affect scales tend to be higher than the means on negative items from the two scales. The means of the 19 positive items averaged around 3.2 and 3.1 at t_1 and T, respectively, whereas the 19 negative items had means that averaged around 1.7 and 1.5 at t_1 and T, respectively. Thus, participants reported much higher levels of positive affect or mood relative to their levels of negative affect or mood. Second, means on all items, whether positive or negative, tended to be about 0.1 to 0.2 lower when computed across all times of measurement, T, when compared to the first time of measurement, t_1, possibly due to some kind of retesting effect, with reporting of all kinds of affect of mood declining over time, positive bias at the initial assessment, or even some type of regression to the mean artifact.

Third, relationship-specific affect items revealed higher levels of positive mood and lower levels of negative mood relative to the non-relationship-specific ratings obtained using the PANAS scales. For relationship-specific affect items, the means for positive items averaged 3.6 and 3.5 at t_1 and T, respectively, and the means for negative items averaged 1.54 and 1.45 at t_1 and T, respectively. Thus, an approximate 2-point mean difference favoring positive items over negative items was found for the relationship-specific items. In

TABLE 6.1
Means and Standard Deviations of Items

Items	t_1 Mean	SD	T Mean	SD
General Affect (PANAS)				
interested	3.03	.97	2.90	1.05
alert	2.74	1.04	2.68	1.10
excited	2.92	1.12	2.78	1.18
inspired	2.36	1.09	2.27	1.15
strong	2.72	1.08	2.50	1.18
determined	2.94	1.12	2.72	1.17
attentive	3.00	.98	2.76	1.09
enthusiastic	2.91	1.17	2.75	1.16
active	2.82	1.15	3.05	1.21
proud	2.68	1.19	2.46	1.22
irritable	2.21	1.13	1.82	1.02
distressed	2.43	1.28	1.98	1.10
ashamed	1.38	.81	1.34	.73
upset	2.01	1.16	1.68	.99
nervous	2.10	1.18	1.76	1.03
scared	1.60	.96	1.49	.88
hostile	1.50	.85	1.39	.78
jittery	1.86	1.05	1.59	.93
afraid	1.57	.97	1.48	.87
guilty	1.48	.96	1.35	.75
Relationship-Specific Affect				
emotionally intimate	3.36	1.10	3.24	1.21
physically intimate	3.09	1.33	2.70	1.39
trusted	3.95	.94	3.86	1.11
committed	4.18	.95	3.95	1.09
free	3.09	1.15	3.07	1.03
loved	4.03	.95	3.88	1.05
happy	3.86	1.04	3.76	1.12
loving	3.84	1.04	3.80	1.08
socially supported	3.35	1.16	3.16	1.27
sad	1.60	1.00	1.54	.89
blue	1.59	.91	1.48	.88
trapped	1.31	.74	1.39	.81
argumentative	1.92	1.12	1.55	.93
discouraged	1.62	.96	1.45	.84
doubtful	1.51	.87	1.41	.81
lonely	1.55	.93	1.58	.98
angry	1.54	.94	1.39	.82
deceived	1.19	.61	1.23	.65

Note. t_1 = data from the first measurement occasion only. T = data from all measurement occasions.

contrast, for PANAS items, the means for positive items averaged 2.8 and 2.7 at t_1 and T, respectively, and the means for negative items averaged 1.8 and 1.6 at t_1 and T, respectively. On PANAS items, the difference in mean levels of endorsement of positive items over negative items was approximately 1 point, about half as large a difference as found for relationship-specific items. These results suggest the following: if PANAS and relationship-specific items do an equally good job of indexing affect or mood, then individuals tend to report higher levels of positive affect or mood and lower levels of negative affect or mood when considering their relationship as contrasted against their general levels of affect or mood during the day. These patterns of scores could represent either artifact—such as the use of rose-colored glasses when viewing one's relationship—or a true difference in the affect or mood tone of the dyadic relationship when compared with other daily experiences. Regardless of the veridicality of the judgments, the higher positive and lower negative affect or mood associated with the dyadic relationship may play a major role in why dyadic relationships last longer than more temporary friendships.

Temporal trends in ratings. In Figure 6.2, plots of positive and negative affect across all 60 days are shown for two couples. With regard to positive affect, the left-hand plot reveals a somewhat U-shaped function, the relatively high levels of positive affect from days 3 through 15, lower levels between days 20 through 40, and then somewhat higher levels after day 45. The right-hand plot reveals a peaking of positive affect between days 10 and 20 and then a slow and relatively linear decline out to day 55. Both plots exhibit patterns of similar tracking of positive affect by the two individuals in a given dyad across time, with similar general trends of increase or decrease over time and some coupling of more restricted up- or down-trends.

Results for the same two couples are shown for negative affect as well. The left-hand figure reveals low and fluctuating levels of negative affect with some disconnect between the peaks for one temporal pattern and those for the other; eventually, one member of the dyad stabilizes at a rather higher level of negative affect than does the other member. The right-hand figure reveals generally much lower levels of negative affect for both members of the dyad, a sudden spike in negative affect for one member around day 20, some instability in ratings between days 30 and 40, and then a gradual dampening of the mean and variability of ratings through the end of the series. As with positive affect, the temporal patterns for negative affect exhibit tracking of negative affect—with unclear lead or lag relations across individuals—and some coupling of the up- and down-trends across time.

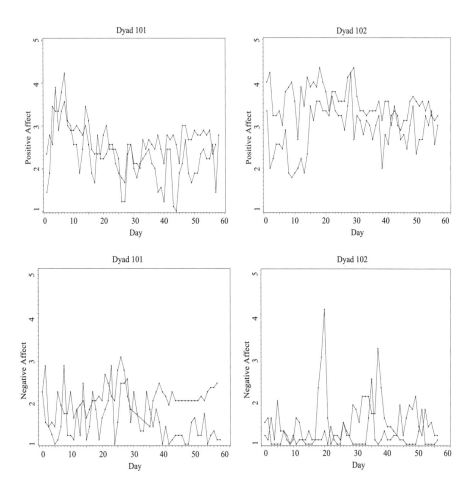

Figure 6.2. Positive and negative affect over time for two dyads.

Exploratory Factor Analysis

Table 6.2 presents the factor loadings from an exploratory factor analysis (with oblique promax rotation) fitted to all of the data, collapsing across both members of each dyad. The 10 positive PANAS items loaded on a Positive General Affect factor, the 10 negative PANAS items on a Negative General Affect factor, the 9 positive relationship-specific items on a Positive Relationship-Specific factor, and the 9 negative relationship-specific items on a Negative Relationship-Specific factor. The standardized values of all defining loadings were quite acceptable, with a range from .528 to .927. The factor loadings therefore indicate that the data provide a clear discrimination

TABLE 6.2
Exploratory Factor Analysis of Items

Positive Affect (General)		Negative Affect (General)		Positive Affect (Relation Specific)		Negative Affect (Relation Specific)	
interested	.687	distress	.792	intimate	.788	sad	.775
excited	.785	upset	.739	trust	.864	blue	.814
strong	.694	guilty	.612	committed	.843	trapped	.684
enthusiastic	.861	scared	.879	physical	.587	argumentative	.732
proud	.850	hostile	.585	free	.528	discouraged	.897
alert	.850	irritable	.648	loved	.927	doubtful	.870
inspired	.593	ashamed	.626	happy	.799	lonely	.660
determined	.693	nervous	.777	loving	.853	angry	.846
attentive	.719	jittery	.650	supported	.547	deceived	.762
active	.532	afraid	.828				

Factor Correlations	$PA_{General}$	$NA_{General}$	$PA_{Specific}$	$NA_{Specific}$
$PA_{General}$	1.000			
$NA_{General}$	-.125	1.000		
$PA_{Specific}$	.408	-.162	1.000	
$NA_{Specific}$	-.126	.492	-.481	1.000

between positive and negative affect and between general and relationship-specific affect. Moreover, the inter-factor correlations indicate a small negative (−.125) correlation between positive and negative general affect, but a rather stronger association (−.481) between positive and negative relationship-specific affect. Because of our interest in affect related to the relationship, we focus on relationship-specific items and latent variables in all subsequent analyses.

Dynamic Factor Analysis of All Dyads

In the first set of DFA analyses, we performed dynamic factor analysis of all 82 dyads simultaneously using data from only the relationship-specific rating scales. To ensure the maximum length of the complete series across all dyads but a balanced set of data points across dyads, we selected the first 52 data points for all dyads. In particular, we fitted exploratory PFA (1,0) and PFA (2,0) DFA models to the data using the DyFA 2.03 program (Browne & Zhang, 2005). The PFA (1,0) model is one incorporating lag-1 relations (or relations from one day to the next) among latent variables and no moving average component, whereas the PFA (2,0) includes both lag-1 and lag-2 relations (or relations from one day to the next day and the day after) among latent variables, but still no moving average components. In DyFA, the exploratory dynamic factor analysis is carried out by specifying a pattern of target loadings (i.e., zero and nonzero) in the factor matrix. The program then generates an exploratory Procrustean or targeted solution, but provides numerical results (i.e., nonzero loadings) for the targeted zero loadings if the original specification is not reasonable. This feature is very useful because it can inform the user about alternative specifications.

Because of our interest in dyadic interactions, in all analyses we examined a model with four hypothesized factors: positive affect for the male, negative affect for the male, positive affect for the female, and negative affect for the female. Each factor was comprised of nine items. A PFA (1,0) model is comprised of two parts: a measurement part that contains the loadings of manifest variables on latent variables, and a time series part that contains the estimates of relations among latent variables. Table 6.3 presents the factor loadings from the first part of the exploratory PFA (1,0) model. The results show a remarkable discrimination between positive and negative affect and between genders. Indeed, the cross-loadings are very small in all cases, indicating that the four-factor solution was a very reasonable specification. For each factor, the factor loadings are listed in decreasing order of magnitude of the defining loadings. For males, the strongest markers of positive affect were feeling committed, trusted, emotionally intimate, loved, loving, and happy. For females, comparable markers were feeling emotionally intimate, loved, loving, physically intimate, happy, and trusted. With regard to the negative affect factor, the strongest markers for males appear to be feeling blue, discouraged, angry, sad, argumentative, and doubtful. These same items appear to be the strongest markers for the negative affect factor for females, although in slightly different order, namely, feeling angry, discouraged, sad, blue, argumentative, and doubtful. Thus, for both genders, it seems that the two items of "social support" and "free" do not load as highly as do the other items on the so-called positive affect factor. Similarly, the three items of "trapped," "deceived," and "lonely" do not load very highly with the other items defining the negative affect factor.

The numerical results from the second, time series part of the PFA (1,0) model are presented in Table 6.4. The first section of Table 6.4 describes the matrix of autoregressive coefficients (sometimes called the transition matrix, especially in the state-space modeling literature, where the equivalence exists for an AR(1) model). In this matrix, the columns represent the latent variables at one point in time, and the rows represent the same factors at the next point in time. Thus, the regression weights represent the direct influence of each column latent variable on each row latent variable. One informative feature of this matrix is comprised of the elements on the diagonal, representing autoregressions of one factor at time t-1 on itself at time t. These coefficients

TABLE 6.3
Factor Loadings of PFA (1,0)

	$Positive(\male)$	$Negative(\male)$	$Positive(\female)$	$Negative(\female)$
committed_m	0.71	0.12	-0.11	-0.11
trust_m	0.68	0.08	-0.08	-0.08
emotion.int_m	0.65	0.07	0.13	0.08
loved_m	0.63	-0.10	0.01	-0.01
loving_m	0.63	-0.05	-0.02	-0.02
happy_m	0.59	-0.22	-0.01	0.00
physical.int_m	0.47	0.00	0.25	0.16
supported_m	0.45	-0.01	0.01	0.00
free_m	0.37	-0.02	-0.19	-0.13
blue_m	0.02	0.71	-0.10	-0.08
discouraged_m	0.02	0.70	0.02	0.01
angry_m	-0.02	0.66	0.07	0.07
sad_m	-0.05	0.63	-0.09	-0.04
argue_m	0.01	0.60	0.08	0.13
doubtful_m	0.01	0.59	0.04	0.02
trapped_m	-0.08	0.43	0.11	0.06
lonely_m	-0.12	0.40	-0.20	-0.20
deceived_m	-0.02	0.39	0.05	0.04
emotion.int_f	0.02	-0.04	0.76	0.17
loved_f	0.01	0.00	0.65	-0.15
loving_f	-0.02	0.00	0.65	-0.18
physical.int_f	0.15	0.02	0.61	0.18
happy_f	0.00	-0.02	0.59	-0.30
trust_f	-0.01	0.02	0.58	-0.11
committed_f	0.00	-0.01	0.55	-0.10
supported_f	0.03	0.00	0.49	-0.07
free_f	-0.08	-0.08	0.25	-0.20
angry_f	-0.06	0.03	-0.01	0.70
discouraged_f	-0.05	-0.01	-0.06	0.67
sad_f	0.01	0.07	-0.15	0.61
blue_f	0.02	0.06	-0.14	0.60
argue_f	-0.01	0.07	0.01	0.57
doubtful_f	-0.02	0.03	-0.10	0.55
trapped_f	-0.02	0.00	-0.07	0.43
deceived_f	-0.05	0.00	0.00	0.45
lonely_f	-0.09	-0.03	-0.29	0.30

TABLE 6.4
Time Series Results From PFA (1,0)

Autoregressive Weights				
	Positive(σ)	*Negative(σ)*	*Positive(φ)*	*Negative(φ)*
Positive(σ)	0.53	0.21	-0.03	-0.08
Negative(σ)	0.07	0.29	-0.07	0.00
Positive(φ)	-0.07	-0.09	0.43	0.12
Negative(φ)	0.01	0.06	0.00	0.18
Lag-0 Factor Correlations (Implied by the Model)				
	Positive(σ)	*Negative(σ)*	*Positive(φ)*	*Negative(φ)*
Positive(σ)	1.00			
Negative(σ)	-0.63	1.00		
Positive(φ)	0.38	-0.24	1.00	
Negative(φ)	-0.17	0.34	-0.50	1.00
Predicted Factor-Covariance Matrix				
	Positive(σ)	*Negative(σ)*	*Positive(φ)*	*Negative(φ)*
Positive(σ)	0.18			
Negative(σ)	-0.03	0.07		
Positive(φ)	0.05	-0.05	0.15	
Negative(φ)	-0.02	0.04	-0.03	0.05
Shock Covariance Matrix				
	Positive(σ)	*Negative(σ)*	*Positive(φ)*	*Negative(φ)*
Positive(σ)	0.82			
Negative(σ)	-0.61	0.93		
Positive(φ)	0.33	-0.19	0.85	
Negative(φ)	-0.14	0.30	-0.47	0.95

indicate moderate and positive lagged (lag-1) autoregressive effects from one day to the next for positive affect for both males ($\beta = .53$) and females ($\beta = .43$), and weaker but still positive autoregressive effects for negative affect (βs $= .29$ and $.18$ for males and females, respectively). Interestingly, no strong cross-regressions (regressions from one latent variable to another) were found, except for relatively weak regressions from negative affect to positive affect for males ($\beta = .21$) and females ($\beta = .12$).

The second section of Table 6.4 summarizes the lag-0 (i.e., concurrent) correlations among the four latent variables, as implied by the model. These values indicate moderately large negative correlations between positive and negative affect for each gender ($rs = -.63$ and $-.50$ for males and females, respectively), smaller but positive correlations between genders for both positive affect ($r = .38$) and negative affect ($r = .34$), and smaller and negative correlations between genders across positive and negative affect.

Next, in the third section of Table 6.4, the predicted factor-covariance matrix is shown. The values in this matrix represent the amount of variance in each factor and in the covariance between each pair of factors explained by the model. Thus, in the current specification, autoregressive effects account for only about 18% and 15% of the variance of the Positive Affect factors and for about 7% and 5% of the variance in the negative affect factors. These relatively small values suggest that most of the temporal variations in the four factors and the covariation among factors is due to forces outside the system, or random shocks. The off-diagonal coefficients in this matrix were uniformly small, varying from –.05 to +.05, suggesting that the trait-like components of the four affect factors are essentially orthogonal.

The parameter estimates associated with the random shocks, due to random influences at a given time of measurement that are independent of the previous day, are shown in the last section of Table 6.4. The diagonal elements of this matrix are the complements of the diagonal elements of the predicted factor-covariance matrix, so the large values on the diagonal here indicate that random shocks explained the vast majority of the variance of the affect factors. Notable in this matrix are the rather large off-diagonal values. First, very large residual covariances were estimated between positive affect and negative affect factors for males ($r = -.61$) and females ($r = -.47$). These values indicate that the very robust negative cross-sectional correlations between Positive and Negative Affect factors found in the lag-0 correlation matrix ($rs = -.63$ and $-.50$ for males and females, respectively) derive almost exclusively from the correlations among state-like random shock influences that fluctuate from day to day and are influenced essentially not at all by stable, trait-like influences from one day to the next. Positive affect for males was relatively highly correlated with positive affect for females ($r = .33$) and the same held across genders for negative affect ($r = .30$). This pattern of results indicates that random shocks lead to opposite changes in positive affect and negative affect for both males and females; that is, if random shocks lead to increased positive affect in an individual, that individual will also tend to experience lower levels of negative affect. In addition, if the random shocks lead to increased positive or negative affect in one member of a dyad, those shocks will be associated with increased Positive or negative affect, respectively, in the other member of the dyad.

The results described above refer to a PFA (1,0) model that was based on data from all dyads as separate units, but included these data as part of a single analysis. That is, we stacked the data for each dyad vertically into a single file, where the first 52 lines of data were from Dyad 1, the next 52 lines of data were from Dyad 2, etc. In this analysis, we can obtain the misfit of the model to the data for each of the dyads. Such misfit values are plotted in Figures 6.3 and 6.4. In both of these figures, the Y axis represents misfit and higher values are worse, and the X axis represents individual dyads using their dyad number. Figure 6.3 displays the misfit due to the time series part of the model for each dyad and for lags 0, 1, 2, and 3 (although not directly

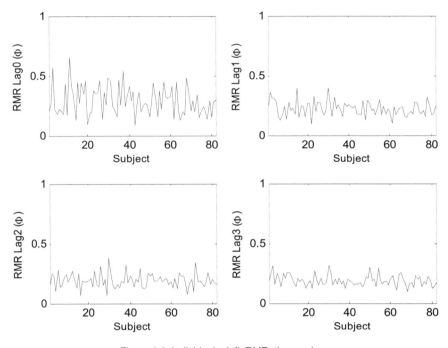

Figure 6.3. Individual misfit RMR time series.

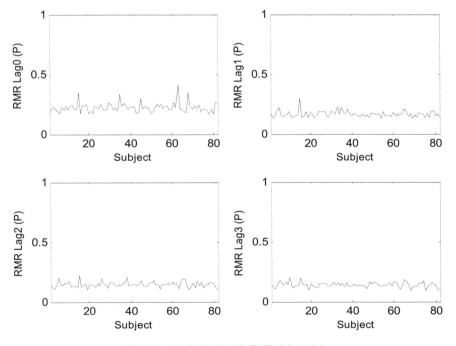

Figure 6.4. Individual misfit RMR full model.

modeled, misfit over lags higher than 1 can be implied by the model). Two features are noticeable here. First, model misfit is largest at lag-0 and diminishes over lags. Second, nontrivial differences in misfit among dyads are apparent, with some dyads having very low levels of misfit and other dyads having much greater levels of misfit.

Figure 6.4 shows misfit to the data due to the full model (i.e., time series plus factor analysis). This plot suggests that misfit is small for all individuals and across all lags. In sum, the misfit for this PFA (1,0) model appears to be primarily a function of the time series and not so much a function of the factor analysis part. These misfit plots, thus, confirm the numerical results presented in Tables 6.3 and 6.4, which indicated a strong factor structure with unambiguous discrimination among factors, but a weak transition matrix of lagged relations among factors.

In the second set of analyses, we fitted a PFA (2,0) model to the same data. That is, we added lagged relations from time t-2 to time t to the PFA (1,0) model. The results from these analyses are presented in Table 6.5 (because the factor loadings for the PFA (2,0) model were almost identical to those for the PFA (1,0) model, we do not report these values here). The first part of Table 6.5 includes the lag-1 and lag-2 regression coefficients. The former resemble the values obtained with the PFA (1,0) model, indicating moderate autoregressive influences for the factors from one day to the next. The latter are also very small and indicate that such autoregressive influences tend to dissipate quickly and are barely perceptible by the second day. The second and third parts of the table describe the amount of variances and covariances predicted by the model. As was the case in the PFA (1,0) analysis, the clear majority of the variances and covariances are predicted by sources outside the dyad, that is, random shocks to the system that vary from day to day.

Dynamic Factor Analysis of Each Dyad

The analyses described above included all the dyads as part of the same sample. Such analyses, thus, yielded aggregate results under the assumption that a single model applies to each dyad. The misfit plots indicated that such an assumption might not be reasonable, especially with regard to the time series part of the model. In the next set of analyses, we examined this issue by conducting an analysis for each dyad separately, instead of pooling all dyads together in the same analysis. In particular, we fitted the same PFA (1,0) model as before to each of the 82 dyads. We then saved the results for the parameter estimates of interest and examined the empirical distributions of these estimates. This, we reasoned, would be indicative of inter-dyad differences in the estimates based on individual (i.e., dyad) information.

TABLE 6.5
Time Series Results From PFA (2,0)

	Positive(σ)	Negative(σ)	Positive($\female$)	Negative($\female$)
Autoregressive Weights (Lag-1)				
Positive(σ)	0.40	0.09	0.08	-0.02
Negative(σ)	-0.04	0.21	-0.07	0.02
Positive($\female$)	0.00	-0.05	0.36	0.08
Negative($\female$)	-0.04	0.05	0.00	0.18
Autoregressive Weights (Lag-2)				
Positive(σ)	0.12	0.10	-0.09	-0.02
Negative(σ)	0.10	0.07	0.01	-0.05
Positive($\female$)	-0.05	-0.01	0.05	0.00
Negative($\female$)	0.03	-0.04	0.01	0.06
Predicted Factor-Covariance Matrix				
Positive(σ)	0.18			
Negative(σ)	-0.05	0.08		
Positive($\female$)	0.06	-0.05	0.13	
Negative($\female$)	-0.03	0.04	-0.03	0.05
Shock Covariance Matrix				
Positive(σ)	0.82			
Negative(σ)	-0.58	0.92		
Positive($\female$)	0.30	-0.19	0.87	
Negative($\female$)	-0.13	0.28	-0.44	0.95

The factor analysis part of the model also yielded large differences between dyads. That is, the highest loading items on each factor varied considerably across dyads, even though the modeling provided clear evidence of four factors for each dyad. For reasons of space, however, we present only results from the time series part of the model. These results are described in Table 6.6. Each entry in this table includes the mean of the parameter estimate (across 82 dyads), the standard deviation, the minimum, and the maximum. Some features are of particular importance here. First, the only elements in the matrix that have mean values that are substantial in magnitude are the values along the diagonal, indicating that only the autoregressive relations of factors seem to have consistent time-lagged relevance across most dyads in these data.

Second, although the means of these estimates are in line with the aggregate results, considerable variability in autoregression estimates is clearly in evidence across dyads. That is, for each of the estimates, the range is very large and includes values of opposite valence. For example, the mean estimate for positive affect for females was .512, a coefficient of substantial magnitude.

TABLE 6.6
Time Series Aggregate Results From PFA (1,0)

Autoregressive Weights (Lag-1)				
	$Positive(\male)$	$Negative(\male)$	$Positive(\female)$	$Negative(\female)$
$Positive(\male)$	.497 (.323)	.049 (.311)	.041 (.292)	.048 (.293)
	(-.38, 1.02)	(-.86, .75)	(-.70, .70)	(-.61, .64)
$Negative(\male)$	.111 (.290)	.338 (.369)	-.047 (.253)	.023 (.302)
	(-.50, .79)	(-.45, .95)	(-.70, .41)	(-.69, .71)
$Positive(\female)$	-.037 (.316)	-.046 (.264)	.512 (.289)	.126 (.304)
	(-.73, .58)	(-.60, .61)	(-.43, .96)	(-.49, .73)
$Negative(\female)$	-.040 (.336)	.043 (.322)	.038 (.262)	.307 (.355)
	(-.79, .65)	(-.70, .78)	(-.54, .50)	(-.52, 1.03)
Predicted Factor-Covariance Matrix				
	$Positive(\male)$	$Negative(\male)$	$Positive(\female)$	$Negative(\female)$
	.524 (.229)	.380 (.223)	.516 (.190)	.400 (.241)
	(.12, .95)	(.01, .92)	(.13, .96)	(.09, .95)

Note. $N = 64$ dyads (NREP $= 0$). The first set of numbers in parentheses are standard deviations. Numbers in parentheses below are minimum and maximum.

But, the SD for this estimate was .289, and the range varied from −.43 to +.96. Similar patterns held for the remaining three factors, with the range of values tending to fall from about −.40 to + 1.0. This indicates that the trait-like transmission of stability from day to day in affective experience varies widely across dyads, a finding masked by the aggregate analyses reported in Tables 6.4 and 6.5.

Third, the mean values of the off-diagonal elements, which represent cross-lagged relations among latent variables from one day to the next, tended to be very small, mimicking the small values for these coefficients reported in Tables 6.4 and 6.5 from the aggregate analyses. However, the SDs for these estimates were rather large, and the range of values for each coefficient was large, even if centered near zero. For example, the mean estimate for the effect of female negative affect on male positive affect was .048, a very modest value. But, the SD for this coefficient was .293, and values varied from −.61 to +.64 across dyads.

Fourth, for all parameter estimates except male and female Positive Affect, the SD for the estimate was larger than the mean estimate. The fluctuation across dyads in the parameter estimates for the autoregression coefficients are displayed in Figure 6.5. These plots visually illustrate the large variation across dyads. Although the mean values for these estimates are centered

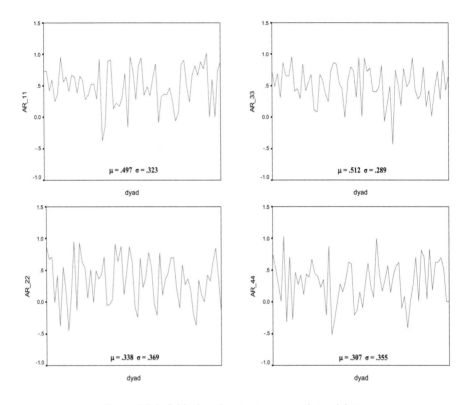

Figure 6.5. Individual analyses—autoregressive weights.

clearly above zero, some dyads have rather negative values. Similar plots for the cross-lagged coefficients would reveal comparable levels of variability across dyads, although the overall level of the profiles would be centered near zero.

The last section of Table 6.6 includes the averages for the predicted factor variances (i.e., diagonal elements in the factor-covariance matrix) across the 82 dyads. In contrast to the aggregate results that yielded predicted factor variances that ranged from 5% to 18%, the mean percentages of predicted variance in factors by the individual-dyad model were substantial, ranging from 38% to 52%. Although the model does not predict much of variance for factors for certain dyads, the model accounts for almost all of the variance in the factors for other dyads. In sum, these results suggest that, although possibly informative of the sample as a whole, the aggregate analysis did not accurately portray any individual dyad.

DISCUSSION

Representing Intraindividual and Dyadic Processes

Our goal in this chapter was to investigate the variability in affective experience of individuals in dyads, examining fluctuations and relationships over time in affect for each dyad, as well as examining differences in such relationships across dyads. We first fitted an exploratory factor model to data to confirm the presence of four affect factors in our data, then fitted a PFA model to the pooled data from all dyads, and finally fitted the same PFA model to each dyad separately. Our main objective here was to generate sample results based on information from each dyad.

One key result of our analyses indicated that a good, clear, and strong factorial structure was evident in the data over time. That is, the data supported a robust discrimination between positive and negative affect and between the two individuals in a dyad. This was true for both the aggregate analyses and the individual dyad analyses. When fitting our PFA models, we used an exploratory approach in which we specified the expected number of factors and a target matrix guiding rotation to simple structure. The results indicated that the data were very much in line with such a specification, with very small cross-loadings of manifest variables on unintended factors.

With regard to the time series part of the model, our results suggested that most of the dynamics in the factors (i.e., positive and negative affect) were not predicted by the trait-like autoregressive part of the model that represents stability of affective experiences from one day to the next, but rather were the result of random shocks to the system that varied from day to day. Moreover, when inspecting either the aggregate results reported in Tables 6.4 and 6.5 or the mean values shown in Table 6.6, the dynamics appeared to be moderate in magnitude and due almost solely to autoregressive influences of each factor at one time to the same factor at the next time, with a virtual absence of cross-lagged influences among factors within or between the individuals comprising a dyad. Based on these estimates, one would conclude that positive affect and negative affect have little in the way of mutual influences and that males and females within dyads have affective experiences that have little interconnection.

When the model was fitted to each dyad separately, however, the results revealed substantial variability in such dynamics across dyads. That is, although some dyads revealed little prediction in dynamics over time, other dyads exhibited very strong and systematic dynamics. When looking at the differences across dyads, important patterns were apparent. For certain dyads, lagged influences between factors over time were very large, suggesting that positive and negative affect had clear effects on each other, both within persons and, importantly, between persons comprising a dyad. These results confirm our everyday phenomenology, in which our affective states seem to influence one another and we engage in interactions with those close to us that produce affective reactions in both partners to the interaction.

Overall, these results suggest that modeling dynamics for all dyads—or, in general, all individuals—appears to be an unreasonable approach, one that is likely to mask interindividual differences across dyads in affective dynamics. The aggregate approach assumes a priori that all dyads have a similar pattern of variability and dynamics and, moreover, cannot adequately represent the dynamics for any particular dyad if the dyad departs from the norm or average. Because of this failure, it seems more reasonable to us to start from the information from each individual dyad and build up to generate results that apply to the sample and, hence, to the population, with results based on the uniqueness of each person's and each dyad's information. The argument of avoiding aggregating individuals before examining their individual information or testing for their homogeneity is not new. For example, based on this same idea, Nesselroade and Molenaar (1999) developed an algorithm to pool subgroups of individuals with homogeneous covariance structures. More recently, several researchers have demonstrated that aggregating data from individuals to express interindividual changes over time fails to characterize accurately how each person changes over time (Hamaker et al., 2005, Molenaar, 2004; Molenaar & Valsiner, 2005; Nesselroade, 2001; 2003). Our results presented in this chapter add further support to the position that one must pay close attention to each individual or dyad and that aggregating data across individuals or dyads may hopelessly confound results.

Methodological Issues

Our results were based on a particular approach to the analyses of the data, and our approach reflects certain methodological options. If the options we selected cannot be fully justified, then other options might be preferred. Here, we discuss several assumptions of our modeling and the options that are available.

Stationarity. One assumption made in all the models examined in this chapter is stationarity. That is, these DFA models assume that the same parameters exist throughout the series. This may be a problematic assumption, especially for short time series like the ones presented here. We consider it likely that individuals in a relationship experience periods of certain length that are different in emotional or affective tone and dynamics from other periods. Further, such differences in the dynamics across various periods can be the very essence of the relationship for certain individuals or dyads. To the extent that this is true, models that relax stationarity assumptions are needed. For example, Molenaar discussed DFA models that can accommodate such conditions in the data (Molenaar, De Gooijer, & Schmitz, 1992; Molenaar & Nesselroade, 2001). Another possibility is to use nonparametric approaches that focus precisely on identifying different segments with discrepant dynamics (Hsieh, Ferrer, & Chen, 2008). Such nonparametric approaches can be useful when trying to find hidden patterns of nonstationarity without any prior knowledge of the dyadic interaction type.

Level of measurement. In the present chapter, we based all of our analyses on individual items, rather than some function of items, such as item parcels. The DyFA program can be employed for conducting analyses at either the item, parcel, or scale level, so we were not compelled to remain at the item level. We selected this approach to remain as close to the original data as possible, but plan to extend our analyses to the parcel level to determine whether the patterns of autoregressive and cross-lagged influences are affected by this change. Because item parcels tend to be more reliable than the individual items that comprise the parcels, analyses are likely to be little affected except for the presence of larger factor loadings and perhaps more precise estimates of autoregressive and cross-lagged effects.

However, one factor that, somewhat surprisingly, may mitigate against the use of item parcels is the relatively small sample size. That is, for each dyad, we had only 50–60 times of measurement, so our PFA models fit to each dyad consisted of 36 manifest variables and the number of observations was only about 1.5 times the number of manifest variables. Because of the small manifest variable:observation ratio, many experts might argue in favor of item parcels, forming three 3-item parcels per factor and thereby reducing the number of manifest variables to 12 (i.e., 3 parcels per factor for 4 factors) and improving the manifest variable:observation ratio to over 4.0. However, among others, Arrindell and Van der Ende (1985) and MacCallum, Widaman, Zhang, and Hong (1999) reported results that question traditional recommendations regarding the manifest variable:observation ratio. Specifically, both Arrindell and Van der Ende and MacCallum et al. argued that a larger, not smaller, number of manifest variables can improve a factor solution if sample size is small, but with this important proviso: the number of latent dimensions should not increase with the increase in the number of manifest variables. In the current situation, we have a choice: nine indicators for each of 4 factors versus three 3-item parcels for each of 4 factors, with the number of observations held constant at about 60. Given this choice, the Arrindell and Van der Ende and MacCallum et al. results suggest that the use of the larger number of indicators might be preferable even if the 3-item parcels improved the reliability of each manifest variable.

Invariance and the metric of parameter estimates. Another issue that is implicit in our approach to modeling data is the issue of invariance of parameter estimates across individuals and dyads. The DyFA program cannot yet accommodate multiple groups or, therefore, factorial invariance constraints across multiple groups (e.g., multiple dyads), constraints that have become common in the use of structural modeling programs. We were therefore unable to invoke any factorial invariance constraints (cf. Widaman & Reise, 1997) across dyads. As a result, latent variable variances were fixed at unity for each dyad, factor loadings varied across dyads, and the resulting autoregressive and cross-lagged paths were reported in a standardized metric, rather than a raw score metric. In typical SEM analyses, great care is often taken to ensure that factor loadings and intercepts of manifest variables are constrained to invariance across groups (e.g., dyads) so that differences in latent variable variances are identified and resulting regression weights for paths between latent variables are on a comparable metric (Widaman & Reise, 1997).

In effect, our approach here flies in the face of usual recommendations for multiple-group analyses, and many experts would conclude that certain key parameter estimates, particularly the autoregressive and cross-lagged path coefficients are likely to be less comparable under our approach. However, Nesselroade (2007) argued explicitly in favor of a quasi-ideographic method such as we have used here, arguing that one should attempt to isolate latent variables for each individual or dyad that reflect the dynamics of that dyad, even if the patterns of loadings preclude strong or explicit factorial invariance constraints. In effect, the latent variables may retain a stronger level of cross-dyad conceptual identity only if one allows mathematical measurement properties such as factor loadings to vary from metric invariance. Moreover, under the Nesselroade approach, standardized regression weights might be more informative than raw score weights that are derived under metric invariance constraints, even though the latter presumably have greater comparability due to being on a "common" metric. Whether this is a major problem is a task for future research to determine, but we encourage researchers to consider various options, because recommendations based on purely statistical arguments may cause one to pursue paths that lead away from fruitful substantive interpretation.

Parameter estimates and their standard errors. Many state-of-the-art statistical approaches provide standard errors for all parameter estimates, so that interval estimates can be derived and the statistical significance of the parameters can be determined. The exploratory approach to analyses we have advocated cannot yet provide standard errors for parameter estimates, although these are under development (Zhang, 2006) and will soon been implemented in DyFA. In effect, this is the standard practice in exploratory factor analysis over the past century—researchers have used the method quite productively even though standard errors for factor loadings and other parameter estimates were not available. In prior research using PFA models, several groups of investigators, including Ferrer and Nesselroade (2003), have used structural equation modeling (SEM) programs to fit PFA models to data, and these studies were able to generate and report standard errors for parameter estimates. But, these ways of adapting SEM programs to fit the PFA model lead to approximations to the proper estimates of the parameters of PFA models, and the DyFA program provides more direct and appropriate estimates of these parameters. Therefore, we opted to employ a modeling approach that provides a closer and more accurate solution for model parameters but fails to provide SEs for parameter estimates over alternative approaches that provide only approximations to solutions yet yields SEs for the inexact parameters in these models (see also Song & Ferrer, in press, for an example of PFA modeling using state-space methodology).

Missing data and subsequent sample selection. Yet another methodological issue concerns the presence of missing data. In our study, we collected data from 235 couples but have reported results from only about one-third of these participants (82 couples). We did this because only 82 couples provided complete daily diary data from each dyad member across at least 54 days, and the DyFA program has no options at present to accommodate the fitting of models to data sets with missing observations. Clearly, if we had opted to use SEM approaches, we could have used full information maximum likelihood estimation to circumvent the problems of missing data. But, the most common way of implementing PFA models using SEM programs requires the use of lagged variables, so our set of manifest variables would have ballooned to 108 manifest variables (i.e., 36 manifest variables at each of three times: times t, t-1, and t-2) if we intended to model lag-2 relations. Given the small number of observations, this matrix would have been non-Grammian, and we would have been forced to use parcels, which, as noted above, is an option that has its own limitations. Clearly, future research should be conducted on this problem to provide guidelines for practicing scientists, noting the options available and the strengths and weaknesses of each option.

Substantive Extensions

In addition to exploring methodological issues, the present results could be exploited in future ways that relate to substantive issues in the study of individuals and dyads. A wide array of substantive extensions could be considered; here we will concentrate on issues related to developmental considerations, the differential importance of information regarding status versus dynamic change, and the role of external variables or covariates.

Developmental considerations. When thinking about how developmental status might moderate relations among affective processes, we think most directly about how to bring indicators of time or age into our equations. The first and most obvious time-related variable is chronological age of the participants. In our current sample, the participants were fairly restricted in chronological age, shown by the SD for age, which was less than 2 years. Because of the restricted age range, we did not pursue analyses to determine whether chronological age was related to the strength of relations among latent variables represented in autoregressive or cross-lagged path coefficients. We are in the process of collecting data from a community sample with much larger age variation, so the effect of chronological age on model parameters will be a focus of our research in the near future. We hypothesize that younger individuals will exhibit greater variability in their affective states and stronger cross-lagged within-individual and within-dyad cross-lagged path coefficients than will older and more mature persons, but future research will be needed to confirm this conjecture.

A second time-related variable that is likely to moderate PFA model parameter estimates is the time point in the dyadic relationship at which data are collected. Some participants in our studies begin filling out their daily diaries at a very early stage of their relationship, even as early as the first month of the relationship, whereas our current community sample includes participants who are in the second or third decade of their relationship. When we have sufficient variability on the dimension of this key variable, we will test our ideas about how simple "time in the relationship" influences autoregressive and cross-lagged influences. With greater time in a relationship, we expect that autoregressive effects will be stronger and cross-lagged influences weaker, because the partners in the dyad know the other partner well and have ready ways of responding to alterations in emotional or affective state of the partner.

A third time-related measure is the duration of the time series. In the study reported in this chapter, we sought to gather data for 60 days and succeeded in doing so for many participants. But, in our current work, we are extending the time series to 3 months (or 90 days) to provide a more stable picture of the dynamic relations between individuals across time. These data will allow us interesting analytic possibilities. For example, we will be able to use only the first 60 days of data if we wish to compare results for the community sample with results for the college sample that served as the basis for this chapter. Furthermore, we could perform comparisons of the quality of results from the first 60 days versus the full 90 days for the community sample, to determine whether increasing the data collection period by 50% provides a noticeable improvement in the quality of parameter estimates. One aim of this research is to determine the optimal amount of data collection time for studies of this sort, to ensure that sufficient data are collected to yield adequate precision for parameter estimates, yet keeping data collection times as short as possible and thereby taxing participants minimally.

Initial status versus dynamic processes. The PFA models we used in this study provide estimates of influences among latent variables that reflect dynamic personal and dyadic processes. Because these dynamics characterize the emotional tone and interactions in the dyadic relationships, our models and their statistical parameters are likely to help predict the stability or breakup of relationships. That is, we expect that relationships that exhibit extreme fluctuations in positive affect and especially in negative affect are the relationships that are most likely headed for an earlier dissolution. Similar predictions hold for relationships in which strong cross-lagged effects are found for negative affect of one partner on the positive affect of the other.

But, we should not lose sight of indicators of initial status or mean level of the variables to which our models of dynamic processes are fit. The dynamic PFA models are traditionally fit to correlation or covariance matrices, and means on manifest variables are taken out when computing such matrices. But, in subtracting means, the researcher may well be discarding information that might be crucial in predicting whether a relationship will endure. Other things being equal, one would predict that dyads that report lower levels of positive affect or higher levels of negative affect with regard to the dyadic relationship would have relationships of shorter duration. Thus, when testing the utility of relationship variables that are useful for predicting longevity of a relationship, we should contrast the predictive power of measures of initial status or mean level of an across-time dynamic profile against the utility of parameter estimates that reflect the dynamics of emotional or affective tone of a relationship.

External variables. A final class of variables that should be investigated comprises external variables that may well play a role in the longevity of a dyadic relationship. Here, we expect to find both main and interactive effects of external variables. For example, extreme fluctuations may be a strong predictor of relationship dissolution, but not for all dyads. Some individuals seem to thrive on emotional upheaval, finding enjoyment in high levels of emotional expression and deriding more flattened affective expression. If such a person were the member of a particular dyad, then heightened levels of variability on emotional dimensions might be a predictor of a more long-lived relationship. Future research will help us uncover how trait-like person variables combine with dyad-level dynamic processes to influence the developmental course and the longevity of dyadic relations.

CONCLUSION

The results we presented in this chapter are clearly exploratory but, we believe, informative of models that can capture fluctuations over time within a person and between the two persons in a dyad. Surely, confirmatory models could be used in such situations, but confirmatory models require theoretical hypotheses about patterns of within- and between-person variability over time. If we had sufficiently specific a priori theory in this domain, alternative confirmatory models could be fitted to the same data and the fit of alternative models compared to refute unreasonable hypotheses. Without clear a priori predictions, exploratory procedures are a reasonable tool. In the case of exploratory approaches, model fit is invariant to the target specification, and no clear methods for comparing alternative models are available. But, we trust that the exploratory results we have reported may provide the beginnings of evidence-based theorizing that will be useful for confirmatory modeling in the future.

ACKNOWLEDGMENTS

We are grateful to Michael Browne, Hairong Song, and Guangjian Zhang for their comments on earlier versions of this article. This research was supported by grant BCS-05-27766 (Ferrer, PI) from the National Science Foundation and also by grants from the National Institute of Child Health and Human Development, the National Institute on Drug Abuse, and the National Institute of Mental Health (HD047573, HD051746, and MH051361; Rand Conger, PI).

REFERENCES

Arrindell, W. A., & Van der Ende, J. (1985). An empirical test of the utility of the observations-to-variables ratio in factor and components analysis. *Applied Psychological Measurement,*, *9*, 165-178.

Browne, M. W., & Nesselroade, J. R. (2005). Representing psychological processes with dynamic factor models: Some promising uses and extensions of ARMA time series models. In Maydeu-Olivares & J. J. McArdle (Eds.), *Advances in psychometrics: A festschrift to Roderick P. McDonald* (pp. 415-451). Mahwah, NJ: Erlbaum.

Browne, M. W., & Zhang, G. (2005). User's Guide: Dyfa: Dynamic factor analysis of lagged correlation matrices, Version 2.03. [WWW document and computer program]. URL http://quantrm2.psy.ohio-state.edu/browne/.

Browne, M. W., & Zhang, G. (2007). Developments in the factor analysis of individual time series. In R. C. MacCallum & R. Cudeck (Eds.), *Factor analysis at 100: Historical developments and future directions*. Mahwah, NJ: Erlbaum.

Cattell, R. B. (1963). The structuring of change by p-technique and incremental r-technique. In C. W. Harris (Ed.), *Problems in measuring change* (pp. 167-198). Madison: University of Wisconsin Press.

Cattell, R. B., Cattell, A. K. S., & Rhymer, R. M. (1947). P-technique demonstrated in determining psychophysical source traits in a normal individual. *Psychometrika, 12*, 267-288.

Engle, R., & Watson, M. (1981). A one-factor multivariate time series model of metropolitan wage rates. *Journal of the American Statistical Association, 76*, 774-781.

Ferrer, E. (2006). Application of dynamic factor analysis to affective processes in dyads. In A. Ong & M. van Dulmen (Eds.), *Handbook of methods in positive psychology* (pp. 41-58). New York: Oxford University Press.

Ferrer, E., & Nesselroade, J. R. (2003). Modeling affective processes in dyadic relations via dynamic factor analysis. *Emotion, 3*, 344-360.

Hamaker, E. L., Dolan, C. V., & Molenaar, P. C. M. (2005). Statistical modeling of the individual: Rationale and application of multivariate stationary time series analysis. *Multivariate Behavioral Research, 40*, 207-233.

Hsieh, F., Ferrer, E., Chen, S., & Chow, S. M. (2008). *Exploring nonstationary dynamics in dyadic interactions via hierarchical segmentation and stochastic small-world networks*. Manuscript submitted for publication.

Immink, K. (1986). *Estimation in Markov models and dynamic factor analysis*. Doctoral dissertation, University of Utrecht, Utrecht.

MacCallum, R. C., Widaman, K. F., Zhang, S., & Hong, S. (1999). Sample size in factor analysis. *Psychological Methods, 4*, 84-99.

McArdle, J. J. (1982). *Structural equation modeling of an individual system: Preliminary results from "A case study of alcoholism."* Unpublished manuscript, University of Denver, Psychology Department.

Molenaar, P. C. M. (1985). A dynamic factor model for the analysis of multivariate time series. *Psychometrika, 50*, 181-202.

Molenaar, P. C. M. (2004). A manifesto on psychology as idiographic science: Bringing the person back into scientific psychology–this time forever. *Measurement, 2*, 201-218.

Molenaar, P. C. M., De Gooijer, J. G., & Schmitz, B. (1992). Dynamic factor analysis of nonstationary multivariate time series. *Psychometrika, 57*, 333-349.

Molenaar, P. C. M., & Nesselroade, J. R. (2001). Rotation in the dynamic factor modeling of multivariate stationary time series. *Psychometrika, 66*, 99-107.

Molenaar, P. C. M., & Valsiner, J. (2005). How generalization works through the single case: A simple idiographic process analysis of an individual psychotherapy. *International Journal of Idiographic Science, Article 1.* Retrieved (10/18/2005) from http://www.valsiner.com/ articles/molenvals.htm.

Nesselroade, J. R. (2001). Intraindividual variability in development within and between individuals. *European Psychologist, 6*, 187-193.

Nesselroade, J. R. (2003). Elaborating the differential in differential psychology. *Multivariate Behavioral Research, 37*, 543-561.

Nesselroade, J. R. (2007). Factoring at the individual level: Some matters for the second century of factor analysis. In R. Cudeck & R. C. MacCallum (Eds.), *Factor analysis at 100: Historical developments and future directions* (pp. 249-264). Mahwah, NJ: Lawrence Erlbaum Associates.

Nesselroade, J. R., McArdle, J. J., Aggen, S. H., & Meyers, J. M. (2002). Alternative dynamic factor models for multivariate time-series analyses. In D. M. Moskowitz & S. L. Hershberger (Eds.), *Modeling intraindividual variability with repeated measures data: Advances and techniques* (pp. 235-265). Mahwah, NJ: Lawrence Erlbaum Associates.

Nesselroade, J. R., & Molenaar, P. C. M. (1999). Pooling lagged covariance structures based on short, multivariate time-series for dynamic factor analysis. In R. H. Hoyle (Ed.), *Statistical strategies for small sample research* (pp. 224-251). Newbury Park, CA: Sage.

Sbarra, D., & Ferrer, E. (2006). The structure and process of emotional experience following non-marital relationship dissolution: Dynamic factor analyses of love, anger, and sadness. *Emotion, 6*, 224-238.

Shifren, K., Hooker, K., Wood, P., & Nesselroade, J. R. (1997). Structure and variation of mood in individuals with Parkinson's disease: A dynamic factor analysis. *Psychology and Aging, 12*, 328-339.

Song, H., & Ferrer, E. (in press). State-space modeling of dynamic psychological processes via the Kalman Smoother algorithm: Rationale, finite sample properties, and applications. *Structural Equation Modeling.*

Watson, D., Clark, L. A., & Tellegen, A. (1988). Development and validation of brief measures of positive and negative affect: The PANAS scales. *Journal of Personality and Social Psychology, 54*, 1063-1070.

Widaman, K. F., & Reise, S. P. (1997). Exploring the measurement invariance of psychological instruments: Applications in the substance use domain. In K. J. Bryant, M. Windle, & S. G. West (Eds.), *The science of prevention: Methodological advances from alcohol and substance use research* (pp. 281-324). Washington, DC: American Psychological Association.

Wood, P., & Brown, D. (1994). The study of intraindividual differences by means of dynamic factor models: Rationale, implementation, and interpretation. *Psychological Bulletin, 116*, 166-186.

Zhang, G. (2006). *Bootstrap procedures for dynamic factor analysis.* Unpublished doctoral dissertation, The Ohio State University, Columbus, OH.

CHAPTER SEVEN

It Takes Two:
A Dyadic, SEM-Based Perspective on
Personality Development

Pamela Sadler

Wilfrid Laurier University

Erik Woody

University of Waterloo

In studying personality traits, developmental researchers examine how traits change across development. One issue is the pattern by which, on average across many individuals, the level of a trait increases or decreases with development. Using the trait of dominance as an example, what is the overall trajectory across time that characterizes the level of this trait? Are there periods of development during which the expression of dominance waxes, and are there other periods during which it wanes? Such patterns can be tracked by looking for changes in the mean of the trait across developmental levels.

Another important issue is the stability of individual differences in a trait. For example, do those who as young children are more dominant than their peers remain more dominant than them in adolescence? Such patterns of stability can be tracked by looking at the consistency in the rank order of individuals on the trait across development. In short, by tracking means on a trait and its correlations with itself over time, stability and change in personality can be charted across developmental level (Caspi, Roberts, & Shiner, 2005; Shiner, 1998; Shiner & Caspi, 2003).

However, traits are mainly interesting to the extent that they underlie behavior and can be used to successfully predict and understand it. Accordingly, this chapter focuses on a somewhat different issue about traits—their relations to behavior, and how these relations change across development. At first blush, tracking this relation may seem methodologically straightforward: Presumably one simply examines the correlation between a measure of the trait and a measure of a behavior; then one can look at how this correlation changes across developmental level. However, our contention in this chapter is that a more sophisticated model of the trait–behavior relation offers considerable advantages and, simply put, is much more interesting. A basic insight of this model is that expression of personality traits, especially in the interpersonal domain, typically involves the traits of two (or more) people, which must be integrated or coordinated in the resulting interaction behaviors.

To introduce this model, we first briefly review relevant literature on the relation of personality traits to behavior, beginning with the near-death of personality in 1968. We embed the main themes of this literature into our proposed structural models, and we show how these models lead to a productive reconceptualization of the issues involved. Then we explore some of the most interesting developmental questions that can be addressed through the use of such models. Finally, we review the statistical methodology needed to apply such models to various types of dyads, including both distinguishable (e.g., male–female) and interchangeable (e.g., female–female) ones.

Sources of Error and Measurement Issues

In his 1968 review of the literature on trait–behavior relations, Mischel famously asserted that the degree of predictability of social behavior that can be achieved with traits is utterly negligible. That is, for any given behavior, personality traits account for only a trivial portion of the variance (Mischel, 1968; see also Peterson, 1968). Therefore, Mischel argued, broad personality traits are not useful for explaining social behavior.

Mischel's critique of personality elicited an important series of responses, some appreciative and some critical. These responses were seminal in helping to clarify crucial underlying issues involved in the study of trait–behavior relations (Kenrick & Funder, 1988).

First, Mischel's assertion that traits do not predict social behavior was highly counterintuitive, because virtually everyone, psychologists and non-psychologists alike, has the striking everyday impression that, for example, some people are consistently more friendly and other people consistently more distant, and that some people are consistently more dominant and others consistently more submissive. If traits are not actually predictive, how do these strong impressions arise?

Nisbett (1980; Nisbett & Ross, 1980) devoted considerable attention to this problem. Strongly endorsing Mischel's position that broad personality traits actually predict social behavior only to a trivial degree, he argued that laypeople (and psychologists) believe otherwise only because they evaluate the evidence in a biased fashion. For example, people's prior expectations may strongly color their social observations; they may form social impressions based on minimal data and then show perseverance of judgment, even in the face of subsequently disconfirming information. Nisbett argued that, partly because of such self-fulfilling biases, people chronically overestimate the impact of personality traits in the explanation of social behavior. Indeed, this tendency is so widespread that Ross (1977) dubbed it the "fundamental attribution error." In short, to some extent people see what they expect to see, whether it is there or not, and they expect to see consistency in people's social behavior.

Unlike Nisbett (1980), we do not believe that such inferential errors explain away the entire problem of trait–behavior relations. However, the evidence that such errors occur is very compelling (see Nisbett & Ross, 1980, for a review). Thus, it is reasonable to assume that whenever a measure of a trait and a measure of a behavior come from the same source—whether self-report, acquaintance, or observer—at least part of the relation may be due to self-fulfilling biases.

To simply ignore this problem of bias seems highly problematic; instead, it needs to be evaluated as a component of the theoretical model used to study trait–behavior relations. Sadler and Woody (2003) pointed out that biases in the perceptions of people involved in social interactions are not merely a nuisance for the researcher. It is true that biases may be a contaminant of obtained trait–behavior relations, which the researcher needs to control to understand what is happening more objectively. However, they may also be an important, intrinsic component of social processes, which the researcher needs to study to understand social interactions more fully. As we will explain in a few moments, we propose that such biases be modeled as systematic errors of measurement, a strategy that allows them simultaneously to be corrected for and studied in their own right. There are other possible modeling strategies, as well; whatever strategy is used, these effects need to be modeled explicitly.

A second important response to Mischel's critique focused on the role of unsystematic, or random, errors of measurement in the study of trait–behavior relations. Epstein and others argued, in effect, that Mischel's position was psychometrically naïve because it ignored the relation-attenuating effects of random measurement errors (Epstein, 1979, 1980; Epstein & O'Brien, 1985; Rushton, Brainerd, & Pressley, 1983). Epstein (1980) likened single samples of behavior to single items on a test, in that they are similarly affected by idiosyncratic influences, or noise. Thus, he argued, behavior in a single situation or on a single occasion should be no more predictable than single items on a test, because, like them, it lacks the requisite reliability. Further, Epstein (1980, p. 790) argued that aggregating behavior measures across situations and/or occasions has the advantage of "canceling out incidental, uncontrollable factors," just as aggregating across items on tests dramatically improves the reliability of the resulting scores. The resulting composite scores show stronger correlations than those found between single behavioral items, and this evidence may be interpreted as indicating that traits are reasonably predictive after all.

   This line of thinking initiated a vigorous debate about its merits. For example, Mischel and Peake (1982) rejected the demonstration of increased correlations with aggregation as a pointless psychometric exercise that sidestepped the real issue. In response to this and other criticisms, Epstein (e.g., 1986) attempted to defend his argument for aggregation. Other commentators have also reconsidered the underlying issues. For example, Tellegen (1991, p. 23) advanced the important point that the increase in reliability of a trait measure due to aggregation should not be confused with the "response penetration" of the trait in predicting behavior. To illustrate, consider a pool of items whose average interitem correlation is a very modest .10. In accordance with the Spearman-Brown prophecy formula, by aggregating many items to form each of two scales, we could achieve scales whose correlation is impressively high, say .80. However, this achievement does not alter the fact that the influence of the underlying construct on each item (its "response penetration") is very small (i.e., explaining about one percent of its variance). The implication is that we need to be very careful about considering how aggregation relates to the particular question being addressed.

   Our own position is that, in the study of trait–behavior relations, some uses of aggregation are legitimate, but others clearly are not. In particular, the types of aggregation used need to fit the conceptual definition of the variable in question.

   To measure a broad, underlying personality trait, virtually all types of aggregation are highly sensible, and some of them are perhaps even necessary. This is because the underlying trait is conceptualized as a general tendency that manifests itself, at least to some extent, across many relevant situations and occasions. Hence, for measuring a trait, aggregating across occasions, situations, and types of measure (e.g., self-report vs. observer) helps crucially to triangulate on the construct of interest.

   However, in measuring the specific behavioral criterion to be predicted by the trait, the issues are quite different. Employing multiple types of measure (self-report vs. observer) is again legitimate for triangulating on the behavior. This is because the behavioral criterion in question should generalize across measurement strategy. In contrast, aggregating over situations or occasions is highly problematic. This is because aggregating over situations or occasions changes the nature of the criterion and, in effect, redefines it. As a rough analogy, consider a meteorologist who argues, in a manner akin to Epstein (1980), that prediction of daily temperature and precipitation is difficult because they are idiosyncratic and noisy; therefore, he or she proposes to predict average monthly temperature and precipitation instead. Such averages are clearly a different variable, not simply a less noisy version of the same variable.

In short, we believe that it is a legitimate and important question to ask how well a general trait, defined as an entity that manifests itself across many situations and occasions, predicts relevant behavior, defined as events occurring on a particular, relevant occasion. A high-quality measure of the general trait should represent, at least in principle, an aggregate across many situations and occasions; in contrast, the behavioral criterion should not be aggregated in this way. Thus, neither the correlation between a type of behavior on two occasions (e.g., Nisbett, 1980) nor the correlation between two scores each aggregated across multiple occasions (e.g., Epstein, 1980) correctly answers the question of trait–behavior relations.

The issue of aggregation is closely related to the principle of disattenuating relations for the limited reliabilities of the measures involved. In the scientific study of personality, questions of how strongly traits predict behavior are best answered in ways that are not arbitrarily affected by known (and, in principle, correctible) limitations of the particular measuring instruments used. That is, our question is not, "Practically speaking (i.e., using these particular measures), how strongly can we predict?" Instead, our question is "How strong is the underlying relation, undistorted by measurement limitations?" Arguments for aggregation partly represent attempts to deal, somewhat incompletely, with this basic distinction. That is, looking beyond the vagaries of practical limitations on prediction, we want to know about the true underlying relation, or best characterization of how the underlying social world actually works.

In accordance with this argument, we propose that questions about trait–behavior relations are best couched in terms of latent variables. These latent variables need to be embedded in a model that accurately represents the practical measurement issues involved. A suitable measurement model specifies the relevant patterns of random and systematic measurement errors, allows the estimation of these errors, and corrects the relations among the latent variables for these errors.

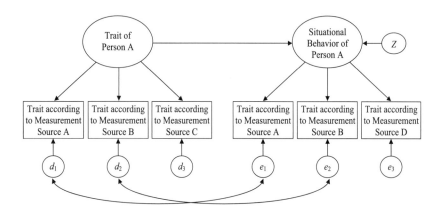

Figure 7.1. Measurement model for the trait–behavior relation.

Figure 7.1 shows the basic form of such a model. The Trait and the Situational Behavior are represented as latent variables, or pure constructs (each within an oval). Each latent variable is connected to a set of fallible measures (shown in rectangles). The model represents each measure as affected both by the relevant construct and by irrelevant errors, shown as the error variables d_1 through e_3. Pairs of measures that have the same source are allowed to have correlated errors (shown by the curved line with arrowheads at both ends). For example, measurement source A could be self-report, and measurement source B the report of an acquaintance. Because pairs of measures sharing the same source may be affected by common biases, they are allowed to correlate in this way, in addition to whatever true underlying relation there may be between the trait and the situational behavior. (As an alternative to correlated errors, another way to represent effects attributable to the same source is with perceiver or perspective factors, as in Kenny's social-relations model—see, e.g., Kenny, 1994; H. Ross, Stein, Trabasso, Woody, & Ross, 2005.) If such a model is specified correctly, then the relation between the Trait and the Situational Behavior (shown by the arrow) is corrected both for systematic biases in social perceptions and for the relation-attenuating effects of random measurement error. (The disturbance, variable Z, represents reliable variance in Situational Behavior that is not explained by the Trait.) Of course, this basic measurement model may be extended in various ways, for example by adding further measures and by adding other traits and behaviors.

In summary, in the study of trait–behavior relations, there has been a long history of concerns about systematic biases and the effects of random measurement error. Our argument is to bring these important issues directly into the light by modeling them as an integral aspect of the theoretical model for investigating trait–behavior relations. As suggested by Figure 7.1, structural equation modeling (SEM), with its flexible capacity to handle latent variables, is ideal for this purpose.

Interactionism and Dyadic Concepts of Trait–Behavior Relations

In his 1968 critique of personality traits, Mischel drew a strong distinction between personality traits and situational factors as the two determinants of behavior. He argued that the "trivial" amount of variance in behavior explained by traits implies that the amount of variance explained by situational forces must be "enormous" (Mischel, 1968, p. 83).

This very strong position of situationism, although endorsed by some commentators (e.g., Nisbett, 1980), was criticized by others (e.g., Bowers, 1973; Endler & Magnusson, 1976). One line of criticism is that, in general, situational forces, even rather powerful ones under experimental control, do not actually explain a larger proportion of variance in behavior than traits (Funder & Ozer, 1983). Another, more important line of criticism is that Mischel had created an artificial dichotomy by pitting personality traits and situational forces against each other in the prediction of behavior. In a famous critique of Mischel, Bowers (1973) argued that traits and situations act together as codeterminants of behavior, such that it is their interaction that is the best predictor of behavior.

Rather than being a unitary concept, interactionism, as advanced by Bowers (1973) and others (e.g., Endler & Magnusson, 1976), actually consists of two separate ideas, neither of which implies the other. First, traits and situations may interact in the statistical sense, whereby each serves as a moderator of the effects of the other. Along these lines, Bowers showed that across a wide range of studies, the statistical interaction of traits and situations explained substantially more variance in behavior than either factor alone (as "main effects"). Endler (1981) dubbed this type of joint effect "mechanistic interactionism."

Second, another type of interactionism posits that traits and situations should not be regarded as separate determinants of behavior because they are interdependent; that is, they have reciprocal influences on each other (Wachtel, 1973). Along these lines, Bowers (1973) argued that the situation is in part a function of the person, in that the person perceives the situation through his or her own perceptual and cognitive filters. Moreover, Bowers argued that much of a person's social environment is selected and created by his or her own behavior: People "foster consistent social environments, which then reciprocate by fostering behavioral consistency" (Bowers, 1973,

p. 329). Thus, as Wachtel (1973) pointed out, although behavioral consistency may stem from being in particular situations repeatedly, these situations are "largely of one's own making and themselves describable as a characteristic of one's personality" (p. 330). Endler (1981) dubbed this type of effect "reciprocal interactionism."

Mischel himself eventually adopted his own version of the interactionist position, best known in his work with Shoda (Mischel & Shoda, 1995; Mischel, 2004). He argues that what is consistent about each person is not a general tendency, as represented in broad personality traits, but each person's profile of behavioral tendencies across relevant classes of situations. For example, John may tend to be dominant in one type of situation, submissive in a second type of situation, and neutral (neither dominant nor submissive) in a third type of situation; whereas, in contrast, Jack may be submissive, neutral, and dominant in the three respective types of situations.

One problem with this idea is the lack of parsimony of positing an unbounded variety of qualitatively different profiles as the representation of individual differences with regard to a class of behavior (e.g., dominance). However, a more basic problem is that Mischel and Shoda (1995) offer no specification of how to determine the relevant classes of situations. They state that these classes should represent "functional equivalence" (Mischel, 2004), but do not tell us what situational features determine functional equivalence. Existing work indicates that the search to devise taxonomies of situations is very challenging (Ten Berge & De Raad, 1999) and readily becomes complexly idiographic (Cervone, 2004).

A quite different, more straightforward approach to interactionism has been advanced by interpersonal theorists, such as Carson (1969) and Kiesler (1983, 1996). The basic insight is that, to a considerable extent, in dyadic social interchanges each person serves as the situation for the other person. With regard to interpersonal behavior, Kiesler (1983, p. 209) argued that "by far the most important class of situations consists of 'other persons,' or, more precisely, of the presenting interpersonal styles of various interactants." Thus, each person's social behavior is a function not only of his or her own traits, but also those of his or her particular interaction partner.

This idea may be represented readily in a structural equation model, as shown in Figure 7.2a. In this figure, all the variables are latent (depicted in ovals); although not shown in Figure 7.2a, we presume that each latent variable is linked to its indicators (e.g., scales) according to an appropriate measurement model, as shown in Figure 7.1. The covariance between the partners' traits, depicted at the left side of the diagram, represents the possibility that the partners' traits are related to each other. This may well be the case for naturally occurring dyads, in which, for example, a process like

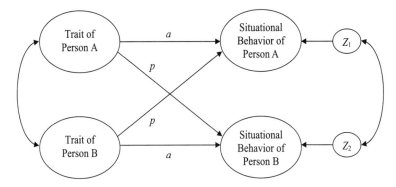

Figure 7.2a. Social behavior as a function of the traits of interaction partners.

assortative mating might lead to similar people pairing together. In contrast, if unacquainted people are paired randomly for the purposes of an experiment, this covariance may be assumed to be zero.

The crucial aspect of the model is that each person's situational behavior is a function of both his or her own trait and that of his or her partner. This type of model is an application of what is called the Actor–Partner Interdependence Model (Cook & Kenny, 2005; Kenny, 1996; Little & Card, 2005). The effects of one's own trait on one's behavior, labeled "a" in the diagram, are termed "actor effects," and the effects of the partner's trait on one's behavior, labeled "p" in the diagram, are termed "partner effects." By supplementing the tendency toward trait–behavior consistency represented by the actor effects, such partner effects are one way of allowing each person to function as the situation for the other. Parenthetically, the covariance between the two disturbances, Z_1 and Z_2, represents residual covariation between the partners' behaviors not explained by the model. If the model captures the phenomena being studied well, this residual covariation may be negligible (and statistically insignificant).

Earlier, we drew a major distinction between two different, basic conceptions of interactionism—what Endler (1981) called "mechanistic" (the statistical interaction of person by situation) versus "reciprocal" (the simultaneous interdependence of person and situation). Using the insight that in social interchanges each person serves as the situation for the other, these contrasting concepts can be represented in structural equation models by appropriately modifying Figure 7.2a. Mechanistic interactionism is depicted in Figure 7.2b, which simply adds the product variable, "Trait of Person A × Trait of Person B," as a third predictor to represent the corresponding statistical interaction. Adding this product variable and the paths labeled "m" on the diagram allows each partner's trait to serve as the moderator of the other person's trait–behavior relation.

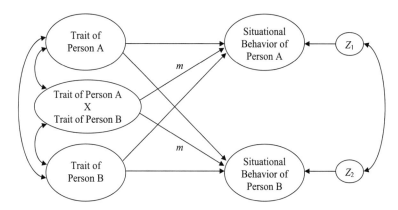

Figure 7.2b. Social behavior as a function of the traits of interaction partners and their statistical interaction.

Alternatively, reciprocal interactionism can be represented with a nonrecursive structural equation model, as shown in Figure 7.2c. Once again, there are actor effects, shown by the paths labeled "a," which represent the impact of each person's trait on his or her own behavior. However, instead of partner effects, there is a simultaneous bidirectional feedback loop, represented by the paths labeled "i," in which the situational behavior of each person reciprocally influences the behavior of the other person. In a sense, the partner effects of the earlier model become indirect in this model, mediated by the partner's situational behavior. Thus, the interpersonal traits of each dyad member have an impact on their own social behaviors, which in turn are mutually influencing such that each person's behavior both shapes and is shaped by the other's behavior. In addition, the feedback loop represents the idea that each person, by influencing the behavior of his or her partner, influences in turn his or her own behavior. Hence, this configuration is consistent with the central concept in reciprocal interactionism that through their behavior, people help create their own social environment, which in turn fosters their behavioral consistency.

This type of model is an application of what Kenny (1996) called the Mutual Influence Model. This terminology is particularly apt, because the model captures one of the "central interpersonal assumptions regarding personality," which Kiesler (1996, p. 4) described as follows:

> Interpersonal transactions consist of two-person mutual influence. Causality is simultaneously bidirectional; it is circular rather than linear. Interpersonal behavior is embedded in a feedback network in which the effect influences or alters the cause—in which Person A both shapes and is shaped by the environment (especially Person B).

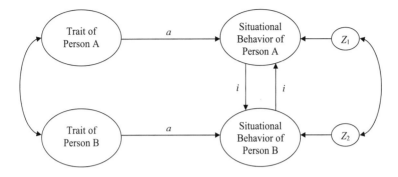

Figure 7.2c. Social behavior as a function of the traits of interaction partners and mutual influence.

In this model, one person's trait is the stable force by which he or she alters the behavior of the other person. Because both people are simultaneously having such an effect on the other, these effects, rather than decreasing predictability due to traits, ought to increase it, so long as the traits of both interaction partners are considered.

In summary, expression of personality traits in the interpersonal domain simultaneously involves the traits of at least two people, with each person serving as the environmental situation for the other and the resulting behaviors becoming interdependent. Structural equation modeling offers a flexible strategy for representing the resulting trait–behavior relations. The Actor–Partner Interdependence Model corresponds well with the concepts of mechanistic interactionism, whereas the Mutual Influence Model corresponds well with the concepts of reciprocal interactionism.

An Example of an Application With Young Adults

As the foregoing discussions demonstrate, SEM offers versatile diagrammatic conventions for clearly representing both theoretical and measurement issues. What is particularly attractive about SEM, however, is that once such a representation has been developed, it can be used to structure complex data analyses in the corresponding, theoretically relevant ways. To illustrate, we next provide a concrete example of how the foregoing dyadic models can be used in data analysis. In addition, the results obtained with young adults are of considerable interest, because they serve as an essential benchmark for our later consideration of possible developmental trajectories.

Our own work has tended to focus on application of the Mutual Influence Model, chiefly because it offers a close conceptual match to the hypotheses of interpersonal theory (e.g., Carson, 1969; Kiesler, 1983, 1996). Interpersonal theorists often portray social-interaction phenomena in a kind of simplifying shorthand, wherein one person's influence on another is described. Likewise, in research on social interactions, the behavior of one of the interaction partners is often scripted, to make the resulting data more amenable to analysis. Nonetheless, all interpersonal theorists recognize that, in real social interactions, influence simultaneously extends in both directions.

Accordingly, we applied the Mutual Influence Model to dyads interacting in a spontaneous, unscripted way (Sadler & Woody, 2003). We collected information about people's trait interpersonal style according to their own report, and also according to their friends. We called them into the lab, two at a time, one male and one female who did not know each other, and gave them a joint task to work on. Specifically, they were asked to work together to figure out the personality of a third person from her answers to five Thematic Apperception Test cards. We videotaped their subsequent 20-minute interaction. Afterwards, we asked them to complete scales about their own interpersonal behavior during the interaction, as well as that of their interaction partner. In addition, trained observers watched the videotaped interactions and completed scales about both participants. Thus, we collected two perspectives on participants' trait interpersonal style (self-report and friend-report), and three perspectives on their interaction behavior in the lab (self-report, partner-report, and observer-report). Interpersonal behavior for all five perspectives was measured using Moskowitz's (1994) Social Behavior Inventory, which allowed us to calculate dominance and friendliness dimension scores for each person from each of the five perspectives.

We wanted to predict peoples' social behavior (their dominance and friendliness) in this situation. Let's first look at the prediction of each person's dominance in the interaction. Figure 7.3 shows the SEM we used to analyze the dominance data. The measures we obtained are depicted in rows of rectangles, the measures for the males toward the top of the diagram and the ones for the females toward the bottom. The four latent (conceptual) variables are depicted in ovals in the central part of the diagram; other ovals around the periphery of the diagram represent various error terms. Our interest was in predicting Male Situational Dominance and Female Situational Dominance, the latent variables shown toward the right. According to interpersonal theory, such dominance behavior has three important determinants, all of which are represented in the SEM by paths among the four latent variables.

First, each person's own level of trait dominance (how dominant he or she is typically) should have a relatively strong impact on his or her situational dominance behavior, reflecting stability in interpersonal style. The path from Male Trait Dominance to Male Situational Dominance represents one of these

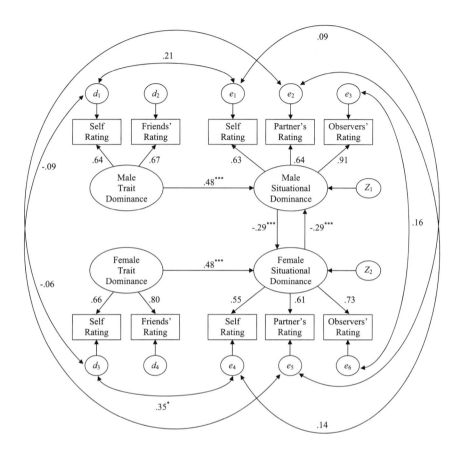

Figure 7.3. Situational dominance as a function of trait dominance and mutual influence.

Note. Coefficients linking latent variables are in a standardized metric obtained by standardizing the measures across the entire sample (males and females combined); coefficients for the measurement model are fully standardized. All paths from latent variables to indicators are significant at $p < .001$. $^*p < .05$; $^{***}p < .001$. Adapted from Sadler & Woody (2003).

actor effects, and the path from Female Trait Dominance to Female Situational Dominance represents the other actor effect. The significant results obtained for these paths, presented on the diagram, show the hypothesized strongly positive trait–behavior relations.

Second, as people interact, they should both affect each other's level of dominance. These reciprocal effects are represented by the two mutual influence paths on the diagram—one from Male Situational Dominance to Female Situational Dominance, and the other from Female Situational Dominance to Male Situational Dominance. Interpersonal theory (e.g., Kiesler, 1983) makes a specific prediction about the nature of this mutual influence: For dominance, people should evoke opposite behaviors in each other—that is, dominance pulls for submission, and vice versa. Therefore, the hypothesis is that these paths should have negative coefficients. This hypothesis is confirmed by the significant negative mutual influence effects that we obtained, as shown on the diagram.

Third, interpersonal theory hypothesizes that people have a consistency-promoting effect on their own behavior, through the feedback loop involving their effect on their partner. For example, the effect of Female Situational Dominance on Male Situational Dominance is fed back (through his reaction towards her) to Female Situational Dominance. The positive product of the two paths along this feedback loop represents this consistency-promoting effect: One's behavior begets one's own behavior by shifting one's partner toward a behavioral style that supports one's own. For example, the female's dominant behavior may push her partner toward more submissive behavior, which supports and further evokes her dominance.

We tested for gender differences in the actor and mutual influence coefficients, but they were clearly not significant. Therefore, we constrained the actor effects to be equal for males and females, and the mutual influence effects to be equal, as well. Setting these equalities increases the precision of estimation for both kinds of effects, resulting in the values shown in Figure 7.3.

The fit of this model was excellent, supporting its plausibility (Sadler & Woody, 2003). In addition, the model explained 37% and 69% of the variance in the situational dominance of males and females, respectively. The remaining variance in situational dominance, not explained by the model, is represented by the disturbances Z_1 and Z_2. To look at the possibility that other variables, not specified by the model, contribute to the relation between Male and Female Situational Dominance, we also estimated a model in which these disturbances were allowed to correlate. This correlation was statistically insignificant, supporting the hypothesis that the variables contributing to the interdependence of Male and Female Situational Dominance are indeed those specified in the model.

The substantive implications of the model depend on the cogency of the measurement part of the model, generally depicted in Figure 7.3 on the periphery of the diagram. We measured each of the four latent variables in more than one way, as shown in the diagram. For trait dominance, we obtained not only self ratings, but also friends' ratings. For situational dominance, we obtained self ratings, partner's ratings, and observers' ratings. For each of these measures, depicted in rectangles, there is a path from the latent variable (construct) that it taps and a path from an error term representing measurement error in that measure.

We handled systematic biases by including correlated measurement errors wherever the informant was the same person for more than one measure. For example, each male participant filled out a self-report about his trait dominance, a self-report about his situational dominance, and a report about his partner's situational dominance. We modeled the resulting possible informant bias by including correlated errors between each pair of these measures. These are denoted by the curved lines with arrowheads at each end. There were three such error correlations for males as informants, and the corresponding three error correlations for females as informants. In addition, the errors for observers' ratings of the male and the female were allowed to be correlated, because observers rated both members of each dyad.

The benefit of having a variety of perspectives and explicitly modeling the relevant biases is that the substantive results, as discussed above, are corrected for both random and systematic measurement error (that is, for unreliability and for informant biases). For the present analysis of dominance, the error correlations obtained were fairly negligible. Only one was significant (between errors for the females' self-ratings of trait and situational dominance), and the omission of all the correlated errors did not significantly reduce the fit. Therefore, the substantive results are quite robust over different assumptions about systematic errors.

In addition to dominance, interpersonal theorists argue that the other major dimension underlying social interactions is affiliation (which is reasonably orthogonal to dominance). Therefore, we completed a very similar SEM analysis for affiliation, shown in Figure 7.4. We expected strongly positive actor effects again, and this is what we obtained, confirming the hypothesis of stability of interpersonal style. However, the prediction for the mutual influence effects was different from that for dominance. Interpersonal theory (e.g., Kiesler, 1983) predicts that friendliness tends to beget friendliness, and hostility begets hostility. Therefore, we expected positive mutual influence effects for affiliation (rather than the negative ones in the dominance model). The results for these paths were indeed positive and significant, consistent with the theory. Similar to the model for dominance, the fit of the model was excellent and the model explained about 60% of the variance in the situational affiliation of males and females.

The role of correlated errors in the affiliation model was much more important than it was in the corresponding dominance model. Most striking were the correlations between the errors of self and partner ratings of affiliation in the situation. These correlations represent a perceiver bias effect: The warmer I think I am being, the warmer I think you are being, holding actual warmth of both partners constant. As can be seen in Figure 7.4, these two error correlations (one for males and one for females) were about .7; thus,

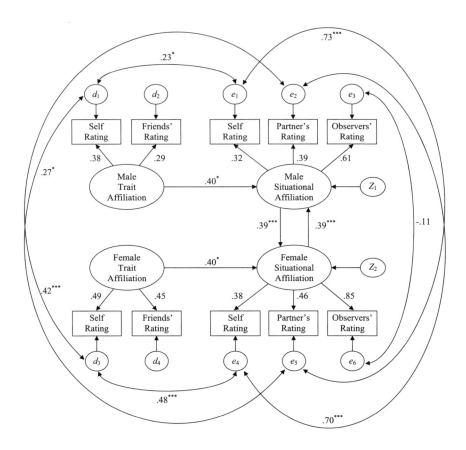

Figure 7.4. Situational affiliation as a function of trait affiliation and mutual influence.

Note. Coefficients linking latent variables are in a standardized metric obtained by standardizing the measures across the entire sample (males and females combined); coefficients for the measurement model are fully standardized. All paths from latent variables to indicators are significant at $p < .05$. *$p < .05$; ***$p < .001$. Adapted from Sadler & Woody (2003).

this type of bias is strong. Using SEM, the results for the latent variables are corrected for this type of systematic bias. These corrections are quite important: Consider that even if no mutual influence in affiliation occurred at all, participant reports would indicate a high degree of correspondence anyway. (Fortunately, this is not a limitation shared by the observer ratings.) However, such participant biases are not just distortions of reality; they may represent an important aspect of how people experience their social world.

Developmental Trajectories in Interpersonal Processes

Our results for these models suggest that social behavior stems from a balance between two processes: (1) trait-like consistency in interpersonal style, represented by the actor effects, and (2) attunedness or adjustment to the style of one's partner during the interaction, represented by the mutual influence effects. It is interesting that interpersonal theorists view the predominance of either type of effect over the other as highly characteristic of problematic or maladjusted interpersonal behavior.

Most frequently discussed as a hallmark of maladaptive social behavior is excessive consistency in interpersonal style across different situations (Carson, 1969; Kiesler, 1996; Mischel, 1973; Wachtel, 1973). For example, Kiesler (1983, p. 209) commented that

> the "radical trait" assumptions of transituationality and transtemporality (Mischel, 1968) more validly apply to maladjusted persons than they do to more normal ... individuals. ... The actions of abnormal individuals tend to override differences in situational parameters, including different styles of interactants.

From the vantage point of our model, we may conceptualize people with rigid and inflexible interpersonal patterns in terms of particularly strong actor effects and particularly weak mutual influence effects.

The opposite imbalance involves excessive adjustments of one's behavior in response to the styles of one's interaction partners. For example, Leary (1957) argued that a maladaptive pattern of "unstable oscillation" stems from "an intensive attempt to adjust to all aspects of the presented environment" (p. 121). Similarly, Andrews (1991) noted that people who respond with excessive flexibility to the demands of interpersonal situations fail to impose a distinctive "self-confirmational stamp" on their actions and therefore lack a "distinctive identity style" (p. 48). From the vantage point of our model, we may conceptualize such people in terms of particularly weak actor effects and particularly strong mutual influence effects.

It seems highly likely that such imbalanced interpersonal patterns in adults essentially represent immature interpersonal behavior—that is, failures to develop more balanced patterns of behavior in which the person both possesses a distinctive personal style and flexibly adapts it to suit particular interaction partners. Unfortunately, however, we know very little about the normal development of these interpersonal processes, which would serve as the necessary foundation for understanding how such development can go astray.

Accordingly, we would propose that the Mutual Influence Model may provide a promising perspective from which to conceptualize developmental issues in interpersonal processes. Specifically, how do trait-driven consistency and attunedness develop? What is the normal developmental sequence of these countervailing tendencies, and how do they change at different developmental levels?

Let's consider interactions between peers from such a developmental perspective. Along the lines of our study of young adults (Sadler & Woody, 2003), consider mixed-sex dyads of children, playing together for the first time. According to the model we have presented, the trait-like consistency of the two children is represented by the actor effects, and the attunedness is represented by the mutual influence effects.

Let's think about how these two processes might develop. There are several interesting questions. When does evidence of actor effects (trait-like consistency) first appear? When does evidence of mutual influence effects (attunedness) first appear? Do these two processes develop at the same time and at the same rate? Or, alternatively, does one process develop earlier than the other? For example, it seems plausible that trait consistency might develop earlier than attunedness, which might depend upon some degree of sophistication in interpersonal perception.

In order to study these sorts of questions, a cross-sectional research design could be used, looking at social interactions between pairs of children of the same age, who have not previously met. For example, pairs of 6-year-olds, 8-year-olds, and 10-year olds could be studied in dyadic social interactions. With several samples like this (grouped by age of children), researchers could evaluate the foregoing questions and study the rates at which actor and mutual-influence effects strengthen as children get older and their personalities become more established.

SEM could be applied to answer these questions by fitting a model, such as the Mutual Influence Model, simultaneously to multiple samples (Kline, 2005). That is, the same model would be evaluated across each group of participants (e.g., 6-year-olds, 8-year-olds, and 10-year-olds) in one analysis. The strength of the actor or trait-like consistency effects could be compared across the peer interactions for different ages, and so could the mutual-influence or attunedness effects. Such an approach could reveal very interesting trajectories of development—for example, perhaps at age 6 there is little trait-to-situational consistency in dominance and little mutual-influence, at age 8 only trait consistency in dominance, and at age 10 both consistency and attunedness in dominance.

Interchangeability of Dyad Members and Other Technical Issues

There are some special statistical issues that come into play when applying SEM models to study personality from a dyadic point of view. Here we briefly review some of the most important and provide references to the appropriate literature.

First, the SEM models we have discussed treat the dyad as the case, rather than the individual participant. For example, if we have 100 males and 100 females who each interact in a mixed-sex dyad, the number of cases is 100, not 200. One set of variables comes from the male in each dyad, and the other set of variables comes from the female in each dyad. In such a study, it is the gender of each dyad member that allows us to distinguish which variable goes with which dyad member.

There are many other possible types of distinguishable dyads. For example, if we study the interactions of children with adults, the dyad members are clearly distinguishable. Likewise, if we study how children who have social problems interact with children who do not have social problems, these dyad members, too, are clearly distinguishable.

More generally, for dyads to be regarded legitimately as distinguishable, there must be a meaningful way to differentiate the two dyad members, such that they represent different categories that have some relevance for the purposes of the research. For example, it would not be legitimate always to assign the first person who arrived for the study as Person A and the second person to arrive as Person B, because this distinction is arbitrary and has nothing to do with the purposes of the research. The issue is that other, equally arbitrary assignment rules would yield somewhat different results (see Woody & Sadler, 2005, for an example).

There are many instances in which dyad members can only be distinguished in some arbitrary way. An example would be same-sex dyads (e.g., boy-boy). In such cases, the two members of the dyad are considered to be interchangeable.

Because interchangeable dyads provide no basis for distinguishing which variable goes with which dyad member, it would appear as if SEM could not be used with them. However, recent methodological advances have overcome this shortcoming. One approach is advanced in detail in Woody and Sadler (2005), which builds on key insights by Kenny (1996). For interchangeable dyads, Kenny suggested setting up two input data matrices: a between-dyad matrix, which is based on the mean of the two partners' scores for each variable; and a within-dyad matrix, which is based on the difference between the difference partners' scores for each variable. For purposes of structural equation modeling, these two input matrices are treated as if they were two independent "groups," and the model is estimated simultaneously for both input matrices, with some equality constraints across the two groups. Woody and Sadler showed that this strategy could be used effectively with a very wide variety of dyadic models, including all those discussed in this chapter and several others.

Partly in response to our work, Olsen and Kenny (2006) devised another method for extending SEM to interchangeable dyads, which is quite versatile. Like Woody and Sadler (2005), they provide very useful examples of analyses involving a variety of models for interchangeable dyads.

In summary, there are two important points: (1) researchers need to determine whether the dyads they are studying are distinguishable or interchangeable, because the two types require somewhat different approaches in SEM; and (2) there are recently developed methods for handling interchangeable dyads in SEM, details of which are provided in Woody and Sadler (2005) and Olsen and Kenny (2006). From a substantive perspective, the ability to apply SEM to interchangeable dyads greatly extends the range of applications. For example, questions about how actor and mutual influence effects develop could be evaluated not only in opposite-sex interactions, as already described, but also in same-sex interactions (boy–boy, girl–girl). To illustrate, we might hypothesize that boys-with-boys could show stronger dominance mutual influence effects, whereas girls-with-girls could show stronger affiliation mutual influence effects.

Another important statistical issue when applying SEM models to the dyadic study of personality is choosing the appropriate model, such that it accurately represents the theoretical concepts underlying the research. For example, earlier in this chapter we advanced different structural equation models for the two different concepts of interactionism: an Actor–Partner Interdependence Model with an interaction term to represent Endler's (1981) mechanistic interactionism, and a Mutual Influence Model with a feedback loop to represent reciprocal interactionism. Illustrative applications of a wide variety of dyadic SEM models may be found in Kenny (1996), Woody and Sadler (2005), and Olsen and Kenny (2006). Researchers need to think carefully about which type of model faithfully represents the ideas they want to evaluate, rather than just arbitrarily picking some model that "works."

A closely related concern is that it is very important to make sure the design for the study meets the assumptions of the chosen model. For example, use of the Mutual Influence Model typically requires the assumption that partner effects are absent (can be assumed to be zero). Referring to Figure 7.2c, the crucial assumption is the absence of a direct effect from Trait of Person A to Situational Behavior of Person B, and from Trait of Person B to Situational Behavior of Person A. In other words, we need to assume that all the effect of the partner's trait is mediated by the partner's behavior. This assumption is plausible for unacquainted dyads, but probably not plausible for pairs of people who already know each other. More detailed discussions of the assumptions required for the Mutual Influence Model are provided in Kenny (1996) and in Woody and Sadler (2005).

Finally, although SEM is a very powerful heuristic for representing the full range of issues involved in studying trait–behavior relations, it would not always provide the best way to analyze a particular data set. In particular, the SEM approaches discussed in this chapter make high demands on the quality of the measures and require relatively large samples (e.g., 100 dyads). For some data sets, alternatives to SEM may be more appropriate, such as regression approaches for dyadic data (Kenny, 1996) and multilevel modeling (Cook & Kenny, 2005; Campbell & Kashy, 2002; see also Kenny, Kashy, & Cook, 2006).

CONCLUSION

Before we can study the development of a phenomenon, we need to devise ways to represent the phenomenon with reasonable fidelity. Our contention is that SEM provides such a representation for social trait–behavior relations in the following important respects:

1. The use of latent variables and multiple measures deals with the issue of random measurement error—that is, the possible attenuation of trait–behavior relations because of limited reliability (Epstein, 1979, 1980). In our view, the SEM approach of linking multiple indicators to specific conceptual variables is more focused and appropriate for managing this issue than the strategy of aggregation used in earlier work.

2. The use of multiple perspectives and the inclusion of error correlations for measures from the same perspective deal with the issue of systematic perceiver biases (Nisbett, 1980). We achieve two benefits with this strategy: the trait–behavior relations are corrected for both random and systematic errors of measurement, and we can study perceiver biases as an important social phenomenon in their own right.

3. Dyadic structural equation models allow us to represent the crucial idea that interaction partners provide the environmental situation for each other. This is one of the most important concepts about personality from interpersonal theory (Carson, 1969; Kiesler, 1983, 1996).

4. The Actor–Partner Interdependence Model with a trait-by-trait product variable allows us to test important hypotheses about the statistical interaction between the traits of partners. Such an interaction is the interpersonal version of what Endler (1981) called "mechanistic interactionism."

5. The Mutual Influence Model allows us to test important hypotheses about reciprocal influence between interaction partners, in which "the interpersonal behavior of each is simultaneously both a cause and an effect of the behavior of the other" (Wagner, Kiesler, & Schmidt, 1995, p. 938).

6. SEM allows us to characterize developmental and other group differences in the countervailing interpersonal processes of trait-like consistency and attunedness to the styles of partners. In addition, we can investigate a wide range of different types of pairings, with members that are either distinguishable or interchangeable.

More generally, the overarching theme of this chapter is that much of personality and its development is inherently dyadic. When the social aspects of personality are being expressed, there are usually two (or more) personalities involved. Through our personalities, we evoke social situations for each other, and, indirectly, for ourselves. We manage a delicate balance between retaining our own distinctive interpersonal style and adapting our behavior to cope with particular partners. How these processes arise and develop is a very promising topic for future research.

REFERENCES

Andrews, J. D. W. (1991). *The active self in psychotherapy: An integration of therapeutic styles.* New York: Gardner.

Bowers, K. S. (1973). Situationism in psychology: An analysis and a critique. *Psychological Review, 80,* 307-336.

Campbell, L., & Kashy, D. A. (2002). Estimating actor, partner, and interaction effects for dyadic data using proc mixed and hlm: A user-friendly guide. *Personal Relationships, 9,* 327-342.

Carson, R. C. (1969). *Interaction concepts of personality.* Chicago: Aline.

Caspi, A., Roberts, B. W., & Shiner, R. L. (2005). Personality development: Stability and change. *Annual Review of Psychology, 56,* 453- 484.

Cervone, D. (2004). The architecture of personality. *Psychological Review, 111,* 183-204.

Cook, W. L., & Kenny, D. A. (2005). The Actor–Partner Interdependence Model: A model of bidirectional effects in developmental studies. *International Journal of Behavioral Development, 29,* 101-109.

Endler, N. S. (1981). Persons, situations, and their interactions. In A. I. Rabin, J. Arnoff, A. M. Barclay, & R. A. Zucker (Eds.), *Further explorations in personality* (pp. 114-151). New York: John Wiley & Sons.

Endler, N. S., & Magnusson, D. (1976). Toward an interactional psychology of personality. *Psychological Bulletin, 83,* 956-974.

Epstein, S. (1979). The stability of behavior: I. On predicting most of the people much of the time. *Journal of Personality and Social Psychology, 37,* 1097-1126.

Epstein, S. (1980). The stability of behavior: II. Implications for psychological research. *American Psychologist, 35,* 790-806.

Epstein, S. (1986). Does aggregation produce spuriously high estimates of behavior stability? *Journal of Personality and Social Psychology, 50,* 1199-1210.

Epstein, S., & O'Brien, E. J. (1985). The person-situation debate in historical and current perspective. *Psychological Bulletin, 98,* 513-537.

Funder, D. C., & Ozer, D. J. (1983). Behavior as a function of the situation. *Personality and Social Psychology, 44,* 107-112.

Kenny, D. A. (1994). *Interpersonal perception: A social relations analysis.* New York: Guilford Press.

Kenny, D. A. (1996). Models of nonindependence in dyadic research. *Journal of Social and Personal Relationships, 13,* 279-294.

Kenny, D. A., Kashy, D. A., & Cook, W. L. (2006). *Dyadic data analysis.* New York: Guilford Press.

Kenrick, D. T., & Funder, D. C. (1988). Profiting from controversy: Lessons from the person-situation debate. *American Psychologist, 43,* 23-34.

Kiesler, D. J. (1983). The 1982 interpersonal circle: A taxonomy for complementarity in human transactions. *Psychological Review, 90,* 185-214.

Kiesler, D. J. (1996). *Contemporary interpersonal theory and research.* New York: John Wiley & Sons.

Kline, R. B. (2005). *Principles and practice of structural equation modeling (2nd edition).* New York: Guilford Press.

Leary, T. F. (1957). *Interpersonal diagnosis of personality.* New York: Ronald Press.

Little, T. D., & Card, N. A. (2005). On the use of Social Relations and Actor-Partner Interdependence Models in developmental research. *International Journal of Behavioral Development, 29,* 173-179.

Mischel, W. (1968). *Personality and assessment.* New York: John Wiley & Sons.

Mischel, W. (1973). Toward a cognitive social learning reconceptualization of personality. *Psychological Review, 80,* 252-283.

Mischel, W. (2004). Toward an integrative science of the person. In S. T. Fiske (Ed.), *Annual Review of Psychology, 5,* 1-22.

Mischel, W., & Peake, P. K. (1982). Beyond déjà vu in the search for cross-situational consistency. *Psychological Review, 89,* 730-755.

Mischel, W., & Shoda, Y. (1995). A cognitive-affective system theory of personality: Reconceptualizing situations, dispositions, dynamics, and invariance in personality structure. *Psychological Review, 102,* 246-268.

Moskowitz, D. S. (1994). Cross-situational generality and the interpersonal circumplex. *Journal of Personality and Social Psychology, 66,* 921-933.

Nisbett, R. E. (1980). The trait construct in lay and professional psychology. In L. Festinger (Ed.), *Retrospections on social psychology* (pp. 109-130). New York: Oxford University Press.

Nisbett, R. E., & Ross, L. (1980). *Human inference: Strategies and shortcomings of social judgment.* Englewood Cliffs, NJ: Prentice-Hall.

Olsen, J. A., & Kenny, D. A. (2006). Structural equation modeling with interchangeable dyads. *Psychological Methods, 11,* 127-141.

Peterson, D. R. (1968). *The clinical study of social behavior.* New York: Appleton-Century-Crofts.

Ross, H. S., Stein, N., Trabasso, T., Woody, E., & Ross, M. (2005). The quality of family relationships within and across generations: A social relations analysis. *International Journal of Behavioral Development, 29,* 110-119.

Ross, L. (1977). The intuitive psychologist and his shortcomings. In L. Berkowitz (Ed.), *Advances in experimental social psychology, vol. 10.* New York: Academic Press.

Rushton, J. P., Brainerd, C. J., & Pressley, M. (1983). Behavioral development and construct validity: The principle of aggregation. *Psychological Bulletin, 94,* 18-38.

Sadler, P., & Woody, E. (2003). Is who you are who you're talking to? Interpersonal style and complementarity in mixed-sex interactions. *Journal of Personality and Social Psychology, 84,* 80-96.

Shiner, R. L. (1998). How shall we speak of children's personalities in middle childhood? A preliminary taxonomy. *Psychological Bulletin, 124,* 308-332.

Shiner, R. L., & Caspi, A. (2003). Personality differences in childhood and adolescence: Measurement, development, and consequences. *Journal of Child Psychology and Psychiatry, 44*, 2-31.

Tellegen, A. (1991). Personality traits: Issues of definition, evidence, and assessment. In W. M. Grove & D. Cicchetti (Eds.), *Thinking clearly about psychology, vol. 2: Personality and psychopathology* (pp. 10-35). Minneapolis: University of Minnesota Press.

Ten Berge, M. A., & De Raad, B. (1999). Taxonomies of situations from a trait psychological perspective: A review. *European Journal of Personality, 13*, 337-360.

Wachtel, P. (1973). Psychodynamics, behavior therapy, and the implacable experimenter: An inquiry into the consistency of personality. *Journal of Abnormal Psychology, 82*, 324-334.

Wagner, C. C., Kiesler, D. J., & Schmidt, J. A. (1995). Assessing the interpersonal transaction cycle: Convergence of action and reaction interpersonal circumplex measures. *Journal of Personality and Social Psychology, 69*, 938-949.

Woody, E., & Sadler, P. (2005). Structural equation models for interchangeable dyads: Being the same makes a difference. *Psychological Methods, 10*, 139-158.

CHAPTER EIGHT

Comparing MLM and SEM Approaches to Analyzing Developmental Dyadic Data: Growth Curve Models of Hostility in Families

Deborah A. Kashy

M. Brent Donnellan

Michigan State University

The kinds of data that developmental psychologists collect are often inherently interdependent. For example, the subdiscipline has been defined, in part, as the study of the changes that occur within individuals across the life span (e.g., Baltes, Reese, & Nesselroade, 1977) and developmentalists often investigate interrelations between individuals and their families and peers. These kinds of data are either interdependent within individuals, across relationship partners, or both. As such, developmental researchers and methodologists who specialize in the analysis of nonindependent data should be natural partners.

In this chapter we discuss how multilevel modeling (MLM; also known as hierarchical linear modeling or mixed modeling) and structural equation modeling (SEM) can be used to analyze over-time dyadic data.[1] We focus our discussion on growth curve models because these models address interesting questions and are becoming increasingly popular in developmental psychology. Growth models address questions of whether or not there is overall change over time in a given sample and whether or not there are intraindividual differences in change. Change parameters from these models can be

---

[1]These are sometimes called latent growth curve models in the SEM literature because the overall growth trends are described by unobserved or latent variables (Bollen & Curran, 2006; Duncan, Duncan, Strycker, Li, & Alpert, 1999).

predicted by covariates or they can be used to predict other variables. In the case of dyadic over-time data, for example, growth curve models can be used to evaluate whether there is evidence that the rate of change for one member of the dyad is associated with the rate of change in the other member.

The MLM and SEM approaches to estimating growth models are equivalent in terms of the underlying statistical model (e.g., Curran, 2003; Hertzog & Nesselroade, 2003); however, there are differences when considering actual data analyses using many of the computer programs associated with one tradition or the other (e.g., SAS Proc Mixed versus AMOS). There are also some "philosophical" differences in terms of the approaches that typical users of MLM and SEM programs take to data analysis. As we will describe, MLM users often focus on parameter estimation whereas SEM users are also concerned with issues related to omnibus model fit. Furthermore, latent variables are easily incorporated into SEM analyses using multiple indicators whereas MLM is generally used with manifest variables. The advantage of latent variables is that they allow researchers to work with variables that have been "corrected" for measurement error; however, the widespread application of growth models in which the key constructs are measured with multiple indicators at each time point is in its infancy (for details see e.g., Bollen & Curran, 2006).

In addition, although both SEM and MLM can be used for distinguishable dyads without difficulty (see below), indistinguishable dyads present some extra analytic challenges for SEM users (e.g., Olsen & Kenny, 2006; c.f. Woody & Sadler, 2005). Finally, if measurement occasions differ for the two dyad members, MLM analyses are straightforward, but SEM approaches can be cumbersome. Thus, there are compelling reasons why researchers would want to develop facility with both kinds of programs. Prior to discussing the MLM and SEM approaches, we begin with a brief discussion of basic issues that arise with over-time dyadic data.

Basic Issues With Longitudinal Dyadic Data

Distinguishability. Any discussion of the analysis of dyadic data needs to begin with the issue of distinguishability because this factor plays a pivotal role in determining the appropriate modeling strategy. Two members of a dyad are said to be conceptually distinguishable if there is a meaningful variable that can be used to identify the two individuals. For example, in research with identical or MZ twins the two siblings would be indistinguishable, but in non-twin sibling research, the siblings can be distinguished by birth order or by gender or by both. Researchers who study adult heterosexual romantic relationships often treat gender as the key distinguishing variable (e.g., husbands versus wives). However, Kenny, Kashy, and Cook (2006) suggest that variables that are treated as distinguishing factors in relationships research from a conceptual point of view often fail to empirically distinguish between dyad members, especially when considering differences in variance/covariance matrices (as opposed to mean-level differences). For example, although researchers sometimes think that husbands differ from wives on a range of factors, there is surprisingly little research that finds evidence that gender moderates the associations under investigation. Thus, although mean differences between men and women are not uncommon, there is far less evidence that gender consistently affects patterns of association.

Distinguishability can be a critical factor in developmental work, particularly in the study of parent–child relationships. In this case the distinguishing variable, family role such as mother or daughter, serves as marker variable for a host of factors, ranging from the obvious age difference to less apparent, but no less real differences in responsibilities, social expectations, life experiences, levels of education, and differences in psychological maturity. Not only might some of these differences result in substantial mean differences across roles, they may also have a systematic impact on variability and measures of association between variables. To be sure, there are also instances in developmental work when individuals are not distinguishable (e.g., research investigating same-sex friendships); however, we suspect that indistinguishable dyads are likely to be less common. Even so, developmental researchers need to be proficient in the tools that are appropriate for analyzing both distinguishable and nondistinguishable dyads.

Our example data set examines the level of hostility that mothers direct toward their adolescent children and the level of hostility adolescents direct towards their mothers. Thus, our example involves distinguishable dyads. The measures of hostility were obtained at four points in time, and so potentially there is nonindependence over time within person (i.e., a child's hostility scores in consecutive years are more similar to one another than are hostility scores that are separated by more than one year). There may also be cross-dyad interdependence such that a mother's general tendency to be hostile is related to the child's general tendency to be hostile. Finally, there may be time-specific cross-dyad interdependence, representing the unique similarity (or dissimilarity) between mother–child hostility scores at a particular point in time.

Data Structures for Over-Time Dyadic Data

Before we turn our attention to growth-curve models, we must briefly consider basic data structure issues. Over-time dyadic data can be difficult to analyze, and the fact that different analyses require different data structures adds to this complexity. There are three data structures for over-time dyadic data: person-period, person (or person-level; e.g., Singer & Willett, 2003), and dyad. A person-period data set has one record for each person at each time point. Thus, with our example data, each family (i.e., mother–adolescent pair) would have eight records in the data set—four for the mother and four for the adolescent, and the focal variable would be the person's hostility at each measurement occasion. There would also be a variable representing which person generated the hostility score (mother or child), and a variable representing time (e.g., year when hostility score was measured). A person data set has one record for each person, and there would be four focal variables (the hostility scores at each of the four time points) for each person. A person data set has two records for each dyad. As was the case for the person-period data set, each record would also include a variable that represents which person generated the four hostility scores. A dyad data set has a single record for each dyad or family (i.e., one record for each mother–child pair in our example), and there are eight variables representing the four focal hostility scores for the mother and the four focal hostility scores for the child. We expect that many developmental researchers will be most familiar with data sets that are organized as dyad data sets. Kenny, Kashy, & Cook (2006, pp.14–18) provide illustrations of these data structures.

The Example Data Set: The Iowa Youth and Families Project

The Iowa Youth and Families Project (e.g., Conger & Conger, 2002; Conger & Elder, 1994) began in 1989 with a sample of 450 two-parent families that included a target adolescent in the 7th grade (52% girls). The sample was reassessed in 1990 (8th grade), 1991 (9th grade), 1992 (10th grade), and 1994 (12th grade). The Iowa Youth and Families Project was originally designed to test a specific model linking economic hardship to family processes called the Family Stress Model (see Conger & Donnellan, 2007). However, the rich data collected to fully evaluate this model turned out to be broadly useful for studying a range of developmental questions. As such, the sample was merged with the Iowa Single Parent Project and rechristened the Family Transitions Project in 1994. The Family Transitions Project is now an ongoing study that examines how the target individual transitions into adult roles and responsibilities (e.g., committed romantic unions, parenthood, and work).

A self-report measure of hostility towards other family members was administered in 1990, 1991, 1992, and 1994. In this chapter we limit our examples to data concerning the mother-adolescent dyad. The hostility scale inc-

TABLE 8.1
Means, Standard Deviations, and Correlations for Mothers' Hostility Toward Their Adolescent
Child and Adolescents' Hostility Toward Their Mother

		Mother's Hostility Toward Adolescent				Adolescent's Hostility Toward Mother			
		1990	**1991**	**1992**	**1994**	**1990**	**1991**	**1992**	**1994**
Mother to Adolescent Hostility	**1990**	1.00							
	1991	.751	1.00						
	1992	.734	.796	1.00					
	1994	.670	.714	.747	1.00				
Adolescent to Mother Hostility	**1990**	.360	.300	.280	.257	1.00			
	1991	.339	.363	.351	.281	.668	1.00		
	1992	.323	.349	.442	.381	.583	.669	1.00	
	1994	.303	.331	.345	.401	.512	.515	.608	1.00
	Mean	2.807	2.790	2.720	2.677	2.935	2.914	3.044	3.006
	SD	.677	.686	.718	.696	.969	1.004	1.012	.962

luded eight items, each measured on a 7-point scale. Example items include: "During the past month, how often did you get angry at [Target]?", "During the past month, how often did you shout or yell at [Target]?", "During the past month, how often did you criticize [Target]?", and "During the past month, how often did you argue with [Target]?" Thus, the mother was asked to report on her hostility towards her adolescent child, and the child was asked to report on his or her hostility towards his or her mother. Reliability coefficients for the mother to adolescent reports ranged from .84 to .87 across the four time points, and the adolescent to mother reports had reliability coefficients ranging from .84 to .89. The means, standard deviations, and correlations for these eight variables are presented in Table 8.1.

GROWTH MODELS

Basic Models for a Sample of Independent Individuals

The univariate growth model (or change model) addresses the question of whether a variable changes in systematic ways as a function of time. A basic linear model might examine whether increases or decreases in hostility occur as a function of time. In this relatively simple model individual trajectories of hostility over time can be characterized by an intercept that measures the individual's hostility at a fixed point in time (e.g., the start of the study) and a slope that measures the person's linear change in hostility. For our example, a linear growth model of the adolescent's hostility would estimate an intercept for each adolescent that measures his or her hostility at time = 0, and a slope that estimates the degree to which the adolescent's hostility changes as time increases by one year.

A basic linear growth model generates at least five parameters of interest: point estimates for the intercept and the slope, variance estimates for the intercept and slope, and a covariance between the intercept and slope. The point estimate for the intercept represents the overall level of hostility at a fixed point in time "averaged" across the sample, whereas the point estimate for the slope represents the direction and amount of linear change "averaged" across the entire sample. The variance for the intercept represents how much variability in the attribute exists at time 0 (akin to a cross-sectional variance at a fixed time point) whereas the variance for the slope represents how much variability exists in within-person increases or decreases in the attribute over time. Finally, the covariance between the intercept and slope measures the association between individuals' rates of change and their positions on an attribute at time 0. A positive value means that individuals with higher scores at time 0 change more rapidly than individuals with lower scores, whereas a negative value indicates that individuals with lower scores at time 0 change more rapidly than individuals with higher scores.

In addition to these parameters, the model estimates residual variances representing unexplained variance in the outcome variable. For example, some of the variance in hostility in 1992 is not explained by the intercept or slope parameters. The residual variances can be handled in different ways. A typical SEM specification is to freely estimate residual variances at each measurement occasion, whereas a typical MLM specification is to constrain the residual variances to the same value. Moreover, residual variances may or may not be allowed to correlate across time (e.g., a first-order autoregressive structure). We revisit issues regarding the various constraints that can be placed on the residuals throughout our discussion.

Given the importance for clear interpretation of growth model parameters, a major issue is the definition of time zero (see e.g., Biesanz, Deeb-Sossa, Papadakis, Bollen, & Curran, 2004). Besides changing the value of the average intercept, the choice of time = 0 affects the variance of the intercepts and the covariance between the intercepts and slopes. Researchers often define time zero to be the first measurement occasion; however, this decision is often arbitrary and other ways to define time zero may lead to more meaningful interpretations of model parameters. Our basic point is that researchers should think carefully about the coding of time zero. In our example, we specify time $= 0$ as the midpoint of the study so that the intercept estimates hostility in 1992. In some developmental contexts, setting time zero to be time of birth or the time when the child enters school might be desirable.

Models for Dyads

Thus far our discussion has focused on growth models based on data from a sample of individuals. At issue here is the application of growth models to the dyadic context. The dyadic case involves computing growth functions for each dyad member, and then estimating parameters that capture the degree of correspondence between growth parameters across dyad members (e.g., the overall association between intercepts for each dyad). Within the context of the mother-adolescent hostility example, dyadic growth curve analysis allows us to estimate the degree to which mothers' and their adolescent children's hostility is similar at time $= 0$ (i.e., the correlation or covariance between the intercepts), and it also allows us to examine whether there is an association between rates of change in hostility for mothers and adolescents (i.e. the correlation or covariance between the slopes). It is important to note that this correlation does not necessarily imply reciprocity (i.e., if one person is hostile, the other person is hostile in return), rather this correlation suggests that the rate of change for the dyad members' outcomes are associated.[2] Dyadic growth curve analyses also allow estimation of the association between one person's intercept and the other person's slope. For our example, it might be that mothers who are generally higher in hostility at time $= 0$ have children whose hostility increases at a greater rate over time.

As mentioned, distinguishability is a critical issue when considering dyadic data analysis. When dyad members are distinguishable, there is a distinct intercept and a distinct slope for each member of the dyad. These intercepts and slopes yield four fixed or average effects, and their corresponding variances. These four variances give rise to six covariances which represent the interrelations between the intercept and slope parameters. Table 8.2 presents a description of the variance and covariance parameters for the intercepts and slopes for our example.

Researchers have many options for placing constraints on the residual variances. These range from very restrictive specifications in which all of the

---

[2]Questions of reciprocity are better addressed in the crossed-lagged model (see Kenny et al., 2006).

TABLE 8.2
Variance and Covariance Parameters in Growth-Curve Analyses With Distinguishable Dyads

		Intercepts		Slopes	
		Mothers	Adolescents	Mothers	Adolescents
Intercepts	**Mothers**	Variance: Are some mothers more hostile at the midpoint than others?			
	Adolescents	Covariance: When mother is high in hostility at the midpoint is the adolescent also high at the midpoint?	Variance: Are some adolescents more hostile at the midpoint than others?		
Slopes	**Mothers**	Covariance: Do mothers who are high in hostility at the midpoint tend to show greater increases in hostility over time?	Covariance: Do adolescents who are high in hostility at the midpoint have mothers whose hostility increases more over time?	Variance: Does the growth/decline of the mother's hostility over time differ across families?	
	Adolescents	Covariance: Do mothers who are high in hostility at the midpoint have adolescents whose hostility increases more over time?	Covariance: Do adolescents who are high in hostility at the midpoint tend to show greater increases in hostility over time?	Covariance: Is mother's change in hostility similar to the adolescent's change in hostility?	Variance: Does the growth/decline of the adolescent's hostility over time differ across families?

residual variances are constrained to the same value, and all the covariances across time and dyad are zero, to specifications in which all the residual variances and covariances are freely estimated. A common MLM specification is to estimate one residual variance for each person in the dyad and one covariance between those residuals. A common SEM specification is to freely estimate residual variances for each person at each time point.

The interpretation of model parameters with indistinguishable dyads turns out to be slightly more complicated. The problem is that any designation as member 1 or member 2 of the dyad is completely arbitrary. For illustrative purposes, consider a longitudinal study of disordered eating habits in female MZ twins. Each twin's over-time trajectory is characterized by an intercept and a slope. However, summary statistics such as the averages and variances of the intercept and slope are computed both across dyads and within dyads. Thus, the indistinguishable case estimates the "average" intercept and slope by pooling across the twins. Likewise, residual variances are constrained to the same value for the two indistinguishable members at each time point.

In addition, there are four covariances between the intercepts and slopes. First there is the between-person covariance of the intercepts that measures the degree to which the twins are similar in their disordered eating scores at time = 0. Next there is the between-person covariance of the slopes that measures the degree of association between the twins' rates of change in disordered eating. Finally, there are both within-person and between-person covariances between the intercepts and slopes. The within-person covariance assesses whether girls who are higher at time = 0 also have greater change in their disordered eating. The between-person covariance measures whether, when one twin is high at time = 0, her sister has greater change as a function of time.

These basic dyadic growth models and extensions can be estimated using either MLM or SEM computer packages. We now turn to the more practical details involved in estimating growth models using these two approaches. Because dyadic growth models in developmental work are most often estimated for distinguishable dyads, such as parent–child dyads, we detail estimation for this type of dyad. Researchers interested in dyadic growth models for the indistinguishable case should consult Kashy, Burt, Donnellan, and McGue (2007).

Estimating Growth Models in the MLM Framework

Multilevel modeling is a statistical technique that is particularly useful for the analysis of over-time data. Over-time or repeated measures data have a hierarchically nested structure such that multiple measures of an outcome are obtained for each individual. Multilevel modeling is also a valuable tool for dyadic data analysis because individuals are nested within dyads. A detailed discussion of basic MLM analyses is beyond the scope of this chapter, however, we refer readers who are not well acquainted with MLM to a number of books describing this approach (e.g., Hox, 2002; Kreft & DeLeeuw, 1998; Bryk & Raudenbush, 2002). Readers who are interested specifically in applications of MLM to dyadic data may also find Kenny et al. (2006) useful.

Dyadic growth curve analyses are based on a combination of the over-time and dyadic data structures. That is, both individuals in the dyad are measured at multiple time points or measurement occasions. In this chapter we assume that the two persons are measured at the same measurement occasions and so the time factor is crossed with individuals within dyads. (If measurement intervals differ across dyad members, the time-specific correlation between the dyad members probably should not be estimated.) Using our example data examining mothers' and adolescents' hostility, we apply a simple linear growth model in which we define time = 0 to be 1992 (the midpoint of the study). The basic level-1 growth equations are

$$Y_{Mti} = c_{Mi} + b_{Mi}T_{ti} + e_{Mti} \tag{1}$$
$$Y_{Ati} = c_{Ai} + b_{Ai}T_{ti} + e_{Ati} \tag{2}$$

These are the lower-level equations for the ith family. Equation 1 models the mother's hostility toward her child as a function of an intercept, c_{Mi}, that estimates the mother's hostility in 1992, a slope, b_{Mi} that estimates the average change in the mother's hostility over the course of one year, and a residual, e_{Mti}, that represents the part of the mother's hostility at time t that is not explained by change over time. The parameters in Equation 2 can be interpreted in a similar fashion for adolescents. The parameters estimated in equations 1 and 2 are typically pooled across families to obtain estimates of the average effects, variances, and covariances.

In the interest of providing an accessible tutorial, we include a brief description of how these models can be estimated using two of the major statistical packages used by social scientists, SPSS and SAS. The first and perhaps most critical element to using these programs is that the data set must have a person-period structure. For the purposes of our example, the outcome variable will be denoted as HOSTILE. The data set also needs to include a FAMILYID variable that identifies families, a YEAR variable that identifies the year of observation, and a ROLE variable that specifies whether the observation is from the mother (ROLE = 1) or the adolescent (ROLE = -1). The data set should also include two dummy variables, ADOL, which is 1 if the observation is from the adolescent and 0 otherwise, and MOM, which is 1 if the observation is from the mother and 0 otherwise. To specify the effect of time, a TIME variable is created. For our example, we created a variable called TIME by recoding the YEAR variable according to this scheme: TIME = -2 when YEAR= 1990, TIME = -1 when YEAR= 1991, TIME = 0 when YEAR = 1992, and TIME = 2 when YEAR = 1994 (note that this makes a one unit increase in TIME equal to a one-year change). Following this scheme it is easy to see how different recode statements could be used to code alternative specifications of TIME = 0.

The SPSS syntax is

```
MIXED
HOSTILE WITH TIME ADOL MOM
/FIXED = MOM ADOL ADOL*TIME MOM*TIME | NOINT SSTYPE(3)
/METHOD = ML
/PRINT = SOLUTION TESTCOV
/RANDOM ADOL MOM ADOL*TIME MOM*TIME | SUBJECT(FAMILYID)
    COVTYPE(UN)
/REPEATED = ROLE | SUBJECT(FAMILYID*YEAR)COVTYPE(CSH).
```

The first line of the syntax specifies the MIXED procedure, and the second line identifies the outcome as HOSTILE and predictors as TIME and the dummy codes indicating which person generated the particular HOSTILE score, ADOL or MOM. There are four predictors in the model specified by the FIXED statement, and the first two are the dummy codes for adolescents (ADOL) and mothers (MOM). Because we specify that the model should be estimated without an intercept (the NOINT option later in this statement), the ADOL effect is the estimated intercept for adolescents and the MOM effect is the estimated intercept for the mothers. We then ask for separate slopes to be estimated for adolescents and mothers by multiplying the two dummy codes with our continuous TIME variable. The METHOD statement requests that maximum likelihood estimation be used rather than the default of restricted maximum likelihood. We chose this method for our example so that the multilevel estimates and SEM estimates would be more comparable. The PRINT statement requests parameter estimates and tests of the covariance parameters.

The last two lines of the SPSS code specify the random components in the model. The RANDOM statement requests that both the intercepts (ADOL and MOM) and slopes (ADOL*TIME and MOM*TIME) be treated as random effects so that variances and covariances are estimated. The SUBJECT(FAMILYID) option specifies the unit at which independence occurs (i.e., from family to family), and the COVTYPE (UN) specifies that the variance-covariance matrix of the random effects is unstructured so that the program estimates each of its parameters. In most applications of MLM, the SPSS code would end with the RANDOM statement. However, because these are dyadic-overtime data, we still need to link the residuals for mothers and their adolescent children. The REPEATED statement treats the mother's and adolescent's scores at each time-point as repeated measurements. Thus, by including ROLE in the repeated statement, we specify a model in which the residuals for the mothers and adolescents are related. The CSH designation of COVTYPE specifies the structure for the residual variances as heterogeneous compound symmetry which allows the residual variances to be different for mothers and adolescents, and also allows for a covariance between the residuals. This covariance estimates the degree to which mothers' and adolescents' residual hostility scores at time t are especially similar to one another. Finally, the SUBJECT(FAMILYID*YEAR) specifies that these residual variances and their covariance should be estimated based on the unique similarity between the mother's and adolescent's scores within the family and across years.

Table 8.3 displays selected SPSS output for this example. The top section reports a set of model-fit statistics that are not interpretable in isolation, but rather provide a way of testing relative model fit for nested models. The next section reports the results from the fixed effects portion of the analysis. That is, this portion reports the average intercepts and average slopes for the growth model. Here we see that the average intercept for adolescents is 2.98 and the parallel value for mothers is 2.73. Thus, the average hostility scores in 1992 were somewhat below the scale midpoint for both mothers and their adolescents. The slopes for adolescents and mothers were .025 and -.038, respectively, and each was significantly different from zero. These values indicate that adolescents tended to show a small increase in hostility over time, whereas mothers tended to show a small decrease in hostility over time.

The next section of the output reports on the variances and covariances for the random effects. The first variances and covariance refer to the residuals after taking the effect of time into account. Var(Role = -1) is the residual variance for adolescents and Var(Role = 1) is the residual variance for mothers. The CSH value is the estimated correlation between the residuals and therefore these values suggest that a) there was considerable variation in hostility that was not accounted for by time, and b) this unexplained hostility was correlated for adolescents and their mothers across time. In other words, at any given time point, after taking the effect of time on hostility into account, if a mother was especially hostile toward her adolescent, the adolescent was also especially hostile at that measurement occasion.

The remaining values in Table 8.3 refer to the variances and covariances of the slopes and intercepts for adolescents and their mothers. Given the ordering of variables in the RANDOM statement, UN(1,1) estimates the variance in the intercepts for adolescents. This large and significant value suggests that there was substantial variation in hostility scores in 1992. For example an adolescent whose hostility at the study midpoint is one standard deviation below the average intercept for the sample would have an intercept of 2.22 whereas an adolescent whose hostility is one standard deviation above average would have an intercept of 3.74. The UN(2,2) value gives the variance in the intercepts for mothers. This value is considerably smaller than that for adolescents, but it still indicates that some mothers were more hostile than others with predicted intercept values for one standard deviation below and above the mean of 2.13 and 3.33, respectively. The UN(3,3) value gives the variance in the time slope for adolescents. Again, converting this variance into a standard deviation we get .131, and so the predicted slope for an adolescent who is one standard deviation below and above the mean would be -.106 and .156, respectively. This suggests that although on average adolescents showed a small positive slope for hostility across the entire sample, there was

TABLE 8.3
Output for Basic Growth Model Examining Mother and Adolescent Hostility From SPSS MIXED

Information Criteria(a)

-2 Log Likelihood	5503.739
Akaike's Information Criterion (AIC)	5537.739
Hurvich and Tsai's Criterion (AICC)	5537.946
Bozdogan's Criterion (CAIC)	5656.745
Schwarz's Bayesian Criterion (BIC)	5639.745

Estimates of Fixed Effects(a)

Parameter	Estimate	Std. Error	df	t	Sig.
MOM	2.731	.032	388.02	86.41	.000
ADOL	2.980	.042	387.36	71.80	.000
ADOL*TIME	.025	.012	371.25	2.02	.044
MOM*TIME	-.0385	.007	372.46	-5.53	.000

Note. a Dependent Variable: HOSTILE.

Estimates of Covariance Parameters(a)

Parameter		Estimate	Std. Error	Wald Z	Sig.
Repeated Measures	Var: [ROLE = -1]	.3459	.0183	18.930	.000
	Var: [ROLE = 1]	.1113	.0058	19.158	.000
	CSH rho	.2015	.0357	5.647	.000
	UN (1,1)	.5781	.0484	11.938	.000
ADOL + MOM +	UN (2,1)	.2217	.0286	7.746	.000
TIME * ADOL + TIME * MOM	UN (2,2)	.3608	.0281	12.856	.000
[subject = FAMILYID]	UN (3,1)	-.0062	.0102	-.606	.545
	UN (3,2)	.0095	.0079	1.202	.229
	UN (3,3)	.0173	.0047	3.623	.000
	UN (4,1)	.0043	.0057	.741	.459
	UN (4,2)	.0044	.0044	1.000	.317
	UN (4,3)	.0037	.0019	1.901	.057
	UN (4,4)	.0052	.0015	3.465	.001

Note. a Dependent Variable: HOSTILE.

wide variation across adolescents in this slope term. In other words, there are individual differences in the change in adolescents' reported hostility as a function of time, with some adolescents showing increases and others showing decreases. The variance of the slopes for mothers is labeled as UN(4,4).

The covariances occur on the off-diagonal of this variance-covariance matrix. Thus, the covariance between the adolescent's intercept and the mother's intercept is UN(2,1) which is .222. This can be transformed into a correlation by dividing by the square-root of the product of the two variances (recall that a correlation is a standardized covariance). As such, the correlation between the intercepts is .486 indicating that adolescents whose hostility was relatively high in 1992 tended to have mothers who were also high in hostility. Similarly, UN(4,3) is the covariance between the slopes which equals .0037 or a correlation of .392, p = .06 in this example. This suggests a trend such that rates of change in hostility were associated within families. The within-person covariance between the intercept and slope is UN(3,1) for adolescents and UN(4,2) for mothers; neither reached statistical significance so there is no evidence that rates of change in hostility are associated with hostility scores in 1992. Finally, the across-person covariances between the intercepts and slopes, UN(4,1) and UN(3,2) were not statistically significant.

The SAS syntax for the same analysis is

```
PROC MIXED COVTEST METHOD = ML;
CLASS FAMILYID ROLE YEAR;
MODEL HOSTILE = ADOL MOM ADOL*TIME MOM*TIME / NOINT
    SOLUTION DDFM=SATTERTH;
RANDOM ADOL MOM ADOL*TIME MOM*TIME / SUB=FAMILYID
    TYPE = UN;
REPEATED ROLE / TYPE=CSH SUBJECT=FAMILYID*YEAR;
RUN;
```

One rather dissatisfying aspect of this analysis is that in estimating separate intercepts and slopes for adolescents and mothers, the analysis fails to test whether these intercepts and slopes really differ across family role. An alternative specification of the syntax provides these direct tests, and researchers should consider specifying the model both ways for maximum interpretability.

The syntax to test for differences across family role in SPSS is

```
MIXED
HOSTILE WITH TIME ROLE
/FIXED = ROLE TIME ROLE*TIME | SSTYPE(3)
/METHOD = ML
/PRINT = SOLUTION TESTCOV
/RANDOM INTERCEPT ROLE TIME ROLE*TIME | SUBJECT(FAMILYID)
    COVTYPE(UN)
/REPEATED = ROLE | SUBJECT(FAMILYID*YEAR) COVTYPE(CSH).
```

The intercept across mothers and adolescents is estimated for the fixed effects because the NOINT option is excluded. In addition, the intercept is now included in the RANDOM statement. The results from this analysis are presented in Table 8.4, and it is important to note that the model fit statistics in Table 8.4 are identical to those in Table 8.3. This indicates that, at a basic level, the two models are identical.

Briefly, the fixed effects parameters include an intercept value which is the grand mean of hostility for 1992 for the data set, as well as a ROLE effect that estimates and tests the degree to which mothers and adolescents differed in their average level of hostility at the study midpoint. Given the way ROLE is coded (Adolescents = -1, Mothers = 1), the significant ROLE effect suggests that adolescents had significantly higher hostility than their mothers in 1992. Similarly, the TIME effect estimates the overall slope, and it suggests that there is no evidence of a general TIME trend. Instead, the ROLE by TIME interaction is significant, indicating that the effect of time differs for mothers and adolescents.

The SAS syntax for the same analysis is

```
PROC MIXED COVTEST METHOD = ML;
CLASS FAMILYID ROLE YEAR;
MODEL HOSTILE = ROLE1 TIME ROLE1*TIME/ SOLUTION
    DDFM=SATTERTH;
RANDOM INTERCEPT ROLE1 TIME ROLE1*TIME / SUB=FAMILYID
    TYPE=UN;
REPEATED ROLE / TYPE=CSH SUBJECT=FAMILYID*YEAR;
RUN;
```

TABLE 8.4
Output for Growth Model Testing for Differences in Mother and Adolescent Hostility
from SPSS MIXED

Information Criteria(a)

-2 Log Likelihood	5503.739
Akaike's Information Criterion (AIC)	5537.739
Hurvich and Tsai's Criterion (AICC)	5537.946
Bozdogan's Criterion (CAIC)	5656.745
Schwarz's Bayesian Criterion (BIC)	5639.745

Estimates of Fixed Effects(a)

Parameter	Estimate	Std. Error	df	t	Sig.
Intercept	2.8554746	.0312468	394.609	91.384	.000
ROLE	-.1244365	.0196068	27.910	-6.347	.000
TIME	-.0066365	.0078640	398.249	-.844	.399
TIME * ROLE	-.0318502	.0063347	261.532	-5.028	.000

Note. a Dependent Variable: HOSTILE.

Estimates of Covariance Parameters(a)

Parameter		Estimate	Std. Error	Wald Z	Sig.
Repeated Measures	Var: [ROLE=-1]	.3458635	.0182710	18.930	.000
	Var: [ROLE=1]	.1113357	.0058114	19.158	.000
	CSH rho	.2014965	.0356823	5.647	.000
Intercept + ROLE + TIME + TIME * ROLE [subject = FAMILYID]	UN (1,1)	.3455611	.0274233	12.601	.000
	UN (2,1)	-.0543111	.0127028	-4.276	.000
	UN (2,2)	.1238839	.0108551	11.413	.000
	UN (3,1)	.0029844	.0048899	.610	.542
	UN (3,2)	.0039438	.0030368	1.299	.194
	UN (3,3)	.0074398	.0018797	3.958	.000
	UN (4,1)	.0013448	.0039330	.342	.732
	UN (4,2)	-.0038749	.0024527	-1.580	.114
	UN (4,3)	-.0030260	.0012269	-2.466	.014
	UN (4,4)	.0037638	.0012447	3.024	.002

Note. a Dependent Variable: HOSTILE.

In this syntax, the variable ROLE1 is identical to the variable ROLE with the exception that ROLE is included in the CLASS statement, thereby defining it as a categorical or classification variable whereas ROLE1 is not. ROLE must be included in the CLASS statement because the REPEATED option requires a classification variable. Similarly, the variable YEAR is identical to TIME.

One nice feature of these models is their ability to incorporate a variety of other covariates into the analysis. For example, it may be that the mothers' and adolescents' intercepts and/or slopes differ depending on either gender of the adolescent (a categorical variable) or income (a continuous variable). In the present data there was little evidence of moderation effects for income, but there was evidence that the mothers' and adolescents' slopes measuring change in hostility over time were moderated by the child's sex. With sex coded as 1 for girls and –1 for boys, the coefficient estimating the sex difference in slopes for mothers versus adolescents is b = .015, p = .015. Combining this with our previous results, we see that in families in which the adolescent was a girl, there was very little change in the child's hostility over time (b = .004), but when the adolescent was a boy, there was a clear increase (b = .047). Child's gender also had an impact on mother's change in hostility, such that in families in which the adolescent was a girl, the mother's hostility showed a small increase over time (b = .018) and in families in which the child was a boy, the mother's hostility decreased over time (b = –.048).

Estimating Growth Models in the SEM Framework

An overall introduction to SEM is beyond the scope of this chapter and interested readers may wish to consult Kline (2005) for a very accessible account, Byrne (e.g., 2001) for a guide to the use of specific SEM programs, or Bollen (1989) for a more statistically demanding treatment. Moreover, Bollen and Curran (2006) and Duncan, Duncan, Strycker, Li, and Alpert (1999) have written book length treatments of growth modeling in the SEM framework. Lastly, Hox (2002) includes a chapter that describes SEM approaches to growth modeling in the context of a multilevel analysis and Ferrer, Hamagami, and McArdle (2004) provide an accessible tutorial for using a variety of packages to estimate growth models including both SEM and MLM packages. Interested readers should consult one or more of these additional sources for a more thorough and technical presentation of growth modeling in the SEM framework.

The input data set for SEM applications is typically a raw dyadic data set where dyad members are assessed at the same intervals on the same variables. Although it is possible to use SEM packages when data are collected at intervals that vary across individuals or across dyads, this approach is fairly cumbersome (see e.g., Mehta & West, 2000) and is sometimes extremely difficult to implement in particular SEM packages. Thus, applied users may find that a MLM program is more efficient for data sets that result from such a design. Moreover, although it is possible to estimate growth models with SEM packages using an input variance/covariance matrix and a vector of scale means, the advantage of using a raw data set is that Full Information Maximum Likelihood (FIML) procedures can be used to estimate parameters in the presence of missing data. Missing data are very common in longitudinal studies and FIML is one of the most recommended techniques for handling missing data when they are ignorable (e.g., Allison, 2003).

We focus our comments on the use of AMOS which is a widely available SEM package that is often bundled with SPSS. Although AMOS has both command language and path diagram input capabilities, we will focus on path diagram input because new users are likely to find path diagram input much easier than command language input. Figure 8.1 displays a path diagram depicting a dyadic growth model. The rectangles represent observed variables and the circles represent latent variables (i.e. unobserved variables). An AMOS file with this input diagram is available from the authors.

As seen in Figure 8.1, a model of linear change was specified by fixing the "Slope" factor loadings to –2, –1, 0, and 2 for the variables assessed at the 1990, 1991, 1992, and 1994 measurement occasions, respectively. This specification has the effect of centering the intercept on the 1992 measurement occasion to correspond to the centering decision we used in the MLM example. As seen in Figure 8.1, the part of the model that specifies a structure for the residuals is readily apparent. This is one advantage of the SEM approach because this transparency facilitates a clear understanding of the structure imposed on the so-called error portion of the model.

To match the "error structure" specified in our MLM example, we imposed certain constraints on the residual variances and covariances. Specifically, we constrained the variances for the residuals associated with the 1990, 1991, 1992, and 1994 measurement occasions for mothers to the same value and likewise we constrained the variances for the residuals associated with 1990, 1991, 1992, and 1994 measurement occasions for adolescents to the same value. These constraints are achieved in AMOS graphics by assigning the same letter to parameters that are to be constrained to the same value. We then constrained the four covariances between the residuals for the measures taken at the same time point (i.e., adolescent hostility in 1990 and maternal hostility in 1990) to the same value. Some of these particular constraints are more typical in multilevel regression analyses (e.g., Hox, 2002, p. 266) and

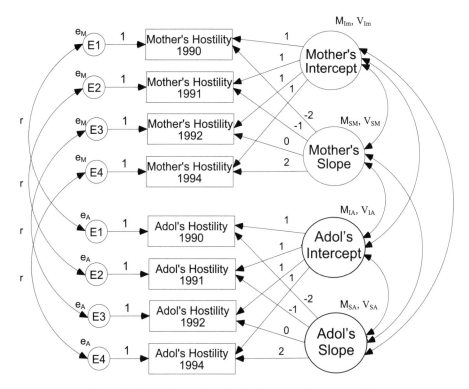

Figure 8.1. Path diagram for a dyadic latent growth curve model.

may strike some experienced SEM users as unnecessarily restrictive; however, the reasonableness of these constraints can be evaluated empirically and making such constraints ensures that we are estimating the heterogeneous compound symmetry (CSH) error structure specified in our MLM example.

Prior to discussing specific parameters, it is instructive to count the degrees of freedom associated with the model depicted in Figure 8.1. Adopting this habit is very useful when trying to estimate models that are depicted in published examples. This also serves as a quick way to catch user errors when estimating models. In our example data set, there are eight manifest variables which yields 36 variances and covariances (8 times 9 divided by 2; see Kline, 2005, p. 100), plus 8 means for a total of 44 pieces of information. The model estimated in Figure 8.1 requires the estimation of 17 parameters: 4 factor variances (i.e., slope and intercept variances for mothers and adolescents), 2 residual variances (1 each for mothers and adolescents based on our constraints), 6 factor covariances (to interrelate slopes and intercepts both within and between mothers and their adolescent children), 1 residual covariance (one for mother's residuals with adolescent's residuals based on our constraints), and 4 factor means (slope and intercept means for mother

TABLE 8.5
Parameter Estimates for Growth Model Examining Mother and Adolescent Hostility
Estimated With SEM

Parameter	Estimate	S.E.	C.R.	P
Means				
Adolescent Intercept	2.980	.042	71.704	< .001
Adolescent Slope	.025	.012	2.019	.043
Mother Intercept	2.731	.032	86.304	< .001
Mother Slope	-.038	.007	-5.522	< .001
Variances				
Adolescent Intercept	.578	.049	11.892	< .001
Adolescent Slope	.017	.005	3.615	< .001
Mother Intercept	.361	.028	12.842	< .001
Mother Slope	.005	.001	3.453	< .001
Adolescent Residual	.111	.006	19.105	< .001
Mother Residual	.346	.018	19.006	< .001
Covariances				
Adolescent Intercept-Adolescent Slope	-.006	.010	-.604	.546
Mother Intercept-Mother Slope	.004	.004	1.006	.315
Adolescent Intercept-Mother Intercept	.222	.029	7.737	< .001
Adolescent Slope-Mother Slope	.004	.002	1.882	.060
Adolescent Intercept-Mother Slope	.004	.006	.744	.457
Adolescent Slope-Mother Intercept	.009	.008	1.207	.228
Adolescent Residual-Mother Residual	.040	.007	5.319	< .001
Correlations				
Adolescent Intercept-Adolescent Slope	-.062			
Mother Intercept-Mother Slope	.102			
Adolescent Intercept-Mother Intercept	.485			
Adolescent Slope-Mother Slope	.390			
Adolescent Intercept-Mother Slope	.078			
Adolescent Slope-Mother Intercept	.120			
Adolescent Residual-Mother Residual	.201			

and adolescents). As such the model estimated in Figure 8.1 has 27 degrees of freedom $(44 - 17 = 27)$.

Table 8.5 provides estimates of key model parameters which are nearly identical to the corresponding parameters reported in Table 8.3. For example, the point estimate for the intercept for mothers was 2.731 in Table 8.5 which is the same value reported in Table 8.3 from the SPSS analysis. Thus, a comparison of Table 8.5 with Table 8.3 provides clear evidence that MLM and SEM approaches result in the same estimates when the exact same model is being estimated. However, one difference between the SEM and MLM approaches is the availability of omnibus indices of overall model fit in SEM. At the outset it is important to acknowledge that there are many controversies and complexities involved in evaluating overall fit in SEM and we refer readers to the general SEM resources that we cited at the beginning of this section for more information.

The model depicted in Figure 8.1 had a significant chi-square value (44.91, $df = 27$) which means that the model did not exactly fit the input data. On the other hand, the RMSEA value (.041, p close $= .740$) suggested that the fit of the model was reasonable. Based on these indices we concluded that although the model fit was more or less acceptable, alternative specifications might improve fit. Indeed, we recommend that researchers who initially make restrictive assumptions in specifying models and subsequently fail to obtain a nonrejectable chi-square value should also attempt to evaluate the source of model misfit. We consider the transparency of the lack of model fit when estimating growth models in SEM to be one of its principal advantages over the MLM framework (see Hox, 2002, pp. 268-269 and 273-274). That is, because omnibus model fit statistics are front and center in SEM, indications that models are somehow inadequate are harder to overlook. The trick is in deciding whether or not the misspecification(s) leading to model misfit are trivial or grave.

Given these considerations, we evaluated some additional models. First, we relaxed all of the constraints on the residual variances and covariances. This resulted in a model with 18 degrees of freedom because we estimated an additional 9 parameters (4 residual variances for adolescents instead of 1, 4 residual variances for mothers instead of 1, and 4 covariances between these residuals instead of 1). This model nonetheless had a significant chi-square value (37.99, $df = 18$; RMSEA $= .053$, p close $= .381$) and the change in chi-square values from the model depicted in Figure 8.1 was not statistically significant ($\Delta\chi^2 = 6.92$, $df = 9$). Thus, there seemed to be little compelling reason to favor this less restrictive model over the more restrictive model depicted in Figure 8.1.

We then tried a second model in which we explored the possibility of non-linear growth without specifying a particular growth function (see Bollen & Curran, 2006, pp. 98–103; Duncan et al., 1999, pp. 24–29; Ferrer et al., 2004; Meredith & Tisak, 1990). To examine this model we changed the "Slope" loadings depicted in Figure 8.1 by fixing the loading of the 1990 occasion to 0 and the loading of the 1994 occasion to 1 for both adolescents and mothers. We then freely estimated the loadings for the 1991 and 1992 occasions separately for adolescents and mothers. Given this change in model specification, it is perhaps better to think about latent "change" variables rather than latent "slope" variables. We also freely estimated all residuals and covariances which resulted in a model with 14 degrees of freedom. One word of caution is warranted: it is our experience that this approach will occasionally produce Heywood cases (i.e., inadmissible solutions such as negative variance estimates) so users should use extra caution and inspect all output carefully.

This second model still produced a significant chi-square value (24.90, $df =$ 14; RMSEA $= .045$, p close $= .588$), although this model was a significantly better-fitting model than our initial model ($\Delta\chi^2=20.01$, $df = 10$). Factor loadings for 1992 and 1994 were -.74 ($p = ns$) and .38, respectively, for adolescents and .14 ($p = ns$) and .60, respectively for mothers. In terms of the variance about the change factor, the amount was marginally significant for adolescents (.088, S.E. $= .038$, C.R. $= 1.789$, $p = .067$) and not statistically significant for mothers (.040, S.E. $= .026$, C.R. $= 1.547$, $p = ns$). As such, one down side to this model is that many of the statistically significant covariances between intercepts and slopes that were displayed in Table 8.5 dropped out of statistical significance. Indeed, there was only evidence for a significant association between intercepts for mothers and adolescents ($r = .46$) and evidence for a significant association between the intercept and change factor for adolescents ($r = -.30$). Thus, the conclusions that can be safely drawn from this model are somewhat less interesting than the interpretation of the model estimated in Figure 8.1.

The point of this discussion of alternative models is to suggest that model misfit should be taken seriously and to alert users of the ability to specify alternative dyadic growth models in SEM. Our hope is that researchers will act judiciously in the face of evidence that their specified model is limited. We also hope that this discussion alerts MLM users to the need to evaluate the adequacy of their models, which can be accomplished by examining residuals.

Some Cautionary Comments

Growth modeling is a fairly recent addition to the toolkit of the developmental scientist and the literature on these models is rapidly expanding. Nonetheless, growth models have gathered attention as perhaps the premier technique for analyzing longitudinal data. Such a designation is probably undeserved given that growth models are useful for addressing certain questions and less useful for addressing other questions. We are also uncomfortable with any suggestion that there is only one way to analyze longitudinal data and a recent simulation study has made us even more wary of the uncritical application of growth modeling. Specifically, Hertzog, Lindenberger, Ghisletta, and von Oertzen (2006) suggest that analyses using multivariate growth models (such as dyadic growth models) are sometimes severely underpowered based on simulation studies. They concluded: "Our results demonstrate that failures to reject the null hypotheses of no covariance in change often do not permit any firm conclusions about the absence of such effects in reality" (p. 248). Given these findings, we encourage users of dyadic growth curve models to exercise restraint in interpreting null results; it is helpful to recall the maxim that the absence of evidence is not evidence of absence.

Beyond low statistical power, we are also concerned when researchers rush to adopt a particular technology without thoroughly evaluating the data requirements that are the prerequisites for these models (see Donnellan & Conger, 2007). Standard growth models assume that variables are measured with interval-level scales (see Singer & Willett, 2003, esp. Chapter 13) and that the properties of the measurement instruments are consistent across waves. There is increasing recognition of the need to evaluate measurement invariance prior to implementing a growth curve analysis. Longitudinal measurement invariance addresses the question of whether or not the same construct is being measured in the same way over time (e.g., Horn & McArdle, 1992; Vandenberg & Lance, 2000). In a nutshell, the ability to draw valid inferences about absolute changes in psychological variables depends on measurement invariance. Indeed, Vandenberg and Lance (2000) noted that "it would seem that establishment of longitudinal [measurement invariance] would be a natural prerequisite to assessment of change using [growth modeling methods], yet curiously, the issue has received scant attention in this context" (p. 41). Thus, good measurement practices are essential to good growth modeling and we hope that these sorts of issues receive the appropriate amount of attention. An analogy might help illustrate this point: Growth modeling on poor measures cannot produce clear and convincing results any more than a shiny new golf club can transform a weekend hacker into Tiger Woods.

CONCLUSION

Our attention in this chapter has focused primarily on basic implementation of dyadic growth curve analyses using either SEM or MLM. We did not cover the extensive exploratory and descriptive analyses that should always precede these sophisticated analyses. Researchers should examine basic descriptive statistics for their measures at each time point. Examination of the standard deviations and reliability coefficients, as well as graphical analyses should be a routine start for growth modeling. We also recommend that before researchers estimate dyadic growth models, they estimate individual-level models (at least when the dyad members are distinguishable). In addition, simple models (e.g., intercept-only models) should be estimated initially and then additional factors can be added. Such analyses provide researchers with information that bears directly on the appropriateness of dyadic growth curve models for their data, and so these analyses create a framework from which the more complex results can be viewed. This can be useful in interpreting results and, perhaps more importantly, in detecting errors or misspecifications. SEM and MLM both offer a great deal to developmental researchers, but these complex approaches should not be undertaken in isolation.

REFERENCES

Allison, P. D. (2003). Missing data techniques for structural equation modeling. *Journal of Abnormal Psychology, 112*, 545-557.

Baltes, P. B., Reese, H. W., & Nesselroade, J. R. (1977). *Life-span developmental psychology: Introduction to research methods.* Monterey, CA: Brooks/Cole.

Biesanz, J. C., Deeb-Sossa, N., Papadakis, A. A., Bollen, K. A., & Curran, P. J. (2004). The role of coding time in estimating and interpreting growth curve models. *Psychological Methods, 9*, 30-52.

Bollen, K. A. (1989). *Structural equations with latent variables.* New York: John Wiley & Sons.

Bollen, K. A., & Curran, P. J. (2006). *Latent curve models: A structural equation perspective.* Hoboken, NJ: John Wiley & Sons.

Bryk, A. S., & Raudenbush, S. W. (2002). *Hierarchical linear models: Applications and data analysis methods.* Newbury Park: Sage.

Byrne, B. M. (2001). *Structural equation modeling with AMOS: Basic concepts, applications, and programming.* Mahwah, NJ: Erlbaum.

Conger, R. D., & Conger, K. J. (2002). Resilience in midwestern families: Selected findings from the first decade of a prospective longitudinal study. *Journal of Marriage and Family, 64*, 361-373.

Conger, R. D., & Donnellan, M. B. (2007). An interactionist perspective on the socioeconomic context of human development. *Annual Review of Psychology, 58*, 175-199.

Conger, R. D., & Elder, J. G. H. (1994). *Families in troubled times: Adapting to change in rural America.* Hillsdale, NJ: Aldine.

Curran, P. J. (2003). Have multilevel models been structural equation models all along? *Multivariate Behavioral Research, 38*, 529-569.

Donnellan, M. B., & Conger, R. D. (2007). Designing and implementing longitudinal studies. In R. W. Robins, R. C. Fraley, & R. F. Krueger (Eds.), *The handbook of research methods in personality psychology.* New York: Guilford Press.

Duncan, T. E., Duncan, S. C., Strycker, L. A., Li, F., & Alpert, A. (1999). *An introduction to latent variable growth curve modeling: Concepts, issues, and applications.* Mahwah, NJ: Lawrence Erlbaum.

Ferrer, E., Hamagami, F., & McArdle, J. J. (2004). Modeling latent growth curves with incomplete data using different types of structural equation modeling and multilevel software. *Structural Equation Modeling, 11*, 452-483.

Hertzog, C., Lindenberger, U., Ghisletta, P., & von Oertzen, T. (2006). On the power of multivariate latent growth curve models to detect correlated change. *Psychological Methods, 11*, 244-252.

Hertzog, C., & Nesselroade, J. R. (2003). Assessing psychological change in adulthood: An overview of methodological issues. *Psychology and Aging, 18*, 639-657.

Horn, J. L., & McArdle, J. J. (1992). A practical and theoretical guide to measurement invariance in aging research. *Experimental Aging Research, 18*, 117-144.

Hox, J. (2002). *Multilevel analysis: Techniques and applications.* Mahwah, NJ: Lawrence Erlbaum.

Kashy, D. A., Burt, S. A., Donnellan, M. B., & McGue, M. (2007). Growth curve models for indistinguishable dyads using multilevel modeling and structural equation modeling: The case of adolescent twins' conflict with their mothers. Unpublished manuscript, Michigan State University.

Kenny, D. A., Kashy, D. A., & Cook, W. L. (2006). *Dyadic data analysis.* Guilford Press.

Kline, R. B. (2005). *Principles and practice of structural equation modeling (2nd edition).* New York: Guilford Press.

Kreft, I., & DeLeeuw, J. (1998). *Introducing multilevel modeling.* London: Sage.

Mehta, P. D., & West, S. G. (2000). Putting the individual back into individual growth curves. *Psychological Methods, 5,* 23-43.

Meredith, W., & Tisak, J. (1990). Latent curve analysis. *Psychometrika, 55,* 107-122.

Olsen, J. A., & Kenny, D. A. (2006). Structural equation modeling with interchangeable dyads. *Psychological Methods, 11,* 127-141.

Singer, J. D., & Willett, J. B. (2003). *Applied longitudinal data analysis: Modeling change and event occurrence.* New York: Oxford University Press.

Vandenberg, R. J., & Lance, C. E. (2000). A review and synthesis of the measurement invariance literature: Suggestions, practices, and recommendations for organizational research. *Organizational Research Methods, 3,* 4-69.

Woody, E., & Sadler, P. (2005). Structural equation models for interchangeable dyads: Being the same makes a difference. *Psychological Methods, 10,* 139-158.

CHAPTER NINE

Techniques for Modeling Dependency in Interchangeable Dyads

James P. Selig
Kelly A. McNamara
Todd D. Little
University of Kansas

Noel A. Card
University of Arizona

The analysis of dyadic data is not new (e.g., Fisher, 1925), but there has been a recent resurgence of interest in the field (Kenny, Kashy, & Cook, 2006). Dyadic data can be especially important in the developmental sciences because development is best considered within an appropriate context and much of this context involves individuals interacting with others. While dyadic data are central to many areas of study, a problem arises because these data often require special treatment due to the fact that they rarely conform to the traditional assumption of noninterdependent data. The purpose of this chapter is to provide a survey of the available methods for analyzing a particular type of dyadic data, that arising from interchangeable dyads. We provide a data example to show how such methods can be used to model data from a developmental perspective and what information can be gleaned from such analyses.

Dyadic Data

As demonstrated throughout this book, the analysis of dyadic data is fundamental to approaches to interdependent data. It can, in fact, be argued that the dyad forms the basis for all social interaction (Kenny et al., 2006) and as such plays a very prominent role in most social sciences. In developmental science in particular, a number of dyadic relationships can have a substantial impact on development, such as those between parent and child, romantic partners, and mutual best friends to name only a few.

Distinguishability

Almost as soon as we begin to consider dyadic data, we are confronted with the issue of distinguishability. Dyads can be classified in two ways, those having members who are distinguishable or who are indistinguishable (also called exchangeable or interchangeable) from one another (see Gonzalez & Griffin, 1997; Kenny et al., 2006; Woody & Sadler, 2005). For example, if we collect data on mother-child dyads, it is clear that the dyad members have distinct roles within the dyads and these distinguishable roles would carry distinct characteristics (in the case of mother-child dyads: age, cognitive capacities, social responsibilities, etc.). Moreover, we would expect each dyad member to differ on the levels of a variable displayed (e.g., a two-year-old may be expected to produce fewer words in a dyadic interaction task than his or her mother) as well as different degrees of variability and relations among those variables (e.g., the two-year-old may respond to a difficult task by crying whereas the mother may respond by increasing her level of verbal support to the child).

In contrast, members of indistinguishable dyads are interchangeable in terms of their roles and defining characteristics. In addition, because they cannot be easily categorized as having distinct roles in the dyad, we have no a priori reason to expect members of such dyads to differ in their levels of a variable or to show different relations among variables than the dyad partner. A common example of such dyads is that of same-sex best friends, which we will use for illustrative purposes in the present chapter. Although such friends are distinct individuals, we view them as interchangeable for purposes of the analysis. The two friends, P and Q, are interchangeable in the sense that their roles in terms of who is friends with whom are arbitrarily determined.

Although there are these clear cases of distinguishable and indistinguishable dyads, it turns out that in many cases distinguishablility is an empirical question (Kenny et al., 2006). Even in instances in which it would seem that dyad members are clearly distinguishable (e.g., heterosexual romantic partners) it is often found that members of the dyads do not differ in the levels of the variables being analyzed (see Kenny et al., 2006, for a thorough treatment of distinguishability and for statistical tests of whether or not dyads are empirically distinguishable).

In the remainder of the chapter, we will describe and demonstrate two approaches to the analysis of data from interchangeable dyads. First, we will cover a method for measuring the degree of association between variables. Although estimating associations is a simple task in nondyadic data requiring only the computation of some form of a correlation coefficient, in the case of indistinguishable dyadic data the procedure is more complicated. Therefore, we will describe work by Griffin and Gonzalez (1995) that shows how to measure associations in interchangeable dyads. Because we are rarely satisfied with assessing only association, we also describe methods for estimating directional/structural models. Specifically, we illustrate the use of the Actor–Partner Interdependence Model (APIM; Cook & Kenny, 2005). This model allows us to move beyond examining associations to look at directional/predictive processes. As demonstrated by Cook and Kenny, the APIM may be particularly valuable to those in the developmental sciences.

Data Structure and Association in Interchangeable Dyadic Data

As is often the case with dyadic data, analyzing distinguishable dyads is much less complicated than analyzing interchangeable dyads. The most common data structure for distinguishable dyads is to have one line of data per dyad with the scores for each member of a dyad represented as separate variables. This data setup is often referred to as the dyad-level structure (Kenny et al., 2006). To examine associations in distinguishable dyads, both within individuals and across individuals, we can simply apply the Pearson product moment correlation (r) to the separate columns of variables that we wish to examine. For example, suppose we wish to know whether mothers who display high levels of positive regard for the child also have children who display high levels of positive regard for the mother in the mother-child scenario presented above. To answer this question, we would simply compute a correlation between the column of mothers' positive regard scores and the column of corresponding children's positive regard scores. Here, the sample size would be the number of mother-child dyads and all significance tests for such correlations would be based on this information because each mother-child dyad is considered an independent draw from the population of mother-child dyads.

The situation is quite different when there are dyads in which members are interchangeable. Consider for example the hypothetical data in Table 9.1 from ten pairs of best friends. For this example suppose each friend rated the aggression of his or her best friend. If we arranged the data in the same dyad-level format (see Chapter 1 of Kenny et al., 2006) as for distinguishable dyads, in which scores from each dyad member were entered as separate var-

TABLE 9.1

Hypothetical Aggression Scores for Ten Pairs of Friends

Dyad	Friend 1	Friend 2	Aggression 1	Aggression 2
1	A	B	9	5
2	C	D	2	5
3	E	F	6	4
4	G	H	1	4
5	I	J	4	1
6	K	L	3	8
7	M	N	4	4
8	O	P	6	10
9	Q	R	4	3
10	S	T	2	7

iables on a single row per dyad (i.e., 10 rows), the data might appear as shown in Table 9.1. We deliberately use the phrase "might appear" here, because the order of the interchangeable dyad members is arbitrary, and it would be just as valid to list, for example, individual B as Friend 1 and individual A as Friend 2. This order would also result in ten pairs of scores with one line of data per dyad, as the data in Table 9.1.

If we computed a Pearson correlation between aggression scores within dyads we would find a correlation of 0.07, suggesting that friends do not show a great deal of similarity in the way they assess each other's aggression. However, the arbitrary nature of ordering the scores from the interchangeable dyads results in inconsistent estimates of this correlation. Suppose we reevaluated our data structure and, since there is no reason that any particular friend should be classified as Friend 1 while the other is designated Friend 2, we decide to rearrange the data so that every other dyad will have its members' scores reversed so that Friend 1 becomes Friend 2 and vice versa. The recomputed Pearson's correlation is 0.70 and now, just by rearranging our arbitrarily ordered dyad members we have a much different story to tell about how members of dyads assess one another's aggression. Because there is no nonarbitrary way to arrange data from interchangeable dyads, an appropriate solution must be found to analyze such data.[1]

Association in Interchangeable Dyads

There are a number of solutions to this problem of analyzing associations. The solutions fall into three categories, one that does not require a restructuring of the data and two others that do. These approaches, which we describe below, are the ANOVA based approach (Kenny et al., 2006), the multilevel modeling approach (Campbell & Kashy, 2002; Kenny et al., 2006), and the pairwise correlational approach (Griffin & Gonzalez, 1995). Before we provide an example illustrating the pairwise correlational approach, we will first briefly describe both the ANOVA and multilevel approaches.

The ANOVA approach as described by Kenny and LaVoie (1985) and Kenny et al. (2006, see Chapters 2 and 4), involves a partitioning of the variance in the data into the variance arising between dyads and that arising within dyads. This partitioning allows us to compute an intraclass correlation that describes the proportion of variance that is due to the fact that individuals are in the same dyad. We can then use an F test based on the ratio of the mean squares between and the mean squares within to determine whether this intraclass correlation is statistically significant. The drawbacks of the ANOVA method include that it requires a series of hand calculations to estimate the intraclass correlation. Though these calculations are not intensive, they are more burdensome than a method that would allow for the direct calculation of the intraclass correlation, such as the pairwise approach described below. Further, if one wished to move beyond a correlational analysis, the ANOVA method is of little use while both the multilevel approach and the pairwise approach offer the ability to estimate regression models.

The multilevel modeling (MLM) approach examines the data as having two levels. This approach would require the dyad-level data set to be restructured so that there were two lines of data per dyad, one containing the information for the first dyad member and the second containing the information for the second member and a variable coding which dyad member is which within the dyad. In this model, level one is that of the individual and level two is that of the dyad. In this way the multilevel approach, similar to the ANOVA approach, partitions the variance into two levels and similarly produces an intraclass correlation. The intraclass correlation describes the variance in the scores that is at the dyad level, or alternatively it can be in-

---

[1] The recent application of SEM to the analysis by Olsen and Kenny (2006) does in fact allow us to compute the maximum likelihood estimate of the correlation coefficient using the dyad-level structure.

terpreted as the correlation between scores for members of a randomly chosen dyad.

The pairwise correlational approach can be traced back to Fisher (1925) who described a solution to the problem of measuring association in interchangeable dyads. Fisher's solution also results in an intraclass correlation by using what Fisher called a symmetrical table. This approach relies on a pairwise or "double entry" data structure (Griffin & Gonzalez, 1995; Kenny et al., 2006), in which the data are reorganized so that each dyad now contributes two lines in the data set. The first line for each dyad contains the scores from both dyad members with one dyad member in the first position and the partner in the second (Individual A as Friend 1 and Individual B as Friend 2), and the second line reverses the order putting the partner in the first position and the member who was first into the second position (Individual B as Friend 1 and A as Friend 2). This restructuring is different from that needed for multilevel modeling in that both lines for each dyad now contain data from both members of the dyad. As mentioned, for the multilevel format the aggression score of friend B is listed on a separate line from that of Friend A but there is not a second column with the partner's score. The multilevel data structure is often referred to as the "tall" format.

Table 9.2 shows the pairwise reorganization of the data from Table 9.1. Because exactly the same data appear in both columns of this new data set, the variables Aggression 1 and Aggression 2 will have the same means and variances. Once the data are reorganized into this pairwise structure we can assess the correlation between the ratings of aggression for best friends by computing a Pearson correlation. Although the data are organized in the pairwise manner, the Pearson correlation is, in fact, the unbiased point estimate of the true association among the scores. The standard error from the Pearson correlation, however, is incorrect if we treat the 20 rows as independent cases (i.e., if we use $df = 20 - 2 = 18$). The Pearson correlation estimated here is an intraclass correlation as described by Fisher (1925). This intraclass correlation is interpreted just as in the other approaches; it is the proportion of variance in aggression scores that is accounted for by dyad membership or, alternatively, as the expected correlation between aggression scores for members of a dyad randomly chosen from the population of best friends. Fisher (1925) presented a significance test for such an intraclass correlation, and Griffin and Gonzalez (1995) present a simpler, though more limited, test of this intraclass correlation and related correlation coefficients. Once the data are restructured, associations of interest are easily calculable within popular software packages. However, the other approaches certainly have their own

TABLE 9.2
Hypothetical Aggression Scores for Ten Pairs of Friends in a Double-Entered Format

Dyad	Friend 1	Friend 2	Aggression 1	Aggression 2
1	A	B	9	5
1	B	A	5	9
2	C	D	2	5
2	D	C	5	2
3	E	F	6	4
3	F	E	4	6
4	G	H	1	4
4	H	G	4	1
5	I	J	4	1
5	J	I	1	4
6	K	L	3	8
6	L	K	8	3
7	M	N	4	4
7	N	M	4	4
8	O	P	6	10
8	P	O	10	6
9	Q	R	4	3
9	R	Q	3	4
10	S	T	2	7
10	T	S	7	2

merits and should be explored as well.[2] For example, for straightforward models like the APIM, MLM and the use of the pairwise approach yield essentially the same information (except MLM will not compute the time 1 ICC as part of the APIM). For more complex models, however, the pairwise approach brings flexibility that can prove beneficial. Therefore, we focus the remainder of our discussion on the pairwise approach.

We will now introduce a data example to illustrate the pairwise approach to analyzing association. The data for this example were drawn from a larger longitudinal study of 6th through 9th graders (see Walls & Little, 2005). The sample included in the current example consisted of 579 boys and 579 girls in the 6th through 8th grades surveyed in the fall of the school year (wave 1) and six months later in the spring of the school year (wave 2). Signed informed parental consent was obtained for approximately 80% of the youth. Socioeconomic status varied from lower class to upper middle class, and the ethnic composition was predominantly European American (64%), followed by approximately 18% African American, 4% Hispanic American, and the remainder were of mixed origins. Participants completed three questionnaires of interest in the current study, a self-report measure of aggression, a friendship questionnaire that encompassed both nominations of best friends and ratings of the best friend's aggression, and a peer-report sociometric instrument.

Students were identified as belonging to a friendship dyad based upon their responses to a set of three questions from the friendship questionnaire asking them, in both the fall and spring, to identify their "very best friend in your school" as well as their "second best friend," and their "third best friend." We defined a friendship dyad as occurring when two students of the same sex mutually nominated each other in one of the three best friend positions at both waves of data collection. We accomplished the identification of such dyads in a sequential manner, whereby we first identified all dyads that nominated one another in the first position and subsequently identified dyads in which the members nominated one another in any of the three positions. In cases where an individual was a member of more than one friendship dyad, we included the dyad with the highest average best friend rank. In this way, although the methods we describe in this chapter address the interdependence resulting from students being nested in friendship dyads, they do not address the interdependence that may arise from the same student being nested within

---

[2]The pairwise method described here will generally yield results similar to that of the ANOVA and multilevel approaches. One potential difference is that the method described here yields a Maximum Likelihood (ML) solution, whereas the ANOVA and multilevel approaches described by Kenny et al. (2006) yield a Restricted Maximum Likelihood(REML) solution. This difference becomes trivial with increasing sample sizes; furthermore, either approach could be adapted to provide either ML or REML solutions, if one solution were preferred over the other.

multiple dyads. This issue, often referred to as one of multiple membership, has been addressed with some success in the field of multilevel modeling; however, it is beyond the scope of the present chapter (see Goldstein, 2003 and Hill & Goldstein, 1998 for a comprehensive treatment of multiple membership models). We identified 121 unique friendship dyads (51 male and 70 female dyads). Ninety-four and 95 of these dyads provided self-reported overt and relational aggression scores; 118 provided best friend-reported aggression scores; and 120 dyads had peer-reported aggression scores.[3]

Aggression Ratings

Both overt and relational aggression (see Card, Stucky, Sawalani, & Little, in press) of participants was assessed by three different reporters. Students reported their own level of overt aggression by responding to six questions (e.g.,"I'm the kind of person who often fights with others."). They also reported their own levels of relational aggression (e.g., "I'm the kind of person who tells my friends to stop liking someone."). Responses for each type of aggression were averaged to create an overall overt aggression score as well as an overall relational aggression score.

Students also reported on the level of overt aggression directed at them by their best friends (e.g., "Does this friend fight with you?"). They also rated the best friends' relational aggression (e.g., "Does this friend gossip or spread rumors about you?") directed at them. The friend-directed overt and relational aggression scores are calculated by averaging the respective overt and relational items.

The entire peer group also provided ratings of adolescents' aggression via a standard sociometric nomination procedure. Peers were asked to nominate students who matched the descriptions provided by four overt aggression items: "Who starts fights to get what they want?"; "Who hurts others to get what they want?"; "Who fights back because they've been hurt?"; and "Who pushes, kicks, or punches others because they've been angered by them?" Additionally, peers nominated students who matched the descriptions provided by four relational aggression items: "Who tells their friends to stop liking someone in order to get what they want?"; "Who ignores or stops talking to others in order to get what they want?"; "Who gossips or spreads rumors about others if they're mad at them?"; and "Who keeps people from being in

---

[3]For simplicity of presentation we will use only complete cases. We note, however, that the pairwise method relies on calculation of a Pearson correlation coefficient and most software packages do not incorporate missing data into the calculation of this correlation coefficient. However, this does not prohibit one from using multiple imputation and subsequently computing the desired correlation coefficient.

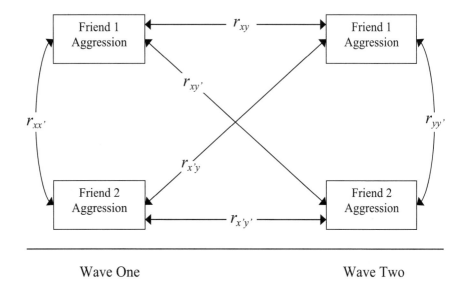

Wave One   Wave Two

Figure 9.1. Relations among best friends' levels of aggression over time.

their group of friends if they've been hurt by them?" Because each classroom could have a different number of students, these nomination scores for each student were standardized within classroom to insure comparability. Overt and relational aggression scores for each individual were found by taking the average of the overt and relational standardized scores, respectively.

Figure 9.1 shows a diagram of the associations among aggression variables at waves one (fall) and two (spring) for best friend dyads. At each wave, each member of the friendship dyad is rated on aggression via the three reporters (self, friend, and peers). This figure, meant to represent any one of the six possible combinations of types of aggression and reporter, depicts six bidirectional paths showing all the possible associations among the four variables in the model. Because the data are structured such that aggression for Friend 1 and Friend 2 at wave 1 are identical in mean and variance (see Griffin & Gonzalez, 1995), two of these paths ($r_{x'y}$ and $r_{x'y'}$) are redundant (i.e., they contain the same information found in $r_{xy'}$ and r_{xy}, respectively). The two nonredundant concurrent paths can be interpreted as follows: $r_{xx'}$ is an intraclass correlation measuring best friends' similarity on levels of aggression at wave one, and $r_{yy'}$ is an intraclass correlation measuring best friends' similarity on levels of aggression at wave two. Based on previous findings (Adams, Bukowski, & Bagwell, 2005; Cairns, Cairns, Neckerman, Gest, & Gariepy, 1988; Card & Hodges, 2006; Cillessen, Jiang, West, & Laszkowski, 2005; Kupersmidt, DeRosier, & Patterson, 1995; Poulin et al., 1997) and the principle of homophily which is the tendency for individuals to affiliate with those who display similar qualities (Kandel, 1978a, 1978b), we would expect best friends to show similar levels of aggression at both waves and for these two intraclass correlations to be sizeable and statistically significant. We can also compare these two intraclass correlations to provide clues regarding selection and socialization effects. Selection is the tendency for individuals to select as friends those who are behaviorally similar to themselves, while socialization refers to the tendency for friends to become more similar to one another in behavior over the duration of the friendship (Hogue & Steinberg, 1995; Kandel, 1978a; Nangle, Erdley, Zeff, Stanchfield, & Gold, 2004). If only selection is working in the best friend dyads, we would expect that the two intraclass correlations (i.e., $r_{xx'}$ and $r_{yy'}$) would remain similar across time; however, if socialization is also playing a role, we would expect friends to become more similar in levels of aggression over time and that the intraclass correlation at wave two $(r_{yy'})$ would be larger in magnitude than the intraclass correlation at wave one $(r_{xx'})$. There are also two nonredundant longitudinal associations in Figure 9.1. The path labeled r_{xy}, following the terminology of Griffin and Gonzalez (1995), is referred to as the overall correlation, and assesses whether individuals show similar levels of aggression across waves of measurement. This path documents the stability of aggression across waves. Previous research has found that levels of aggressive behavior are moderately stable over time (e.g., Olweus, 1979), and therefore we would expect that this relationship would be sizable and significant in the present data. Finally, the estimate labeled $r_{xy'}$ is the cross-intraclass correlation. It assesses whether friends are similar in levels of aggression across waves (i.e., is aggression in one friend at wave one correlated with aggression in the other friend at wave two?). To the degree that best friends are similarly aggressive at both waves, we would expect there to be a sizable cross-intraclass correlation in that friends' scores are similar and scores within individuals are stable.

As mentioned, in the following analyses we examine two types of aggression, overt and relational; assessed at two waves, fall and spring semesters; by three different reporters, self, best friend, and peers; to evaluate these patterns of similarity within best friend dyads. The combination of aggression type by reporter yields six sets of scores that cover both waves of measurement. We will elaborate on the methods used to analyze association in the first combination, self-reported overt aggression (from 94 dyads), and then report the results from the other five combinations.

As previously mentioned, data for these analyses are "double entered" so that each dyad is represented by two lines of data, the first line with one friend in the first position and the other in the second and the second line with the order of the friends' scores reversed. Therefore each line contains four self-reported overt aggression scores, one for each friend at wave one and one for each friend at wave two. After rearranging the data in the pairwise structure, the four correlations—the concurrent intraclass correlations at waves one and two, the stability correlation, and the cross-intraclass correlation—can be computed in any software package that can compute Pearson product moment correlations (i.e., r). However, the significance tests reported by the software will not be correct. Because the program assumes each line of data represents an independent case, we will need to compute corrected standard errors and significance tests by hand following the formulas from Griffin and Gonzalez (1995).

First, we examine the within-person longitudinal correlation between self-reported overt aggression at waves one and two. Since we are examining the same variable over time, we can think of this as a stability coefficient answering the question of how stable overt aggression is between the fall and spring semesters. The information for this correlation comes from 94 dyads; however, the significance tests reported by the data analysis program assume that there are 188 independent observations because our data are entered in 188 rows. Therefore, the reported p value would be based on more information (i.e., more dfs) than we actually have. The one exception to this is when scores from the dyad members are not correlated (i.e., dyad members are more or less as similar as random pairings). In this special case, dyad membership gives no additional information about the scores and the appropriate sample size is in fact equal to the number of individuals. In the much more common case, wherein dyad members are more similar to each other than to other members of the population, we need a way to adjust the sample size used in significance testing to reflect the amount of redundancy provided by entering each dyad twice in the data set. Following this logic, we can see that the adjusted sample size can generally range in value from N (in the case where dyad members are perfectly correlated) to $2N$ (where there is no correlation between the scores of dyad members) (see below for an exception to this general range).The formula for this corrected sample size, from Griffin and Gonzalez (1995) is as follows:

$$N^* = 2N/(1 + r_{xx'}r_{yy'} + r_{xy'}^2) \qquad (1)$$

Where N^* is the adjusted sample size, N is the number of dyads, $r_{xx'}$ is the intraclass correlation in self-reported overt aggression at wave one, $r_{yy'}$ is the intraclass correlation in self-reported overt aggression at wave two, and $r_{xy'}$ is the cross-intraclass correlation between one friend's self-reported overt aggression at wave one and the other friend's self-reported overt aggression at wave two.

TABLE 9.3
Associations among Friends' Aggression Levels by Reporter and Aggression Type

Rater	Aggression Type	$r_{xx'}$	r_{xy}	$r_{xy'}$	$r_{yy'}$
Self	Overt	0.23*	0.50*	0.10	0.30*
	Relational	0.17*	0.47*	0.04	0.13
Friend	Overt	0.10	0.35*	-0.00	0.07
	Relational	0.17*	0.37*	0.18*	0.24*
Peer	Overt	0.36*	0.60*	0.28*	0.16*
	Relational	0.46*	0.62*	0.38*	0.38*

Note. $^{*}p < .05$.

Table 9.3 shows the four nonredundant correlations available from these data for self-reported overt aggression (as well as for the other combinations of reporter and type of aggression); these are used to compute the adjusted sample size for the within-person longitudinal correlation between waves one and two self-reported overt aggression. Using these values, we find that the adjusted sample size is calculated as follows:

$$N^* = 2(94)/(1 + .2281 * .2968 + .1011^2) = 174.41 \qquad (2)$$

The correct standard error used in evaluating the statistical significance of this correlation is $\sqrt{1/N^*}$ and in this case is equal to $\sqrt{1/174.41}$, or .0757. The test statistic for this correlation is $z = 0.4973/0.0757 = 6.57$ which has a p value of less than .001. Though not directly addressed by Griffin and Gonzalez (1995), given a small sample size it might be more appropriate to compare the test statistic to the t distribution with degree of freedom equal to $N^* - 2$. However, given the current sample size and for the sake of consistency we will continue to use the z distribution.

Next, we describe the two concurrent intraclass correlations for these data, the one describing the relationship between friends' self-reported overt aggression at wave one and the second describing the same relationship at wave two. These intraclass correlations have an asymptotic standard error equal to $1/\sqrt{N}$, where N is again the number of unique dyads. We can assess the significance of the first intraclass correlation by computing $z = 0.2281/(1/\sqrt{94}) = 2.21$ ($p = 0.014$). Similarly, we can compute a test of significance of the second intraclass correlation as $z = 0.2968/(1/\sqrt{94}) = 2.88$ ($p = 0.002$).

Finally, we come to the cross-intraclass correlation that measures the similarity between one friend's self-rated aggression at wave one and the second friend's self-rated aggression at wave two. Note again that there is only one cross-intraclass correlation given the interchangeable nature of these dyads (see Figure 9.1). Very much like the adjusted sample size for the within-person longitudinal correlation, the sample size for this across-person longitudinal correlation must be adjusted according to the degree of similarity of dyad members. The formula for the adjusted sample size for the cross-intraclass correlation is:

$$N^* = 2N/(1 + r_{xx'}r_{yy'} + r_{xy}^2) \qquad (3)$$

with all terms being the same as those in Equation 1 with the exception of the last term r_{xy}, that takes the place of $r_{xy'}$ in the prior equation. The adjusted sample size for the cross-intraclass correlation for self-reported overt aggression is then:

$$N^* = 2(94)/(1 + .2281 * .2968 + .4973^2) = 142.97 \qquad (4)$$

As for the overall correlation, the correct standard error for the cross-intraclass correlation is $\sqrt{1/N^*}$ and in this case is equal to $\sqrt{1/142.97}$, or .0836. The test statistic for this correlation is $z = 0.1010/0.0836 = 1.21$, which has a p value of 0.1134.

Table 9.3 shows the results for all combinations of raters and aggression types. Beginning with the concurrent intraclass correlations (i.e., $r_{xx'}$ and $r_{yy'}$), which describe the dyad members' similarity in aggression scores at waves one and two, respectively, we see that, in support of our hypotheses based on the principle of homophily, dyad members' levels of aggression at wave one are correlated in all instances except overt aggression reported by one's friend. Four of the six aggression types by reporter combinations (2 types by 3 reporters) are also correlated at wave two. These results demonstrate some degree of homophily in self-reported overt aggression, friend-reported relational aggression, and peer-reported overt and relational aggression at wave 2. This pattern of results could be interpreted as support for both the selection and socialization components of homophily, but we must be cautious in the interpretation of these results in regard to socialization. For example, a more thorough test of the socialization hypothesis (that friends become more similar in levels of aggression over time) would require us to establish that $r_{xx'}$ and $r_{yy'}$ are statistically different, specifically that $r_{yy'}$ is significantly greater than $r_{xx'}$. We will defer any such test to the Actor–Partner Interdependence Model (APIM) model as it is much easier to conduct such a test in the context of a structural model.

Moving next to the stability correlations (r_{xy}), which gives information about whether individuals are similar across waves in levels of aggression, we see that there is good evidence for stability for all examined combinations of aggression type and reporter. This stability is not surprising as it suggests that individuals see themselves and their friends as stable in levels of aggression from the fall to the spring semester of the school year. Additionally, this finding demonstrates that peers rate their classmates as displaying similar levels of aggression throughout the school year.

Finally, we examine the cross-intraclass correlation ($r_{xy'}$) that describes whether one friend's level of aggression at wave one is correlated with his or her friend's level of aggression at wave two. These results are mixed in that for three reporter by aggression combinations this relationship is significant while for the other three it is not. The significant findings for the cross-intraclass correlation suggest that friends' levels of aggression are similar across both waves of data collection. Specifically, an individual's level of relational aggression at wave one is significantly correlated with his or her friend's level of relational aggression at wave two as reported by friend and peers. Additionally, peer-reports of overt aggression at wave one are significantly correlated with friend's overt aggression at wave two. Again we must be cautious in interpreting this relationship as the best test would be one in which one friend's wave one aggression is used to predict the other friend's aggression at wave two. The APIM to be demonstrated next will provide us with this information.

Actor–Partner Interdependence Model for Interchangeable Dyads

While each of the methods for analyzing associations can be fruitfully employed, none of the three can be used to model directional relations among variables. For example, there is no straightforward way to extend the pairwise approach to a multiple regression framework. As with models for association, there are a handful of methods for directional/predictive models using data from interchangeable dyads. One such method developed by Kenny (Kashy & Kenny, 2000) is a pooled regression method that requires the estimation of separate between-dyad (using dyad means) and within-dyad (using dyad difference scores) models. Results from both models are then pooled to provide estimates of the parameters from the APIM. A second approach is to use standard multilevel modeling. In this approach, as when estimating the intraclass correlation using a multilevel model, individuals are the level one unit and dyads are the level two unit. Recently, a third method for estimating the APIM has been introduced that capitalizes on the flexibility of structural equation modeling (SEM; Olsen & Kenny, 2006).[4] While the Olsen and Kenny (2006) approach has broad applications, we will discuss it here only in the context of the APIM.

Olsen and Kenny (2006), in describing their approach to using SEM for interchangeable dyadic data, point out that these models are by no means intractable and in many cases just require a thoughtful consideration of the data at hand and placing the appropriate constraints on parameters of the model as well as adjusting the default model fit results provided by most SEM packages. Their model can be used with either the pairwise data structure used throughout this chapter or the dyad-level structure as illustrated by Table 9.1. As an aside, the Olsen and Kenny (2006) method can be used with dyad-level data to estimate the intraclass correlations we found in the previous analysis, but this approach does not address the sample size adjustment made explicit in the pairwise method.

Figure 9.2 shows a path diagram of the APIM in which the nondirectional arrows from the previous model have now been changed to predictive paths. The stability correlations from the association model are now referred to as actor effects and the cross-intraclass correlations are now referred to as partner effects. To facilitate the transition to SEM, we now use the Y-side LISREL notation for the parameter estimates in the model, and for simplicity's sake leave out the mean structure. As noted before when describing association, many of the parameters in this model are redundant. For example $\psi_{1,1}$ is equal to $\psi_{2,2}$, $\psi_{3,3}$ is equal to $\psi_{4,4}$, $\beta_{3,1}$ is equal to $\beta_{4,2}$, and $\beta_{3,2}$ is equal to $\beta_{4,1}$. Therefore, although it may at first appear as if there are ten parameters to estimate in this model, there are in fact only six. While more complicated models such as those containing latent variables with multiple indicators will require a more complex set of constraints, not to mention those that must be added to account for longitudinal measurement invariance, the constraints for this simple path model are relatively easy to understand.

Having discussed the appropriate constraints to the model, the next issue to consider when employing the Olsen and Kenny (2006) approach is that of model fit. The problem with assessing model fit for models with interchangeable dyadic data is that the independence, or null, and the saturated models used to compute a number of model fit indices are not correctly estimated by SEM software. For example, in the APIM model, the independence model estimated as the default in standard SEM packages would include four variances, one for each friend's score at the two waves and no covariances. This model would have six degrees of freedom. However, given that the pair of

---

[4]Woody and Sadler (2005) also have presented an approach to using SEM for interchangeable dyadic data that involves the use of multilevel SEM.

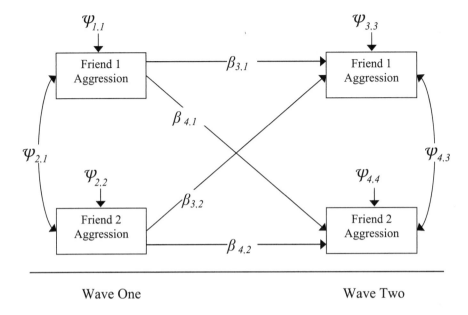

Wave One   Wave Two

Figure 9.2. Actor–Partner Interdependence Model for best friends' aggression over time.

wave one aggression scores and the pair of wave two aggression scores contain the same scores, there are only two unique variances to estimate and the independence model should have eight degrees of freedom. Similarly, the saturated model, in which all variables are allowed to freely covary, produced as a default by SEM programs will have zero degrees of freedom. Again, after we account for the nonindependence of the scores in the model, we see that the adjusted saturated model will have four degrees of freedom. The procedure described by Olsen and Kenny (2006) uses the information about model fit to adjust the model χ^2 and degrees of freedom to properly account for the nonindependence inherent in the dyadic data. Specifically, any model using such data should have its fit adjusted by subtracting the saturated model χ^2 from the model χ^2 and the saturated model degrees of freedom subtracted from the model degrees of freedom. When using the pairwise data structure as we are in this chapter, the saturated model χ^2 will be equal to the default saturated model χ^2 but the degrees of freedom will not be correct.

The APIM path models examined here are in fact saturated models and so model fit is not of the foremost concern. Instead we will be primarily interested in interpreting the parameter estimates and their accompanying standard errors. Using the sufficient statistics computed from the double entered data, we used LISREL to estimate path models examining the predictive paths between each friend's own aggression as well as the effect that

an individual's aggression has on his or her friend's aggression. LISREL
syntax, including the sufficient statistics for each model, can be found at
Quant.KU.edu. Because we input the sufficient statistics (instead of the raw
data) into our LISREL syntax, we must also input the sample size for each
model. Inputting the data in this format is advantageous over reading in the
raw data because we can adjust the sample size and tell the program what the
adjusted sample size should be. For the initial models, we input the sample
size as equal to the number of dyads (a conservative sample size if there is
little or no dependency in the data). However, had we read in the raw data,
the sample size would be determined as the number of records in the data file
(i.e., two times the number of dyads because of the pairwise method of data
entry).

In this example, we employ a longitudinal application of the APIM in
which an individual's aggression level at wave one affects not only his or her
subsequent levels of aggression but also his or her partner's level of aggression
at wave two. These models are saturated in that we begin with six pieces of
information for each dyad (one variance at each time, two concurrent intraclass covariances, one actor effect, and one partner effect) and estimate the
corresponding paths within each path model. Therefore, the fit is perfect for
each model. Table 9.4 shows the standardized regression coefficients from the
path models.

As before, there is evidence for similarity in levels of aggression at wave
one ($\Psi_{xx'}$) for three of the six aggression types by rater combinations, which
again supports the principle of homophily as it applies to levels of aggression
and friends. At wave two, the concurrent covariance ($\Psi_{yy'}$) now describes the
relationship between residual variance in the aggression scores after controlling for one's own and one's friend's level of aggression at wave one. Only
one of these remains significant (self-reported overt aggression).

The actor effects (β_{xy}) for all combinations are significant suggesting that
one's previous level of aggression does in fact predict one's current level of
aggression regardless of type of aggression or reporter. We also see evidence
for partner effects ($\beta_{xy'}$) such that a friend's report of one's relational aggression at wave two is predicted by that friend's report at wave one. The same
relationship holds for the peer-reports of relational aggression.

Effective Sample Size

The attentive reader will note an important difference between the Griffin and Gonzalez (1995) method for assessing association and the Olsen and
Kenny (2006) approach using SEM to estimate an APIM model. This difference is that much of the emphasis of the Griffin and Gonzalez (1995) method

TABLE 9.4
Standardized Regression Weights From Path Models

Rater	Aggression Type	$\psi_{xx'}$	β_{xy}	$\beta_{xy'}$	$\psi_{yy'}$
Self	Overt	.23*	.50*	-.01	.25*
	Relational	.17 [a]	.48*	-.04	.13 [a]
Friend	Overt	.10	.35*	-.04	.09
	Relational	.17† [a]	.35*	.12*	.14† [a]
Peer	Overt	.36*	.58*	.07	-.04
	Relational	.46*	.57*	.12*	.09† [a]

Note. *$p < .05$; †$p < .10$; [a] Path becomes significant using adjusted N.

is on computing the effective sample size that is used to compute the appropriate standard error for each type of correlation. While Olsen and Kenny (2006) do briefly note that the effective sample size for each model ranges between the number of dyads and the number of individuals, no mention is given of whether effective sample size may vary by parameter. Part of this lack of mention may stem from the fact that standard errors in SEM are taken from the inverse of the information matrix and it would not be possible to calculate standard errors within a single model that are based on varying sample sizes. However, as a way of examining the effect of varying effective sample sizes for different parameters in the model, we ran each model a number of times. Each time we used the adjusted sample size calculated from the formulas provided by Griffin and Gonzalez (1995) and then recorded only the standard error of the model parameter that corresponds to the adjusted sample size. Rather than reporting the full results from all these separate analyses, we note that for these analyses five paths changed from being nonsignificant to being significant at the $p < .05$ level when using the adjusted sample size based on the Griffin and Gonzalez (1995) calculations instead of the most restricted sample size (number of dyads). The changing paths are noted in Table 9.4. One point to be made here is that the effect size (i.e., estimated correlation or semipartial regression weight) does not change in these models, only the significance level based on the adjusted sample size changes. Therefore, researchers should pay particular attention to effect size in interpreting results from these models.

CONCLUSION

Our purpose in this chapter was to present two approaches to treating data from interchangeable dyads. The first pairwise approach for measuring association can be very useful in describing relationships among variables within the context of dyads. It is limited in the same way that all measures of association are limited in that it does not estimate predictive/directional relationships. The APIM as modeled within a SEM framework does allow the researcher to model interesting directional relationships and in the present case make useful statements about longitudinal change within dyads.

Generally speaking, the pairwise entry method presented Griffin and Gonzalez (1995) merged with the SEM analytic logic of the APIM provides researchers with a flexible way to estimate more interesting and complex developmental questions about the nature of dyadic associations. Such models can include latent variables, hierarchical models, models with covariates and other exogenous predictors, as well as latent growth curve models. Our goal for this chapter was to carefully describe the basic logic of these two approaches. We provide some examples of more complex models on the support pages for this chapter at Quant.KU.edu.

REFERENCES

Adams, R. E., Bukowski, W. M., & Bagwell, C. (2005). Stability of aggression during early adolescence as moderated by reciprocated friendship status and friend's aggression. *International Journal of Behavioral Development, 29*, 139-145.

Cairns, R. B., Cairns, B. D., Neckerman, H. J., Gest, S. D., & Gariépy, J.-L. (1988). Social networks and aggressive behavior: Peer support or peer rejection? *Developmental Psychology, 24*, 815-823.

Campbell, L., & Kashy, D. A. (2002). Estimating actor, partner, and interaction effects for dyadic data using proc mixed and hlm: A user-friendly guide. *Personal Relationships, 9*, 327-342.

Card, N. A., & Hodges, E. V. E. (2006). Shared targets for aggression by early adolescent friends. *Developmental Psychology, 42*, 1327-1338.

Card, N. A., Stucky, B. D., Sawalani, G. M., & Little, T. D. (in press). Direct and indirect aggression during childhood and adolescence: A meta-analytic review of gender differences, intercorrelations, and relations to maladjustment. *Developmental Psychology.*

Cillessen, A. H. N., Jiang, X. L., West, T. V., & Laszkowski, D. K. (2005). Predictors of dyadic friendship quality in adolescence. *International Journal of Behavioral Development, 29*, 165-172.

Cook, W. L., & Kenny, D. A. (2005). The actor-partner interdependence model: A model of bidirectional effects in developmental studies. *International Journal of Behavioral Development, 29*, 101-109.

Fisher, R. A. (1925). *Statistical methods for research workers.* Edinburgh: Oliver and Boyd.

Goldstein, H. (2003). *Multilevel statistical models* (3rd ed.). London: Hodder Arnold.

Gonzalez, R., & Griffin, D. W. (1997). On the statistics of interdependence: Treating dyadic data with respect. In S. Duck (Ed.), *Handbook of personal relationships* (2nd ed., pp. 271-302). New York: John Wiley & Sons.

Griffin, D. W., & Gonzalez, R. (1995). Correlational analysis of dyad-level data in the exchangeable case. *Psychological Bulletin, 118*, 430-439.

Hill, P. W., & Goldstein, H. (1998). Multilevel modeling of educational data with cross classification and missing identification of units. *Journal of Educational and Behavioral Statistics, 23*, 117-128.

Hogue, A., & Steinberg, L. (1995). Homophily of internalized distress in adolescent peer groups. *Developmental Psychology, 31*, 897-906.

Kandel, D. B. (1978a). Homophily, selection, and socialization in adolescent friendships. *American Journal of Sociology, 84*, 427-436.

Kandel, D. B. (1978b). Similarity in real-life adolescent friendship pairs. *Journal of Personality and Social Psychology, 36*, 306-312.

Kashy, D. A., & Kenny, D. A. (2000). The analysis of data from dyads and groups. In H. Reis & C. Judd (Eds.), *Handbook of research methods in social and personality psychology*. New York: Cambridge University Press.

Kenny, D. A., Kashy, D. A., & Cook, W. L. (2006). *Dyadic data analysis*. New York: Guilford Press.

Kenny, D. A., & La Voie, L. (1985). Separating individual and group effects. *Journal of Personality and Social Psychology, 48*, 339-348.

Kupersmidt, J. B., DeRosier, M. E., & Patterson, C. P. (1995). Similarity as the basis for children's friendships: The roles of sociometric status, aggressive and withdrawn behavior, academic achievement and demographic characteristics. *Journal of Social and Personal Relationships, 12*, 439-452.

Nangle, D. W., Erdley, C. A., Zeff, K. R., Stanchfield, L. L., & Gold, J. A. (2004). Opposites do not attract: Social status and behavioral style concordances and discordances among children and the peers who like or dislike them. *Journal of Abnormal Child Psychology, 32*, 425-434.

Olsen, J. A., & Kenny, D. A. (2006). Structural equation modeling with interchangeable dyads. *Psychological Methods, 11*, 127-141.

Olweus, D. (1979). Stability of aggressive reaction patterns in males: A review. *Psychological Bulletin, 86*, 852-875.

Poulin, F., Cillessen, A. H. N., Hubbard, J. A., Coie, J. D., Dodge, K. A., & Schwartz, D. (1997). Children's friends and behavioral similarity on two social contexts. *Social Development, 6*, 224-236.

Walls, T. A., & Little, T. D. (2005). Relations among personal agency, motivation, and school adjustment in early adolescence. *Journal of Educational Psychology, 97*, 23-31.

Woody, E., & Sadler, P. (2005). Structural equation models for interchangeable dyads: Being the same makes a difference. *Psychological Methods, 10*, 139-158.

CHAPTER TEN

Variance Component Analysis of Generalized and Dyadic Peer Perceptions in Adolescence

Thomas E. Malloy

Rhode Island College

Antonius H. N. Cillessen

University of Connecticut

Peer perception in childhood and adolescence has received considerable research attention during the past 40 years (Dubin & Dubin, 1965; Livesley & Bromley, 1973; Selman, 1980; Shantz, 1983; Yarrow & Campbell, 1963). Guided initially by Piagetian theory (Inhelder & Piaget, 1964), social stimuli were thought to be equivalent to objects; processes that explained cognition about objects were assumed to operate similarly in social cognition. A second wave of research on peer perception then ensued that emphasized the interpersonal dyadic context (Dornbusch, Hastorf, Richardson, Muzzy, & Vreeland, 1965; Livesley & Bromley, 1973). This theoretical advancement led to the use of new research designs and analytic methods developed specifically for dyadic research (Malloy, Sugarman, Montvilo, & Ben-Zeev, 1995; Malloy, Yarlas, Montvilo, & Sugarman, 1996). We extend this work in a study of generalized and dyadic perceptual phenomena in adolescence; the former are general processes that involve multiple peers, whereas the latter involve specific dyads.

Components of Adolescents' Peer Perceptions

Perceiver and target effects. A milestone in peer perception research was the simultaneous focus on the perceiver that forms an impression and the target of judgment (Dornbusch et al., 1965; Livesley & Bromley, 1973). This focus distinguished object perception, which is unidirectional, from interpersonal perception, which is dyadic and reciprocal. Livesley and Bromley (1973) identified multiple components of interpersonal perceptions that included the "objective stimulus characteristics" of the target, features of the target to which the perceiver attends, perceiver characteristics that affect interpretation of target information, and the unique relationship between the perceiver and the target. Shantz (1983) concluded "What one perceives in the social word is best conceived as a joint function of the characteristics ... of the perceiver and the characteristics of the perceived" (p. 505). Moreover, the perceiver judges the target and the target judges the perceiver; peer perception is reciprocal.

Dyadic effects. Further theoretical analysis of the dyadic context was accomplished in Selman's (1980) 5-stage developmental model of interpersonal understanding. In Stage 0 (roughly 3 to 6 years), interpersonal understanding is egocentric and without a clear differentiation of the child's own and another person's perspective. In Stage 1 (roughly 6 to 8 years), another person's perspective is recognized but not clearly understood. In Stage 2 (roughly 8 to 10 years), children can take the perspective of someone else and understand that the other can take their own perspective. Here for the first time, interpersonal understanding is reciprocal rather than unidirectional. In Stage 3 (roughly 10 to 12 years), interpersonal understanding is characterized by mutual perspective taking. Selman theorized that the early adolescent can "abstractly step outside an interpersonal interaction and simultaneously and mutually coordinate and consider the perspectives (and their interactions) of self and other(s)" (p. 39). Early adolescents can understand that they are both a perceiver and a target of perception and that participants in a social interaction have a perspective and a meta-perspective (i.e., knowledge of another's perspective on the self). Finally, in the stage of societal perspective taking (Stage 4, 12 to 15 years and older), adolescents understand the perspective of the "generalized other." Interestingly, adolescents' interpersonal understanding shows more complexity when reasoning about peers than about adults (Selman, Beardslee, Schultz, Krupa, & Podorefsky, 1986), suggesting that interpersonal understanding and perception in the peer context is unique.

Generalized Perceiver and Target Effects in Peer Perceptions

The theoretical analyses of Dornbusch et al. (1965), Livesley and Bromley (1973), and Selman (1980) focused attention on perceiver, target, and perceiver-target relationship effects in peer perceptions. The Dornbusch et al. (1965) study of perceiver and target effects considered children's verbal descriptions of peers. Results indicated that "the most powerful influence on interpersonal description is the manner in which the perceiver structures his interpersonal world" (p. 440), whereas the target of judgment had a much weaker effect.

Malloy et al. (1995) conducted a longitudinal study of children's and preadolescents' interpersonal perceptions with rating scales rather than verbal descriptions. In contrast to Dornbusch et al. (1965), Malloy and colleagues found that target effects (i.e., the effects of the characteristics of the perceived) were greater than perceiver effects, and that the ratio of target effects to perceiver effects increased with development. Target effects were highly consistent over time: Targets were perceived similarly (i.e., consensually) by different groups of perceivers who made judgments one year apart, over the course of three years. Perceiver effects were much less consistent over time.

Research has also assessed the accuracy of peer perceptions in childhood and preadolescence (Malloy et al., 1996). To be accurate, peer judgments must show an association with a validity criterion, such as teacher ratings or standardized test scores. Indeed, in this study peer perceptions on multiple dimensions (cognitive, behavioral, status, affect, and attractiveness) were reliably related to teacher judgments. Moreover, judgments of cognitive abilities (math and reading) were strongly related to standardized test scores. Thus, peer perceptions were not only consensual, but also accurate.

Meta-accuracy, defined as the accurate awareness of others' judgments of one self, has been addressed as well. Malloy, Albright, and Scarpatti (2007) examined participants' predictions of their peers' judgments of themselves (i.e., meta-perception) on cognitive, behavioral, and status dimensions and found that children and preadolescents showed accurate awareness of others' judgments of themselves. Meta-accuracy was statistically reliable at all grade levels, but somewhat greater in later grades (5 and 6). A structural equation model of the process of achieving accurate meta-perception showed that self, peer, and teacher perceptions of academic ability were associated with actual academic ability, but that only self-perceptions were associated with meta-perceptions. This finding replicated what was found with adults (Kenny, 1994). Meta-perceptions were accurate because academic ability was associated with others' perceptions and self-perceptions; the self-perceptions, in turn, determined the predictions of others' judgments. Consequently, predictions of others' judgments were accurate.

Dyadic Effects in Peer Perceptions

When peer perception is affected uniquely by a specific partner the phenomenon is dyadic. Individual and dyadic processes operate simultaneously, although little attention has been directed to dyadic phenomena in peer perception. One exception is research that has focused explicitly on the dyadic nature of aggression in boys. Recognizing that "it takes two to fight," studies have focused on mutually aggressive dyads rather than aggressive individuals only (Coie et al., 1999; Dodge, Price, Coie, & Christopoulos, 1997). Dyadic effects accounted for as much variance in aggression as either actor or partner effects. In hostile dyads, members were biased in their interpretations of verbalizations and gestures by the other indicating that social-cognitive processes leading to aggression were also dyadic. In a further test of the hypothesis that social-cognitive processes and aggression are related at the dyadic level, Hubbard, Dodge, Cillessen, Coie, and Schwartz (2001) confirmed that social cognitions varied reliably across dyadic relationships and that peers develop dyadic mental representations of each other.

Children's awareness of others' liking of them also appears to be dyadic (Cillessen & Bellmore, 1999). In a study of 644 fourth-graders, peers indicated whom they liked most and least, and who they thought liked them the most and the least. Results showed that accuracy for affect was dyadic; peers knew specifically who liked them the most and the least.

Variance Component Analysis of Individual and Dyadic Effects

Research on peer perception is enhanced by a simultaneous focus on individual and dyadic processes that can be addressed using unique designs and a general analytic approach called *variance component analysis* (Kenny, West, Malloy, & Albright, 2006). Imagine a dyad in which adolescent A rates adolescent B a 9 on a 10-point scale ranging from "un-cool" (1) to "cool" (10). This rating of 9 is composed of effects due to the perceiver (A), the target (B), and the perceiver's unique reaction to target B (compared with A's judgment of C). However, if the study is designed so that A only rates B and B only rates A, the estimation of these separate effects is impossible. Instead, a design is required in which peers' rate and are rated by multiple others (Malloy & Albright, 2001). Two such designs were used in this study: the *round-robin* design, in which all members of a group rate each other, and the *asymmetric block* design, in which the members of one group rate the members of another group. The variance components in these data can be calculated using the Social Relations Model (Kenny, 1994) that produces estimates of perceiver and target effects, as well as dyadic relationship effects.

The separate estimation of these effects is an important advancement of the social relations analysis as it eliminates the statistical confounding and conceptual confusion of effects that results when dyadic data are not decomposed (Gage & Cronbach, 1955; Kenny, Kashy, & Cook, 2006). A detailed presentation of the Social Relations Model can be found elsewhere (Kenny, 1994; Kenny & La Voie, 1984; Malloy & Kenny, 1986).

Hypotheses at the Individual Level of Analysis

Assimilation. Assimilation occurs when a perceiver judges multiple targets similarly. There may still be variation between perceivers, showing that perceivers differ in how they organize the same social information (Bruner, 1957). In studies of adults, about 20% of the variance in the perception of others is due to the perceiver (Kenny, 1994). Malloy et al. (1995) also found assimilation in a sample of children and preadolescents. Therefore, we anticipated evidence of assimilation in adolescents' peer perceptions as well (hypothesis 1). The evidence for assimilation is even greater in meta-perceptions; about 55% of the variance in meta-perceptions is due to the perceiver (Kenny, 1994). Therefore, we expected that adolescents' meta-perceptions would be strongly determined by perceiver-based variance (hypothesis 2).

Consensus. Consensus occurs when perceivers agree in their judgments of targets. In their study with children in Grades 1 through 6, Malloy et al. (1995) found consistently high consensus in children's judgments of their peers' classroom conduct across grades. Consensus for ratings of cognitive abilities (reading and math) increased from Grade 1 to Grade 2 and then reached substantial levels (40-50% of the variance). Consensus in judgments of physical ability and peer status (popularity and number of friends) increased linearly with grade to about 50% of the variance by Grade 6. Consensus in judgments of attractiveness increased in preadolescence to 43% of the variance in Grade 6 (Malloy et al., 1995). The interpersonal goals that are most salient at a developmental level determine the dimensions on which peers reach consensus at that level. In the current study, peers rated each other's personalities and peer status—dimensions that are highly relevant to the high school population. Therefore, we predicted reliable consensus in these perceptions, and particularly for the judgments of peer status (hypothesis 3).

Effects of sex on assimilation and consensus. Although interactions and relationships with other-sex peers increase in adolescence, there is still more shared time and familiarity with same-sex peers (Maccoby, 1988). Indeed, Card, Hodges, Little, and Hawley (2005) found that early adolescents were more likely to name same-sex peers than cross-sex peers for both positive and negative traits. From an intergroup processes perspective, same-sex peers may be seen as the in-group whereas other-sex peers are the out-group. Research has documented (e.g., Linville, Fischer, & Salovey, 1989; Park & Rothbart, 1982) that judgments of in-group members show less stereotyping (i.e., heterogeneity) than judgments of out-group members, that show more stereotyping (i.e., homogeneity). In our study, perceiver and target effects were estimated within and between sexes. We expected in-group judgments to show greater consensus (target variance) and less assimilation (perceiver variance) than out-group judgments (hypothesis 4).

Mean levels of self and peer perceptions. People in general judge themselves more positively on personality factors than they judge others (Kenny, 1994). One exception to this self-enhancement bias involves Factor IV (emotional stability) of the Big Five. People believe that others are, on average, more emotionally adjusted than they themselves are. This judgement difference may occur because people have direct access to their own emotional state but not to the emotional state of others, and sharing of emotional difficulties is restricted to a few select others. Therefore, we anticipated self-enhancement for trait judgments, except for Factor IV, where others would be judged more positively than the self (hypothesis 5).

Association of self and peer perception. In addition to addressing the levels of self- and peer-perceptions, we examined the association between them. There has been much interest in this association (cf. L. Ross, Greene, & House, 1977), ever since Cronbach (1955) warned that social perception is characterized by *assumed similarity*—the phenomenon that individuals assume that others are like them. There is clear evidence for assumed similarity in Big Five judgments (Kenny, 1994), with the greatest association between perceptions of self and others found for Factor II (agreeableness). Consequently, we anticipated assumed similarity for adolescents' peer judgments of personality factors (hypothesis 6).

In adolescence, the status hierarchy of the peer group and one's position in it are highly salient. Explicit cues provide objective information about the status of self and others (e.g., one is or is not a varsity athlete or a national merit finalist). Therefore, we expected weaker assumed similarity for judgments on dimensions of peer status than for personality traits (hypothesis 6a).

We also reasoned that self-knowledge is more relevant for judgments of same-sex peers than other-sex peers and that this would impact assumed similarity. Because adolescents are more similar to their same-sex peers and spend more time with them, we expected that assumed similarity would be stronger for same-sex peers than for other-sex peers (hypothesis 6b).

Self and other agreement. Do adolescents judge themselves as their peers judge them? Symbolic interactionism (Mead, 1934) predicts that beliefs about others' judgments of oneself affect one's self-perceptions. The reverse causal ordering has also been presented, that is, people actively try to make others perceive them as they see themselves (Swann, 1990). A third possibility is that behavior affects the self and others simultaneously (Bem, 1967; Felson, 1981). Malloy et al. (2007) found that judgments of academic ability by self, peers, and teachers were reliably related to standardized measures of academic ability. Among well-acquainted college students, self–other agreement was substantial with correlations for Big Five factors ranging from .39 to .70 for factors III (conscientiousness) and I (extroversion), respectively (Kenny, 1994). These theoretical perspectives and empirical findings led to the prediction that self–other agreement should be evident in adolescents' perceptions of their peers (hypothesis 7). Because more social interaction occurs with same-sex peers, we predicted that self–other agreement would be greater for same-sex than for other-sex peers (hypothesis 7a).

Generalized meta-accuracy. Abundant evidence shows that people (including children) know accurately how others in general judge them (Kenny, 1994; Kenny & DePaulo, 1993; Malloy et al., 2007). Similarly, adolescents know how their parents perceive them (Cook & Douglas, 1998). Individuals' predictions of how others judge them are strongly associated with their self-perceptions and are highly stable across multiple peers. Because people believe that others perceive them as they see themselves, generalized meta-accuracy is achieved when self and others are similarly affected by one's behavior (Albright & Malloy, 1999). Consequently, we anticipated generalized meta-accuracy among adolescents (hypothesis 8). Furthermore, we anticipated that generalized meta-accuracy would be higher for same-sex than for other-sex peers (hypothesis 8a), again due to actual similarity and greater association.

Hypotheses at the Dyadic Level of Analysis

Uniqueness. To the extent that peers make judgments of one another that differ from generalized perceiver and target effects, there is uniqueness in judgment. Selman's (1980) theory predicts that adolescent interpersonal judgments should be increasingly dyadic. Livesley and Bromley (1973) made a similar prediction. Moreover, judgments of aggressive intent are unique within dyads and a determinant of dyadic aggression (Coie et al., 1999) and social cognition (Hubbard et al., 2001).

People show an egocentric bias by overestimating the attention that others pay to their actions and appearance (Gilovich et al., 2000) and the salience of their presence and absence in a group (Savitsky et al., 2003). This over-estimation is termed the *spotlight bias*. Similarly, Elkind (1967) argued that adolescents are keenly attuned to the views of others and believe they are the constant focus of others' attention (i.e., the *imaginary audience*). One's position relative to others in the status hierarchy is highly salient in adolescence because it determines with whom one can form a friendship or romantic relationship (Dornbusch et al., 1981). If two peers are seen as "cool" in the peer group and both are aware of their status, their interpersonal judgments should be characterized by dyadic reciprocity. Person 1 might reason, "I'm cool and so are you, and I know that you think I'm cool." Person 2 will reason similarly, thereby producing dyadic reciprocity of both perception and meta-perception. A similar process should operate among those with lower status. Thus, although dyadic reciprocity in trait perception among adults is essentially zero (Kenny, 1994), the special nature of adolescent social cognition (Selman et al., 1986) and the salience of status for relationship formation (Dornbusch et al., 1981) led us to predict dyadic reciprocity in perception (hypothesis 9) and meta-perception (hypothesis 9a).

If adolescents are highly attentive to and actively seek information regarding others' judgments of them, there should also be evidence of dyadic meta-accuracy. Not only should adolescents be accurately aware of how others judge them in general (see hypothesis 8), they should also be accurately aware of how specific others judge them (hypothesis 10), particularly same-sex peers (hypothesis 10a) who are their competitors in the peer system.

METHOD

Participants

Participants were 293 high-school students (155 females, 138 males) in Grades 9 ($n = 78$), 10 ($n = 77$), 11 ($n = 81$), and 12 ($n = 57$) at a private coeducational institution in Rhode Island. Participants were informed that the study focused on peer perceptions of high school students. Parental and student consent was obtained for all participants.

Procedures and Measures

Mixed-sex groups were formed randomly within homerooms, with the constraint that each group had at least four members. A total of 47 groups were formed of between four and nine persons. There were 3 groups of 4, 11 of 5, 16 of 6, 8 of 7, 7 of 8, and 2 of 9 persons. Because the groups of four did not permit estimation of variance components by sex, they did not contribute to those analyses.

Peer perceptions were measured using 10 bipolar rating scales with scores ranging from 1 to 7. Five scales measured the Big Five personality factors. The bipolar adjectives for these scales were unsociable–sociable (Factor I), irritable–good natured (Factor II), irresponsible–responsible (Factor III), anxious–calm (Factor IV), and unintelligent–intelligent (Factor V). The remaining five scales measured constructs relevant to social status; the bipolar adjectives for these scales (1 through 7) were unattractive–attractive, unpopular–popular, unathletic–athletic, uninvolved–involved, and uncool–cool. *Peer perceptions* were obtained by asking participants to rate each group member on all 10 scales. *Self-perceptions* were measured by asking students to rate themselves on the same scales. *Meta-perceptions* were measured by asking students to predict how the group members rated them on each of the 10 dimensions. We also recorded grade (9–12) and academic ability level (1 = highest, 4 = lowest) based on school records.

Research Designs and Social Relations Analyses

Each group formed a round-robin in which all members of the group rated all other group members and themselves. Consider an 8-person group of four males (A–D) and four females (E–H). As seen in Table 10.1, each person is both a perceiver and a target. Embedded within the overall round-robin design (for groups of size 6 or greater) were two other designs: the asymmetric block design and the within-sex round-robins. The asymmetric block design had two subgroups (males and females) and each subgroup rated all members of the other subgroup. In Table 10.1, measurements labeled x and y form the data of the asymmetric block. The within-sex round-robins are restricted to peers of one's own sex.

The variances and covariances of the components of the Social Relations Model can be estimated with the round-robin and asymmetric block designs (Malloy & Albright, 2001). The components have different meaning in each design. For a dyad of persons i and j in a randomly formed round-robin, a perception on dimension X yielding X_{ij} can be represented by

$$X_{ij} = \mu + \alpha_i + \beta_j + \gamma_{ij} + \varepsilon \tag{1}$$

where α_i is the consistency of i's responses to multiple partners including j, β_j is the consistency of j's effect on responses elicited from multiple partners, and γ_{ij} is i's unique response to j after controlling for α_i and β_j. The constant μ is the average of intergroup responses, and ε is random error. Terms of the

TABLE 10.1
Round-Robin Design With Symmetric and Asymmetric Blocks

		Male Targets				Female Targets			
		A	**B**	**C**	**D**	**E**	**F**	**G**	**H**
	A	s	m	m	m	x	x	x	x
Male Perceivers	**B**	m	s	m	m	x	x	x	x
	C	m	m	s	m	x	x	x	x
	D	m	m	m	s	x	x	x	x
	E	y	y	y	y	s	f	f	f
Female Perceivers	**F**	y	y	y	y	f	s	f	f
	G	y	y	y	y	f	f	s	f
	H	y	y	y	y	f	f	f	s

Note. m: male's judgment of male; f: female's judgment of female; x: male's judgment of female; y: female's judgment of male; s: self-rating.

model are assumed to be normally distributed random variables. Likewise, j's response to i is represented by

$$X_{ji} = \mu + \alpha_j + \beta_i + \gamma_{ji} + \varepsilon \qquad (2)$$

The variances of the components (α, β, and γ) quantify the consistency of perceptions made (perceiver variance), the consistency of perceptions elicited (target variance), and unique perceptions of specific partners (uniqueness). The variance components are random effects and generalize to people in general because the groups were formed randomly. The null hypothesis tested is that a variance component equals zero.

In an asymmetric block design, members of one subgroup respond to members of another subgroup. The interpretation of the variance components differs from the round-robin. In the current study the intergroup responses were reciprocal, but the model can also be applied if they are unidirectional (Malloy & Albright, 2001). Consider a dyad composed of male M and female F. The response of M to F on dimension X (X_{mf}) is represented by Equation 3:

$$X_{mf} = \mu + \alpha_m + \beta_f + \gamma_{mf} + \varepsilon \qquad (3)$$

where μ is the average rating of females by males on dimension X, α_m is a measure of the consistency of M's perceptions of different females (perceiver effect), β_f is the consistency of perceptions of F by multiple males (target effect), γ_{mf} is the unique response of M to F (relationship effect), and ε is the random error component. Likewise, the response of F to M (X_{fm}) is represented by Equation 4:

$$X_{fm} = \mu + \alpha_f + \beta_m + \gamma_{fm} + \varepsilon \qquad (4)$$

where the subscripts now indicate the perceiver effect for F judging males, the consistency of perceptions of M by multiple females, and the unique response of F to M. The grand mean μ is the average rating of males by females.

The individual level effects (α and β) are termed *perceiver* and *target* while the dyadic effect (γ) is termed *relationship*. The perceiver effect is the tendency for a perceiver to judge targets similarly on a dimension when they in fact vary, and is an "eye of the beholder" effect. The target effect measures agreement among multiple judges when rating a common target. The relationship effect is a specific judge's reaction to a specific target after controlling for their respective perceiver and target effects. In the random round-robin these effects generalize to people in general, whereas in the asymmetric block design the effects are group specific.

Perceiver variance quantifies a phenomenon termed *assimilation*. If this variance component is different from zero, perceivers vary in their judgments of the same set of peers, and show consistency across targets. Target variance quantifies a phenomenon termed *consensus*; that is, multiple peers judge other peers similarly. Relationship variance quantifies a phenomenon termed *uniqueness*, which occurs when there is reliable variation in judgments of specific targets by specific perceivers. Detailed discussions of the SRM and the perceptual phenomena quantified by the model's parameters are available (Kenny, 1994; Kenny, Kashy, & Cook, 2006; Kenny & La Voie, 1984; Malloy & Albright, 1990; Malloy & Kenny, 1986).

RESULTS

Perception of Peers at the Individual Level of Analysis

Table 10.2 includes the standardized perceiver and target variances for each variable. These are the proportions of the total variance for each variable that are due to each source and add up to 1 in each row. The results are illustrated by the findings for sociability. The relative perceiver and target variances for this trait were .16 and .35, respectively, indicating that 16%

of the total variance in peer judgments of sociability was due to perceiver effects and 35% was due to target effects. Both variance components were reliably different from zero, indicating both assimilation and consensus in peer perceptions of sociability. Relationship and error accounted for the remaining 49% of the variance.

A 4 (grade) x 4 (Academic Ability Level) MANOVA was run on the 10 perceiver variance components and on the 10 target variance components. Group was the unit of analysis and the dependent measure was the unstandardized (not the standardized) variance component for each group. There were no reliable differences ($p > .05$) due to grade, ability level, or their interaction in the perceiver or target variances for the personality or social status variables.

Assimilation. As predicted, statistically reliable ($p < .05$) assimilation was observed for all 10 dimensions. Relative perceiver variances ranged from .15 (popular) to .30 (involved) with a median of .21. Adolescents' perceptions of their peers were significantly affected by stable differences between perceivers when judging the same classmates, providing support for hypothesis 1. There was also statistically reliable assimilation in meta-perceptions for all variables. Perceiver variances ranged from .50 (sociability) to .79 (athletic) with a median of .65. Adolescents predicted that multiple peers judged them similarly, thereby supporting hypothesis 2. Inspection of the variances by variable type suggests that perceiver variance in meta-perceptions may be greater for status (median .70) than for personality variables (median .58).

Consensus. We predicted (hypothesis 3) and found reliable consensus on the 10 dimensions with greater consensus for social status dimensions than for personality traits. Target variances ranged from .10 (good-natured) to .35 (sociability) with a median of .17 for the traits, and from .26 (cool) to .45 (popular) with a median of .32 for the status variables (see Table 10.2). Notice in Table 10.2 that no reliable consensus (target variance) was found for meta-perceptions.

Effects of perceiver and target sex. We anticipated greater consensus and less assimilation for same-sex than for other-sex judgments. To test this prediction, planned contrasts were run separately for the personality and social status variables. The variance components from each group are the dependent measures in this analysis. There were no reliable differences ($p > .05$) due to sex of peer (same vs. other) in the perceiver variances of personality variables for males, $t_{(43)} = .69$, or females, $t_{(43)} = .44$. The same was true for the status variables, with $t_{(43)} = .52$ for males and $t_{(43)} = .11$ for females. However, for target variances, among both males, $t_{(43)} = 2.07$, $p = .04$, and females, $t_{(43)} = 3.00$, $p = .004$, there was reliably greater consensus when judging the personality traits of same-sex peers than other-sex peers. For

TABLE 10.2
Relative Perceiver, Target, and Uniqueness/Error Variance:
Interpersonal Perceptions and Meta-Perceptions for Males and Females Combined

	Interpersonal Perceptions		
Variable	Perceiver	Target	Uniqueness/Error
Sociability	.16*	.35*	.49
Good-natured	.21*	.10*	.69
Responsible	.25*	.17*	.58
Calm	.18*	.12*	.69
Intelligent	.27*	.18*	.55
Attractive	.22*	.32*	.46
Popular	.15*	.45*	.40
Athletic	.16*	.44*	.40
Involved	.30*	.28*	.42
Cool	.21*	.26*	.53
	Meta-Perceptions		
Variable	Perceiver	Target	Uniqueness/Error
Sociability	.50*	.00	.50
Good-natured	.53*	.01	.46
Responsible	.63*	.00	.37
Calm	.67*	.00	.33
Intelligent	.58*	.00	.42
Attractive	.70*	.00	.30
Popular	.69*	.01	.30
Athletic	.79*	.00	.21
Involved	.75*	.00	.25
Cool	.62*	.00	.38

Note. $*p < .05$, $df = 46$ (number of groups -1).

TABLE 10.3
Effects of Perceiver and Target Sex on Assimilation and Consensus

		Assimilation Target Sex		Consensus Target Sex	
		Male	Female	Male	Female
Perceiver Sex	Male	.23	.30	.30	.24
	Female	.31	.28	.27	.35

Note. Entries are mean relative perceiver and target variance components.

the status variables, reliable differences in target variance were not observed for males, $t_{(43)} = .24$, $p = .81$, or females, $t_{(43)} = 1.82$, $p = .08$. These results partially supported hypothesis 4. Both males and females demonstrated greater consensus in judgments of same-sex peers than other-sex peers, but assimilation did not vary by the sex of peers (Table 10.3).

Self and Peer Perceptions

Mean levels of self and peer perceptions. We expected that self-perceptions would be greater than peer perceptions except for judgments of emotional adjustment where the reverse was predicted (hypothesis 5). Results were generally consistent with this prediction (see Table 10.4). For 9 of the 10 variables the means for self-ratings were reliably greater than the means for peer ratings. Cohen's effect size estimator d ranged from 1.84 (Factor III, responsibility) to 6.93 (Factor II, good-natured) with a mean d of 2.71 for these nine variables. On average, self-perceptions were about $2^{3}/_{4}$ standard deviations higher than peer perceptions. The mean self and peer ratings for the variable calm, an indicator of Factor IV, were 4.81 and 4.96, respectively. The difference was in the direction predicted but not significant, $t_{(46)} = -1.91$, $p > .05$, $d = -.55$.

The relationship of self and peer perceptions. We predicted and found that self and peer perceptions of Big Five traits were characterized by a pattern of assumed similarity (hypothesis 6), estimated by correlating self-ratings with perceiver effects for each dimension. For the traits, these correlations ranged from .17 (Factor IV, calm) to .39 (Factor II, good-natured) with a median of .20. All estimates were statistically reliable ($p < .05$). Consistent with hypothesis 6a, weaker assumed similarity correlations were found for judgments of social status, ranging from .05 (popularity) to .29 (involvement

TABLE 10.4
Means for Self and Peer Perceptions: Males and Females Combined

Variable	Self	Peer	t
Sociability	5.5836	4.8506	11.39*
Good-natured	5.7406	5.1722	7.00*
Responsible	5.6451	5.1203	6.40*
Calm	4.8123	4.9606	-1.91
Intelligent	5.7713	5.3414	7.09*
Attractive	4.9898	4.2578	8.04*
Popular	5.0546	4.5200	9.00*
Athletic	5.0956	4.0136	10.65*
Involved	4.8259	4.0847	7.74*
Cool	5.3823	4.5656	11.13*

Note.*$p < .05$, $df = 46$.

in school activities) with a median correlation of .10. Only one of the five estimates was reliably different from zero (see Table 10.5). Hypothesis 6b predicted moderation of assumed similarity as a function of perceiver and target sex, and results showed more assumed similarity in same-sex dyads (MM, $r= .63$, $p = .05$, and FF, $r = .78$, $p = .007$) than in other-sex dyads (MF, $r = .16$, $p = .67$, and FM, $r = .40$, $p = .25$).

Self and other agreement. We anticipated that adolescents' self-perceptions would be reliably related to how they are judged by their peers (hypothesis 7). Self and other agreement was estimated by correlating self-ratings on a trait with the target effect derived from judgments on that trait by multiple peers. Results in Table 10.6 showed that all 10 estimates of self and other agreement were statistically reliable, ranging from $r = .22$ (intelligent) to $r = .62$ (athletic), with a median $r = .35$. Substantial self–other agreement was observed. We also predicted greater self–other agreement for same-sex than other-sex peers (hypothesis 7a). Median correlations across traits were .32 and .39 for male and female same-sex dyads, respectively, and were reliably different from zero ($p < .05$), whereas self and other agreement in other-sex dyads did not differ from zero (r of .17 and .19 for MF and FM dyads, respectively, $p > .05$). Only same-sex peers were judged as similar to the self.

TABLE 10.5
Correlations of Self-Ratings With Perceiver Effects Based on
Ratings of Multiple Peers

Variable	Combined (df = 245)	MM (df = 85)	FF (df = 85)	MF (df = 90)	FM (df = 107)
Sociability	.21*	.25*	.20*	-.00	.36*
Good-natured	.39*	.60*	.22*	.16*	.14
Responsible	.20*	.27*	.17	.07	-.04
Calm	.17*	.11	.44*	-.01	.11
Intelligent	.19*	.24*	.33*	.12	.07
Attractive	.08	.06	.22*	-.03	.01
Popular	.05	.48*	-.08	-.01	.17
Athletic	.10	.19	-.14	.16*	-.09
Involved	.29*	.52*	.07	.15	.11
Cool	.12	.30*	.27*	.06	.05

Note. * $p < .05$, $df = (N - G - 1 \text{ or } 293 - 47 - 1) = 245$ for the combined data.

TABLE 10.6
Correlations of Self-Ratings With Target Effects
Based on Ratings of Multiple Peers

Variable	Combined	MM	FF	MF	FM
Sociability	.57*	.44*	.30*	.30*	.33*
Good-natured	.34*	.14	.08	.08	.10
Responsible	.32*	.14	.51*	.10	.22*
Calm	.29*	.19	.66*	-.04	.04
Intelligent	.22*	-.19	.48*	.10	.14
Attractive	.25*	.40*	.11	.23*	.12
Popular	.53*	.52*	.19	.43*	.21*
Athletic	.62*	.56*	.50*	.39*	.28*
Involved	.53*	.53*	.49*	.26*	.21
Cool	.35*	.24*	-.06	.11	.16

Note. * $p < .05$.

TABLE 10.7
Generalized Meta-accuracy

Variable	Combined	MM	FF	MF	FM
Sociability	.51*	.50*	.32*	.33*	.34*
Good-natured	.40*	.35*	.29*	-.02	.22*
Responsible	.54*	.35*	.61*	.45*	.31*
Calm	.20	.12	.70*	-.05	.03
Intelligent	.53*	.36*	.47*	.24*	.41*
Attractive	.46*	.46*	.17	.39*	.32*
Popular	.61*	.68*	.37*	.51*	.45*
Athletic	.72*	.66*	.56*	.58*	.45*
Involved	.57*	.47*	.59*	.37*	.25*
Cool	.54*	.52*	.20*	.54*	.32*

Note. $* p < .05$.

Generalized meta-accuracy. Participants' awareness of how they were seen by others in general was estimated by correlating the perceiver effect of meta-perceptions with the target effect of peer perceptions. As predicted (hypothesis 8), meta-accuracy at the individual level was statistically reliable for 9 of the 10 dimensions (see Table 10.7). The statistically reliable correlations ranged from $r = .40$ (good-natured) to $r = .72$ (athletic), with a median r of .54. Adolescents knew how peers perceived their traits, but did not accurately predict others' judgments of their emotional stability (calm; $r = .20$, $p > .05$). Hypothesis 8a that generalized meta-accuracy would be greater for same-sex than other-sex peers was not confirmed. Median generalized meta-accuracy correlations across traits were .47, .42, .38, and .32 for the MM, FF, MF, and FM combinations, respectively. These median correlations were all different from zero ($p < .05$).

Generalized reciprocity. Generalized reciprocity is the association between how one perceives others in general and how one is generally perceived by others. Seven of the ten generalized reciprocity correlations were negative (see Table 10.8), and two were statistically reliable (popular, $r = -.34$, and athletic, $r = -.23$). The remaining reliable estimate was positive (Factor II, good-natured, $r = .30$). Adolescents who were judged as popular by others (i.e., their target effect on this variable was high) tended to judge others as unpopular (i.e., their perceiver effect was low). Thus, for status, generalized reciprocity was characterized by contrast.

TABLE 10.8
Generalized Reciprocity:
Correlations Between Perceiver and Target Effect Estimates

Variable	Combined	MM	FF	MF	FM
Sociability	-.18	.00	.07	-.23*	.16
Good-natured	.30*	.26	.43*	.12	.11
Responsible	.01	.32	.05	.14	-.07
Calm	-.13	.30	-.04	.05	.06
Intelligent	.03	.35	.04	.15	-.02
Attractive	-.02	.14	-.22	-.09	.04
Popular	-.34*	-.59*	-.72*	-.19	-.09
Athletic	-.23*	-.40*	-.23	.02	-.10
Involved	-.03	.13	-.16	.22*	-.11
Cool	-.13	.02	-.17	-.07	.16

Note. $* p < .05$.

Peer Perception at the Dyadic Level

Dyadic reciprocity of perception and meta-perception. Because adolescents are sensitive to their position in the status hierarchy and to how others see them, we anticipated dyadic reciprocity for peer perceptions and meta-perceptions. Dyadic reciprocity may be positive or negative, indicating either similarity or contrast of unique judgments. All dyadic reciprocity correlations in the total sample were positive, ranging from .04 (popularity) to .21 (cool). Seven of the 10 dyadic reciprocity correlations were statistically reliable, with a median r of .15 (see Table 10.9). For example, the dyadic reciprocity correlation for cool was .21 ($p < .05$), showing that judgments of coolness were reciprocal within specific dyads. In support of hypothesis 9, adolescents' perceptions were characterized by dyadic reciprocity across a broad range of dimensions, indicating similarity of unique judgments at the dyadic level. Dyadic meta-perceptions were also characterized by positive reciprocity (hypothesis 9a). Six of the ten reciprocity correlations in the total sample were reliable, ranging from .17 (popularity) to .31 (sociability). The remaining estimates ranged from .02 to .08. Positive reciprocity was greater within sex (particularly among females where 4 of 10 dyadic reciprocity coefficients were

TABLE 10.9
Dyadic Reciprocity for Interpersonal Perceptions and Meta-Perceptions

	Interpersonal Perceptions			
Variable	Combined	Across Sex	MM	FF
Sociability	.15*	.29	.11	-.05
Good-natured	.19*	.31*	.15	.38
Responsible	.09	-.11	-.06	.07
Calm	.09	.14	.16	.03
Intelligent	.15*	.05	.04	-.04
Attractive	.14*	.18	.03	.33*
Popular	.04	.18	.07	.25
Athletic	.15*	.16	.26	-.04
Involved	.18*	.05	.05	.32*
Cool	.21*	.26	.10	.45
	Meta-Perceptions			
Variable	Combined	Across Sex	MM	FF
Sociability	.31*	.16	.13	.65*
Good-natured	.27*	.15	.30*	.47*
Responsible	.15*	.18	.07	.20
Calm	.02	.02	-.15	-.02
Intelligent	.07	.23	.02	.20
Attractive	.10*	.14	.14	.25
Popular	.17*	.09	.26	.45*
Athletic	.08	-.04	.17	.18
Involved	.02	-.04	.16	.19
Cool	.20*	.05	.07	.39*

Note. *p < .05, df = 46 for combined data, 15 for MM, 10 for FF (G - 1 within sex), 43 (G - 1) across sex. Entries are correlations of the uniqueness components of a variable with group as unit of analysis.

TABLE 10.10
Dyadic Meta-Accuracy: Correlations Between the Uniqueness Effects of
Meta-Perceptions and Judgments

Variable	Combined	MM	FF	MF	FM
Sociability	.21*	.07	.30*	.01	.02
Good-natured	.16*	.09	.35*	.01	.01
Responsible	.13*	.13	-.07	.00	.01
Calm	.08	-.03	.07	.01	.00
Intelligent	.07	.07	.16	.00	.01
Attractive	.11*	.24*	.32*	.00	.01
Popular	.16*	.13	.35*	.01	.00
Athletic	.17*	.23	.28*	-.01	.00
Involved	.07	.09	.14	.00	.01
Cool	.25*	.16	.42*	.02	.00

Note. $* p < .05$.

reliable) than between sex, although no predictions had been made in this regard.

Accuracy of dyadic meta-perception. We predicted that adolescents know accurately how specific peers judge their traits (hypothesis 10), especially in same-sex dyads (hypothesis 10a). Results for males and females combined (see Table 10.10) showed that 7 of the 10 dyadic meta-accuracy correlations were positive and reliably different from zero ($p < .05$). Dyadic meta-accuracy between the sexes showed no statistically reliable estimates for MF or FM dyads. Among males only one estimate was statistical reliability (attractive at $r = .24$). Among females, however, 60% of the dyadic meta-accuracy correlations were reliably different from zero, ranging from .28 (athletic) to .42 (cool). Reliable dyadic meta-accuracy was observed on two of the Big Five factors (I and II) and on 4 of the 5 status measures (attractive, popular, athletic, and cool). Support for hypothesis 10a was found only among females.

DISCUSSION

The goal of this chapter was to examine adolescents' peer perceptions at the individual and dyadic levels. The data were collected with round-robin and asymmetric block designs, and the Social Relations Model was used to simultaneously estimate a broad range of phenomena. While the social perception phenomena focused upon here have been considered theoretically in the past, this research is one of the first studies to estimate them empirically in adolescence.

Adolescents' Peer Perceptions at the Individual Level

Assimilation. Assimilation occurs when perceivers do not differentiate among a group of targets on a certain dimension on which they actually vary. Although the participants of the present study were well-acquainted peers, we saw evidence for assimilation with median perceiver variance of about .21 across 10 trait dimensions. Assimilation did not vary reliably as a function of sex of perceiver or target. Given this evidence for assimilation among well-acquainted peers, the findings by Dodge and Coie (1987) take on added significance. They showed that boys who are seen as aggressive by their peers are inclined to judge the intent of those peers as hostile. That is, aggressive boys show high assimilation by overestimating the hostility directed to them in the peer group. This perceptual process may be a precursor of actual interpersonal conflict among peers in general and among marginalized peers in particular (Dodge & Coie, 1987).

In a review of 15 studies, Kenny, 1994 found that 55% of the variance in meta-perceptions is due to the perceiver. Our estimate was 65%. Thus, adolescents believed that peers in general judged them similarly on personality and status variables. The fact that the level of assimilation was somewhat higher among the adolescents of our study than among adults may reflect a relative insensitivity to the degree of differentiation of their traits by different peers.

Consensus. Based on data from five studies that included 645 well-acquainted persons, the average level of consensus across the Big Five personality factors was .28, documenting agreement in trait judgment (Kenny, Albright, Malloy, & Kashy, 1994). Our consensus estimate across the Big Five factors in the total sample was .18, although our estimate across the status variables was higher at .35 (range .26 for cool to .45 for popular).

Why was consensus higher for social status variables than for personality variables in our study? There are two answers to this question. First, dimensions of social status such as athleticism, physical attractiveness, and even popularity are more directly visible than personality traits. Second, discrimination among peers based on status in the social hierarchy is highly relevant for adolescents, as it has implications for friendship formation, peer influence, social power, and dating. Consistent with this idea, Malloy et al. (1995) found that consensus for judgments of attractiveness and popularity increased strongly across the transition from middle childhood to early adolescence. Adolescents more than children attend to the features of others that determine their status in the peer group because of the implications it has for themselves.

There was greater consensus in trait judgments within sex than between sex, due in part to greater familiarity and differential association with same-sex peers (Linville, Fischer, & Yoon, 1996). Attention to the characteristics of same-sex peers may serve a specific developmental function in adolescence. A same-sex peer is a potential competitor for relationships with other-sex peers and, as a result, a great deal of attention may be directed to the competition in order to clearly understand one's own position within the status hierarchy. Relationships form among persons who share similarity on a broad array of dimensions (Byrne, 1971) and if one is aware of one's own standing in the same-sex group, then one can know with greater certainty which members of the other sex are the most likely partners for personal relationships.

Mean levels of self and peer perceptions. Self-enhancement, or the tendency to judge oneself more positively than others, is common. Kenny's (1994) review showed that people judge themselves more positively than others on four of the Big Five factors, except for emotional stability where they judge themselves lower. The exact same pattern was found for the adolescents in our study. In general, others do not have access to our private emotional experiences unless we share them, which typically occurs only with close friends. Similarly, while adolescents know their own anxieties, insecurities, and conflicts, they do not necessarily know those of their peers and also presume that their own personal distress is not shared widely. When sex was taken into account, we observed that females rated both female and male peers higher on Factors IV (calm) and V (intelligent) than they rated themselves. Males, however, rated themselves higher on all dimensions, suggesting an overall tendency toward greater self-enhancement compared with females.

The relationship of self-perception and peer perception. There is a long research tradition documenting the correspondence between self-perceptions and perceptions of others. Since Cronbach's (1955) discussion of *assumed similarity*, there has been sustained interest in the relationship between perceptions of self and others (see, e.g., L. Ross et al., 1977). In a review of studies with college students, Kenny (1994) found that the correlation between self-perceptions and the perceiver effect on ratings of the Big Five factors ranged from .27 for Factor I (extroversion) to .65 for Factor II (agreeableness), with a mean of about .40 across all factors. In the combined sample of this study, the correlations between self-perceptions and perceiver effects were statistically reliable for all Big Five factors, ranging from .17 for Factor IV to .39 for Factor II. The same correlations for the social status variables, however, were low, with an average of about .09, showing that self- and peer perceptions of these dimensions were independent. When broken down by sex, average assumed similarity correlations across all dimensions was .30 and .17 for MM and FF dyads, but only .07 and .09 for MF and FM dyads.

Although adolescents' peer perceptions showed assumed similarity, several caveats must be considered. First, assumed similarity is much stronger within than between sex because adolescents of the same sex are objectively more similar and also have more information about each other because they interact more. Second, assimilation is stronger for ratings of personality (Big Five) than for ratings of peer status (e.g., popularity). In a context where unambiguous information about the characteristics of peers is available, adolescents rely less on personal stereotypes and self-knowledge. One would not use self-knowledge to judge the athletic ability of an all-state athlete or the intellectual achievements of a national merit finalist because unambiguous external information is available. For less visible personality traits, however, information about the self provides a reference point that influences judgment.

Self and peer agreement in trait perception. Adolescents' judgments of a peer are reliably correlated with that peer's self-judgment (average r about .40). This finding replicates those with younger participants (Malloy et al., 1996) and is consistent with a model that posits that self–other agreement is the result when behavior affects both self and others similarly (Malloy et al., 2007). This mutual influence occurs when explicit cues in the environment offer clear information about someone's characteristics, and also explains why the strongest self and peer agreement was found for ratings of athletic abilities. More frequent associations with, and hence more information about, same-sex peers than other-sex peers also influences agreement. The average self-peer agreement was $r = .32$ in same-sex dyads versus $r = .18$ in mixed-sex dyads.

Generalized meta-accuracy. Children (Malloy et al., 2007) and adults (Kenny, 1994; Kenny & DePaulo, 1993) are accurately aware of how others generally judge their traits and abilities. Adolescents are accurately aware of their sociometric status (Ausubel, Schiff, & Gasser, 1952), and children are accurately aware of how much they are liked by peers (Cillessen & Bellmore, 1999). Children know accurately how their parents (Cook & Douglas, 1998) and teachers (Felson, 1989) judge them. Among adults, Kenny (1994) reported an average meta-accuracy of $r = .51$ across six studies. In our study, across sex and dimensions, the average meta-accuracy estimate was also $r = .51$. This finding is consistent with Selman's (1980) prediction that coordination of interpersonal perspectives increases with development. Accumulating evidence suggests that people, including 1st grade children, have the capacity to know accurately how peers judge them. Adolescents' meta-accuracy was equivalent to that for adults, but larger than children's. Awareness of peers' judgments of oneself was also stronger within sex than between sex. In adolescence, same-sex peers interact more and have more information about each other than other-sex peers (Berndt, 1982; Camarena, Sarigiani, & Petersen, 1990), resulting in greater consensus, self-peer agreement, and meta-accuracy.

Peer Perception at the Dyadic Level

Research of children's and adolescents' peer perceptions and behaviors at the dyadic level is relatively recent (e.g., Cillessen & Bellmore, 1999; Coie et al., 1999; Hubbard et al., 2001; H. S. Ross & Lollis, 1989). This research has shown that social behavior is not only consistent across partners but also dyadic; that is, unique in response to particular partners. Because behavior affects interpersonal perception (Kenny & Malloy, 1988), there should also be evidence of dyadic processes in perception. The evidence for this, however, has remained elusive.

This study included five social status measures that form one status construct. About 16% of the variance in perceptions of status and about 10% of the variance in meta-perceptions of status was due to adolescents' unique responses to specific peers. This amount is consistent with the average relationship variance for interpersonal perceptions of .20 across 10 studies with adults (Kenny, 1994). Our findings are also consistent with Coie et al.'s (1999) relative relationship variances of .16 for total aggression, .12 for proactive aggression, and .16 for reactive aggression among boys. Thus, 15 to 20% of the variance in behavior and perception is due to the unique reactions of peers to specific others. In our study, the uniqueness effect for the social status construct was larger than its assimilation estimate (.11), but weaker than its consensus (.25). These data add to the growing awareness that uniqueness in perception and its impact on behavior deserves more empirical attention (Coie et al., 1999; Hubbard et al., 2001).

Dyadic reciprocity. Reciprocity is a norm that governs social interaction (Gouldner, 1960) and interpersonal behavior is reciprocal (Kenny, Mohr, & Levesque, 2001). Although dyadic reciprocity of behavior is well documented, there is no evidence for dyadic reciprocity of perception. Based on data from 12 studies reported by Kenny (1994), the average dyadic reciprocity correlation for trait judgments was .04. We nevertheless anticipated dyadic reciprocity in adolescent's interpersonal judgments based on the spotlight bias (Gilovich et al., 2000; Savitsky et al., 2003), the special characteristics of adolescent social cognition, particularly Elkind's (1967) imaginary audience concept, and the finding by Ausubel and colleagues (1952) that adolescents are highly aware of their peer group status. In early adolescence there is heightened vigilance and attention to how one is judged by peers (Cillessen &

Bellmore, 1999). In the adolescent culture the status hierarchy is important, known to self and others, and has implications for interpersonal behavior. High status peers are likely to form friendships and to be among the first to begin dating (Dornbusch et al., 1981).

Our finding of reliable dyadic reciprocity in trait perception and meta-perception is noteworthy given the general failure to find this in adults. In fact, 70% of the dyadic reciprocity correlations we estimated were statistically reliable, although the effects were small and within a fairly restricted range ($r = .14$ to $.21$). These estimates are consistent with a mathematically derived expected value for dyadic reciprocity of $r = .20$ proposed by Kenny (1994). For meta-perceptions, 60% of dyadic reciprocity correlations were statistically reliable, ranging from $.10$ to $.31$. Dyadic reciprocity was uniformly weak for both perceptions and meta-perceptions across sex and only moderate within sex, although stronger for females than for males.

Overall, dyadic reciprocity of perception and meta-perception is a fairly weak phenomenon. What is important is that it was observed at all. Adolescents spend considerable time with peers who are similar to them (Montemayor & Van Komen, 1985) and share personal information in these relationships (Berndt, 1982; Douvan & Adelson, 1966). Consequently, when these dyad members make interpersonal judgments they are characterized by reciprocity. In this study, however, the dyadic reciprocity occurred among classmates and we hypothesize that estimates based only on friends would yield even stronger results.

Dyadic meta-accuracy. Adolescents knew accurately how specific other adolescents judged them. This conclusion, however, is limited by two conditions. First, dyadic meta-accuracy was restricted to same-sex dyads. When adolescents predicted how other-sex peers judged them, dyadic meta-accuracy was essentially zero. Second, dyadic meta-accuracy is much stronger among female than male adolescents. Among females, dyadic meta-accuracy was apparent on two Big Five factors (I and II) and on four status variables (all except involved). The average meta-accuracy across the six dimensions was $r = .34$.

What is the basis of this sex difference? Adolescent friends spend more time together than with other classmates and have more specific knowledge about each other (Diaz & Berndt, 1982; Newcomb & Bagwell, 1995). Further, adolescents seek information about how their friends view them (Douvan & Adelson, 1966) and trust that communications from friends will be honest (Rawlins & Holl, 1987). If one has more information about specific others who are friends (Funder & Colvin, 1988), dyadic meta-accuracy should emerge. However, in our study it emerged only among females. Females self-disclose more (Berndt, 1982; Douvan & Adelson, 1966) and are more emotionally expressive than males (Hall & Halberstadt, 1981; Kring & Gordon, 1998). This emotional expression most likely occurs with other females (Snodgrass, Hecht, & Ploutz-Snyder, 1998). While there is insufficient data to fully explain the sex difference in dyadic meta-accuracy, we hypothesize that it is due to greater expressiveness (particularly with friends), greater attention to others (Fiske, 1993), and more intimate self-disclosure among females. Males, on the other hand, emphasize mutual involvement in activities (Camarena et al., 1990) rather than intimate self-disclosure.

CONCLUSION

Initial research on the development of social cognition and peer perception focused only on the perceiver and the perceived (Dornbusch et al., 1965). Later theories specified that the unique relationship between the perceiver and the target should also be taken into account (e.g., Hinde & Stevenson-Hinde, 1987; Livesley & Bromley, 1973; Selman, 1980; Shantz, 1983). The methodological advances needed to study these effects developed more slowly. The current study confirmed that both generalized and dyadic interpersonal processes occur simultaneously (see also Coie et al., 1999; Dodge & Coie, 1987; Hubbard et al., 2001). While the generalized (individual level) phenomena were stronger than the dyadic phenomena, this difference may be due to the particular context of this study. Dyads were formed randomly within homerooms and did not necessarily pair adolescent friends. Studies of adolescents who share a close or an acrimonious relationship should yield even stronger evidence of dyadic peer perception.

Peer relations research should explicitly consider individual and dyadic phenomena to attain precision and conceptual clarity. A statistically refined focus on individual and dyadic processes became possible when Kenny (1981), guided by Cronbach (1955; see also Cronbach, Glesser, Nanda, & Rajaratnam, 1972), introduced the Social Relations Model. The Social Relations Model defines an array of individual and dyadic phenomena and provides a method for their estimation. In spite of an awareness of the importance of dyads, the dominant analytic focus in developmental social psychology was on the individual (cf. Rogosch & Newcomb, 1989; Scarlett, Press, & Crockett, 1971; Yarrow & Campbell, 1963), in large part, because methods to manage the complexity of dyadic research were unavailable. This situation has now changed (see also Kenny, Kashy, & Cook, 2006). Appelbaum and McCall (1983) lamented: "Given the litany of cautions, the reader may decide to avoid the study of social interaction at all costs," but added "that would be unfortunate" (p. 468). We agree. Peer perception in the dyadic context operates simultaneously at multiple levels of analysis. We demonstrated one method for managing this inherent complexity, and showed the rich texture that can be unraveled with multiple interaction designs and variance component analysis.

REFERENCES

Albright, L., & Malloy, T. E. (1999). Effect of self-observation on meta-perception. *Journal of Personality and Social Psychology, 77*, 726-734.

Appelbaum, M. I., & McCall, R. B. (1983). Design and analysis in developmental psychology. In W. Kessen (Ed.), *Handbook of child psychology* (Vol. 1, pp. 415-476). New York: John Wiley & Sons.

Ausubel, D. P., Schiff, H. M., & Gasser, E. B. (1952). A preliminary study of developmental trends in socioempathy: Accuracy of perception of own and others' sociometric status. *Child Development, 23*, 111-128.

Bem, D. J. (1967). Self perception: An alternative interpretation of cognitive dissonance phenomena. *Psychological Review, 74*, 183-200.

Berndt, T. J. (1982). The features and effects of friendships in early adolescence. *Child Development, 53*, 1447-1461.

Bruner, J. (1957). On perceptual readiness. *Psychological Review, 64*, 123-152.

Byrne, D. (1971). *The attraction paradigm.* New York: Academic Press.

Camarena, P. M., Sarigiani, P. A., & Petersen, A. C. (1990). Gender-specific pathways to intimacy in adolescence. *Journal of Youth and Adolescence, 19*, 19-32.

Card, N. A., Hodges, E. V. E., Little, T. D., & Hawley, P. H. (2005). Gender effects in peer nominations for aggression and social status. *International Journal of Behavioral Development, 29*, 146-155.

Cillessen, A. H. N., & Bellmore, A. D. (1999). Accuracy of social self-perceptions and peer competence in middle childhood. *Merrill-Palmer Quarterly, 45*, 650-676.

Coie, J. D., Cillessen, A. H. N., Dodge, K. A., Hubbard, J. A., Schwartz, D., Lemerise, E. A., et al. (1999). It takes two to fight: A test of relational factors and a method for assessing aggressive dyads. *Developmental Psychology, 35*, 1179-1188.

Cook, W. L., & Douglas, E. M. (1998). The looking-glass-self in family context: A social relations analysis. *Journal of Family Psychology, 12*, 299-309.

Cronbach, L. J. (1955). Processes affecting scores on "understanding of others" and "assumed similarity". *Psychological Bulletin, 52*, 177-193.

Cronbach, L. J., Glesser, G. C., Nanda, H., & Rajaratnam, N. (1972). *The dependability of behavioral measurements: Theory of generalizability for scores and profiles.* New York: John Wiley & Sons.

Diaz, R. M., & Berndt, T. J. (1982). Children's knowledge of a best friend: Fact or fancy? *Developmental Psychology, 18*, 787-794.

Dodge, K. A., & Coie, J. D. (1987). Social-information-processing factors in reactive and proactive aggression in children's peer groups. *Journal of Personality and Social Psychology, 53*, 1146-1158.

Dodge, K. A., Price, J. M., Coie, J. D., & Christopoulos, C. (1997). On the development of aggressive dyadic relationships in children's peer groups. *Human Development, 33*, 260-270.

Dornbusch, S. M., Carlsmith, L., Gross, R. T., Martin, J. A., Jenning, D., Rosenberg, A., et al. (1981). Sexual development, age, and dating: A comparison of biological and sociological influences upon the set of behaviors. *Child Development, 52*, 179-185.

Dornbusch, S. M., Hastorf, A. H., Richardson, S. A., Muzzy, R. E., & Vreeland, R. S. (1965). Development and validation of brief measures of positive and negative affect: The Panas scales. *Journal of Personality and Social Psychology, 1*, 434-440.

Douvan, E., & Adelson, J. (1966). *The adolescent experience.* New York: John Wiley & Sons.

Dubin, R., & Dubin, E. R. (1965). Children's social perceptions: A review of research. *Child Development, 36*, 809-838.

Elkind, D. (1967). Egocentrism in adolescence. *Child Development, 38*, 1025-1034.

Felson, R. B. (1981). Self- and reflected appraisal among football players: A test of the median hypothesis. *Social Psychology Quarterly, 44*, 116-126.

Felson, R. B. (1989). Parents and the reflected appraisal process: A longitudinal analysis. *Journal of Personality and Social Psychology, 56*, 965-971.

Fiske, S. T. (1993). Controlling other people: The impact of power on stereotyping. *American Psychologist, 48*, 621-628.

Funder, D. C., & Colvin, C. R. (1988). Friends and strangers: Acquaintanceship, agreement, and the accuracy of personality judgment. *Journal of Personality and Social Psychology, 55*, 149-158.

Gage, N. L., & Cronbach, L. J. (1955). Conceptual and methodological problems in interpersonal perception. *Psychological Review, 62*, 411-422.

Gilovich, T., Medyec, V. H., & Savitsky, K. (2000). The spotlight effect in social judgment: An egocentric bias in estimates of the salience of one's own actions and appearance. *Journal of Personality and Social Psychology, 78*, 211-222.

Gouldner, A. W. (1960). The norm of reciprocity: A preliminary statement. *American Sociological Review, 25*, 161-178.

Hall, J. A., & Halberstadt, A. G. (1981). Sex roles and nonverbal communication skills. *Sex Roles, 7*, 273-287.

Hinde, R. A., & Stevenson-Hinde, J. (1987). Interpersonal relationships and child development. *Developmental Review, 7*, 1-21.

Hubbard, J. A., Dodge, K. A., Cillessen, A. H. N., Coie, J. D., & Schwartz, D. (2001). The dyadic nature of social information processing in boys' reactive and proactive aggression. *Journal of Personality and Social Psychology, 80*, 268-280.

Inhelder, B., & Piaget, J. (1964). *The early growth of logic in the child: Classification and seriation.* Routledge: London.

Kenny, D. A. (1981). Interpersonal perception: A multivariate round robin analysis. In M. B. Brewer & B. E. Collins (Eds.), *Knowing and validating in the social sciences: A tribute to Donald T. Campbell* (pp. 288-309). San Francisco: Jossey-Bass.

Kenny, D. A. (1994). *Interpersonal perception: A social relations analysis*. New York: Guilford Press.

Kenny, D. A., Albright, L., Malloy, T. E., & Kashy, D. A. (1994). Consensus in interpersonal perception: Acquaintance and the big five. *Psychological Bulletin, 116*, 245-258.

Kenny, D. A., & DePaulo, B. M. (1993). Do people know how others view them? An empirical and theoretical account. *Psychological Bulletin, 114*, 145-161.

Kenny, D. A., Kashy, D. A., & Cook, W. L. (2006). *Dyadic data analysis*. New York: Guilford Press.

Kenny, D. A., & La Voie, L. (1984). The Social Relations Model. In L. Berkowitz (Ed.), *Advances in experimental social psychology* (Vol. 18, pp. 142-182). Orlando, FL: Academic Press.

Kenny, D. A., & Malloy, T. E. (1988). Partner effects in social interaction. *Journal of Nonverbal Behavior, 12*, 34-57.

Kenny, D. A., Mohr, C. D., & Levesque, M. J. (2001). A social relations variance partitioning of dyadic behavior. *Psychological Bulletin, 127*, 128-141.

Kenny, D. A., West, T. V., Malloy, T. E., & Albright, L. (2006). Componential analysis of interpersonal perception data. *Personality and Social Psychology Review, 10*, 282-294.

Kring, A. M., & Gordon, A. H. (1998). Sex differences in emotion: Expression, experience, and physiology. *Journal of Personality and Social Psychology, 74*, 686-703.

Linville, P. W., Fischer, G. W., & Salovey, P. (1989). Perceived distributions of the characteristics of in-group and out-group members: Empirical evidence and a computer simulation. *Journal of Personality and Social Psychology, 57*, 165-188.

Linville, P. W., Fischer, G. W., & Yoon, C. (1996). Perceived covariation among the features of ingroup and outgroup members: The outgroup covariation effect. *Journal of Personality and Social Psychology, 70*, 421-436.

Livesley, W. J., & Bromley, D. B. (1973). *Person perception in childhood and adolescence*. London: John Wiley & Sons.

Maccoby, E. E. (1988). Gender as a social category. *Developmental Psychology, 24*, 755-765.

Malloy, T. E., & Albright, L. (1990). Interpersonal perception in a social context. *Journal of Personality and Social Psychology, 58*, 419-428.

Malloy, T. E., & Albright, L. (2001). Multiple and single interaction designs for dyadic research: Conceptual and analytic issues. *Basic and Applied Social Psychology, 23*, 1-19.

Malloy, T. E., Albright, L., & Scarpatti, S. (2007). Awareness of peers' judgments of oneself: Accuracy and process of metaperception. *International Journal of Behavior Development, in press*.

Malloy, T. E., & Kenny, D. A. (1986). The social relations model: An integrative method for personality research. *Journal of Personality, 54*, 199-223.

Malloy, T. E., Sugarman, D. B., Montvilo, R. K., & Ben-Zeev, T. (1995). Children's interpersonal perceptions: A social relations analysis of perceiver and target effects. *Journal of Personality and Social Psychology, 68,* 418-426.

Malloy, T. E., Yarlas, A., Montvilo, R. K., & Sugarman, D. B. (1996). Agreement and accuracy in children's interpersonal perceptions: A social relations analysis. *Journal of Personality and Social Psychology, 71,* 692-702.

Mead, G. H. (1934). *Mind, self, and society.* Chicago: University of Chicago Press.

Montemayor, R., & Van Komen, R. (1985). The development of sex differences in friendship patterns and peer group structure during adolescence. *Journal of Early Adolescence, 5,* 285-294.

Newcomb, A. F., & Bagwell, C. L. (1995). Children's friendship relations: A meta-analytic review. *Psychological Bulletin, 117,* 306-347.

Park, B., & Rothbart, M. (1982). Perceptions of out-group homogeneity and levels of social categorization: Memory for the subordinate attributes of in-group and out-group members. *Journal of Personality and Social Psychology, 42,* 1051-1068.

Rawlins, W. K., & Holl, M. (1987). The communicative achievement of friendship during adolescence: Predicaments of trust and violation. *Western Journal of Speech Communication, 51,* 345-363.

Rogosch, F. A., & Newcomb, A. F. (1989). Children's perceptions of peer reputations and their social reputations among peers. *Child Development, 69,* 597-610.

Ross, H. S., & Lollis, S. P. (1989). A social relations analysis of toddler peer relationships. *Child Development, 60,* 1082-1091.

Ross, L., Greene, D., & House, P. (1977). The false consensus effect: An egocentric bias in social perception and attribution processes. *Journal of Experimental Social Psychology, 13,* 279-301.

Savitsky, K., Gilovich, T., Berger, G., & Medyec, V. H. (2003). Is our absence as conspicuous as we think? Overestimating the salience and impact of one's absence from a group. *Journal of Experimental Social Psychology, 39,* 386-392.

Scarlett, H. H., Press, A. N., & Crockett, W. H. (1971). Children's descriptions of peers: A Wernerian developmental analysis. *Child Development, 42,* 439-453.

Selman, R. L. (1980). *The growth of interpersonal understanding: Developmental and clinical analyses.* New York: Academic Press.

Selman, R. L., Beardslee, W., Schultz, L. H., Krupa, M., & Podorefsky, D. (1986). Assessing adolescent interpersonal negotiation strategies. *Developmental Psychology, 22,* 450-459.

Shantz, C. U. (1983). Social cognition. In J. H. Flavell & E. M. Markman (Eds.), *Handbook of child psychology* (Vol. 3, pp. 495-555). New York: John Wiley & Sons.

Snodgrass, S. E., Hecht, M. A., & Ploutz-Snyder, R. (1998). Interpersonal sensitivity: Expressivity or perceptivity? *Journal of Personality and Social Psychology, 74,* 238-249.

Swann, J. W. B. (1990). To be adored or to be known? The interplay of self-enhancement and self-verification. In E. T. Higgins & R. M. Sorrentino (Eds.), *Handbook of motivation and cognition: Foundations of social behavior* (Vol. 2, pp. 408-448). New York: Guilford Press.

Yarrow, M. R., & Campbell, J. D. (1963). Person perception in childhood. *Merrill-Palmer Quarterly, 9*, 57-72.

CHAPTER ELEVEN

Using the Bivariate Social Relations Model to Study Dyadic Relationships: Early Adolescents' Perceptions of Friends' Aggression and Prosocial Behavior

Noel A. Card

University of Arizona

Todd D. Little

James P. Selig

University of Kansas

How adolescents view one another plays a critical role in their interpersonal behaviors and relationships. This intuitive statement is supported by research on adults' interpersonal perceptions (see Kenny, 1994) as well as related research on adolescents' social cognitions (see Crick & Dodge, 1994; Gifford-Smith & Rabiner, 2004). However, empirical evaluation of this statement requires the use of specialized models, with the Social Relations Model (SRM) being an especially flexible model for studying interpersonal perceptions. In this chapter, we will first describe the SRM, focusing on the bivariate SRM. Our main goal of this chapter, however, is to show how the bivariate SRM can be used to study dyadic relationships in which some individuals are in multiple relationships. In our view, this situation is common when studying adolescent friendships, yet existing dyadic data analysis methods are limited. We illustrate how the bivariate SRM can be used to study interpersonal perceptions within early adolescent friendships, using data on sixth graders' friendships and perceptions of aggression and prosocial behavior. We

conclude that the SRM, although typically considered an approach to studying small groups, can also be a useful tool for studying dyadic relationships,
overcoming some difficulties inherent in other models.

The Social Relations Model

The Social Relations Model (SRM), developed by David Kenny and colleagues in the late 1970s and early 1980s (Kenny & La Voie, 1984; Malloy
& Kenny, 1986; Warner, Kenny, & Stoto, 1979) and refined over the past
three decades (see Kenny, 1994; Kenny, Kashy, & Cook, 2006), represents
a powerful conceptual and analytic approach to understanding interpersonal
perception and dyadic behaviors. Given the value of this model, it is not
surprising that it has been used in over 200 studies (for a bibliography of
SRM, see David Kenny's Web site: http://davidakenny.net/kenny.htm). In
the following, we describe the details of the SRM as applied to univariate
and bivariate data analysis (for fuller details, see Kenny, 1994). We describe
these in the context of interpersonal perception both because this has been
the most common application in the previous literature and because this is a
focus of the illustrative example described later.

Univariate SRM

The simplest, and likely most common, use of the SRM is in univariate
analyses, in which three key variance estimates and two covariance estimates
are made from a round-robin design with a single dyadic variable. Specifically,
interpersonal perceptions are characterized by three influences that affect one
individual's perceptions of another (target) individual: the individual's tendencies to perceive others in a certain way, the target's tendencies to be
perceived by others in certain ways, and the unique perceptions that occur
specific to the dyadic relationship between the two individuals (see Kenny,
1994). One useful way to conceptualize these influences, and to analyze data
regarding these influences, is through the SRM. As shown in Figure 11.1, the
data for the SRM is a square sociomatrix representing individuals' perceptions (or other dyadic variables) within a round-robin design (similar analytic
strategies exist for other designs; see Kenny, 1994; Kenny et al., 2006). The
SRM partitions variability in these perceptions into three components reflecting the three perception influences: (a) variance due to individual differences
among perceivers (termed actor variance), (b) variance due to individual differences among those being perceived (partner variance), and (c) variance in
the dyadic perception scores that is not accounted for by actor and partner
effects (unique variance).

	1	2	3	4	5	6	Total
1	--	X_{12}	X_{13}	X_{14}	X_{15}	X_{16}	$M_{1\bullet}$
2	X_{21}	--	X_{23}	X_{24}	X_{25}	X_{26}	$M_{2\bullet}$
3	X_{31}	X_{32}	--	X_{34}	X_{35}	X_{36}	$M_{3\bullet}$
4	X_{41}	X_{42}	X_{43}	--	X_{45}	X_{46}	$M_{4\bullet}$
5	X_{51}	X_{52}	X_{53}	X_{54}	--	X_{56}	$M_{5\bullet}$
6	X_{61}	X_{62}	X_{63}	X_{64}	X_{65}	--	$M_{6\bullet}$
Total	$M_{\bullet 1}$	$M_{\bullet 2}$	$M_{\bullet 3}$	$M_{\bullet 4}$	$M_{\bullet 5}$	$M_{\bullet 6}$	$M_{\bullet\bullet}$

Figure 11.1. Parameter estimates in univariate SRM. Adapted from Kenny et al. (1994).

Actor effect for adolescent $i = \hat{a}_i = \dfrac{(n-1)^2}{n(n-2)}M_{i\bullet} + \dfrac{n-1}{n(n-2)}M_{\bullet i} - \dfrac{n-1}{n-2}M_{\bullet\bullet}$

Partner effect for adolescent $i = \hat{b}_i = \dfrac{(n-1)^2}{n(n-2)}M_{\bullet i} + \dfrac{n-1}{n(n-2)}M_{i\bullet} - \dfrac{n-1}{n-2}M_{\bullet\bullet}$

Unique effect of adolescent i toward adolescent $j = \hat{g}_{ij} = X_{ij} - \hat{a}_i - \hat{b}_j - M_{\bullet\bullet}$

Relationship variance $= s_g^2 = \dfrac{1}{2}\left(\dfrac{2\sum\left(\frac{\hat{g}_{ij}+\hat{g}_{ji}}{2}\right)^2}{\left[\frac{(n-1)(n-2)}{2}\right]-1} + \dfrac{\sum(\hat{g}_{ij}-\hat{g}_{ji})^2}{(n-1)(n-2)} \right)$

Relationship covariance $= s_{gg'} = \dfrac{1}{2}\left(\dfrac{2\sum\left(\frac{\hat{g}_{ij}+\hat{g}_{ji}}{2}\right)^2}{\left[\frac{(n-1)(n-2)}{2}\right]-1} - \dfrac{\sum(\hat{g}_{ij}-\hat{g}_{ji})^2}{(n-1)(n-2)} \right)$

Actor–partner covariance $= s_{ab} = \dfrac{\sum(\hat{a}_i\hat{b}_i)}{n-1} - \dfrac{s_{gg'}(n-1)}{n(n-2)} - \dfrac{s_g^2}{n(n-2)}$

Actor variance $= s_a^2 = \dfrac{\sum\hat{a}_i^2}{n-1} - \dfrac{s_g^2(n-1)}{n(n-2)} - \dfrac{s_{gg'}}{n(n-2)}$

Partner variance $= s_b^2 = \dfrac{\sum\hat{b}_i^2}{n-1} - \dfrac{s_g^2(n-1)}{n(n-2)} - \dfrac{s_{gg'}}{n(n-2)}$

Imagine that the data in Figure 11.1 are a group of adolescents' perceptions of one another as aggressive, with X_{ij} representing Adolescent i's perception of Adolescent j's aggression. We see that Adolescent 1 has perceptions
of all other adolescents in the group $(X_{12}, X_{13}, \ldots, X_{16})$, but self-perceptions
are not included so there are missing data along the diagonal of the sociomatrix (it is possible to incorporate self-perceptions within SRM, but these are
generally considered as fundamentally different types of perceptions that are
not included in the sociomatrix; see chapter 9 of Kenny, 1994). We can obtain
a rough idea of how Adolescent 1 perceives others in general by considering
the average of his or her perceptions of other group members $(M_{1\cdot})$, but a
correction needs to be made to account for the fact that Adolescent 1 did
not provide ratings of himself or herself (e.g., if Adolescent 1 was perceived
by others as very aggressive, then Adolescent 1 would have a downwardly
biased mean perception, $M_{1\cdot}$, relative to others in the group because he or
she did not have the opportunity to provide ratings of this highly aggressive
self). This correction is made by including Adolescent 1's mean perceptions
by others (discussed next) when estimating how Adolescent 1 perceives others in general. Typically the average perceptions of all members in the group
is subtracted, so that negative scores denote lower-than-average perceptions
of others as aggressive, whereas positive scores represent higher-than-average
perceptions of others as aggressive. Therefore, how adolescent i tends to perceive others as aggressive, which is called an *actor effect* $(\hat{a}_i)$, is estimated
using the following formula (see Kenny, 1994):[1]

$$\hat{a}_i = \frac{(n-1)^2}{n(n-2)}M_{i\bullet} + \frac{n-1}{n(n-2)}M_{\bullet i} - \frac{n-1}{n-2}M_{\bullet\bullet} \qquad (1)$$

where, n = number of individuals in group
$M_{i\cdot}$ = row mean of individual i
$M_{\cdot i}$ = column mean of individual i
$M_{\cdot\cdot}$ = grand mean across all individuals

Similarly, we can compute an estimate of how Adolescent 1 is perceived by
others, called a *partner effect* $(\hat{b}_i)$. Positive values imply that the adolescent
tends to be perceived as highly (relative to others) aggressive by others in
general, whereas negative values imply that the adolescent is perceived as
low in aggression by others. The formula for the partner effect of Adolescent
i is similar to that for actor effects (Equation 1), but with emphasis on the
column means from Figure 11.1 (with a correction for the adolescent's row

---

[1]The equations reported here were adapted directly from Appendix B of Kenny (1994)
and generally follow his notation (with some minor deviations for the bivariate covariances).

mean as the second term, and centering around the grand mean with the third term):

$$\hat{b}_i = \frac{(n-1)^2}{n(n-2)}M_{\bullet i} + \frac{n-1}{n(n-2)}M_{i\bullet} - \frac{n-1}{n-2}M_{\bullet\bullet} \qquad (2)$$

After accounting for the perceiver i's tendencies to see others in general as aggressive or nonaggressive (i.e., actor effects), and target j's tendencies to be seen by others in general as aggressive or nonaggressive (i.e., partner effects), we can consider the unique perception one adolescent has toward a particular other adolescent. Specifically, the unique effect (also called the relationship effect) of Adolescent i toward Adolescent j, removing the individual tendencies of Adolescent i to view others as aggressive and others to view Adolescent j as aggressive (and the group mean), is computed as:

$$\hat{g}_{ij} = X_{ij} - \hat{a}_i - \hat{b}_j - M_{\bullet\bullet} \qquad (3)$$

This unique effect, g_{ij}, consists of reliable perceptions that are unique to the dyadic relationship (termed relationship effects) and random measurement error. When one has multiple indicators of the same construct (e.g., one has perceptions of different aspects of aggressive behavior) it is possible to separate the variance in this unique effect that is reliable from that due to random error. In the example below, we are unable to separate these two sources of variance because we do not have sufficient indicators.[2] In this case, we assume that measurement error is minimal and that this unique effect, g_{ij}, is largely veridical. The degree to which this assumption is violated will attenuate effect size estimates and is thus a conservative (i.e., low power) bias.

From these three effect estimates (i.e., actor, partner, and unique effects), one estimates three variance and two covariance terms: actor variance, partner variance, relationship variance, actor–partner covariance, and dyadic covariance (see Figure 11.1). Because it is used in subsequent equations, we first consider relationship variance, s_g^2, which is the amount of variability in the unique effects across all possible dyads:

$$s_g^2 = \frac{1}{2}\left(\frac{2\sum\left(\frac{\hat{g}_{ij}+\hat{g}_{ji}}{2}\right)^2}{\left[\frac{(n-1)(n-2)}{2}\right]-1} + \frac{\sum(\hat{g}_{ij}-\hat{g}_{ji})^2}{(n-1)(n-2)}\right) \qquad (4)$$

---

[2]We actually do use dichotomous responses (nominations versus lack of nominations) from multiple items, but chose to average these items to form a single variable rather than to treat these items as multiple indicators. Our reason for this is to obtain a more continuous single variable, given that some have recommended against using the SRM with dichotomous data (but see footnote 2 in Lashley & Bond, 1997).

We compute the dyadic covariance using a similar expression (except the second term within the large parentheses is subtracted from, rather than added to, the first). The dyadic covariance represents the extent to which Adolescent i's unique perception of Adolescent j is associated with Adolescent j's unique perception of Adolescent i. In other words, if Ike views Jake as uniquely aggressive (above and beyond Ike's tendency to see others in general as aggressive, and Jake's tendency to be viewed as aggressive by others), does Jake also tend to view Ike as uniquely aggressive (implying a positive dyadic covariance)? This dyadic covariance, $s_{gg'}$, is computed as:

$$s_{gg'} = \frac{1}{2} \left(\frac{2 \sum \left(\frac{\hat{g}_{ij} + \hat{g}_{ji}}{2} \right)^2}{\left[\frac{(n-1)(n-2)}{2} \right] - 1} - \frac{\sum (\hat{g}_{ij} - \hat{g}_{ji})^2}{(n-1)(n-2)} \right) \tag{5}$$

We can also compute another covariance, called the actor–partner covariance. This covariance indexes the association between individuals' perceptions of others in general with how individuals are perceived by others in general. For example, are adolescents who perceive their peers (in general) as highly aggressive perceived by their peers (in general) as enacting high (positive actor–partner covariance) or low (negative covariance) levels of aggression? This actor–partner covariance differs from the dyadic covariance in that the former involves perceptions of (and by) *others in general*, whereas the latter involves perceptions of (and by) *specific others*. The actor–partner covariance is computed as a function of the actor effect by partner effect products, removing the dyadic covariance and relationship variance:

$$s_{ab} = \frac{\sum (\hat{a}_i \hat{b}_i)}{n-1} - \frac{s_{gg'}(n-1)}{n(n-2)} - \frac{s_g^2}{n(n-2)} \tag{6}$$

Finally, we can compute the two most basic variance terms, the actor and partner variances. Actor variance can be conceptualized as the amount of interindividual variability in tendencies to perceive others as high or low in, for example, aggression (as well as an index of *assimilation*, which is the tendency to see others in a similar way). Partner variance can be conceptualized as the amount of interindividual variability in tendencies to be perceived *by others* as high or low in, for example, aggression (as well as an index of *consensus*, which is the tendency for individuals to agree in their perceptions). Estimates of actor variance, s_a^2, and partner variance, s_b^2, can be made with the following two equations:

$$s_a^2 = \frac{\sum \hat{a}_i^2}{n-1} - \frac{s_g^2(n-1)}{n(n-2)} - \frac{s_{gg'}}{n(n-2)} \tag{7}$$

$$s_b^2 = \frac{\sum \hat{b}_i^2}{n-1} - \frac{s_g^2(n-1)}{n(n-2)} - \frac{s_{gg'}}{n(n-2)} \qquad (8)$$

To summarize, the SRM of univariate round-robin data allows us to estimate five key parameters. The three variance terms are actor variance, partner variance, and relationship variance (with the latter variance comprised of both reliable and unreliable components unless multiple indicators of each construct are used to separate these sources of variance). The two covariance terms are the actor–partner covariance and the dyadic covariance.

Bivariate SRM

When the SRM is applied to multiple constructs, one can estimate far more parameters. If we consider just two constructs, a total of 16 unique parameter estimates are possible. These include the five univariate estimates (three variances and two covariances) for each of the two variables and six cross-variable covariances. Consider the example of adolescents' perceptions of others' aggression and prosocial behavior. As described in the previous section, we could make the following parameter estimates from the data involving aggression: actor variance (s_a^2), partner variance (s_b^2), relationship variance (s_g^2), actor–partner covariance (s_{ab}), and dyadic covariance ($s_{gg'}$). We could make estimates for these same five univariate parameters for the perceptions of prosocial behavior, which we could denote as s_c^2, s_d^2, s_h^2, s_{cd}, and $s_{hh'}$, respectively. Of the six possible cross-variable covariances, two are at the dyadic level and four are at the individual level.

The first dyadic covariance that we consider is the intrapersonal covariance, s_{gh}. This covariance evaluates whether the unique effects of individual i perceiving person j for two variables are associated. For example, this covariance would evaluate whether the extent to which Ike perceives Jake as uniquely aggressive (above and beyond Ike's perceptions of others in general as aggressive and Jake's being perceived by others as aggressive) is related to Ike also perceiving Jake to be uniquely high (positive covariance) or low (negative covariance) in prosocial behavior. This intrapersonal covariance, s_{gh}, is computed as:

$$s_{gh} = \frac{\sum\left(\frac{(\hat{g}_{ij}+\hat{g}_{ji})(\hat{h}_{ij}+\hat{h}_{ji})}{4}\right)}{\left(\frac{(n-1)(n-2)}{2}-1\right)} + \frac{\sum(\hat{g}_{ij}-\hat{g}_{ji})(\hat{h}_{ij}+\hat{h}_{ji})}{2(n-1)(n-2)} \qquad (9)$$

The other bivariate dyadic covariance is the interpersonal covariance, $s_{gh'}$. This covariance is interpreted as the association of individual i's unique perception of individual j (i.e., relationship effect) on one variable with individual j's unique perception of individual i on the other variable. Continuing the example of aggression and prosocial behavior, this interpersonal covariance answers the question: If Ike perceives Jake to be particularly aggressive (above and beyond Ike's actor effect and Jake's partner effect), does Jake tend to view Ike as particularly high (positive covariance) or low (negative covariance) on prosocial behavior? The formula for this interpersonal correlation is similar to Equation 9, but here the second portion of the equation is subtracted from the first:

$$s_{gh'} = \frac{\sum \left(\frac{(\hat{g}_{ij}+\hat{g}_{ji})(\hat{h}_{ij}+\hat{h}_{ji})}{4} \right)}{\left(\frac{(n-1)(n-2)}{2} - 1 \right)} - \frac{\sum (\hat{g}_{ij}-\hat{g}_{ji})(\hat{h}_{ij}+\hat{h}_{ji})}{2(n-1)(n-2)} \quad (10)$$

The four individual-level bivariate covariances are more straightforward. Two of these effects simply involve the cross-variable covariances in actor effects or partner effects. The actor–actor covariance, s_{ac}, represents that association of the actor effects of one variable with the actor effects of the other; for example, if Ike tends to see others in general as aggressive, does Ike also tend to see others as high (positive covariance) or low (negative covariance) in prosocial behavior? Similarly, the partner–partner covariance, s_{bd}, represents the association of the partner effects of one variable with the partner effects of the other; for example, if Ike is perceived by others as aggressive, is Ike also perceived as high (positive covariance) or low (negative covariance) in prosocial behavior? The computation of actor–actor covariances (s_{ac}) and partner–partner covariances (s_{bd}) is as follows:

$$s_{ac} = \frac{\hat{a}_i \hat{c}_i}{n-1} - \frac{s_{gh}(n-1)}{n(n-2)} - \frac{s_{gh'}}{n(n-2)} \quad (11)$$

$$s_{bd} = \frac{\hat{b}_i \hat{d}_i}{n-1} - \frac{s_{gh}(n-1)}{n(n-2)} - \frac{s_{gh'}}{n(n-2)} \quad (12)$$

The remaining two bivariate covariances are the actor–partner covariance and the partner–actor covariance. The actor–partner covariance (s_{ad}) indexes the association of individual i's perceptions of others in general on the first variable with how others perceive individual i on the second variable; for example, if Ike tends to view others as aggressive, do others perceive Ike as high (positive covariance) or low (negative covariance) in prosocial behavior? The partner–actor covariance (s_{bc}) is similar except that the order of the variables is reversed; for example, if Ike views others as high in prosocial behavior, do others tend to view Ike as high (positive covariance) or low (negative covariance) in aggression? As might be expected, the formulas for the actor–partner (s_{ad}) and the partner–actor (s_{bc}) covariances are similar:

$$s_{ad} = \frac{\hat{a}_i \hat{d}_i}{n-1} - \frac{s_{gh(n-1)}}{n(n-2)} - \frac{s_{gh'}}{n(n-2)} \tag{13}$$

$$s_{bc} = \frac{\hat{b}_i \hat{c}_i}{n-1} - \frac{s_{gh(n-1)}}{n(n-2)} - \frac{s_{gh'}}{n(n-2)} \tag{14}$$

Using SRM to Study Adolescent Interpersonal Perceptions

Having described the SRM, we now turn toward its application in study-ing interpersonal perception. As mentioned, the SRM has been used to study interpersonal perception among adults in numerous studies (for reviews see Kenny, 1994; Kenny, Albright, Malloy, & Kashy, 1994; on the topic of accu-racy see Kenny & Albright, 1987; on meta-accuracy see Kenny & DePaulo, 1993). In contrast, the SRM has been infrequently used to study interpersonal perception, or other aspects of peer relations, among children or adolescents. Given the importance of interpersonal perceptions during this developmen-tal period, the potential of SRM in shedding new light on these perceptions, and the settings in which children interact (e.g., classrooms) that provide naturalistic round-robin designs, this infrequency is somewhat disappointing.

The literature using the SRM to study peer relations during childhood or adolescence is limited,[3] and can be summarized briefly (see also Little & Card, 2005). H. S. Ross & Lollis (1989) studied young (20- to 30-months) children's play behaviors using SRM, finding modest actor and partner variances for both play and conflict. In artificial play groups of third grade boys, SRM of aggressive behaviors (Coie et al., 1999) and aggression-encouraging social cognitions (Hubbard et al., 2001) has revealed significant actor, partner, and (especially) relationship variance components. These studies demonstrate the value of SRM in developmental research, but both focused on behaviors rather than interpersonal perceptions.

We are aware of only three studies that have used the SRM to study chil-dren's or adolescents' interpersonal perceptions. The first (Malloy, Sugarman,

---

[3]This review considers only peer relations research and does not consider the numer-ous studies that have examined behaviors and interpersonal perceptions within families including children and adolescents. Readers interested in this topic should see works by Branje (Branje, Finkenauer, & Meeus, chapter 12; Branje, van Aken, & van Lieshout, 2002; Branje, van Lieshout, & van Aken, 2002; Branje, van Aken, van Lieshout, & Mathijssen, 2003; Finkenauer, Engels, Branje, & Meeus, 2004), Cook, 1993, 1994, 2000, 2001, 2005; Cook & Dreyer, 1984; Cook & Kenny, 2004; Cook, Kenny, & Goldstein, 1991), and others (e.g., Buist et al., 2004; Delsing et al., 2003, 2005; Hoyt, Fincham, McCullough, Maio, & Davila, 2005; Hsiung & Bagozzi, 2003; Ross, Stein, Trabasso, Woody, & Ross, 2005; Stevenson, Leavitt, Thompson, & Roach, 1988).

Montvilo, & Ben-Zeev, 1995) examined actor and partner variances among
first through sixth graders' ratings of peers' academic ability, positive affect,
attractiveness, popularity, physical strength, and positive behavior (i.e., "well
behaved"). Their results generally indicated greater partner than actor variance, more so for academic ability and physical strength but less so for affect
and popularity. Importantly, Malloy and colleagues (1995) studied a range of
age cohorts longitudinally, thus allowing them to consider developmental processes of interpersonal perception. Comparisons across age indicated that the
relative variance due to partner (i.e., target, compared to actor, or perceiver)
was greater among older children than among younger children. Longitudinal
analyses revealed fairly low stability in actor (perceiver) effects, but more substantial stability in partner (target) effects. This stability of partner effects
was especially strong for certain characteristics (e.g., academic ability). Further analyses relating these partner effects to external teacher reports (Malloy,
Yarlas, Montvilo, & Sugarman, 1996) suggest that certain characteristics are
more readily perceived (and presumably therefore more stable) than others.

The second study (Card, Romero, & Weissman, 2004) fit SRM to sixth
through eighth graders' peer nominations for aggression and victimization.
The results indicated reliable actor (15% and 9% of reliable variance in aggression and victimization nominations, respectively) and partner variance
(16% and 27% for perceptions of aggression and victimization). The actor
effects indicate reliable individual differences in perceptions (consistent with
work on hostile attributional biases, e.g., Dodge, 1980; see Crick & Dodge,
1994), and the partner effects indicate consensus in peer perceptions (thereby
also supporting the use of peer nomination inventories as internally consistent measures of behavior and peer experiences). However, the majority
of variance in interpersonal perception was due to relationship effects, with
these effects accounting for 69% and 64% of the reliable variance in aggression and victimization nominations, respectively. There was no evidence of
within-construct reciprocity (either actor–partner or dyadic), but bivariate
SRM revealed evidence of two cross-construct actor–partner correlations: (1)
a positive correlation ($r = .23$) between actor effects in perception of others
as victimized and partner effects in viewing others as aggressive; and (2) a
positive correlation ($r = .20$) between actor effects in perceptions of others
as aggressive and partner effects in viewing others as victimized. The former
correlation suggests that adolescents who are perceived as aggressive tend
to see victimization risk in others (presumably because they themselves are
motivated to target these victims). The latter correlation, which is consistent with prior theory and literature, links experiences of victimization with
hostile attributional biases (e.g., Schwartz et al., 1998).

Finally, Card, Hodges, Little, and Hawley (2005), applied SRM to sixth graders' peer nominations of various aspects of aggression and social status. Within mixed-sex classrooms, the authors found evidence of reliable actor and partner variance in all variables studied. Actor–partner correlations were less consistent, but significant positive correlations emerged for perceptions of relational aggression, peer influence, and social preference, whereas a negative correlation was found for perceptions of peer victimization. The authors also found dyadic reciprocity, with perceptions of instrumental aggression, peer influence, and social preference exhibiting significant positive correlations. The remainder of these authors' analyses focused on comparing same- and cross-sex perceptions, which we will not describe here.

Studying Early Adolescent Friendships Using SRM

Although the SRM is commonly thought of as an analytic tool for small-group data, we will use the SRM to address questions about interpersonal perception and dyadic relationships. Specifically, we will consider the bivariate associations of dyadic friendship relationships with interpersonal perceptions of aggression and prosocial behavior among early adolescents.

Why go through the trouble of adapting the SRM to study dyadic relationships when methods of studying dyads already exist? We believe that the tendency of early adolescents' to have multiple friendships necessitates such adaptation. Traditional dyadic methods, such as the Actor–Partner Interdependence Model (Cook, 2005; Kashy & Kenny, 2000; Kenny, 1996), Mutual Influence Model (Sadler & Woody, chapter 7; Woody & Sadler, 2005), and methods of pairwise data analysis (Gonzalez & Griffin, 1997; Griffin & Gonzalez, 1995; Selig, McNamara, Card, & Little, chapter 9) are well suited for analyzing dyads in which each individual is in one and only one dyad. However, inferential tests using these methods generally assume that the dyads are independent in terms of the individuals involved, and are not yet easily adapted for situations in which Adolescent 1 is a member of both Dyad 1 and Dyad 2 (i.e, the two dyads are nonindependent in their members).

The restriction of these methods to nonoverlapping individuals limits their use in studying adolescent friendships, in which there are very likely individuals in multiple dyads. Various "fixes" to this problem have been used, including (a) ignoring this violation, (b) randomly selecting friendships so that the dyads do not contain overlapping individuals (e.g., Adams, Bukowski, & Bagwell, 2005,), and (c) studying only best-friendships in which each individual is limited to one friendship dyad (e.g., Cillessen, Jiang, West, & Laszkowski, 2005). The first method is unacceptable in that it biases inferences made from the analyses. The second approach is justifiable in that it would not be expected to bias parameter estimates, although the random exclusion of dyads introduces some imprecision in these estimates and results in lower statistical power. The third approach is appropriate if the researcher is truly interested in exclusive best friendships, but this decision should be made based on conceptual interest rather than statistical convenience. During adolescence multiple friendships are common (e.g., Cairns, Leung, Buchanan, & Cairns, 1995; Card & Hodges, 2006; for a review see Rubin, Bukowski, & Parker, 1998). Therefore, if we are to understand the common occurrence of adolescents having multiple friendships, it is necessary to use analytic strategies that allow for overlap of individuals across dyads.

We propose a modification of the bivariate SRM as a tool for studying these overlapping dyads. The key to this approach is creating a symmetric sociomatrix that represents the occurrence of reciprocal friendships. This symmetric relationship matrix is then examined in conjunction with other dyadic qualities, such as interpersonal perception, using bivariate SRM. The advantages of this approach include

(a) Allowing for the possibility that some individuals may be engaged in relationships with multiple others. For example, this approach allows for the possibility that some adolescents will have numerous friendships.

(b) Including individuals who are not engaged in the relationship studied. Although some adolescents have numerous friends and others may only have one, the modified bivariate SRM allows adolescents with no friendships to be included in the analysis. This flexibility is advantageous over excluding individuals without the type of relationship under study because it allows stronger inferences and greater generalization of findings.

(c) Consideration of both individual-level and dyad-specific effects. Analysis of individual-level effects allows the researcher to examine whether the number of relationships in which the individual is engaged is associated with (a) the individuals' perceptions of (or behaviors toward) others, and (b) the individuals' perceptions (or behaviors) received by others. Dyad-level effects are those that are often considered in relationship research, and address questions such as "Do adolescents tend to perceive their friends as more prosocial than they perceive their nonfriends?" With traditional dyadic analysis techniques it is unclear whether differences between friends and nonfriends are due to the relationship (a dyadic effect) or the individuals in the relationships (an individual effect). For example, it may be the case that adolescents who are viewed as prosocial are engaged in many friendships; therefore, the tendency to find higher perceptions of prosocial behavior between friends relative to nonfriends is due to the individuals being perceived (i.e., those who are seen as highly prosocial have more friendships than those who are seen as less prosocial) rather than the context of friendships. The approach we describe next separates the individual- and dyad-level effects.

The modified bivariate SRM for studying associations between relationships (e.g., friendships) and dyadic features (e.g., perceptions of aggression and prosocial behavior) is shown in Figure 11.2. The matrix on the left is now a symmetric matrix, given that if Adolescent 1 has a friendship with Adolescent 2, then Adolescent 2 necessarily has a friendship with Adolescent 1. In other words, this approach is for nondirectional relationships (e.g., reciprocal rather than unrequited friendships), specifically those that can be considered indistinguishable (see Gonzalez & Griffin, 1997; Kenny et al., 2006; Sadler & Woody, chapter 7; Selig, McNamara, Card, & Little, chapter 9).

In contrast to the standard bivariate SRM with five within-variable parameter estimates per variable and six cross-variable estimates, using a symmetric relationship matrix reduces the number of parameters. Specifically, the symmetric friendship matrix of Figure 11.2 has only two meaningful parameter estimates: individual variance and unique variance. The *individual variance* is analogous to the actor and partner variance of a traditional SRM. Because the actor and partner effects are necessarily equal in a symmetric matrix (and the amount of actor and partner variance is therefore also equal), these two parameters are estimated as one common "individual variance" parameter. The *unique variance* of the symmetric friendship matrix is equivalent to that in the traditional SRM. However, the two covariances typically estimated in a univariate SRM are not estimated here because the symmetry of the friendship matrix necessitates that these are perfect 1.0 correlations.

Reducing the estimated parameters in the symmetric relationship (e.g., friendship) matrix also reduces the cross-matrix (cross-variable) associations from six to three. The separate actor–actor and partner–actor covariances estimated in traditional bivariate SRM are now replaced by a common individual–actor covariance. Returning to the example of friendships and perceptions of aggression, this covariance indicates whether individuals with more friendships tend to perceive others (in general) as more (positive covariance) or less (negative) aggressive than do individuals with fewer friendships. Similarly, the separate actor–partner and partner–partner covariances estimated in traditional bivariate SRM are replaced by a single covariance, the individual–partner covariance. Considering again friendships and perceptions of aggression, this covariance would indicate whether individuals with more

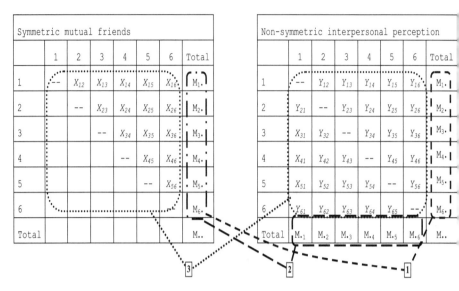

Figure 11.2. SRM associations between friendship matrices and nonsymmetric interpersonal perception matrices.

friends are perceived by others (in general) as more (positive) or less (negative) aggressive than are individuals with fewer friends. Finally, the intrapersonal and interpersonal covariances estimated in a traditional bivariate SRM are also replaced by a common covariance given the symmetry of the friendship matrix. This covariance evaluates whether perceptions of aggression tend to be higher (positive) or lower (negative) in friendships relative to nonfriends, accounting for the individual tendencies (perceiving others and being perceived by others in general) of those involved in friendships.

1) Associations of friendship individual differences with actor (perceiver) effects of interpersonal perception.

$$
\mathrm{cov}(\hat{a}_x, \hat{a}_y) = \frac{\displaystyle\sum_{i>j} \hat{a}_{xi}\hat{a}_{xy}}{n-1}
$$

$$
-\left(\frac{n-1}{2n(n-2)}\right)\left(\frac{2\displaystyle\sum_{i>j}\left[\left(\frac{\hat{g}_{xij}+\hat{g}_{xji}}{2}\right)\left(\frac{\hat{g}_{yij}+\hat{g}_{yji}}{2}\right)\right]}{\left[\frac{(n-1)(n-2)}{2}\right]-1} + \frac{\displaystyle\sum_{i>j}\left[(\hat{g}_{xij}+\hat{g}_{xji})(\hat{g}_{yij}+\hat{g}_{yji})\right]}{(n-1)(n-2)}\right)
$$

$$
-\left(\frac{1}{2n(n-2)}\right)\left(\frac{2\displaystyle\sum_{i>j}\left[\left(\frac{\hat{g}_{xij}+\hat{g}_{xji}}{2}\right)\left(\frac{\hat{g}_{yij}+\hat{g}_{yji}}{2}\right)\right]}{\left[\frac{(n-1)(n-2)}{2}\right]-1} - \frac{\displaystyle\sum_{i>j}\left[(\hat{g}_{xij}+\hat{g}_{xji})(\hat{g}_{yij}+\hat{g}_{yji})\right]}{(n-1)(n-2)}\right)
$$

2) Associations of friendship individual differences with partner (target) effects of interpersonal perception.

$$\mathrm{cov}(\hat{a}_x, \hat{a}_y) = \frac{\displaystyle\sum_{i>j} \hat{a}_{xi}\hat{a}_{xy}}{n-1}$$

$$\left(\frac{n-1}{2n(n-2)}\right)\left(\frac{2\displaystyle\sum_{i>j}\left[\left(\frac{\hat{g}_{xij}+\hat{g}_{xji}}{2}\right)\left(\frac{\hat{g}_{yij}+\hat{g}_{yji}}{2}\right)\right]}{\left[\frac{(n-1)(n-2)}{2}\right]-1} - \frac{\displaystyle\sum_{i>j}\left[(\hat{g}_{xij}+\hat{g}_{xji})(\hat{g}_{yij}+\hat{g}_{yji})\right]}{(n-1)(n-2)}\right)$$

$$\left(\frac{1}{2n(n-2)}\right)\left(\frac{2\displaystyle\sum_{i>j}\left[\left(\frac{\hat{g}_{xij}+\hat{g}_{xji}}{2}\right)\left(\frac{\hat{g}_{yij}+\hat{g}_{yji}}{2}\right)\right]}{\left[\frac{(n-1)(n-2)}{2}\right]-1} + \frac{\displaystyle\sum_{i>j}\left[(\hat{g}_{xij}+\hat{g}_{xji})(\hat{g}_{yij}+\hat{g}_{yji})\right]}{(n-1)(n-2)}\right)$$

3) Associations of friendship (dyads) with the unique effects of interpersonal perception.

$$\mathrm{cov}(\hat{g}_x, \hat{g}_y) =$$

$$\left(\frac{n-1}{2n(n-2)}\right)\left(\frac{2\displaystyle\sum_{i>j}\left[\left(\frac{\hat{g}_{xij}+\hat{g}_{xji}}{2}\right)\left(\frac{\hat{g}_{yij}+\hat{g}_{yji}}{2}\right)\right]}{\left[\frac{(n-1)(n-2)}{2}\right]-1} + \frac{\displaystyle\sum_{i>j}\left[(\hat{g}_{xij}+\hat{g}_{xji})(\hat{g}_{yij}+\hat{g}_{yji})\right]}{(n-1)(n-2)}\right)$$

An Illustrative Example From Adolescents' Views of Their Friends

In this section, we briefly report results involving early adolescents' interpersonal perceptions in relation to mutual friendships. The data used for these analyses are the same as those used in Card et al. (2005), who also fit SRM to peer nomination data. However, the results reported here answer very different questions than those of the previous study by focusing on bivariate associations between dyadic friendships and two aspects of interpersonal perception, perceptions of aggression and prosocial behavior. We turn to those results after briefly reporting the methodology of this study.

METHOD

Participants. Participants were 371 sixth grade (M age = 10.5 years) boys ($n = 177$) and girls ($n = 194$) from 17 classes within 9 elementary schools located in a mid-sized city in the northeastern United States. Representative of the population of these schools, participants were 68% Caucasian, 22%

African American, 5% Hispanic, and 5% of other or mixed ethnicity. The communities in which these schools were located are generally lower to upper middle class.

Measures. Participants completed a peer nomination instrument. One item assessed liking ("Who do you like the most?") and was used to establish mutual friendships by assigning a one within the friendship sociomatrix if both children nominated each other. For dyads in which reciprocal friendship nominations were not made, we assigned a zero to that cell of the sociomatrix (unilateral nominations were not considered here).[4]

Other items on the peer nomination instrument were used to measure interpersonal perceptions of aggression and prosocial behavior. *Aggression* was assessed in a general way, combining across forms (overt and relational; see Card, Stucky, Sawalani, & Little, 2007) and functions (instrumental and reactive; see Card & Hodges, 2006) by nominations on eight items, two nominations on each of four form-function combinations: overt-instrumental (e.g., "Who starts fights to get what they want?"), overt-reactive (e.g., "Who pushes, kicks, or punches others because they've been angered by them?"), relational-instrumental (e.g., "Who ignores or stops talking to others in order to get what they want?"), and relational-reactive (e.g., "Who keeps people from being in their group of friends if they've been hurt by them?"). *Prosocial behavior* was assessed by nominations on two items, "Who is nice to others?" and "Who is most friendly to others?" Scores (x_{ij}) were computed as the percentage of items of each construct on which adolescent i nominated peer j.

Data analytic strategy. Separate SRMs were evaluated for each of 33 sex by classroom combinations (note that one class contained only three participating girls and was dropped because at least four participants are required to estimate all SRM parameters; Kenny, 1994; see also Card et al., 2005). Thus, only same-sex relationships and interpersonal perceptions were used (which is reasonable given that friendships at this age occur primarily with same-sex peers; see Maccoby, 1998). Results from each of the 33 SRMs were combined to yield averaged parameter estimates and standard errors for significance tests (see Lashley & Bond, 1997, for a description of this and other methods of significance testing in SRM).

An illustrative example. In order to demonstrate the analyses performed to answer these questions, we will present results of analyses involving one

---

[4]Algebraically, creation of the mutual friendship ($\boldsymbol{F}$) sociomatrices is equivalent to squaring the liking ($\boldsymbol{L}$) matrices, so that $\boldsymbol{F} = \boldsymbol{L}^2$ (see Wasserman & Faust, 1994). The use of these symmetric friendship matrices precludes consideration of unilateral relationships (i.e., unreciprocated friendships).

group, a class of 10 boys. The data analyzed in this example are the reciprocal friendship patterns and perceptions of aggression shown in Figure 11.3.

Perceptions of aggression. We first examined the univariate SRM for the matrix to the right—perceptions of aggression. We begin with this matrix because it most directly parallels the traditional univariate SRM described above. We see that Adolescent 1 nominated his peers, on average, for 6.94% of the aggression items. This percentage cannot yet be contrasted with the group average of 3.19%, until we have formally computed his actor effect. Using Equation 1 above, we compute an actor effect for Adolescent 1 ($\hat{a}_1$) of 3.75 (row mean = 6.94, column mean = 2.78, group mean = 3.19, $n = 10$). This actor effect accounts for the fact that this boy did not evaluate himself (i.e., it corrects for the fact that we do not have a measure of his perceptions of someone like himself, someone just below the group mean in being perceived as aggressive) and subtracts the group mean (i.e., the positive actor effect indicates that this adolescent had higher than average perceptions of others as aggressive). Similarly, we see that Adolescent 1 was nominated for 2.78% of the aggression items, average across the nine peers rating him (i.e., the column mean). To compute this adolescent's partner effect, or tendency to be perceived by others as aggressive, we employ Equation 2 above, which weights this column mean, corrects for the fact that this boy (who tends to perceive others as aggressive) did not report on himself, and subtract the group mean. This results in a partner effect for Adolescent 1 ($\hat{b}_1$) of 0.00— this adolescent can be considered average within this group in how aggressive others perceive him. Actor and partner effects for each of the other nine adolescents in the group would be computed.

We would next compute the unique effects across each of the 90 [10 * (10-1)] directional dyadic relationships. Consider the perceptions of Adolescent 1 toward Adolescent 2. We see that Adolescent 1 nominated Adolescent 2 on 25% of the aggression items. In order to evaluate the extent to which Adolescent 1 views Adolescent 2 as uniquely aggressive, we must compute the unique effect ($\hat{g}_{12}$) using Equation 3 above. Specifically, this effect is 25 − 3.75 − 5.00 − 3.19 = 13.06. Because this value is positive, we can conclude that Adolescent 1 views Adolescent 2 as especially aggressive, above and beyond (a) Adolescent 1's tendencies to view others as aggressive, (b) the tendency of Adolescent 2 to be viewed as average in aggression by others, and (c) the average levels of perceived aggression in this group of boys. The remaining 89 unique effects would be computed.

Next we compute the variance and covariance terms for this group. Paralleling the order of Equations 4 through 8 above, we compute the following. Because this term is used in subsequent equations, we begin by using Equation 4 to compute the amount of variance that is due to unique/relationship

Nonsymmetric (directional) matrix of perceptions of aggression

	1	2	3	4	5	6	7	8	9	10	M_i.	a_i
1	--	25.0	0.0	12.5	12.5	12.5	0.0	0.0	0.0	0.0	6.94	3.75
2	12.5	--	0.0	0.0	0.0	0.0	0.0	0.0	0.0	0.0	1.39	-1.25
3	12.5	12.5	--	0.0	0.0	0.0	0.0	0.0	0.0	12.5	4.17	0.78
4	0.0	0.0	0.0	--	0.0	0.0	0.0	0.0	12.5	12.5	2.78	-0.47
5	0.0	0.0	0.0	12.5	--	0.0	0.0	0.0	0.0	12.5	2.78	-0.63
6	0.0	12.5	0.0	0.0	0.0	--	0.0	0.0	25.0	0.0	4.17	1.09
7	0.0	25.0	12.5	0.0	0.0	25.0	--	0.0	0.0	0.0	6.94	3.44
8	0.0	0.0	0.0	0.0	0.0	0.0	0.0	--	0.0	12.5	1.39	-2.19
9	0.0	0.0	0.0	0.0	0.0	0.0	0.0	0.0	--	0.0	0.00	-2.97
10	0.0	0.0	0.0	0.0	0.0	0.0	0.0	0.0	12.5	--	1.39	-1.56
M_.i	2.78	8.33	1.39	2.78	1.39	4.17	0.00	0.00	5.56	5.56	3.19	
b_i	0.00	5.00	-1.72	-0.47	-1.88	1.09	-2.81	-3.44	2.03	2.19		

Symmetric matrix of reciprocal friendships

	1	2	3	4	5	6	7	8	9	10	M_i.	a_i
1	--	1	0	0	1	1	0	0	0	1	.44	.28
2	1	--	0	0	0	0	0	0	0	0	.11	-.10
3	0	0	--	0	0	0	0	0	0	0	.00	-.23
4	0	0	0	--	0	0	0	0	1	0	.11	-.10
5	1	0	0	0	--	1	1	0	0	1	.44	.28
6	1	0	0	0	1	--	0	0	0	0	.22	.02
7	0	0	0	0	1	0	--	0	0	0	.11	-.10
8	0	0	0	0	0	0	0	--	0	0	.00	-.23
9	0	0	0	1	0	0	0	0	--	1	.22	.02
10	1	0	0	0	1	0	0	0	1	--	.33	.15
M_.i	.44	.11	.00	.11	.44	.22	.11	.00	.22	.33	.20	
b_i	.28	-.10	-.23	-.10	.28	.02	-.10	-.23	.02	.15		

Figure 11.3. Illustrative data from a class of 10 boys.

Univariate SRM

Unique variance:

$$s_g^2 = \frac{1}{2}\left[\frac{2\sum\left(\frac{\hat{g}_{ij}+\hat{g}_{ji}}{2}\right)^2}{\left[(n-1)(n-2)\right]\big/2} - 1\right] + \frac{\sum(\hat{g}_{ij}-\hat{g}_{ji})^2}{(n-1)(n-2)} = .136$$

$$s_g^2 = \frac{1}{2}\left[\frac{2\sum\left(\frac{\hat{g}_{ij}+\hat{g}_{ji}}{2}\right)^2}{\left[(n-1)(n-2)\right]\big/2} - 1\right] + \frac{\sum(\hat{g}_{ij}-\hat{g}_{ji})^2}{(n-1)(n-2)} = 36.89$$

Relationship covariance: *(necessarily, r = 1.0)*

$$s_{gg'} = \frac{1}{2}\left[\frac{2\sum\left(\frac{\hat{g}_{ij}+\hat{g}_{ji}}{2}\right)^2}{\left[(n-1)(n-2)\right]\big/2} - 1\right] - \frac{\sum(\hat{g}_{ij}-\hat{g}_{ji})^2}{(n-1)(n-2)} = 6.510$$

Actor variance:

$$s_a^2 = \frac{\sum \hat{a}_i^2}{n-1} - \frac{s_g^2(n-1)}{n(n-2)} - \frac{s_{gg'}}{n(n-2)} = .017$$

$$s_a^2 = \frac{\sum \hat{a}_i^2}{n-1} - \frac{s_g^2(n-1)}{n(n-2)} - \frac{s_{gg'}}{n(n-2)} = .868$$

Partner variance:

$$s_b^2 = \frac{\sum \hat{b}_i^2}{n-1} - \frac{s_g^2(n-1)}{n(n-2)} - \frac{s_{gg'}}{n(n-2)} = .017 \ \text{(equal to actor)}$$

$$s_b^2 = \frac{\sum \hat{b}_i^2}{n-1} - \frac{s_g^2(n-1)}{n(n-2)} - \frac{s_{gg'}}{n(n-2)} = 2.604$$

Actor-partner covariance: *(necessarily, r = 1.0)*

$$s_{ab} = \frac{\sum(\hat{a}_i\hat{b}_i)}{n-1} - \frac{s_{gg'}(n-1)}{n(n-2)} - \frac{s_g^2}{n(n-2)} = -3.038$$

263

Bivariate SRM

Individual-actor covariance:

$$\text{cov}(\hat{a}_x, \hat{a}_y) = \frac{\sum_{i>j} \hat{a}_{xi} \hat{a}_{yi}}{n-1} - \left(\frac{n-1}{2n(n-2)}\right) \left\{ \frac{2\sum_{i>j}\left[\left(\frac{\hat{g}_{xij}+\hat{g}_{xji}}{2}\right)\left(\frac{\hat{g}_{yij}+\hat{g}_{yji}}{2}\right)\right]}{\left[\frac{(n-1)(n-2)}{2}\right]-1} + \frac{\sum_{i>j}\left[(\hat{g}_{xij}+\hat{g}_{xji})(\hat{g}_{yij}+\hat{g}_{yji})\right]}{(n-1)(n-2)}\right\}$$
$$- \left(\frac{1}{2n(n-2)}\right)\left\{\frac{2\sum_{i>j}\left[\left(\frac{\hat{g}_{xij}+\hat{g}_{xji}}{2}\right)\left(\frac{\hat{g}_{yij}+\hat{g}_{yji}}{2}\right)\right]}{\left[\frac{(n-1)(n-2)}{2}\right]-1} - \frac{\sum_{i>j}\left[(\hat{g}_{xij}+\hat{g}_{xji})(\hat{g}_{yij}+\hat{g}_{yji})\right]}{(n-1)(n-2)}\right\} = .072$$

Individual-partner covariance:

$$\text{cov}(\hat{a}_x, \hat{b}_y) = \frac{\sum_{i>j} \hat{a}_{xi} \hat{b}_{yi}}{n-1} - \left(\frac{n-1}{2n(n-2)}\right)\left\{\frac{2\sum_{i>j}\left[\left(\frac{\hat{g}_{xij}+\hat{g}_{xji}}{2}\right)\left(\frac{\hat{g}_{yij}+\hat{g}_{yji}}{2}\right)\right]}{\left[\frac{(n-1)(n-2)}{2}\right]-1} + \frac{\sum_{i>j}\left[(\hat{g}_{xij}+\hat{g}_{xji})(\hat{g}_{yij}+\hat{g}_{yji})\right]}{(n-1)(n-2)}\right\}$$
$$- \left(\frac{1}{2n(n-2)}\right)\left\{\frac{2\sum_{i>j}\left[\left(\frac{\hat{g}_{xij}+\hat{g}_{xji}}{2}\right)\left(\frac{\hat{g}_{yij}+\hat{g}_{yji}}{2}\right)\right]}{\left[\frac{(n-1)(n-2)}{2}\right]-1} + \frac{\sum_{i>j}\left[(\hat{g}_{xij}+\hat{g}_{xji})(\hat{g}_{yij}+\hat{g}_{yji})\right]}{(n-1)(n-2)}\right\} = .089$$

Dyadic-dyadic covariance:

$$\text{cov}(\hat{g}_x, \hat{g}_y) = \left(\frac{n-1}{2n(n-2)}\right)\left\{\frac{2\sum_{i>j}\left[\left(\frac{\hat{g}_{xij}+\hat{g}_{xji}}{2}\right)\left(\frac{\hat{g}_{yij}+\hat{g}_{yji}}{2}\right)\right]}{\left[\frac{(n-1)(n-2)}{2}\right]-1} + \frac{\sum_{i>j}\left[(\hat{g}_{xij}+\hat{g}_{xji})(\hat{g}_{yij}+\hat{g}_{yji})\right]}{(n-1)(n-2)}\right\} = .067$$

effects, or the relationship variance, s_g^2. We find that the variance due to unique perceptions of particular adolescents in this group toward particular peers is 36.89. By itself, this value is difficult to interpret, but it will be compared below to the amount of actor and partner variance in order to determine its relative effect. Using the similar Equation 5, we compute the relationship covariance, $s_{gg'} = 6.51$. This covariance is the unstandardized association between how a particular adolescent perceives a particular peer (e.g., how Adolescent 1 perceives Adolescent 2) and how that particular peer perceives the adolescent (e.g., how Adolescent 2 perceives Adolescent 1). To calculate this association in standardized form (i.e., the relationship correlation) this covariance is divided by the relationship variance: $6.51/36.89 = 0.18$. This correlation is interpreted as a small-to-moderate association between how one adolescent perceives another and how that other perceives the adolescent as aggressive.

Having obtained estimates of the dyad-level variance and covariance, we can compute the individual-level variances and covariance. We first consider the actor variance, or the variance due to individual differences in perceptions of others as aggressive (and the tendency of adolescents to perceive others in an assimilated way). Using Equation 7, we obtain an estimated actor variance $(s_a^2) = 0.89$. Similarly, we estimate the partner variance, or variance due to individual differences in being perceived by others as aggressive (and the tendency for consensus among these adolescents perceptions of aggression), using Equation 8: partner variance $(s_b^2) = 2.60$. With these three variance terms (actor, partner, and unique/relationship) from the univariate SRM, we can compute the relative amounts of variance accounted for by each effect. Dividing each variance term by the sum of these three variances [e.g., relative actor variance $= 0.89/(0.89 + 2.60 + 36.89) = .022$], we find that 2.2% of the variance in perceptions of aggression in this group is due to actor effects, 6.5% due to partner effects, and 91.4% due to unique/partner effects. Clearly, unique perceptions held by particular adolescents toward particular peers predominate in this group, although—as we will see below when we aggregate across all groups—we should be cautious about dismissing the individual differences (actor and partner variance) found here.

Finally, we can compute the actor–partner covariance, which indexes the magnitude of association between how an adolescent perceives his peers in general and how that adolescent is perceived by his peers in general. Applying Equation 6, we find that the actor–partner covariance (s_{ab}) equals –3.04. As with the relationship covariance, it aids interpretation to compute the standardized version of this association by dividing by the relevant variances. Here, we compute the actor–partner correlation by dividing this covariance by the square root of the product of actor and partner variances: $-3.04/\sqrt{(0.87}$

* 2.60) $= -2.02$. Here, the implied actor–partner covariance is out of bounds (illustrating to the reader, we hope, that we did not select a "perfect case" for this illustration). In this situation, we cannot interpret the actor–partner correlation. We can speculate that the reason for this out-of-bounds estimate is the relatively small amount of individual-level (i.e., actor and/or partner) variance, probably in this case the small actor variance estimate. In situations of out-of-bounds (i.e., negative) variance estimates, it is best not to compute the associated covariances (i.e., do not compute the actor–partner covariance with inadmissible actor or partner variances, or the relationship covariance with inadmissible unique variance); when these variance estimates are small, the associated covariances should be interpreted cautiously, and perhaps not interpreted at all if the overall (aggregated across groups, see below) variance terms are not significantly greater than zero.

Reciprocal friendships. In the friendship matrix to the left in Figure 11.3, we see that Adolescent 1 was engaged in reciprocal friendships with 4 of his 9 classmates, so his row and column mean is 4/9, or 0.44. We compute his individual effect using Equation 1 (for actor effects) above, which adjusts this mean level to account for the fact that this adolescent did not have the opportunity to befriend himself and subtracts the group mean, and obtain an actor effect for this adolescent $(\hat{a}_1)$ of .28. This positive value indicates that Adolescent 1 has somewhat more reciprocal friends than is average for his class. Note that the column mean and computed partner effect for Adolescent 1 are identical to his actor effect. The duplicity of row and column means (and therefore the actor and partner effects) is due to the symmetry of this reciprocal friendship matrix. Therefore, rather than computing separate actor and partner effects for each adolescent, we compute a common individual effect. Similarly, rather than estimating separate actor and partner variances, we estimate a common individual variance. The fact that actor and partner effects are identical also implies that they are perfectly correlated, so the standardized actor–partner association is necessarily 1.0.

For each of the 45 $[(10 * (10\text{-}1))/2]$ possible reciprocal relationships, we can compute a unique or relationship effect. Considering the friendship between Adolescents 1 and 2, we decompose the existing friendship (i.e., x_{12}) into that which is due to (a) the unique relationship, (b) the tendencies of Adolescents 1 and 2 to have many or few friends (i.e., their individual effects), and (c) the group average number of friends. In other words, the unique effect of the friendship between Adolescents 1 and 2 (from Equation 3) is $g_{12} = 1 - .28 - (-.10) - .20 = .62$. Similar unique effects between the 44 remaining pairs of boys are also computed. Using these values, we can then compute the amount of variance in the occurrence of reciprocal friendships that is due to unique effects using Equation 4, yielding a unique variance estimate (s_g^2) of .136.[5]

To summarize, we have two meaningful, nonduplicated parameters that are estimated in this univariate analysis of the reciprocal friendship nominations: an individual variance estimate (the identical actor and partner variances) and the unique or relationship variance. The relative proportion of variance in the friendships accounted for at each level indicates that individual differences account for 11.2% [.017 / (.017+.136)] of this variance whereas unique effects account for 88.8% [.136 / (.017+.136)]. Here, the occurrence of friendships is largely a dyadic phenomenon more so than one dependent on some adolescents having many friends and others few.

Bivariate associations between friendship and perceptions of aggression. We now consider the three bivariate covariances that can be computed between the symmetric friendship matrix and the nonsymmetric (directional) perceptions of aggression matrix of Figure 11.3. In the following paragraphs, and in the formulas at the bottom of Figure 11.3, we denote the friendship effects and parameters as X and those for perceptions of aggression as Y. This notation is simply for clarity; it should be noted that we are evaluating covariances (not regression paths) between variables measured at the same point in time. Therefore, our notation should not be assumed to denote causal relations.

The first of the three bivariate associations is the individual-level covariance between individual variance in friendships (some individuals have more whereas some have fewer friendships) and the actor effects for perceptions of aggression (individual differences in tendencies to see peers in general as more or less aggressive). Because Equations 11 and 14 yield identical estimates given the identical actor and partner effects of the symmetric friendship matrix, the more general equation (first bivariate equation) of Figure 11.3 is used. We find that, for this group of adolescent boys, the individual–actor covariance is .072. To obtain a more interpretable metric, we compute the standardized correlation by dividing this covariance by the square root of the product of the two relevant variances (individual variance in friendship and actor variance in perceptions of aggression): $r = .072/\sqrt{(.017 * .868)} = .591$.

---

[5]Note that the similar equation (Equation 5 above) for relationship covariance necessarily yields an identical value (i.e., $s_{gg'} = .136$; because the difference scores that form the second part of Equations 4 and 5 are zero given the symmetry of this matrix), so if we attempted to compute this association, the standardized value would necessarily be 1.0. This also makes sense conceptually because Adolescent i's friendship toward j is necessarily the same as Adolescent j's friendship toward i when we are considering reciprocal relationships.

This correlation indicates that there is a strong tendency for the boys with more friends to perceive others as more aggressive than do boys with fewer friends.

The second bivariate association we can consider is the relation between number of friends adolescents have and how they are perceived by others. Here we use the second bivariate equation in Figure 11.3 (taken from Equations 12 and 13 above), which differs from the first in that the first term involves the product of the individual friendship effects with the partner effects of aggression. This covariance is .089 and when converted to a standardized metric yields $r = .089/\sqrt{(.017 * 2.604)} = .42$. This correlation indicates that, within this group of boys, adolescents who have more friends tend to be perceived by others (in general) as more aggressive than are adolescents with fewer friends.

The third covariance to compute is between the unique effects of the friendship and perceptions of aggression matrices. This covariance is the combined intrapersonal and interpersonal covariances of traditional bivariate SRM (Equations 9 and 10), which are equivalent given the symmetry of the reciprocal friendship matrix. The equation for computing this dyadic–dyadic covariance is shown at the bottom of Figure 11.3 and yields a covariance of .067. To put this in a standardized metric, we divide this value by the square root of the product of the two unique variances (from friendships and perceptions of aggression): $r = .067/\sqrt{(.136 * 36.89)} = .03$. This correlation is essentially zero, so would not be interpreted. For illustrative purposes, however, a meaningful positive association would indicate that perceptions within friendships tend to be of higher aggression than are perceptions outside of friendship (again, this is a very small effect in this group).

Aggregated Univariate SRM Results

Although it is informative to step through the calculations and results for one particular group, we draw more reliable conclusions by aggregating results across all groups in a study (33 in this example). A second important advantage of aggregating across groups is that it allows us to estimate the statistical significance of these parameters (cf. alternative methods of significance testing by Lashley & Bond, 1997). Before turning to the bivariate SRM results that are our focus, we describe briefly the univariate results. We consider first the univariate SRM of the perceptions of aggression and prosocial behavior and then the univariate SRM of the symmetric reciprocal friendship matrices.

Aggression. Analysis of perceptions of aggression indicates significant (all $p < .05$) variability due to individual differences in how adolescents perceive others in general (actor effects) and how adolescents are perceived by others in general (partner effects). Specifically, 4.8% of variability in perceptions of aggression is due to perceiver differences, and 25.0% is due to individual differences in being perceived as aggressive. However, the majority (70.2%) of variance in interpersonal perceptions of aggression is due to relationship effects.

The actor–partner covariance was not significant, indicating no evidence that adolescent who perceive others (in general) as aggressive tend to be perceived by others as especially high or low in aggression. A marginal effect for dyadic covariance in perceptions of aggression ($p = .059$) emerged, suggesting that when adolescents perceived a particular peer as aggressive, that particular peer also tended to view the adolescent as aggressive (i.e., if Adam views Billy as aggressive, Billy tends to view Adam as aggressive; standardized $r = .10$).

These reliable actor, partner, and unique effects replicate those of Card et al. (2004) and provide further support for the importance of considering (a) individual differences in adolescents' perceptions of others as aggressive (consistent with evidence of individual differences in hostile attributional biases; e.g., Dodge, 1980); (b) individual differences in adolescents' being perceived by others as aggressive (consistent with common usage of peer nomination instruments to measure aggression); and, especially, (c) the unique perceptions certain adolescents have of certain peers as being aggressive. Card et al. (2004) did not find evidence of dyadic reciprocity in perceptions of aggression, so we should be cautious in interpreting the marginal association found here.

Prosocial Behavior. The perceptions of others as prosocial also indicated significant actor (9.5%) and partner (11.9%) variance, and that a majority of variance was due to unique perceptions that certain adolescents have of certain peers (i.e., relationship variance, 78.6%).[6] As with perceptions of aggression, the univariate SRM of prosocial behavior indicates that (a) there are reliable individual differences in adolescents' tendencies to view others as prosocial, (b) there are reliable individual differences in adolescents' tendencies to be viewed as prosocial by peers, but (c) perceptions of prosocial behavior during early adolescence are primarily due to dyad-specific perceptions.

We also tested for potential reciprocity of perceptions of prosocial behavior at the general (actor–partner covariance) and dyadic (dyadic reciprocity covariance) levels. As was the case for perceptions of aggression, we found no

---

[6]To our knowledge, this is the first empirical presentation where the variance of perceptions of prosocial behavior toward peers has been portioned in the SRM (Malloy et al., 1995, examined perceptions of others as "well behaved").

evidence for an actor–partner association. But we did find evidence of dyadic reciprocity, such that adolescents who perceived a particular peer as prosocial tended to also be viewed as prosocial by that peer, $r = .16$.

Reciprocal Friendships. Univariate analysis of the symmetric friendship matrices yields two meaningful parameters: individual variance (the actor and partner variances in a nonsymmetric SRM, which are necessarily equal given the symmetry of the reciprocal friendship matrices analyzed) and relationship variance (again, the actor–partner and dyadic reciprocity correlations are necessarily 1.0 given the symmetry of these matrices). There was evidence for significant individual differences in the numbers of reciprocal friendships, supporting the commonsense notion that some adolescents tend to have more friends than others. However, the proportion of variance due to individual effects was small, 5.4%. Instead, the vast majority of variance (94.6%) in the occurrence of reciprocal friendships is unique variance, supporting the idea that friendships are a dyadic phenomenon.

Aggregated Bivariate SRM Results

We now present results of bivariate SRMs examining the associations of friendships with perceptions of aggression and prosocial behavior. Paralleling the three meaningful covariances that emerge from these results, we will present these findings in three sections.

How adolescents with mutual friends perceive others. The first set of bivariate SRM associations considered are between the individual effects of having more versus fewer reciprocal friends with individual differences in perceiving others as aggressive and prosocial (i.e., association of individual friendship effects with actor effects in perceptions). Individual differences in having friends were not significantly associated with perceptions of others as aggressive, but were associated with perceptions of others as prosocial. Specifically, adolescents with more reciprocated friends tended to see others (in general) as more prosocial than did adolescents with fewer friends ($r = .59$).

How adolescents with mutual friends are perceived by others. The next set of bivariate SRM associations are between the individual effects of having more versus fewer reciprocal friends with individual differences in being perceived by others as aggressive and prosocial (i.e., association of individual friendship effects with partner effects in perceptions). Here, we find that individual differences in having friends are not significantly associated with being perceived by others (in general) as either aggressive or prosocial.

Perceptions within friendships. Perhaps of most interest are the associations between unique friendship effects and unique perceptions of aggression and prosocial behavior. These associations indicate the extent to which perceptions within friendships are unique, after accounting for the individual-level tendencies of those in the relationships. Results indicated significant effects for both aggression and prosocial behavior. Adolescents were significantly more likely to view their friends as aggressive relative to nonfriends, $r = .11$. The effect for perceptions prosocial behavior were more pronounced, with perceptions of prosocial behavior being especially high within friendships, $r = .37$. These results indicate that adolescents are especially likely to view their friends, relative to nonfriends, as being both aggressive and prosocial.

CONCLUSION

The goal of this chapter was to describe a modification of the bivariate SRM that can be applied to the study of relationships in which members overlap (i.e., individuals are involved in more than one relationship). We demonstrated the use of this approach in studying early adolescent friendships; specifically in examining associations between early adolescents' engagement in reciprocal friendships and their interpersonal perceptions of aggression and prosocial behavior. We believe that this approach has several advantages over other methods of studying dyadic relationships—including the allowance that individuals may have multiple relationships, that some individuals may not be involved in any relationships, and the separation of individual- and dyad-level effects—which make this approach useful in studying adolescent friendships.

We believe that there are several important steps in further developing this modified bivariate SRM for studying dyadic relationships. One task may be to adapt alternative methods of significance testing that can be used with single groups and might have greater statistical power (Lashley & Bond, 1997) for use with the bivariate SRM (for preliminary work in this area, see Bond & Malloy, 2007).

A second important future direction in quantitative research is to extend this modified bivariate SRM to longitudinal analysis. In the illustrative example, we evaluated only concurrent links between friendships and perceptions; thus, we were not able to infer directions of effect. With two time points, it might be possible to evaluate whether friendships predict (at the individual- and/or dyad-level) increases or decreases in perceptions of aggression and prosocial behavior (i.e., friendships predicting perceptions), and whether perceptions in these constructs predict changes in friendships (i.e., perceptions predicting the formation and/or termination of friendships). Both processes might be plausible, but it will be necessary to extend the bivariate SRM to a more general multivariate regression model in order to test these processes. With increasing time points, it might also be possible to model growth curves of friendships and perceptions, and examine the associations across these curves. These longitudinal extensions of the SRM in general, and to the modified bivariate SRM described here in particular, will be important if these techniques are going to be used in developmental research.

In the illustrative example of this chapter, we considered adolescent friendships. However, this approach might be fruitfully applied to other types of relationships. For example, antipathetic relationships—relationships based on dislike—have been shown to be a common and influential type of relationship experienced during adolescence (see Card, 2007; Hartup & Abecassis, 2002; Hodges & Card, 2003). Both friendships and antipathetic relationships can be considered nondirectional (i.e., indistinguishable) types of dyads, but the modified bivariate SRM could also be applied to directional (i.e., distinguishable) dyads as well by using a nonsymmetric matrix of relationships (i.e., the left matrix of Figure 11.3). This extension would also accommodate situations in which some dyads are directional whereas others are nondirectional, such as aggressor–victim relationships (which are most commonly unilateral, but some can be mutually aggressive relationships; see Card & Hodges, 2007)—a situation for which traditional methods of dyadic data analysis have not been well adapted (see Kenny et al., 2006).

In sum, we believe that the modified bivariate SRM described in this chapter is a useful approach to studying dyadic relationships in which individuals may variously be in no, one, or multiple relationships, such as is the case for adolescent friendships. As described in this section, however, this approach is new and there is a need for further quantitative development and application in developmental research. Nevertheless, we hope that readers will consider this approach as a viable alternative to studying dyadic relationships in developmental research.

272   CARD, LITTLE, AND SELIG

REFERENCES

44

Adams, R. E., Bukowski, W. M., & Bagwell, C. (2005). Stability of aggression during early adolescence as moderated by reciprocal friendship status and friend's aggression. *International Journal of Behavioral Development, 29,* 139-145.

Bond, C. F., Jr., & Malloy, T. E. (2007). *Social relations analysis of arbitrary data structures.* Manuscript submitted for publication.

Branje, S. J. T., Finkenauer, C., & Meeus, W. H. J. (chapter 12). Modeling interdependence using the social relations model: The investment model in family relationships. In N. A. Card, J. P. Selig, & T. D. Little (Eds.), *Modeling dyadic and interdependent data in the developmental and behavioral sciences.* New York, NY: Routledge/Taylor & Francis Group.

Branje, S. J. T., van Aken, M. A. G., & van Lieshout, C. F. M. (2002). Relational support in families with adolescents. *Journal of Family Psychology, 16,* 351-362.

Branje, S. J. T., van Aken, M. A. G., van Lieshout, C. F. M., & Mathijssen, J. J. J. P. (2003). Personality judgments in adolescents' families: The perceiver, the target, their relationship, and the family. *Journal of Personality, 71,* 49-81.

Branje, S. J. T., van Lieshout, C. F. M., & van Aken, M. A. G. (2002). Relations between agreeableness and perceived support in family relationships: Why nice people are not always supportive. *International Journal of Behavioral Development, 29,* 120-128.

Buist, K. L., Dekovic, M., Meeus, W. H., & van Aken, M. A. G. (2004). Attachment in adolescence: A social relations model analysis. *Journal of Adolescent Research, 19,* 826-850.

Cairns, R. B., Leung, M.-C., Buchanan, L., & Cairns, B. D. (1995). Friendships and social networks in childhood and adolescence: Fluidity, reliability, and interrelations. *Child Development, 66,* 1330-1345.

Card, N. A. (2007). "I hated her guts!": Emerging adults' recollections of the formation, maintenance, and termination of antipathetic relationships during high school. *Journal of Adolescent Research, 22,* 32-57.

Card, N. A., & Hodges, E. V. E. (2006). Shared targets for aggression by early adolescent friends. *Developmental Psychology, 42,* 1327-1338.

Card, N. A., & Hodges, E. V. E. (2007). Victimization within mutually antipathetic peer relationships. *Social Development, 160,* 479-496.

Card, N. A., Hodges, E. V. E., Little, T. D., & Hawley, P. H. (2005). Gender effects in peer nominations for aggression and social status. *International Journal of Behavioral Development, 29,* 146-155.

Card, N. A., & Little, T. D. (2006). Proactive and reactive aggression in childhood and adolescence: A meta-analysis of differential relations with psychosocial adjustment. *International Journal of Behavioral Development, 30,* 466-480.

Card, N. A., Romero, P. A., & Weissman, S. E. (2004). *Peer nominations of aggression and victimization: A social relations analysis.* Paper presented at the 10th biennial meeting of the Society for Research on Adolescence, Baltimore, MD.

Card, N. A., Stucky, B. D., Sawalani, G. M., & Little, T. D. (in press). Direct and indirect aggression during childhood and adolescence: A meta-analytic review of gender differences, intercorrelations, and relations to maladjustment. *Developmental Psychology.*

Cillessen, A. H. N., Jiang, X. L., West, T. V., & Laszkowski, D. K. (2005). Predictors of dyadic friendship quality in adolescence. *International Journal of Behavioral Development, 29*, 165-172.

Coie, J. D., Cillessen, A. H. N., Dodge, K. A., Hubbard, J. A., Schwartz, D., Lemerise, E. A., et al. (1999). It takes two to fight: A test of relational factors and a method for assessing aggressive dyads. *Developmental Psychology, 35*, 1179-1188.

Cook, W. L. (1993). Interdependence and the interpersonal sense of control: An analysis of family relationships. *Journal of Personality and Social Psychology, 64*, 587-601.

Cook, W. L. (1994). A structural equation model of dyadic relationships within the family system. *Journal of Consulting and Clinical Psychology, 62*, 500-509.

Cook, W. L. (2000). Understanding attachment security in family context. *Journal of Personality and Social Psychology, 78*, 285-294.

Cook, W. L. (2001). Interpersonal influence in family systems: A Social Relations Model analysis. *Child Development, 72*, 1179-1197.

Cook, W. L. (2005). The SRM approach to family assessment: An introduction and case example. *European Journal of Psychological Assessment, 21*, 216-225.

Cook, W. L., & Dreyer, A. (1984). The Social Relations Model: A new approach to the analysis of family-dyadic interaction. *Journal of Marriage and the Family, 46*, 679-687.

Cook, W. L., & Kenny, D. A. (2004). Application of the Social Relations Model to family assessment. *Journal of Family Psychology, 18*, 361-371.

Cook, W. L., & Kenny, D. A. (2005). The Actor-Partner Interdependence Model: A model of bidirectional effects in developmental studies. *International Journal of Behavioral Development, 29*, 101-109.

Cook, W. L., Kenny, D. A., & Goldstein, M. J. (1991). Parental affective style risk and the family system: A Social Relations Model analysis. *Journal of Abnormal Psychology, 100*, 492-501.

Crick, N. R., & Dodge, K. A. (1994). A review and reformulation of social information-processing mechanisms in children's social adjustment. *Psychological Bulletin, 115*, 74-101.

Delsing, M. J. M. H., Oud, J. H. L., De Bruyn, E. E. J., & van Aken, M. A. G. (2003). Current and recollected perceptions of family relationships: The Social Relations Model approach applied to members of three generations. *Journal of Family Psychology, 17*, 445-459.

Delsing, M. J. M. H., van Aken, M. A. G., Oud, J. H. L., De Bruyn, E. E. J., & Scholte, R. H. J. (2005). Family loyalty and adolescent problem behavior: The validity of the family group effect. *Journal of Research on Adolescence*, *15*, 127-150.

Dodge, K. A. (1980). Social cognition and children's aggressive behavior. *Child Development*, *51*, 162-170.

Finkenauer, C., Engels, R. C. M. E., Branje, S. J. T., & Meeus, W. H. J. (2004). Disclosure and relationship satisfaction in families. *Journal of Marriage and Family*, *66*, 195-209.

Gifford-Smith, M. E., & Rabiner, D. L. (2004). Social information processing and children's social adjustment. In J. B. Kupersmidt & K. A. Dodge (Eds.), *Children's peer relations: From development to intervention* (pp. 61-79). Washington, DC: American Psychological Association.

Gonzalez, R., & Griffin, D. W. (1997). On the statistics of interdependence: Treating dyadic data with respect. In S. Duck (Ed.), *Handbook of personal relationships, 2nd ed.* (pp. 271-302). New York: John Wiley & Sons.

Griffin, D. W., & Gonzalez, R. (1995). Correlational analysis of dyad-level data in the exchangeable case. *Psychological Methods*, *118*, 430-439.

Hartup, W. W., & Abecassis, M. (2002). Friends and enemies. In P. K. Smith & C. H. Hart (Eds.), *Blackwell handbook of childhood social development* (pp. 285-306). Oxford: Blackwell.

Hodges, E. V. E., & Card, N. A. (Eds.). (2003). Enemies and the darker side of peer relations. *New Directions for Child and Adolescent Development*, *102*. San Francisco: Jossey-Bass.

Hoyt, W. T., Fincham, F. C., McCullough, M. E., Maio, G., & Davila, J. (2005). Responses to interpersonal transgressions in families: Forgivingness, forgivability, and relationship-specific effects. *Journal of Personality and Social Psychology*, *89*, 375-394.

Hsiung, R. O., & Bagozzi, R. P. (2003). Validating the relationship qualities of influence and persuasion with the family social relations model. *Human Communication Research*, *29*, 81-110.

Hubbard, J. A., Dodge, K. A., Cillessen, A. H. N., Coie, J. D., & Schwartz, D. (2001). The dyadic nature of social information processing in boys' reactive and proactive aggression. *Journal of Personality and Social Psychology*, *80*, 268-280.

Kashy, D. A., & Kenny, D. A. (2000). The analysis of data from dyads and groups. In H. T. Reis & C. M. Judd (Eds.), *Handbook of research methods in social and personality psychology* (pp. 451-477). New York: Cambridge University Press.

Kenny, D. A. (1994). *Interpersonal perception: A social relations analysis*. New York: Guilford Press.

Kenny, D. A. (1996). Models of nonindependence in dyadic research. *Journal of Social and Personal Relationships*, *13*, 279-294.

Kenny, D. A. (1998). *SOREMO* (Version 2) [Computer software and manual]. University of Connecticut.

Kenny, D. A., & Albright, L. (1987). Accuracy in interpersonal perception: A social relations analysis. *Psychological Bulletin, 102*, 390-402.

Kenny, D. A., Albright, L., Malloy, T. E., & Kashy, D. A. (1994). Consensus in interpersonal perception: Acquaintance and the big five. *Psychological Bulletin, 116*, 245-258.

Kenny, D. A., & DePaulo, B. M. (1993). Do people know how others view them? An empirical and theoretical account. *Psychological Bulletin, 114*, 145-161.

Kenny, D. A., Kashy, D. A., & Cook, W. L. (2006). *Dyadic data analysis.* New York: Guilford Press.

Kenny, D. A., & La Voie, L. (1984). The Social Relations Model. In L. Berkowitz (Ed.), *Advances in experimental social psychology* (Vol. 18, pp. 142-182). Orlando, FL: Academic Press.

Lashley, B. R., & Bond, C. F., Jr. (1997). Perceived distributions of the characteristics of in-group and out-group members: Empirical evidence and a computer simulation. *Psychological Methods, 2*, 278-291.

Little, T. D., & Card, N. A. (2005). On the use of Social Relations and Actor-Partner Interdependence Models in developmental research. *International Journal of Behavioral Development, 29*, 173-179.

Maccoby, E. E. (1998). *The two sexes: Growing up apart, coming together.* Cambridge, MA: Harvard University Press.

Malloy, T. E., & Kenny, D. A. (1986). The Social Relations Model: An integrative method for personality research. *Journal of Personality, 54*, 199-223.

Malloy, T. E., Sugarman, D. B., Montvilo, R. K., & Ben-Zeev, T. (1995). Children's interpersonal perceptions: A social relations analysis of perceiver and target effects. *Journal of Personality and Social Psychology, 68*, 418-426.

Malloy, T. E., Yarlas, A., Montvilo, R. K., & Sugarman, D. B. (1996). Agreement and accuracy in children's interpersonal perceptions: A social relations analysis. *Journal of Personality and Social Psychology, 71*, 692-702.

Ross, H., Stein, N., Trabasso, T., Woody, E., & Ross, M. (2005). The quality of family relationships within and across generations: A social relations analysis. *International Journal of Behavioral Development, 29*, 110-119.

Ross, H. S., & Lollis, S. P. (1989). A social relations analysis of toddler peer relations. *Child Development, 60*, 1082-1091.

Rubin, K. H., Bukowski, W. M., & Parker, J. G. (1998). Peer interactions, relationships, and groups. In W. Damon (Ed.), *Handbook of child psychology: Vol. 3, Social, emotional, and personality development* (pp. 619-700). New York: John Wiley & Sons.

Sadler, P., & Woody, E. (chapter 7). It takes two: A dyadic, SEM-based perspective on personality development. In N. A. Card, J. P. Selig, & T. D. Little (Eds.), *Modeling dyadic and interdependent data in the developmental and behavioral sciences.* New York, NY: Routledge/Taylor & Francis Group.

Schwartz, D., Dodge, K. A., Coie, J. D., Hubbard, J. A., Cillessen, A. H. N., Lemerise, E. A., et al. (1998). Social-cognitive and behavioral correlates of aggression and victimization in boys' play groups. *Journal of Abnormal Child Psychology, 26*, 431-440.

Selig, J. P., McNamara, K. A., Card, N. A., & Little, T. D. (chapter 9). Techniques for modeling dependency in interchangeable dyads. In N. A. Card, J. P. Selig, & T. D. Little (Eds.), *Modeling dyadic and interdependent data in the developmental and behavioral sciences.* New York, NY: Routledge/Taylor & Francis Group.

Stevenson, M. B., Leavitt, L. A., Thompson, R. H., & Roach, M. A. (1988). A Social Relations Model analysis of parent and child play. *Developmental Psychology, 24*, 101-108.

Warner, R. M., Kenny, D. A., & Stoto, M. (1979). A new round robin analysis of variance for social interaction data. *Journal of Personality and Social Psychology, 37*, 1742-1757.

Wasserman, S., & Faust, K. (1994). *Social network analysis: Methods and applications.* New York: Cambridge University Press.

Woody, E., & Sadler, P. (2005). Structural equation models for interchangeable dyads: Being the same makes a difference. *Psychological Methods, 10*, 139-158.

CHAPTER TWELVE

Modeling Interdependence Using the Social Relations Model: The Investment Model in Family Relationships

Susan J. T. Branje

C. Finkenauer

W. H. J. Meeus

University of California, Davis

When studying family relationships, researchers often are interested in relational phenomena at an individual level, such as whether an individual child thrives in a particular family context; relational phenomena at the dyadic level, such as whether the mother is more committed than the father to the relationship; and relational phenomena at the familial level, such as whether some families are more satisfied with their relationships than other families. These three levels of relational phenomena, that is, individuals, dyadic relationships, and groups have to be distinguished and are reciprocally related within the family system (Hinde, 1997; Laursen & Bukowski, 1997). However, their theoretical and methodological interdependence represents a challenge for empirical investigation. The family as a group includes the individual family members and relationships, but these parts combine in such a way that new structures emerge which have their own meaning and are more than a collection of its members and relationships and which may affect relationships and the relationship partners (Reis, Collins, & Berscheid, 2000). Both statistical methods and theoretical frameworks are needed that allow us to disentangle the three levels and the influence they exert on each other and to capture the truly social nature of family relationships.

The interdependence of the three levels is apparent in family members' behavior toward other family members and their perceptions of other family members. These behaviors and perceptions simultaneously reflect a family member's individual characteristics, individual characteristics of the other family members, characteristics of the particular actor–partner relationship, and characteristics of the family as a system (Cook, 1994; Kashy & Kenny, 1990). Thus, when people are asked to rate their family members, each rating comprises aspects of the rating person, his or her rated partner, their dyadic relationship, and the family in which they are embedded. A statistical and methodological tool to distinguish these aspects of ratings and thereby differentiate between different levels of influences is the *Social Relations Model* (SRM). This model was originally proposed by Kenny and La Voie (1984), and extended to the family context by Cook (1993, 1994) and Kashy and Kenny (1990).

This chapter aims to provide an overview of the unique and exciting possibilities that the SRM offers to researchers interested in the empirical investigation of family relationships. For a comprehensive understanding of theoretical and statistical interdependence, it begins by presenting a relational theory, specifically Rusbult's *investment model* (Rusbult, 1983) and applies it to the family. It will then highlight how the hypotheses that can be derived from the investment model translate into SRM. Subsequently, it will describe the SRM and its methodological requirements in more detail and illuminate the possibilities that SRM offers for family researchers. To illustrate some applications of the SRM, the chapter will present three applications of the SRM to findings on the investment model in families. Specifically, the chapter will first examine how the SRM allows us to disentangle and quantify the influence of the three different levels of relational phenomena in the investment model in families. Then, it will show how the SRM can be used to examine specific hypotheses and longitudinal relations in the investment model. Finally, the chapter will present one example of how the SRM can be used to examine individual outcomes by considering all levels of influence in a family over time. To this end, we will present our findings on how relational phenomena predict adolescent depression over time. The chapter will conclude by portraying some of the theoretical and practical implications of the use of SRM for theories and future research.

A Theoretical Framework: The Investment Model

According to the investment model (e.g., Rusbult, 1983), individuals are committed to their relationship to the extent that they are satisfied with the relationship. They are also more committed to the relationship if they have made investments in the relationship that may be lost if the relationship ends, and they are more committed to the relationship if they have poor alternatives to the relationship. Thus, relationship *satisfaction* and *investments* are positively related to relationship *commitment*, whereas *quality of alternatives* is negatively related to relationship commitment (Rusbult, 1983; Rusbult, Johnson, & Morrow, 1986). The investment model has proved fruitful to explain processes in romantic and marital relationships. To explore the extent to which the investment model is applicable to explain commitment in family relationships, we used SRM. On a theoretical level family relationships are characterized by different levels of equality and voluntariness. In the following, we will first focus on the theoretical implications of these differences and consider their implications for SRM.

Differences in family relationships. Family relationships can be distinguished in terms of equality or whether they are *horizontal or vertical*. Although parent–child relationships may become more horizontal during adolescence, parent–child relationships can be regarded as more vertical and asymmetrical than marital relationships (e.g., Hartup, 1989; Maccoby, 1992; Russell, Pettit, & Mize, 1998). Parent–child relationships are marked by unequal exchanges: Parents usually have more knowledge and social power than their children and are also expected to provide security and warmth for their children. Marital relationships are typically horizontal: They are characterized by equality, symmetry, mutual liking, and reciprocity between the marital partners (Laursen & Bukowski, 1997). The horizontal versus vertical nature of different relationships in a family may affect the way the investment model explains relationship processes. Because of the vertical nature of their relationship with their children, parents may invest in their children independent of how satisfied they are with the relationship. In contrast, because of the horizontal nature of their relationship, marital partners may invest in their relationship to the extent to which they perceive their partner to invest in the relationship. Horizontal relationships are based more on mutuality and reciprocity than vertical relationships. Horizontal relationships, more than vertical relationships, need to be perceived as equitable to be satisfactory. Put differently, the benefits that one partner experiences in the relationship need to equal his or her costs or contributions to the relationship. Not only does the investment model differ across vertical and horizontal relationships, it is also likely to differ within vertical relationships. Specifically, while parents may invest in the relationship with their child independent of their satisfaction with the relationship, children's investment may well be contingent on their level of relationship satisfaction with their parents. Adolescents often make a point of being treated fairly by their parents and expect their parents to treat them like equal partners (Collins, Laursen, Mortensen, Luebker, & Ferreira, 1997).

Another important difference between different types of relationships in a family is *voluntariness*. In involuntary relationships terminating the relationship is not an option. Marital relationships can be regarded as voluntary because marital partners have the possibility to divorce. This choice may be more difficult to make when there are children involved, but the choice is there. The relationship between parents and children can be regarded as involuntary. Parents and children are stuck to each other for better and worse. Parents and/or children may choose never to see each other again, for example, but they will always remain parents and children. Due to these differences in voluntariness across family relationships, quality of alternatives may not similarly apply to the parent–child relationship as to marital relationships. Further, parents are socially expected to invest in, take responsibility for, and care for their children. Parental investment also has an evolutionary basis and is directed at reproductive success (Kenrick, Sadalla, Groth, & Trost, 1990). Therefore parents are likely to unconditionally invest in their children regardless of the costs of the relationship. This implies that satisfaction, investments, and quality of alternatives may be less related to commitment in parent–child relationships than in marital relationships. The SRM offers a unique opportunity to explore these suggestions and the investment model in families. Before presenting an empirical study, however, for comprehensive understanding of the SRM and its application to family relationships, we will first focus on SRM in more detail.

The Social Relations Model in Three-Person Families

To be able to use the SRM to examine family relationships, data must be collected within a round-robin design: Each participating family member has to rate the characteristics of each of the other family members, or evaluate his or her relationship with each of the other family members. In a three-person family with two parents and one child, this means that data on six dyadic family relationships (three family members × two partners) are needed for a round-robin design. Family members have clearly assigned roles, such as mother, father, and adolescent. In family research, therefore, the different family members are not interchangeable. Because the individuals within families can be distinguished by their role, different effects for each of these roles can be estimated.

Within the SRM, each dyadic score can be disentangled into four different components: actor, partner, relationship, and family effects (see Figure 12.1). As an example, consider the father's commitment to his adolescent child.

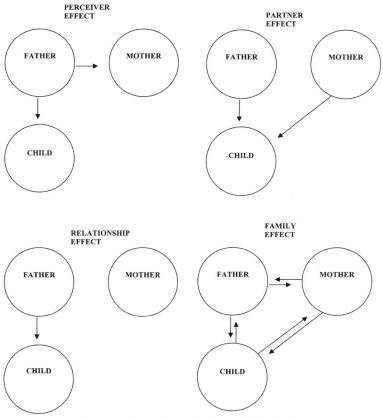

Figure 12.1. The Social Relations Model effects.

The *actor effect* reflects a family member's tendency to act to all other family members in a particular manner. In the example, the actor effect describes the father's tendency to be committed to all family members. The *partner effect* reflects a tendency for a family member to be regarded by all family members in a particular manner. In the example, the partner effect measures the tendency for the adolescent child to elicit commitment from all other family members. The *relationship effect* describes the unique aspects of the relationship between two individuals after both actor and partner effects have been statistically removed. In the example, the relationship effect measures the father's commitment to the adolescent after controlling for the father's general tendency to be committed to other family members in general and the adolescent's general tendency to elicit commitment from other family members. Note that the relationship effect is directional in that the relationship effect for the father with the adolescent may differ from the relationship effect for the adolescent with the father. The *family effect* represents the unique aspects of the family as a group. In the example, it reflects the general level of commitment in the family, that is, the commitment of all family members to all family members. Additionally, the SRM considers error variance which reflects any remaining variance that is due to error.

These different effects in dyadic scores can be described by the following formula:

$$X_{ijk} = \mu_k + \alpha_{ik} + \beta_{jk} + \gamma_{ijk} + \varepsilon_{ijk},$$

in which X_{ijk} is the reported dyadic score (for example the commitment in a family dyad of actor i with partner j in family k) and ε_{ijk} represents the error term. The actor effect is α_{ik}, β_{jk} is the partner effect, and γ_{ijk} is the relationship effect. Usually, μ represents the constant term, but when groups such as families are studied, μ_k represents the mean level of scores within the family as a whole, or the family effect.

Generally, there will be variability across families in the measured variables. For example, typically fathers will differ across families in the commitment to their adolescent children. The SRM is used to identify the sources of this variability. In three-person families, each of the possible six relationships consists of four sources of variance: actor variance, partner variance, relationship variance, and family variance. The actor variance for any given role measures the degree of variation in actor effects for that role. Using the commitment example, a very small estimate of actor variance for adolescents would indicate that adolescents across all families tend to be similarly committed to all other family members. Similarly, the partner variance measures the variability in partner effects for each role. For example, large estimates of partner variance for adolescents would indicate that some adolescents elicit much commitment from all other family members, whereas other adolescents do not elicit much commitment from all other family members. Relationship variance for each dyadic combination of roles (e.g., mothers' commitment to fathers, mothers' commitment to adolescents) can also be estimated. For example, large relationship variance for mothers' commitment to fathers would indicate that in some families, mothers are very committed to fathers, whereas in other families, mothers are not committed to fathers. Finally, variance in the family means can be estimated. This would reflect the extent to which commitment differs across families. For example, all members of a family are more committed to each other compared to all members of other families.

In addition to these four effects, the SRM enables estimation of various meaningful correlations between effects. Two of these important correlations are individual and dyadic reciprocity. *Individual reciprocity* refers to the correlation between a person's actor effect and that person's partner effect.

For example, positive individual reciprocity for mothers examines whether mothers who are committed to all their family members elicit commitment from all their family members as well. *Dyadic reciprocity* refers to the correlation between two persons' relationship effects and measures the degree of similarity or dissimilarity between two individuals' relationship effects. For example, positive dyadic reciprocity for the mother–adolescent dyad examines whether mothers are committed to their adolescent when their adolescent is committed to them. Individual and dyadic reciprocity can also be negative, for example, if the father is committed to others, but others tend to be less committed to the father.

OVERVIEW

As we have shown the SRM provides us with the unique opportunity to theoretically and methodologically disentangle different levels of influence in family relationships. In the following we will present a study that allows us to illustrate different applications of the SRM to family relationships. Rather than applying the SRM to the investment model in general, we will focus on three specific applications of the SRM to highlight its usefulness for the empirical investigation of truly relational phenomena and independent data. Specifically, after having introduced the study, we will present findings on the univariate SRM analyses of the investment model to demonstrate how the SRM allows us to disentangle and quantify actor, partner, relationship, and family effects in the investment model in families. Then, we will present findings of the multivariate analyses of aspects of the investment model to demonstrate the utility of the SRM for the investigation of longitudinal relations. Finally, we will present one example of how the SRM can be used to examine individual outcomes by considering all levels of influence in a family over time. Specifically, we will present our findings on how relationship commitment and satisfaction may predict adolescent depression over time.

Our aims of the presentation of this selection of applications of the SRM to the investment model in families are threefold. First, we want to provide readers with a general overview of how the SRM can be used in the family context. Second, we aim to explain and describe the SRM in such a fashion that the model become more accessible to researchers investigating relational phenomena with interdependent data. Third, we aim to shed some light on the practicality and rich possibilities the SRM offers for empirical research on relational phenomena.

METHOD

Participants. Data of this study come from the first and second wave of the family sample of the CONAMORE study (CONflict And Management Of Relationships, Meeus et al., 2004), in which 1313 early and middle adolescents participated longitudinally. At the first measurement, all early adolescents received a letter including an invitation to participate with both parents during annual home-visits as well. Of the families invited, 491 families initially agreed to participate. Due to our restriction of including only two-parent families, 90 one-parent families who agreed to participate were not able to take part in this additional research project. Finally, after some families had decided to withdraw from participation, 323 families participated in the study from wave two onwards. The current study uses data from this family sample, in which father, mother, and adolescent participated. The vast majority (99%) of the adolescents in the family sample was of Dutch origin. Adolescents came from 12 schools in Utrecht and surroundings. Different educational levels were represented, with approximately 1/3 of the adolescents being in schools preparing for blue collar work, 1/3 of the adolescents in schools preparing for higher professional education, and 1/3 of the adolescents in schools preparing for university (because classes are often combinations of different school levels, exact numbers cannot be provided).

Procedure. Before the start of the study, students and their parents received written information and, if the students agreed to participate, were required to provide written informed consent; less than 1% refused to participate. Written informed consent was also obtained at all the participating schools. In each of the two waves with a one-year interval, interviewers visited schools and asked participating adolescents to fill out a battery of questionnaires after school hours. During school visits the interviewer started with an explanation of the project and instruction about filling out the questionnaire. Anonymity and confidentiality were guaranteed explicitly. The interviewer asked the adolescents to fill out the questionnaires individually. The presence of the interviewer encouraged complete responding and prevented collaboration among the adolescents as they completed the questionnaire. In both waves, respondents received € 10 after completing the questionnaires.

Measures. Participants completed a large battery of questionnaires including measures on relationship satisfaction, quality of alternatives, investment level and relationship commitment. Adolescents rated these measures for father and mother and parents rated their spouse and child.

Investment model scale. Investment model variables were assessed by a Dutch adaptation of the Investment Model Scale (Rusbult, Martz, & Agnew, 1998), an instrument designed to measure commitment level, satisfaction level, investment size, and quality of alternatives that has good reliability and validity. Commitment level refers to the intent to maintain a relationship and to feel attached to it, and was assessed with four items. For example: "I wish the relationship with my ..... were to stay the way it is." Satisfaction assesses the extent to which participants are satisfied with their relationship or experience positive and negative affect in their relationship. This scale was assessed with four items. An item example is: "I am satisfied with the relationship with my ..." Investment size refers to the number, magnitude, and importance of resources that are put into a particular relationship that cannot be retrieved if the relationship ends, and was assessed with five items. An example item is: "I lose a lot if the relationship with my ..... gets worse." Quality of alternatives assesses the rewards and costs that are expected in the alternatives participants have for the relationship, or the perceived desirability of the best available alternative for the relationship, and was assessed with five items. For example: "I have many opportunities to do things with others than my ....." All items were answered on 5-point Likert scales. Across relationships, reliability coefficients (Cronbach's alphas) ranged from .82 to .94 for satisfaction (from .82 to .94 for parents and from .91 to .94 for adolescents), from .56 to .85 for investment (from .56 to .73 for parents and from .81 to .85 for adolescents), from .36 to .80 for alternatives (from .36 to .66 for parents and from .68 to .80 for adolescents), and from .65 to .89 for commitment (from .65 to .87 for parents and from .85 to .89 for adolescents). Lowest reliabilities appeared for Alternatives as perceived by parents.

Depression was measured with the Children's Depression Inventory (CDI; Kovacs, 1985, 1992), a symptom-based measure consisting of 27 items rated on a 3-point Likert scale ranging from not true to very true. Sample items are: "I worry all the time about all kind of things," "I feel tired all the time", and "I don't have any friends." The CDI has adequate to good internal consistency and test-retest reliability (Finch, Saylor, Edwards, & McIntosh, 1987) and adequate factor validity (Craighead, Smucker, Craighead, & Ilardi, 1998). Cronbach's alpha for this measure in the current sample was .92.

RESULTS

Univariate SRM Analyses

Description of analyses. Social Relations Models in families are commonly estimated using confirmatory factor analysis, although other methods are available (see for example, Kenny, 1994; Snijders & Kenny, 1999). The actor, partner, relationship, and family effects technically constitute separate factors or latent variables within a confirmatory factor analysis (see Figure 12.2;

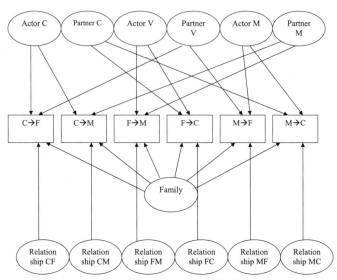

Figure 12.2. Parameters of the LISREL model.

Note. F = father, M = mother, C = child; FM = fathers' perception of mother, FC = fathers' perception of child, MF = mothers' perception of fathers, and so forth. Rectangles represent the observed measures; ellipses represent the latent SRM components. Double-headed arrows represent dyadic reciprocity correlations. All of the observed variables loaded on the latent SRM component "family variance," which is not included in the figure. Figure 12.2 displays the parameters for one indicator of perceived support only; the other indicator loads on the same latent factors in a similar manner.

Cook, 1994). A structural equation modeling program can be used to perform the confirmatory factor analysis (e.g., LISREL, Jöreskog & Sörbom, 1996). A minimum sample size of 50 families is required to have enough power for an SRM analysis (Kashy & Kenny, 1990). A sample size of 323 families, such as in the present study, is therefore more than adequate.

In a three-person family, six variables are obtained. In families composed of a mother (M), a father (F), and a child (C), these variables are, for example, mother's commitment to father (MF), mother's commitment to the adolescent child (MC), father's commitment to mother (FM), and so on. Thus, in a round-robin design, the six observed variables include MF, MC, FM, FC, CM, and CF. Note that in these abbreviations the first letter corresponds to the actor (the person making the rating), and the second letter corresponds to the partner (the person being rated). The variables are asymmetric in that MF is not necessarily the same as FM. The SRM components are estimated from the covariance matrix of these observed variables.

To partition the observed variance in the investment model variables in the SRM variance components, one has to specify which variable loads on

TABLE 12.1
Parameters of the LISREL Model

Observed Variables	Actor Effects			Partner Effects			Relationship Effects						Family Effects
	F	M	C	F	M	C	FM	FC	MF	MC	CF	CM	
FM	1	0	0	0	1	0	1	0	0	0	0	0	1
FC	1	0	0	0	0	1	0	1	0	0	0	0	1
MF	0	1	0	1	0	0	0	0	1	0	0	0	1
MC	0	1	0	0	0	1	0	0	0	1	0	0	1
CF	0	0	1	1	0	0	0	0	0	0	1	0	1
CM	0	0	1	0	1	0	0	0	0	0	0	1	1

The header row "SRM Components (Latent Factors)" spans the Actor, Partner, Relationship, and Family effect columns.

Note. F = father; M = mother; C = child. Direction is presented as follows: FM = father's commitment to mother, FC = father's commitment to the child, MF = mother's commitment to father, and so forth.

which factors, or latent variables, in the confirmatory factor analysis. In the basic three-person family design, each observed variable loads on four general factors which represent the four effects described above: an actor factor, a partner factor, a relationship factor, and a family factor. For example, the commitment of mother to father loads on the mothers' actor factor, the fathers' partner factor, the mother→father relationship factor, and the family factor.

Similarly, the commitment of mother to the adolescent loads on the mothers' actor factor, the adolescents' partner factor, the mother→adolescent relationship factor, and the family factor. All six of the observed variables load on the family mean factor. The factor loadings (i.e., paths from the latent variables to the observed variables) are usually fixed at 1.0, and the SRM factor variances are the parameters to be estimated (Kashy & Kenny, 1990).

Table 12.1 shows how the observed variables load on the latent variables. Forcing the observed variables to load on the appropriate factors enables us to estimate the amount of variance in the observed variable accounted for by each of the factors. The variance of each factor (e.g., the mother actor factor) estimates the variance in the corresponding SRM component (e.g., the variance in the actor effects across mothers). In this design there are three factors for actor (F, M, and C actor), three factors for partner (F, M, and C partner), six relationship factors (one for each unidirectional relationship), and one family mean factor. Estimates of the actor and partner variance for each role, the six relationship variances, and the family variance can be found on the diagonal of the factor-by-factor covariance matrix.

Relationship variance describes variance in the unique level of commitment of one family member (e.g., mother) to another (e.g., adolescent). For the three-person family design, there are six relationship variances, one for each variable. However, to reliably estimate the six relationship components (that is, without random error), at least 12 variables are needed. In order to separate true relationship effects from error, replications of each of the observed variables need to be obtained. One option is to measure each variable at two or more times. Another option is to use two or more different measures and treat these as indicators of one theoretical construct. In the current study, the second option was used and two parcels were created for each of the investment model variables. The two or more replications are considered as indicators of a relationship factor as well as indicators of the relevant actor, partner, and family factors (Cook, 1993, 1994, 2000).

To be able to reliably estimate all SRM variance components as well as all possible correlations between these variance components, at least four members of each family have to participate in the study (Cook, Kenny, & Goldstein, 1991; Kashy & Kenny, 1990). To be able to estimate all SRM variance components in three-person families, one cannot estimate all possible correlations between variance components. Therefore, we did not estimate all possible correlations. For example, we did not estimate correlations between relationship effects of children with fathers and mother (so-called *intergenerational assimilation*) or correlations between relationship effects of fathers and mothers with children (so-called *intergenerational consensus*). Instead, only individual and dyadic reciprocity for significant variance components were estimated.

Thus, in four separate SRM analyses, for satisfaction, investments, alternatives, and commitment, we explored the extent to which variance in commitment, satisfaction, investment, and quality of alternatives in each of the six family relationships is due to actor, partner, relationship, and family effects. All these effects are estimated independently, controlling for all remaining effects. That is, a relationship effect is estimated after controlling for actor, partner, and family effects. We allowed for correlations among measurement errors for each indicator per rating family member (e.g., for each indicator of father's commitment, we allowed father's measurement errors for their commitment to mother and adolescent to correlate). The different variances were simultaneously estimated using structural equation modeling with maximum likelihood estimation procedures (LISREL 8.54, Jöreskog &

Sörbom, 1996). Missing data were estimated in LISREL using the FIML approach.

After estimating the SRM variance components, the correlations between different significant variance components can be specified, for example to estimate individual and dyadic reciprocity effects. Estimates of individual reciprocity for each role (the covariance between actor and partner effects such as the covariance between the mother actor factor with the mother partner factor) and the three measures of dyadic reciprocity (the covariance between relationship effects MF–FM, MC–CM, and FC–CF) can be found in the off-diagonal of the factor covariance matrix.

The statistical significance of each parameter estimate (i.e., actor, partner, relationship, and family variances) can be evaluated. For tests of variance, the key question is whether the variance is greater than zero, since the estimated variances must be positive. In testing for the significant presence of SRM variance components, the tests should be one-tailed, assuming that the estimated variances are positive.

In addition to the individual parameter tests, the overall fit of the model is generally evaluated by a chi-square goodness-of-fit test or other goodness-of-fit indices such as the Root Mean Square Error of Approximation (RMSEA) (M. Browne & Cudeck, 1989; M. W. Browne & Cudeck, 1993; Kenny, 2001, February 22). These indices assess the success of the proposed model to adequately reproduce the observed covariation among the variables. RMSEA values up to .05 represent a close fit and values up to .10 represent reasonable errors of approximation in the population (M. Browne & Cudeck, 1989; M. W. Browne & Cudeck, 1993; Hu & Bentler, 1999; Kenny, 2001, February 22). Also, it is possible to use goodness-of-fit tests to compare two alternative models, one of which is a simpler version of the other. In this way, an initial model can be modified by making it more complex or simple, and these changes can be statistically evaluated.

Once the basic model has been estimated, simpler versions of the model can be estimated and compared with the basic model. In equality-of-parameter tests, one takes a given set of parameters (e.g., actor variances) and forces them to equal the same value. This allows one to test whether or not the parameters differ significantly by family role (e.g., whether mother's actor variance actually differs from father's actor variance). Similarly, sets of parameters (e.g., actor variances) can be fixed to zero to evaluate whether a given component (e.g., actor variance) or correlation between components (e.g., dyadic reciprocity) is supported by the data. By comparing the fit of these restricted versions of the model (the models in which some components are set to zero or set equal) to the fit of the unrestricted model, one can evaluate whether the unrestricted model is indeed the best fitting model. If

TABLE 12.2
Fit Indices of SRM Analyses

	χ^2	df	RMSEA
Univariate SRM Analyses			
Satisfaction	91.93**	43	.06
Investments	71.18**	46	.04
Quality of Alternatives	91.15*	47	.05
Commitment	101.29**	47	.06
Commitment T2	102.62**	45	.06
Multivariate longitudinal SRM Analyses			
Commitment→ Commitment T2	603.73**	242	.07
Satisfaction→ Commitment T2	1574.98**	578	.07
Investments → Commitment T2	1376.82**	580	.06
Quality of Alternatives → Commitment T2	1223.47**	582	.06

the chi-square is significantly higher in the restricted model, the restriction on the model significantly worsens the fit. One can then conclude that a variance component is supported by the data, or that there is a difference between variance components for family members with different roles.

Univariate SRM analyses of the investment model. Separate SRM analyses were performed for each investment model variable to partition the variance in satisfaction, investments, quality of alternatives, and commitment into actor variance, partner variance, relationship variance, and family variance. We allowed for correlations among measurement errors for each indicator per rating family member (e.g., we allowed correlations between measurement errors for the two indicators of father's commitment to mother). The goodness-of-fit indices are presented in Table 12.2. These indices showed that the fit of these models was fairly acceptable, indicating that the SRM components can be used to adequately represent the investment model in families.

Results of the univariate SRM analyses are displayed in Table 12.3 (the first four columns present the results for Time 1). For each of the six dyadic relationships, the percentage of the variance in the investment model variables explained by the SRM components was calculated. For example, the total explained variance in fathers' commitment to mothers consists of four variance components: (1) the actor variance among the fathers (see Table 12.3, .09), (2) the partner variance of the mothers (.00), (3) the father→mother relationship variance (.19), and (4) the family variance (.02). The relative

TABLE 12.3
SRM Variance Estimates for Satisfaction, Investments, Quality of Alternatives, and
Commitment and Correlations Between SRM Components

	Satisfaction	Investments	Quality of Alternatives	Commitment	Commitment T2
Actor Variance					
Child	.24**	.29**	.24**	.25**	.27**
Father	.08**	.09**	.06**	.09**	.08**
Mother	.07**	.07**	.04**	.08**	.08**
Partner Variance					
Child	.09**	.01	.00	.00	.02
Father	.08**	.02	.02	.01	.02
Mother	.00	.00	.01	.00	.07**
Relationship Variance					
Child-father	.11**	.13**	.08**	.17**	.24**
Child-mother	.12**	.02	.00	.09**	.00
Father-child	.08**	.05**	.02	.09**	.07**
Mother-child	.10**	.04**	.04*	.12**	.11**
Father-mother	.41**	.17**	.09**	.19**	.26**
Mother-father	.43**	.13**	.08**	.21**	.33**
Family Variance	.08**	.03**	.03**	.02**	.01
Individual Reciprocity Correlations					
Father	.31	-	-	-	-
Mother	-	-	-	-	.12
Child	-.21	-	-	-	-
Dyadic Reciprocity Correlations					
Father-mother ↔ Mother-father	.72**	.64**	.83**	.64**	.73**
Child-father ↔ father-child	-.24	-.06	-	.06	.20
Child-mother↔ mother-child	.10	-	-	-	-

Note. Dashes indicate covariances that were not estimated because there was no significant variance in one or both of the variables.
*$p < .05$; **$p < .01$.

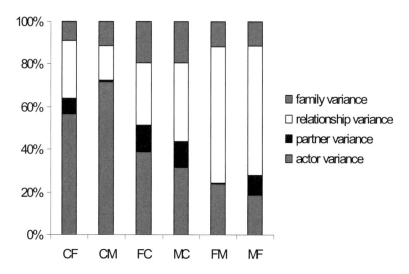

Figure 12.3. Percentage of variance explained by SRM components.

Note. FM = fathers' perception of mother, FC = fathers' perception of child, MF = mothers' perception of fathers, and so forth.

actor variance in fathers' commitment to mothers is computed by dividing the fathers' actor variance by the total explained variance in fathers' commitment to mothers (i.e., .09/.30 = 30%). The contributions of the different SRM components to the variance in the dyadic relationships were next averaged across the four variables of the investment model. In Figure 12.3, the relative amounts of variance accounted for by the four SRM components are presented. The mean relative actor variance, partner variance, relationship variance, and family for each of the six unilateral relationships are presented separately.

For each of the three family members, significant actor variance was found as indicated by the t-values of the coefficients in the psi-matrix. This means that differences in relationship satisfaction, investment, quality of alternatives, and commitment across families are at least in part due to differences in the actors' generalized tendency to be satisfied, to invest, to have alternatives, or to be committed. Some fathers, mothers, and adolescents report more satisfaction, investment, quality of alternatives, and commitment to all family members than other fathers, mothers, and adolescents. Actor variance was much higher for adolescents than for parents, explaining on average 64% of the total explained variance in adolescents' relationships (Figure 12.3). Actor effects contributed especially to variance in children's relationship with mothers. Actor effects contributed least to the variance in the horizontal marital relationship (on average 21%). Actor effects might contribute more to the variance for children than for parents because in this study children rate two persons in a comparable role (i.e., parents) whereas parents rate two persons in different roles (i.e., spouse and child). However, other studies have found comparable differences in the contribution of actor variance to ratings of children versus parents in four-person families (Branje, van Aken, & van Lieshout, 2002; Branje, van Aken, van Lieshout, & Mathijssen, 2003).

Significant partner variance was found only for satisfaction of fathers and children. This indicates that characteristics of fathers and children in part account for the satisfaction that family members experience in their relationships with fathers and children. Some fathers and adolescents elicit more satisfaction from all family members than other fathers and adolescents. On average, partner effects only explained 7% of the total explained variance. For mothers, no significant partner variance was found in Time 1 investment model variables. Also, for the other investment model variables, no significant partner variance was found. These nonsignificant partner variances indicate that there is little consensus among family members regarding their satisfaction with, investments to, alternatives for, and commitment to specific individual family members. Put differently, in all families certain roles elicit different responses or perceptions from all other family members such that for mothers for example no partner variances are observed.

Differences in investment model variables can be attributed to differences in the particular combination of actor and partner in all dyadic family relationships, as indicated by the significant relationship variances (Table 12.3). For example, the significant relationship variance for fathers' commitment to children indicates a unique component in the commitment that fathers have to their child when compared to the commitment that fathers have to their spouse. The contribution of relationship effects to the total variance varied a lot, ranging from 0% to 72%. Relationship variance was particularly large in the marital relationship, explaining on average 62% of the variance. In the relationships of parents to children and of children to fathers, relationship effects explained on average 31% of the variance and in the relationship of children to mothers relationship effects explained the least amount of variance, on average 16%. In other words, in the horizontal marital relationship much of the behavior and perception is determined by the specific relationship, above and beyond any other influence. Thus, relationships between marital partners are relationship specific and do not generalize to other types of relationships.

Differences in investment model variables can also be attributed to differences in the mean family level of these variables across families, as indicated by significant family variance. The family effect explained on average 14% of the total explained variance (see Table 12.3). It can be concluded that families clearly differ in the level of commitment and investment variables within the family as a whole. Family variance explained most of the total explained variance in parents' relationships with their children.

We also estimated individual and dyadic reciprocity correlations for significant SRM variances. These correlations are estimated as the relations among the latent variables in the CFA. The correlations between significant actor and partner variances (i.e., individual reciprocity) and significant relationship variances (i.e., dyadic reciprocity) are presented in Table 12.3. Results show that actor and partner variances were not significantly related. Relationship variances were significantly and strongly related within the marital relationship only. These findings indicate that dyadic reciprocity is important in the marital relationship but not in other family relationships. So, if mother is especially satisfied with her relationship with father, father is especially satisfied with his relationship with mother too.

To summarize, the SRM can be meaningfully applied to disentangle and quantify the influence of different levels of relational phenomena in the family. The results provide unique insights in differences between different relationship types. Specifically, in our findings, horizontal relationships between marital partners show distinct patterns of influences as compared to vertical relationships between parents and children. Marital relationships seem to be more strongly determined by the specific interaction between the relationship partners, whereas in parent–child relationships the individual characteristics of the child play an important role.

Multivariate SRM Analyses: Concurrent and Longitudinal Associations of Satisfaction, Investments, and Alternatives With Commitment

To demonstrate the utility of SRM for concurrent and longitudinal research, we estimated the links between SRM components of the investment model variables with commitment both concurrently and over time in multivariate SRM analyses. Because a model including commitment at both time points as well as satisfaction, investments, and alternatives in a single comprehensive model would be too complicated, we opted for a stepwise and pairwise procedure. First, we examined the stability of the SRM variances of commitment over time. Next, we performed three separate multivariate analyses that included satisfaction, investments, and alternatives with commitment at both time points in a pairwise fashion.

First, we estimated a stability model of commitment, in which significant Time 2 SRM variance components of commitment were predicted from sig-

TABLE 12.4
Correlations Between SRM Components Across Investment Model Variables

		Correlating Commitment T1 With:			Predicting Commitment T2 From:			
		Satisfaction	Investment	Quality of Alternatives	Commitment	Satisfaction	Investment	Quality of Alternatives
Actor Variance Associations								
	Child	.81**	.79**	-.42**	.56**	.04	-.01	-.04
	Father	.68**	.70**	-.42**	.61**	.07	.07	.03
	Mother	.46**	.73**	-.02	.62**	.08	.06	.05
Family Variance Associations		1.01**	1.01**	-.67**	-	-	-	-
Relationship Variance Associations								
	Father-Mother	.97**	1.00**	-.20**	.66**	-.13**	-.13*	-.19**
	Mother-Father	.96**	1.04**	-.25**	.64**	-.05	-.10	-.16**
	Mother-Child	.24	.83**	-.31	.56**	-.03	.02	-.04
	Child-Mother	.69**	-	-	-	-	-	-
	Father-Child	.42**	.55**	-	.56**	.01	.21	-
	Child-Father	1.09**	.75**	-.15	.41**	.04	.05	-.06

Note. Dashes indicate covariances that were not estimated because there was no significant variance in one or both of the variables.
$p < .05$; $**p < .01$.

nificant Time 1 SRM variance components of commitment. That is, we estimated the directional effect of the commitment family variance Time 1 on the commitment family variance Time 2, the directional effect of the commitment father–actor variance Time 1 on the commitment father–actor variance Time 2, etc. Values for SRM variances were fixed at the estimates from the univariate models of commitment Time 1 and Time 2. Errors of the two indicators of each relationship within time points were again allowed to correlate, as well as errors of similar indicators across time (e.g., measurement errors of the first indicator of fathers' commitment to mother at Time 1 and Time 2 were allowed to correlate). Fit indices of this model are displayed in Table 12.2 and results are presented in Table 12.4, fifth column with the heading Commitment. Results indicate that all variance components are moderately stable over a one year period, ranging from .41 to .66.

Second, we estimated relations of satisfaction, investments, and alternatives with commitment both concurrently and over time. To be able to esti-

mate this model, values for SRM variances were fixed at the estimates from
the univariate models, and the stability effects of the SRM commitment variances from Time 1 to Time 2 were fixed at the values found in the stability
model. Again, errors of the two indicators of each relationship within time
points as well as errors of similar indicators across time were allowed to correlate. Thus, three separate SRM analyses were performed with Time 1 and
Time 2 commitment and either Time 1 satisfaction, investments, or alternatives, to relate the significant actor, partner, relationship, and family effects
of commitment to the significant SRM effects of the other investment model
variables. More specifically, the family variance of one variable was related to
the family variance of the other, the father–actor variance of one variable with
the father–actor variance of the other, etc. The models showed an acceptable
fit with our data set given the complexity of the models and the number of
variables involved (see Table 12.2).

   Concurrent relations between investment model variables in family rela-
tionships. We will first discuss concurrent links between investment model
variables in family relationships (see Table 12.4, 2nd to 4th column). To examine whether more committed family members generally invest more, are
more satisfied and have less alternatives as has been found in romantic relationships (cf., Rusbult, 1983), the correlations between a family member's
actor effect for commitment and that family member's actor effect for satisfaction, investment and alternatives were computed. Errors of the two indicators of each relationship within time points were again allowed to correlate,
as well as errors of similar indicators across time. The significant and strong
correlations of actor effects indicate that individuals who are more committed
to all their family members are more satisfied with, invest more, and—to a
lower extent—have less alternatives to all family members. The correlations
of partner variances were not computed because most of these variances were
nonsignificant.

   The family effect for commitment significantly and very strongly correlated with the family effect for satisfaction, investment, and alternatives,
suggesting that in families where individuals are generally more committed the individuals are also generally more satisfied, invest more and have
fewer alternatives. These relations generalize to the family as a group. As
Jöreskog (1999) describes, these coefficients are structural coefficients, and
can be larger than one in magnitude in the completely standardized solution.

   The correlations between a family member's relationship effect for commitment and that family member's relationship effect for satisfaction, investment, and alternatives revealed that relationship effects were most strongly
related in the horizontal marital relationship, followed by the child–father
relationship. This shows that in particular marital partners who are more

committed to their marital partner are also more satisfied, invest more, and have fewer alternatives for their partner. In the vertical mother–child, father–child, and child–mother relationship, relationship variances were generally less strongly related, although it should be noted that not all these relations could be estimated due to nonsignificant variances.

Overall, these findings indicate that the investment model can be extended to family relationships. It holds for individual members within the family but also for families as a group. Moreover, in line with our speculations, it seems to apply more in marital relationships than in parent–child relationships.

Longitudinal relations between investment model variables and commitment. Because the relationships between parents and children may become more horizontal over time, it is interesting to explore whether the concurrent results generalize over time. To explore these questions, in the same models, we also estimated the links of satisfaction, investment, and alternatives with commitment at Time 2 (Table 12.4, 6th to 8th column). Most of these effects over time were nonsignificant, except for the relationship-specific effects of quality of alternatives to commitment in the marital relationship and the relationship-specific effects of satisfaction and investments of fathers to their spouse to commitment to their spouse. Marital partners who have more alternatives are less committed to their marital partner over time. Also, but in contradiction to our hypotheses, men who are more satisfied with and invest more in the relationship with their spouse are less committed over time. The fact that most longitudinal effects occur in the marital relationship indicates that the investment model is most suited to predict commitment in marital relationships. Perhaps when children become young adults, the investment model will be more suited to predict commitment in the parent–child relationship.

Overall, SRM analyses suggest that the investment model can predict marital commitment over time. It is well suited for horizontal relationships between equal partners, but seems less suited for vertical relationships between unequal partners. Additionally, the analyses suggest that there is little variation across parent–child relationships neither concurrently nor over time. In the SRM, the absence of an effect may be interpreted in two ways. On the one hand, it is possible that the investment model is less important in parent–child relationships than it is in other relationships. Parent–child relationships are involuntary, that is neither parents nor children can choose to leave the relationship. Rather, they must continue to live with each other in good times and in bad times. On the other hand, the absence of SRM effects may also indicate that parent–child relationships are rated in a comparable fashion across all families who participated in our study. Because the social relations model does not allow us to distinguish between these two explanations, research must be designed to systematically compare the investment model in different family relationships with the investment model in other types of relationships that vary in voluntariness (e.g., adolescent friendships, romantic relationships, sibling relationships).

Concurrent and Longitudinal Associations of Satisfaction and Commitment With Adolescents' Depression

To illuminate the usefulness of SRM for family research, the last application that we want to describe here concerns the prediction of individual outcomes by considering different familial influences over time. For this illustration, we will focus specifically on two variables in the investment model, namely commitment and relationship satisfaction. Depression in adolescence has consistently been found to be related to the quality of children's relationship with their parents (Branje, Hale III, & Meeus, 2008). The question that has remained unanswered, however, is whether adolescent depression is predicted by the quality of specific relationships the child has with his or her parents or by the quality of the relationships of the family as a group. This question can be tackled by using the SRM.

To predict adolescents' depression at Time 2 from the Time 1 SRM variance components of commitment and satisfaction, we estimated separate models for commitment and satisfaction. Values for SRM variances were again fixed at the estimates from the univariate models, and errors of the two indicators of each relationship within time points were allowed to correlate. We first estimated a baseline model with the SRM variances for either commitment or satisfaction and the stability of depression from Time 1 to Time 2 ($\beta = .46$). Next, correlations of depression Time 1 with child actor variance, child partner variance, child–father and child–mother relationship variance, and family variance were added stepwise. Subsequently, effects of child actor variance, child partner variance, child–father and child–mother relationship variance, and family variance on depression Time 2 were added stepwise. Chi-square difference tests were performed to examine whether inclusion of a correlation or an effect improved model fit, and if not, the effect was removed from the model. Table 12.5 presents the fit statistics and model comparisons of these models.

Using the SRM to predict adolescent depression with commitment. For commitment, child actor variance was significantly related to depression Time 1, as well as child–mother relationship variance (see Table 12.5, models 2 and 4 for commitment). When child actor variance and child–mother relationship variance were entered together in the model, model fit did not improve compared to a model with only one of these variances (see Table 12.5, model 6),

and the correlation of child–mother relationship variance became nonsignificant. When adding effects on depression Time 2 while controlling for the
correlation of the specific variable with depression Time 1, model comparisons revealed that child actor variance and child–mother relationship variance significantly predicted depression at Time 2 (see Table 12.5, models 7
and 10). However, when child actor variance and child–mother relationship
variance were entered together in the model, model fit did not improve compared to a model with only one of these variances (see Table 12.5, model 11),
and the effect of child actor variance became nonsignificant. Thus, the final
model was model 10, including a significant negative correlation of child actor
variance with depression Time 1 ($r = -.31$) and a significant positive effect
of child–mother relationship variance on depression Time 2 ($\beta = .28$) while
controlling for the correlation of child–mother relationship variance with depression Time 1. These results indicate that the child's general tendency to
be committed to parents is negatively related to depression, and suggest that
children who are more committed to mother have lower levels of depression.
However, children who are more specifically committed to mother have higher
levels of depression over time.

 Using the SRM to predict adolescent depression with satisfaction. For satisfaction, child actor variance was significantly related to depression Time 1,
as well as child–mother relationship variance, child–father relationship variance, and family variance (see Table 12.5, models 2, 4, 5, and 6 for satisfaction). When child actor variance and child–mother relationship variance or
child–father relationship variance were entered together in the model, model
fit did not improve compared to a model with only one of these variances (see
Table 12.5, models 7 and 8), and the correlations of child–mother relationship
variance and child–father relationship variance became nonsignificant. When
child actor variance and family variance were entered together in the model,
model fit improved compared to a model with only one of these variances
(see Table 12.5, model 9), and both correlations remained significant. When
adding effects on depression Time 2 while controlling for the correlation of
the specific variable with depression Time 1, model comparisons revealed that
child–father relationship variance and child–mother relationship variance significantly predicted depression at Time 2 (see Table 12.5, models 13 and 14).
However, when child–father relationship variance and child–mother relationship variance were entered together in the model, model fit did not improve
compared to a model with only one of these variances (see Table 12.5, model
15), and both effects became nonsignificant. Therefore, we will discuss the
results of models 13 and 14, including a significant negative correlation of
child actor variance and family variance with depression Time 1 ($r = -.27$
and $r = -.32$, respectively), a significant positive effect of child–mother rela-

TABLE 12.5
Fit Indices and Model Comparisons of SRM Analyses Predicting Depression

	χ^2	df	$\Delta\chi^2 / \Delta df$	RMSEA
Commitment				
1. Baseline model	284.57**	110		.07
2. Model 1 + child actor effect T1	265.61**	109	18.96/1**	.07
3. Model 1 + child–father relationship effect T1	282.53**	109	2.04/1	.07
4. Model 1 + child–mother relationship effect T1	277.91**	109	6.66/1**	.07
5. Model 1 + family effect T1	283.86**	109	.71/1	.07
6. Model 2 + child–mother relationship effect T1	265.48**	108	.13/1	.07
7. Model 2 + child actor effect T2	261.14**	108	4.47/1*	.07
8. Model 2 + family effect T1+2	262.87**	107	2.74/2	.07
9. Model 2 + child–father relationship effect T1+2	262.12**	107	3.49/2	.06
10. Model 2 + child–mother relationship effect T1+2	252.80**	107	8.57/2*	.06
11. Model 10 + child actor effect T2	252.68**	106	.12/1	.07
Satisfaction				
1. Baseline model	275.25**	110		.07
2. Model 1 + child actor effect T1	250.13**	109	25.12/1**	.06
3. Model 1 + child partner effect T1	272.80**	109	2.45/1	.07
4. Model 1 + child–father relationship effect T1	271.14**	109	4.11/1*	.07
5. Model 1 + child–mother relationship effect T1	268.44**	109	6.81/1**	.07
6. Model 1 + family effect T1	252.36**	109	22.89/1**	.06
7. Model 2 + child–father relationship effect T1	250.08**	108	.05/1	.06
8. Model 2 + child–mother relationship effect T1	250.08**	108	.05/1	.06
9. Model 2 + family effect T1	239.45**	108	10.68/1**	.06
10. Model 9 + child actor effect T2	239.22**	107	.23/1	.06
11. Model 9 + family effect T2	237.87**	107	1.58/1	.06
12. Model 9 + partner effect T1+2	239.21**	106	.24/1	.06
13. Model 9 + child–father relationship effect T1+2	233.32**	106	6.13/1*	.06
14. Model 9 + child–mother relationship effect T1+2	230.88**	106	8.57/1**	.06
15. Model 13 + child–father and child–mother relationship effect T1+2	228.39**	104	4.93/2	.06

Note. *p < .05; **p < .01.

tionship variance on depression Time 2 ($\beta = .22$), and a significant negative effect of child–father relationship variance on depression Time 2 ($\beta = -.21$) while controlling for the correlation of child–mother relationship variance with depression Time 1. These results indicate that the child's general tendency to perceive satisfaction from parents and the general level of satisfaction at the family level are negatively related to depression, and children who perceive more specific satisfaction with father have lower levels of depression over time, while children who perceive more specific satisfaction with mother have higher levels of depression over time.

More generally, these findings yield new insights in how the quality of family relationships can contribute to child depression. For both commitment and satisfaction it seems that good relationships in the entire family and good relationships with both parents serve as a protective factor. However, especially good relationships with one single parent may render an adolescent child more vulnerable to depression over time. The SRM thereby allows us to paint a more complete picture of how familial relationships may contribute to the development of depression in adolescents.

CONCLUSION

The selection of analyses presented in the current chapter show that the Social Relations Model can be used to estimate interdependent processes in family relationships. The SRM allows one to estimate four sources of variance at the level of the individual, the dyad, and the group (Kenny, 1994; Kenny & La Voie, 1984). The actor effect reflects the tendency of the actor to judge all family members similarly. The partner effect reflects the extent to which all family members perceive a specific family member similarly. The relationship effect reflects whether a family member perceives specific relationship partners uniquely. Finally, the family effect reflects the extent to which all family members perceive all other members similarly. It thereby offers researchers interested in family relationships the possibility to disentangle the influence of different levels of influence and shed new light on relational phenomena that are inherently interdependent.

We began by investigating whether differences in the investment model can be attributed to differences in individual actors, individual partners, specific relationships, and family characteristics. The results of the Social Relations Analyses showed that family members' perceptions of investment model variables are more determined by the actor (or perceiver) than by the partner. The relatively strong influence of actor characteristics showed perceptions of others to be highly idiosyncratic, and may reflect a kind of working model based on earlier experiences that affects the expectations of all family members and relationships (Sarason, Pierce, & Sarason, 1990). This underlines the importance of examining the subjective meanings that experiences and circumstances in the family have for individual family members. Because similar experiences may have very different meanings for different individuals, the same experiences may lead to different outcomes for different individuals. Family member's expectations about the partners' behavior might affect interactions and relationships between family members (Collins, 1991; 1997). These findings underline the importance of including multiple reporters within the family in a round-robin design. The SRM offers researchers the possibility to deal with the associated interdependence. The findings we obtained by using the SRM indicate that relying on single reports of others about a target individual may paint an incomplete picture of the relational influences at work in families. The results regarding family effects and relationship effects provide further support for this conclusion.

The family as a whole also contributed to differences in the investment model variables, which might indicate the importance of a general family climate. In some families, members seem to be more committed to and satisfied with each other, invest more and have fewer alternatives for their family relationships than in other families. In other words, some families are closer than others.

Although the characteristics of the perceiving individual and the family as a whole appeared to be important determinants of judgments about the investment model, characteristics of the specific dyadic family relationships also contributed to differences in judgments. Family members make unique responses to specific dyadic partners as shown by relationship effects. Horizontal marital relationships were characterized by higher relationship effects than vertical parent→child and child→parent relationships, indicating that the specific dyadic relationships were more important for horizontal relationships than for vertical relationships. In contrast to vertical relationship partners, horizontal relationship partners mutually reciprocate their unique perceptions. This shows the horizontal relationships to be largely dependent on the specific match between actor and partner.

These findings are compatible with our suggestions that horizontal relationship partners are more equal with regard to power, expertise, authority, and the exchange of affect than vertical relationship partners (Bugental & Goodnow, 1998; Hartup, 1989). Moreover, they have important theoretical implications for the investment model in family relationships. In horizontal relationships, both partners have to continuously invest in their marital relationship and mutually coordinate and adjust their behavior, and the extent to which they do so may have the character of an exchange relationship more than in vertical relationships (Clark & Jordan, 2002). If individuals in a horizontal relationship do not perceive the investment in the relationship to be reciprocated, then they may subsequently invest less and be less committed as a result. Because the horizontal relationship between marital partners is voluntary, the consequences of such a negative sequence of behavior may be dramatic. In the vertical parent–child relationship, however, parents may be committed to their children regardless of the investment of the children. The same might be the case for children toward parents, as children are typically loyal to their parents regardless of parental behaviors.

It should be noted, however, that the interpretation of SRM variance components in a three-person family differs from the interpretation in a four-person family. In a four-person family with two parents and two children, judgments are balanced over generations, with each family member judging one family member of his or her own generation (i.e., the spouse or the sibling) and two members of the other generation (i.e., the two parents or the two children). In three-person families, adolescents judge two similar relationships (two parents) and father and mother judge two different relationships (spouse and child). The child actor effect may therefore reflect a "relationship type" effect and represent the child's general perception of parents. Thus, results of SRM analyses cannot be directly compared across studies examining families of different sizes or different composition, and researchers should always keep in mind the specifics of the families in their study to be able to interpret the results.

In four-person families, children's general perception of parents can be assessed as well, by correlating the relationship effects of child to father and child to mother. These correlations are referred to as *intergenerational assimilation* and measure the degree to which a person from one generation sees the persons of the other generation as similar (Branje, van Aken, & van Lieshout, 2002; Finkenauer, Engels, Branje, & Meeus, 2004; Kashy & Kenny, 1990). For example, the degree to which the adolescent is equally committed to mother and father, or the degree to which mother is equally committed to both children. Another correlation assessing intergenerational interdependency that may be relevant in families in which the generation of the children may be distinguished from the generation of the parents, is *intergenerational consensus,* which measures the degree to which individuals from one generation view an individual from another generation as similar. For example, mother and father agree about how committed they are to the adolescent.

To demonstrate SRM's utility for the examination of the investment model in families both concurrently and longitudinally, we examined the relations of the variables of the investment model to commitment concurrently and over time. Based on these analyses, one can draw conclusions about whether associations between variables are stronger at the individual level, the dyadic level, or the family level. In the present study, concurrent associations between satisfaction, investment, and alternatives with commitment were strongest at the level of the family, indicating that families that are more committed also invest more, are more satisfied, and have fewer alternatives than families that are less committed. Concurrent relations were also strong at the level of the individual actor, and at the dyadic level for the marital relationship in particular. Relationship effects appeared to be the strongest predictors of commitment over time, but only in horizontal marital relationships. Please note that these covariances of relationship effects are evaluated after controlling for individual- and family-level covariances. These findings are in line with the idea that the investment model works best for exclusive dyadic relationships, although the direction of effects was sometimes opposite to our expectations (Lin & Rusbult, 1995).

To demonstrate a third application of the SRM to family relationships, we predicted child depression over time from the SRM variance components of commitment and satisfaction. These analyses enable us to examine whether fathers and mothers have similar effects on child depression or whether it is important to distinguish between father and mother effects. As judgments of the child's relationship with father and mother are often highly related, it is difficult to decide how to handle these scores when using traditional analytic strategies. For example, entering scores on the relationship with father and mother in the same regression might lead to multicollinearity, performing separate analyses entails the risk that one is assessing the same relation two times, and combining or averaging father and mother scores might obscure differences in effects of father and mother. The SRM enables us to assess the effect of the child's general relationship with parents as well as the effect of the child's specific relationship to father and mother, thereby offering unique and exciting insights into the relation between family functioning and adolescent depression. Specifically, results indicated that concurrent relations with depression are due to the child's general relationship with both parents while effects over time are due to the child's specific relationship with mother or father. These results further underline the importance of considering different types of influence of relationships to enhance our understanding of the link between relationships and individual outcomes in general, and relationship quality and the development of adolescent depression in particular.

The current chapter only shows a few of the possibilities of the SRM in family relationships. The SRM could be extended in several ways. For example, instead of only correlating the same variances of different variables to each other (e.g., the child's actor variance of variable X to the child's actor variance of variable Y), one could estimate correlations between different variances. An example is the work of Branje, van Lieshout, and van Aken (2002), who examined dyadic reciprocity across variables and found that individuals who are perceived as more agreeable by specific relationship partners perceive these relationship partners as more supportive. The SRM variances could also be related to self-judgments to examine assumed similarity (do family members perceive others as similar to themselves?) and self–other agreement (do family members perceive themselves similar as other members do?) (Kenny, 1994). For example, on most personality factors, the judgments of adolescents revealed a higher degree of self–other agreement and a lower degree of assumed similarity than those of parents (Branje et al., 2003). Further, Cook and colleagues (Cook & Kenny, 2004) have focused on the SRM effects in individual families, which offer important possibilities for clinical practice.

To conclude, the SRM does not capture all possible complexity of family relationships but the model is certainly much more powerful for the study of complex family relationships than models that are typically used. In particular, instead of using just the judgment of single family members or aggregating judgments of several family members, the SRM enables one to assess the independent effects of the actor, the partner, their relationship, and the family on the interdependent judgments of all members in the family.

REFERENCES

Bentler, P. M., & Bonett, D. G. (1980). Significance tests and goodness-of-fit in the analysis of covariance structures. *Psychological Bulletin, 88*, 588-606.

Branje, S. J. T., Hale, W., III, & Meeus, W. H. J. (2008). Reciprocal development of parent-adolescent support and adolescent problem behaviors. In M. Kerr, H. Stattin, & R. Engels (Eds.), *What can parents do? New insights into the role of parents in adolescent problem behaviour*. New York: John Wiley & Sons.

Branje, S. J. T., van Aken, M. A. G., & van Lieshout, C. F. M. (2002). Relational support in families with adolescents. *Journal of Family Psychology, 16*, 351-362.

Branje, S. J. T., van Aken, M. A. G., van Lieshout, C. F. M., & Mathijssen, J. J. J. P. (2003). Personality judgments in adolescents' families: The perceiver, the target, their relationship, and the family. *Journal of Personality, 71*, 49-81.

Branje, S. J. T., van Lieshout, C. F. M., & van Aken, M. A. G. (2002). Relations between agreeableness and perceived support in family relationships: Why nice people are not always supportive. *International Journal of Behavioral Development, 29*, 120-128.

Browne, M., & Cudeck, R. (1989). Single sample cross-validation indices for covariance structures. *Multivariate Behavioral Research, 24*, 445-455.

Browne, M. W., & Cudeck, R. (1993). Alternative ways of assessing model fit. In K. A. Bollen & J. S. Long (Eds.), *Testing structural equation models* (pp. 132-162). Beverley Hills, CA: Sage.

Bugental, D. B., & Goodnow, J. J. (1998). Socialization processes. In W. Damon (Ed.), *Handbook of child psychology* (5th ed.; Vol. 3, pp. 389-465). New York: John Wiley & Sons.

Clark, M. S., & Jordan, S. D. (2002). Adherence to communal norms: What it means, when it occurs, and some thoughts on how it develops. *New Directions for Child and Adolescent Development, 95*, 3-25.

Collins, W. A. (1991). Shared views and parent-adolescent relationships. *New Directions for Child Development, 51*, 103-110.

Collins, W. A. (1997). Relationships and development during adolescence: Interpersonal adaptation to individual change. *Personal Relationships, 4*, 1-14.

Collins, W. A., Laursen, B., Mortensen, N., Luebker, C., & Ferreira, M. (1997). Conflict processes and transitions in parent and peer relationships: Implications for autonomy and regulation. *Journal of Adolescent Research, 12*, 178-198.

Cook, W. L. (1993). Interdependence and the interpersonal sense of control: An analysis of family relationships. *Journal of Personality and Social Psychology, 64*, 587-601.

Cook, W. L. (1994). A structural equation model of dyadic relationships within the family system. *Journal of Consulting and Clinical Psychology, 62*, 500-509.

Cook, W. L. (2000). Understanding attachment security in family context. *Journal of Personality and Social Psychology, 78*, 285-294.

Cook, W. L., & Kenny, D. A. (2004). Application of the Social Relations Model to family assessment. *Journal of Family Psychology, 18*, 361-371.

Cook, W. L., Kenny, D. A., & Goldstein, M. J. (1991). Parental affective style risk and the family system: A Social Relations Model analysis. *Journal of Abnormal Psychology, 100*, 492-501.

Craighead, W. E., Smucker, M. R., Craighead, L. W., & Ilardi, S. S. (1998). Factor analysis of the Children's Depression Inventory in a community sample. *Psychological Assessment, 10*, 156-165.

Finch, J. J., Jr., Saylor, C. F., Edwards, G. L., & McIntosh, J. A. (1987). Children's depression inventory: Reliability over repeated administrations. *Journal of Clinical Child Psychology, 16*, 339-341.

Finkenauer, C., Engels, R. C. M. E., Branje, S. J. T., & Meeus, W. H. J. (2004). Disclosure and relationship satisfaction in families. *Journal of Marriage and Family, 66*, 195-209.

Hartup, W. W. (1989). Social relationships and their developmental significance. *American Psychologist, 44*, 120-126.

Hinde, R. A. (1997). *Relationships: A dialectic perspective.* Hove, East Sussex: Psychology Press.

Hu, L. T., & Bentler, M. P. (1999). Cut-off criteria for fit indexes in covariance structure analysis: Conventional criteria versus new alternatives. *Structural Equation Modeling, 6*, 1-55.

Jöreskog, K. G. (1999). *How large can a standardized coefficient be?* [Online]. Retrieved from http://www.ssicentral.com/lisrel/column2.htm.

Jöreskog, K. G., & Sörbom, D. (1996). *LISREL 8: User's reference guide* (2nd ed.). Chicago, IL: Scientific Software International.

Kashy, D. A., & Kenny, D. A. (1990). Analysis of family research designs: A model of interdependence. *Communication Research, 17*, 462-482.

Kenny, D. A. (1994). *Interpersonal perception: A social relations analysis.* New York: Guilford Press.

Kenny, D. A. (2001). *Measuring model fit* [Online]. Retrieved [2/22/01] from http://nw3.nai.net/~dakenny/fit.htm.

Kenny, D. A., & La Voie, L. (1984). The Social Relations Model. In L. Berkowitz (Ed.), *Advances in experimental social psychology* (Vol. 18, pp. 142-182). San Diego, CA: Academic Press.

Kenrick, D. T., Sadalla, E. K., Groth, G., & Trost, M. R. (1990). Evolution, traits, and the stages of human courtship—Qualifying the parental investment model. *Journal of Personality, 58*, 97-116.

Kovacs, M. (1985). The Children's Depression Inventory. *Psychopharmacology Bulletin, 21*, 995-998.

Kovacs, M. (1992). *Children's Depression Inventory manual.* Los Angeles: Western Psychological Services.

Laursen, B., & Bukowski, W. M. (1997). A developmental guide to the organisation of close relationships. *International Journal of Behavioral Development, 21,* 747-770.

Lin, Y. W., & Rusbult, C. E. (1995). Commitment to dating relationships and cross-sex friendships in America and China. *Journal of Social and Personal Relationships, 12,* 7-26.

Maccoby, E. E. (1992). The role of parents in the socialization of children: An historical overview. *Developmental Psychology, 28,* 1006-1017.

Meeus, W., Akse, J., Branje, S. J. T., Ter Bogt, T., Delsing, M. J. M. H., & Doorn, M. (2004). [Codebook of the research project CONflicts and MAnagement of Relationships (CONAMORE). First wave: 2001]. Unpublished manuscript, Utrecht University, The Netherlands.

Reis, H. T., Collins, W. A., & Berscheid, E. (2000). The relationship context of human behavior and development. *Psychological Bulletin, 126,* 844-872.

Rusbult, C. E. (1983). A longitudinal test of the investment model: The development (and deterioration) of satisfaction and commitment in heterosexual involvement. *Journal of Personality and Social Psychology, 45,* 101-117.

Rusbult, C. E., Johnson, D. J., & Morrow, G. D. (1986). Predicting satisfaction and commitment in adult romantic involvements: An assessment of the generalizability of the investment model. *Social Psychology Quarterly, 49,* 81-89.

Rusbult, C. E., Martz, J. M., & Agnew, C. R. (1998). The investment model scale: Measuring commitment level, satisfaction level, quality of alternatives, and investment size. *Personal Relationships, 5,* 357-391.

Russell, A., Pettit, G. S., & Mize, J. (1998). Horizontal qualities in parent-child relationships: Parallels with and possible consequences for children's peer relationships. *Developmental Review, 18,* 313-352.

Sarason, B. R., Pierce, G. R., & Sarason, I. G. (1990). Social support: The sense of acceptance and the role of relationships. In B. R. Sarason, I. G. Sarason, & G. R. Pierce (Eds.), *Social support: An interactional view* (pp. 97-128). New York: John Wiley & Sons.

Snijders, T. A. B., & Kenny, D. A. (1999). The Social Relations Model for family data: A multilevel approach. *Personal Relationships, 6,* 471-486.

CHAPTER THIRTEEN

Methods for Detecting Subgroups in Social Networks

Jonathan Templin

University of Georgia

It can be safely said that social network research has a relatively long past, yet a relatively short history. Although studies using social network methodology date from the early part of the 20th century (for instance, see Criswell, 1939; Evans-Pritchard, 1929; Moreno, 1934), such methods seem to be sparsely used in modern research. Such scarcity could stem in part from several problematic hurdles which researchers must overcome when choosing social networks as a method to study developmental phenomena, the biggest of which are inherent in data collection and data analysis. Data collection difficulty stems from the amount and type of information needed to fully assemble a network of relations among individuals. Additional concerns regarding consent of individuals named within a network complicate such efforts. Once network data have been collected, however, additional challenges meet researchers in the form of selecting the right type of statistical analysis to cull information from the network data. The following chapter seeks to present a survey of tools used for extracting groups of similarly behaving individuals from social network data. The methods presented in the chapter are aligned into two general categories: nonstochastic groups of individuals formed by meeting definitional requirements and stochastic groups of similarly behaving individuals. Following a brief introduction about statistical methods used in social network analysis, methods for each type of category are presented, framed in the context of the analysis of a social network data set.

Social Networks

A social network is a collection of individuals (commonly called actors) and an enumeration of the relations (or ties) among such individuals. The term social network is attributed to Barnes (1954) who used it in reference to the social relations found in a community in Bremmes, Norway. Ever since, the term has come to be associated with many different types of relations among many different types of individuals, from people connected by marriage (for example, see Padgett & Ansell, 1993) to user profiles connected on online "social-networking" sites such as MySpace (for example, see Finin, Ding, Zhou, & Joshi, 2005). Network relations can be denoted in many differing ways: as merely existing or not (a binary or dichotomous variable), as a valued relation (such as the amount of money exchanged among countries), or even as a count (such as the number of times email was exchanged among individuals). In the analysis of social network data, such relations are typically stored in a square matrix, forming what is called a sociomatrix. Typically, each row and column of a sociomatrix represents an individual in a social network. The entries in the matrix are the values of the relational ties among individuals. Because relations can be directional, the matrix is not necessarily symmetric (for instance, Individual A may choose Individual B as a friend, but Individual B may not think Individual A is a friend). Although the topics discussed in this paper will work with most types of matrix data, for simplicity, binary relations among individuals will be the only relations considered within this chapter.

Social networks present challenges for statistical analyses because of the interrelatedness of the ties and the individuals within the network. Modeling the probability a tie is present between two individuals (for a directional binary relation) is not as simple as plugging the data into a logistic regression package and selecting a set of meaningful covariates (such an analysis treats all ties as independent). Because of the interconnectedness of the data, the likelihood of the relation being present is influenced by other ties within the network. To illustrate, consider "love" as a relation being measured. Love is a relation which is directional (love can be unrequited), but is more likely to exist if a given pair of individuals *both* profess their love for each other. Therefore, the existence of a directional tie between two individuals (Individual A loves Individual B) is highly associated with the existence of reciprocity (the tendency for individuals to have network relations in either direction) of another tie within the network (Individual B loving Individual A). Furthermore, additional relations between two or more individuals within a network (such as transitivity or intransitivity) can also influence the existence of a relational tie. Transitivity is a network characteristic between any triple of individuals. A transitive triplet is one where Individual A has a tie with Individual B, Individual B has a tie with Individual C, *and* Individual A has a tie with Individual C. How such dependencies are addressed is the focus of many of the statistical techniques developed to treat social network data.

Over the past 30 years, statistical methods have been developed to model relational network behavior and to investigate network tendencies for association beyond that of a pair of individuals. One set of statistical methods for the analysis of social network data is the family of exponential random graph models (for example, Frank & Strauss, 1986; also, see references for p^*, Wasserman & Pattison, 1996; or an application of p^* by Zijlstra, Veenstra & Van Duijn., chapter 15). Although such models have been greatly expanded from their original form, the most basic use of such models is to determine if a given network effect (such as reciprocity or transitivity) happens more often than chance would predict for a network of a given size. Part of the difficulty with the widespread application of exponential random graph models stems from the lack of stable algorithms to estimate such models. Although recent work has focused on such problems, and holds great promise (see, for example, Snijders, Pattison, Robins, & Handcock, 2006), easily accessible estimation of such models is currently not available.

Other methods for social network analysis attempt to model network dependencies by use of latent spaces. The p_2 model for social networks incorporates random effects for individuals (for example, see Van Duijn, Snijders, & Zijlstra, 2004). Another model for the relations present in networks is the Generalized Bilinear Mixed-Effects Model (Hoff, 2005). The GBME uses a Euclidean approach to modeling the dependency present in network data. The approach places individuals on a latent Euclidean space with the distance among individuals being the key to modeling the likelihood of a tie between individuals (or strength of a tie for nonbinary relations).

The modeling methods for social networks are necessary tools which can be used in stochastic algorithms for detecting network subgroups (or blockmodels). Although, in theory, any statistical model for network data could be generalized into a mixture model for detecting groups, the estimation difficulty inherent in the exponential random graph models limit their current application as such. Instead, the stochastic group method portion of this chapter will focus on the expansion of Euclidean methods for network modeling to detect clusters of similarly performing individuals (Handcock, Raftery, & Tantrum, 2005).

OVERVIEW

The focus of this chapter is on methods for detecting groups of similarly relating individuals within social network data. To this end, two types of methods will be considered: nonstochastic (definitional or graph-theoretic) and stochastic (blockmodel or positional methods). The nonstochastic methods determine group membership for a set of individuals in an all-or-none fashion, by comparing the set of ties among individuals to definitions of what comprises a "group." Such methods produce groups under commonly used names such as cliques or clans. Stochastic methods group individuals by use of a statistical model for the ties of individuals from within a group. Such methods define a group by evaluating the statistical likelihood of an individual being a group member in comparison with similarly positioned individuals within a network (individuals with similar numbers of ties to and from other commonly tied individuals). In stochastic methods, individuals are not placed into groups with certainty: resulting from the stochastic methods is the estimated probability a given individual is a member of a given group. Both types of methods for detecting groups in social network data are presented to highlight the differences between the two, and to draw comparisons to features they have in common. Nonstochastic methods are presented first, followed by stochastic methods.

To illustrate the methods used for detecting groups in social network data, an example data set will be used throughout the chapter (and was used by Card, Little, & Selig in chapter 11). The data were collected as part of a study of middle school children in the New England region of the United States. A total of 59 students from a single school were used in the analysis (25 boys and 34 girls). The students were all in the sixth grade, and came from three differing classrooms (such information will be used to help describe and validate how individuals are grouped in our data). As part of the study, students were asked (1) to name up to 10 other students whom they identified as friends and (2) to name up to 10 other students whom they "hung out with." If a student identified another student on either of the two network relation questions, then a tie was given among the students in the sociomatrix (a binary relation denoted by a one). Figure 13.1 provides the relational structure of the school network in a diagram (produced by the NetDraw program, Borgotti, 2002).

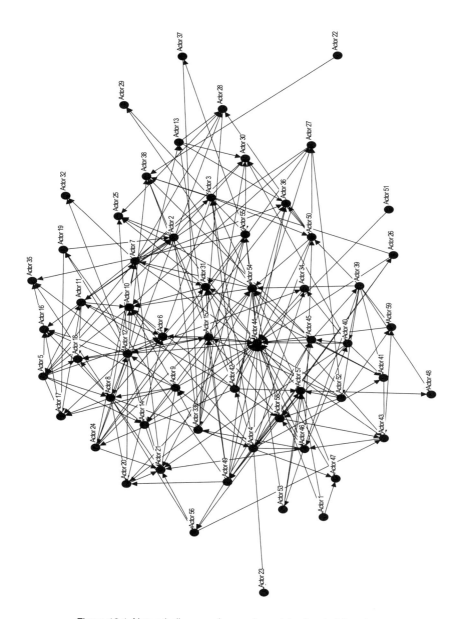

Figure 13.1. Network diagram of example social network data set.

NonStochastic Methods for Group Detection

The survey of grouping methods for social network data begins with methods which are nonstochastic, or definitional in nature. Such methods place individuals into groups when a given group exhibits a prespecified network structure. As such, individuals are placed into each group with absolute certainty: for each group, each individual either is a member or is not a member. The most commonly used nonstochastic methods rely on graph-theoretic notions of grouping to assign individuals, omitting other structural information regarding an individual's relative position within a network. In a sense, then, the nonstochastic methods to be highlighted subsequently are markedly different from the stochastic methods which assign group member-ship based on network position. After detailing the benefits and detriments to using nonstochastic methods to find groups, several nonstochastic methods are highlighted: cliques, clans, plexes, and other (mainly permutation-based) approaches.

Perhaps the single biggest benefit to using nonstochastic group detection methods comes with its simplicity: all subgroups identified will have a known structure. Search algorithms for finding such groups are well known and easily obtainable by using programs such as UCINET (Borgatti, Everett, & Freeman, 2002b). Furthermore, there is no uncertainty regarding the group(s) to which an individual belongs. If the set of an individual's relational ties with other potential group members meets the definition for inclusion, then the individual is included; otherwise, the individual is excluded from the group. No further investigation is required to determine why such a group was formed.

One of the largest detriments to many of the nonstochastic methods (par-ticularly those based on network definitions) is in the way that individuals can be a member of multiple groups, simultaneously. For instance applying a basic method for group detection using our example data set (as will be shown subsequently), some individuals appeared in up to 17 such "groups." Such information can be overwhelming to a researcher, and does not speak to what each of the multiple groups may have in common (or if some groups are highly overlapping—containing many of the same members). Furthermore, the overall number of such groups in a network may be extremely large. Using a slightly different method for group membership (which will be illustrated subsequently) with our example data resulted in nearly 800 such groups which were formed from the 59 individuals in the sample. Therefore, knowledge of group membership using definitional approaches can be helpful to describe if a person is a part of some type of group, but beyond that, such information can become unwieldy.

As an alternative to the pitfalls of the definitional nonstochastic methods, search algorithms have been created to parse smaller numbers of groups of individuals. Such searches typically focus on maximizing the number of network ties within a group while minimizing the number of ties among groups. Such methods are very promising at solving some of the excessive grouping problems inherent in the definitional approaches, but still have some problems related to the algorithms. Primarily, depending on how the algorithm penalizes between-group ties compared to within-group ties, differing clustering solutions can come about. Furthermore, most algorithms are prone to having multiple solutions (some because of how the algorithm decides to end – optimality issues; some because of the network structure). Depending on the size of the network and the density (or frequency) of the relations present, such problems can lead to issues of group validity when examining the output of such methods.

In all, it seems that nonstochastic methods are the primary choice of researchers seeking to find groups in social networks. Within the chapter, the more commonly used nonstochastic methods are presented first: cliques, clans, and plexes. Following a review of such methods, I present a few nonstochastic grouping methods based on search/permutation procedures. Although the network relations for the example data are directional, for convenience in showing the definitional methods (cliques, clans, and plexes), all ties will be considered symmetric.

Cliques. A clique is a set of three or more individuals with relational ties to all other individuals within the set. Given the graph-theoretic notions of what entails a clique, another term for clique is a maximally complete subgraph (Wasserman & Faust, 1994). Taking the example data set, a total of 98 different cliques were found. As is typical, many cliques had overlapping individuals. For instance, one clique consisted of Students 4, 9, 33 and 44 whereas another clique consisted of Students 4, 33, 44, and 46 – only the lack of a relational tie between Students 9 and 33 kept both individuals from being part of the same clique. Figure 13.2a shows a network diagram of one of the cliques from within the data set.

Although it was not the case with our example data set, the definition of a clique is fairly strict: all individuals must have ties to all other individuals in the clique. Because of the strict definition of a clique, many sparse network data sets may have very few cliques. For that reason, a more general clique definition exists, that of an *N*-clique. An *N*-clique is a set of three or more individuals that are separated by no less than *N* relational ties. For instance, a 2-clique would have individuals who are either direct friends with other

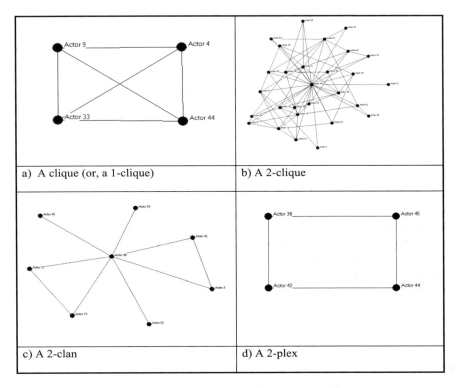

| a) A clique (or, a 1-clique) | b) A 2-clique |
| c) A 2-clan | d) A 2-plex |

Figure 13.2. Diagrams of nonstochastic group results.

individuals or are friends of other individual's friends. In this sense, the clique definition from the proceeding paragraph could also be called a 1-clique. Because of the loosening of the definition of what consists of a clique, there tends to be more N-cliques present in a given network as N increases. For instance, our example data had 98 cliques (or 1-cliques), whereas a total of 792 2-cliques were found. Furthermore, the typical number of individuals in a clique increases as N increases. To illustrate, Figure 13.2b contains the network diagram of one of the identified 2-cliques. A total of 29 individuals were contained within this specific 2-clique. By comparison, the two largest (1-) cliques contained a total of five individuals each.

Clans. With the definition of a clique sometimes being too restrictive and the generality of N-cliques being sometimes too admissive, other types of groups have been defined. Clans are groups of individuals that are all separated by *at most* N separations from each other (Alba, 1973). The idea of separation is more commonly referred to as the diameter of a graph, the maximum number of relational ties between any two individuals in a network. So, an N-clan is an N-clique that has a diameter of no more than N directional ties separating any two individuals. By adding the additional consideration of diameter, the number of N-clans that exist in a network will tend to be much less than the number of N-cliques in the network. For instance, in our example data set, a total of 14 2-clans were found. Figure 13.2c illustrates one of the 2-clans found in the data set. Illustrated in the figure is that each individual is no more than two relational ties apart from each other individual. Because of the N-clan definition, as the choice of N increases, the number of individuals in a clan increases (while the overall number of unique clans decreases). For a network where all individuals are connected in some way to all other individuals (in network terms, were reachable), the choice of N being equal to the network diameter will result in a single clan containing all individuals in the network.

Plexes. Another type of nonstochastic grouping method based on network definitions is that of a K-plex. A K-plex is a group of N individuals (N being greater than three) that are connected to at least N - K other individuals in the group. To illustrate a K-plex, Figure 13.2d gives a network diagram of one of the 2-plexes found in the example data set. A total of four different individuals are present in the figure, Students 38, 42, 44, and 45. By definition of the 2-plex, each of these four individuals must be connected to at least two (or, using the notation of the K-plex, $4 - 2$) individuals in the group. From the figure, one can see that each individual is connected to exactly two other individuals, satisfying the definition of the 2-plex. For small numbers of K, K-plexes tend to exist in large quantities in networks. For instance, a total of 1,192 2-plexes were found in our example network data set. Increasing K will result in even larger numbers of groups identified in the data set.

Nonstochastic Structural Approaches

The definitional approaches to groups in networks have two features which tend to make their widespread application in research somewhat difficult: first individuals can be part of multiple groups, and second, enormous numbers of groups can exist in a single data set. In addition, cliques, clans, plexes, and other such approaches ignore the relative positions in the network of the individuals that they contain. Specifically, it makes no difference if an individual is chosen by many other individuals in the network (although that individual will often appear in many of the definitional groups found in the network).

Substantively, perhaps more important than determining the number of definitional groups an individual is part of is determining the set of individuals in similar positions within the network. To this end, the notion of structural equivalence plays a role. For our purposes, I will provide a loose definition of structural equivalence—structurally equivalent individuals are individuals with similar patterns of ties to other similarly positioned individuals within the network. Knowing how many groups of structurally equivalent individuals there are present, which individuals are in each group, and the attributional characteristics of each group may provide researchers with more meaningful information about the structure of the network of interest.

For the remainder of the chapter, I will focus on methods for determining the number of and composition of structurally equivalent groups of individuals in a social network. To this end, I categorize the first set of methods into the nonstochastic family of group search algorithms due to the manner which such methods determine group membership. It is worth noting that, unlike the definitional approaches where the number of groups meeting a given definition (clique, clan, or plex) was counted, for each structural equivalence method the number of groups must be specified at the beginning of each run of the algorithm. As will be shown and discussed, the ultimate choice of the number of groups to extract is then found by a series of successive runs of each algorithm, and by checking diagnostic measures for when to stop extracting groups. Such approaches are similar to what is done in methods such as k-means clustering, latent class analysis, and other exploratory procedures for understanding the group structure of data.

To limit our discussion on nonstochastic approaches for finding groups of structurally equivalent groups, I discuss a generic search algorithm. Other methods include extracting groups through procedures such as CONCORR (Convergence of iterated Correlations; Breiger, Boorman, & Arabie, 1975). The differentiating feature behind such nonstochastic procedures for structural grouping and stochastic procedures is that nonstochastic procedures try to permute the sociomatrix such that the overall density within groups is high and between groups is low. Statistical models for group membership are not present in nonstochastic methods, and as such, each individual can belong to only one group.

In the nonstochastic search algorithm, a cost or loss function is created—a function containing the number of "errors" or "atypical results" present in any given permutation of the matrix. One type of error would be that of having individuals within a group who did not share any relations. Another type of error would be individuals in differing groups having relational ties. The algorithm then tries to permute individuals between the different groups so that the cost function is minimized. Critical differences between algorithms include the cost function weighting of errors present in any one solution, the way individuals are permuted between groups, and the stopping criteria for the algorithm. Because of the approach taken by each such algorithm, a given "final" solution may not have arrived at the overall minimum for the cost function. As such, users are encouraged to try multiple algorithm runs with differing starting values for a given number of groups being extracted. Further confounding the results is the possibility that multiple configurations of individuals and groups may have the minimum cost function value, making the choice of any one of these solutions arbitrary. I note that the multiple optima problem is also present in the model-based stochastic methods which are discussed in the next section.

To demonstrate one of the nonstochastic methods for grouping structurally equivalent individuals, I will apply an algorithm found in UCINET to our example data. The algorithm uses binary-valued relations, which can be directional (I will be using directional relations for this example). The algorithm was run eight different times attempting to extract two through ten groups, successively. For each group level, the algorithm was run with 10 random starts, each with a different starting configuration and random number seed (the results to be discussed came from stable results exhibited by more than three different iteration runs). Because of the selection of the cost function, methods for evaluating the number of groups are not well defined, and any result must be validated with external information. The cost function for the algorithms attempts to minimize the total number of "errors" (ties between individuals of differing groups or the absence of ties between individuals within the same group). Figure 13.3 provides the count of the errors for the final solution for each number of groups extracted (in a plot similar to the scree plots common in exploratory factor analysis). Although the metric of "errors" is not too reliable, some information can be obtained from such a plot—specifically, that after four groups, the number of errors only diminishes slightly for each successive group extracted. For this reason, I will consider the four group solution to describe our network.

To get a picture of how the groups differ, Table 13.1 lists, for each extracted group, descriptive counts of group members by gender and classroom affiliation. Each group has roughly about the same number of individuals—a condition enforced by the algorithm. The gender ratio for each group is not skewed widely in either direction, as perhaps having a single group consisting of only one gender would indicate. Rather, it appears that there is a rather large tendency for the individuals in the network to form groups with respect to classroom affiliations. Group 1 has 11 students from Classroom 3, Group 2 has 10 students from Classroom 2, and Group 4 has 12 students from Classroom 1. Group 3 has a mixture of students, mainly from Classrooms 2 and 3. From this post-hoc inspection of the groups, it seems that structural positions are tied to classroom affiliation. Understanding the structure of the school would go farther in validating the grouping result, yet it seems to be consistent (or perhaps make sense anecdotally) that most elementary/middle

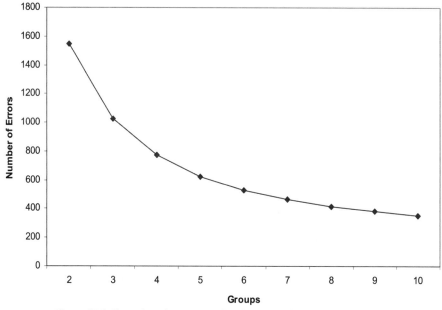

Figure 13.3. Error chart from nonstochastic structural grouping algorithm.

school students tend to have friendship relations with their fellow classmates. To further illustrate the clustering result, Figure 13.4 provides a network diagram for the entire social network, with differing shaped symbols representing the different groups. With a few notable exceptions, group members tend to have more ties than individuals from differing groups, which is verified by looking at the density portion of Table 13.1, which illustrates the proportion of relational ties between and within each group.

Stochastic Methods for Group Detection

The algorithm used to parse individuals into groups through permutations was neither model-based, nor stochastic in nature. The resulting output was an arrangement of individuals into groups with complete certainty. However, not all individuals are equally likely to be in each group. As an alternative, stochastic methods for network group detection attempt to place individuals into a prespecified number of groups by weighting an individual's relational profile (the list of other individuals to whom the individual has relations) compared with the profile of individuals from within a group. By analogy, the nonstochastic structural algorithm for finding groups was similar to a k-means cluster analysis: all individuals were assigned to the "closest" group (in our case, the group that produced the fewest number of errors), and then the group composition was assessed. There was no uncertainty about

TABLE 13.1
Nonstochastic Structural Group Algorithm Density Results

Measure	Group 1	Group 2	Group 3	Group 4
N	15	14	15	15
Gender (M/F)	6 / 9	4 / 10	7 / 8	8 / 7
Classroom (1/2/3)	1 / 3 / 11	3 / 10 / 1	2 / 5 / 8	12 / 3 /0

Density	Group 1	Group 2	Group 3	Group 4
Group 1	0.16	0.03	0.04	0.05
Group 2	0.04	0.14	0.03	0.05
Group 3	0.05	0.01	0.25	0.06
Group 4	0.04	0.04	0.04	0.14

the group assignment: all individuals were placed into a single group only. Continuing with the analogy, stochastic methods for detecting groups are more similar to finite mixture models (such as latent class models or growth mixture models), where individuals each have a specific probability that they fall into each prespecified group. Individuals exhibiting similar profiles to those already in the group will tend to have higher probabilities of belonging to the group. Individuals exhibiting profiles that are not similar to many of the groups will tend to have an equal probability of falling into any of the groups. Stochastic methods provide the potential for more detailed analyses because of the statistical (or distributional) assumptions they employ. To demonstrate the use of such methods, I present a recently developed method for detecting groups stochastically, as constructed by Handcock, Raftery, and Tantrum (2005). Prior to detailing the method, application, and analysis, I discuss some background information regarding stochastic methods for group detection: specifically, historical issues and the pros and cons for applying such approaches.

Stochastic methods for grouping individuals according to structural equivalence (or the role which they play within a network) have also been developed under the term blockmodel. A blockmodel is a model for network data that specifies a set of groups (consisting of similarly behaving individuals) and a set of relations between the blocks. Although not all blockmodels are stochastic (for example, see Breiger, Boorman, & Arabie, 1975), I limit the

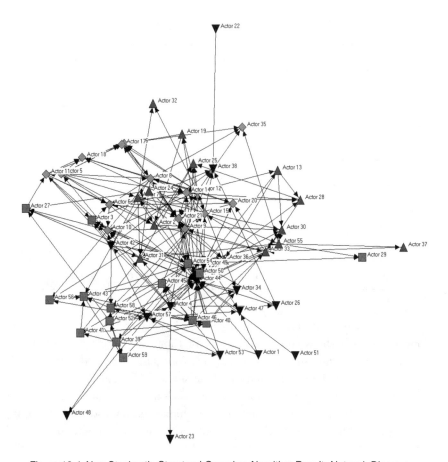

Figure 13.4. Non-Stochastic Structural Grouping Algorithm Result: Network Diagram.

brief discussion of such methods to stochastic blockmodels. Stochastic versions of blockmodels, such as those developed by Fienberg and Wasserman (1981), Wasserman and Anderson (1987), and Snijders and Nowicki (1997) parse individuals into groups based on relational similarities of the individuals in the network. Of the varying models created for detecting groups (or blocks), each makes different assumptions about how social network trends (such as transitivity) affect the tendencies for ties between individuals. The model presented in this chapter uses a novel approach to address the influence of such network tendencies, by developing a latent social space onto which individuals are projected and then modeling the tendency for a relational tie to exist between any pair of individuals as a function of the social space distance between those individuals.

The stochastic methods for determining groups from network data share many of the benefits and deficiencies with the nonstochastic algorithm for determining groups of structurally equivalent individuals. Specifically, unlike the definitional approaches, in nearly all stochastic methods the number of groups is determined from characteristics of the data (and with successive runs of the algorithm). Additionally, another consideration of the stochastic model presented is the time it takes for an algorithm to converge. Depending upon the size of the network and the number of groups to be extracted, the algorithm may take upwards of several hours for a single run (for a fixed number of groups to extract). If multiple runs are needed (and they are if the number of groups is unknown at the start), then it is within reason that determining how many groups exist in a data set may take several days of continuous computation.

Alternatively, when applied correctly, the stochastic approach to determining groups can provide rich information regarding the structure of the social network data. For instance, in the model that will be presented, one can additionally model the tendency for ties to be present based on network covariates (such as individuals sharing the same gender or classroom, often called homophily of attributes). Also, for the current model, a spatial mapping of individuals using the statistical model is produced, allowing a visual display of a network diagram based on the observed tendencies of the individuals and the estimates of the model. Finally, the probability any given individual belongs to any group is obtained, providing more evidence about each individual as to how closely they resemble the group.

As mentioned previously, the stochastic model for detecting groups is based on the GBME (Hoff, 2005). Prior to introducing the model (and then applying it to our example data set), I review the GBME.

Generalized Bilinear Mixed-Effects Model (Hoff, 2005)

The generalized version of the Bilinear Mixed-Effects Model is a stochastic model for the value of a relation between any two individuals. The word generalized is included to indicate the model can be used for differing types of network relations (valued or binary). For our presentation, I will present the GBME as a model for the logit of the probability of a tie between any two given individuals. Let $\mathbf{W}$ denote a sociomatrix with elements w_{ij} representing a tie between any two individuals i and j (here, w_{ij} is the binary indicator of a tie between individuals i and j being present). The GBME models the probability of w_{ij} as

$$P(w_{ij} = 1 | z_i, z_j, \mathbf{x}_{ij}, \beta) = \frac{\exp\left(\beta_0' \mathbf{x}_{ij} - \beta_1 | z_i - z_j |\right)}{1 + \exp\left(\beta_0' \mathbf{x}_{ij} - \beta_1 | z_i - z_j |\right)} \qquad (1)$$

where z_i and z_j are latent variables which are the coordinates of individuals i and j in what Hoff defines as the "latent social space," $|z_i - z_j|$ is the Euclidean distance between individuals i and j in the "latent social space," and β is the vector of regression weights (with $\mathbf{x}_{ij}$ being the network-based covariate information for individuals i and j).

The concept of the latent social space is one that is used to allow the GBME to stochastically model the ties between the individuals. Given the entire set of positions in the latent social space, the ties between any two individuals are assumed to be independent. Such a conditional independence assumption is prominent in other latent variable modeling techniques, such as confirmatory factor analysis (when residuals are uncorrelated) and item response theory. By constructing the model in this manner, network tendencies that may influence the probability a tie exists between any two individuals are already incorporated. The modeled probability is a function of the Euclidean distance between any two individuals, multiplied by the β_1 model parameter. If β_1 is zero, then the distance between any two individuals does not influence the probability of a tie between them (essentially, this indicates other network tendencies do not play a role in the analysis). Alternatively, as β_1 grows large and greater than zero, the distance between any two individuals directly affects the likelihood the individuals have a relational tie. When β_1 is positive, as the distance between any two individuals increases, the probability of a tie decreases. The number of dimensions present in the latent social space can be set by the user, although for simplicity, I use two throughout our analysis in this chapter. The reader is directed to Hoff (2005) for more information about dimensionality (and for information pertaining to the constraints necessary to identify the model).

The other model parameters, β_0, determine the level of influence between any network-based covariate and the likelihood of a tie being present. Such covariates can include an overall intercept (to model the overall tendency of a tie being present), and indicators of network homophily for various covariates. Interpretation of these regression weights proceeds similar to interpretation for regression weights in a logistic regression model. For each covariate, a positive value of β_0 indicates an increased tendency for a tie to be present between two individuals. Similarly, negative values of β_0 indicate a decreased tendency for a tie to be present between any two individuals. For applications of the GBME in other settings, please see Hoff (2005).

Extending the GBME to Detect Network Groups (Handcock et al, 2005)

Although the GBME model presented by Hoff did not directly parse individuals into groups, the model has been extended by Handcock et al. (2005) to be used to detect group structures in network data. As a brief overview, the extension of the GBME comes from the modeling of the latent social space as with a finite mixture model. Finite mixture models are stochastic models which specify the likelihood of observed data as a function of multiple groups. For instance, latent class models (see, for example, Lazarsfeld & Henry, 1968) provide a method for determining the likelihood any given observation falls into one of a prespecifed number of classes by comparing the observed values with that of distributions which characterize each class (distributions with parameters estimated simultaneously by the model).

Similarly, in converting the GBME into a model for multiple groups, distributional assumptions are made regarding the latent social space. Specifically, an individual's position (denoted by the vector $\mathbf{z}_i$ with elements representing the coordinate of the individual in each of the d dimensions) in the latent social space (the coordinates in the dimension) is said to be distributed as

$$\mathbf{z}_i : \sum_{g=1}^{G} \lambda_g f(\mathbf{z}_i; \mu_g, \sigma^2 \mathbf{I}_d), \tag{2}$$

where λ_g is the probability of any individual being a member of group g ($g = 1, \ldots, G$, with $\sum_{g=1}^{G} \lambda_g = 1$), and $f(\mathbf{z}_i; \mu_g, \sigma^2 \mathbf{I}_d)$ is the likelihood value of $\mathbf{z}_i$ being a member of group g, as expressed as a multivariate normal distribution with mean vector μ_g and (spherical) covariance matrix $\sigma^2 \mathbf{I}_d$. For the model, λ_g, μ_g, and σ^2 are estimated for each group g, and help to define the probability an individual falls into group g. Types of output emanating from the model include the individual estimates of group membership in the forms of (posterior) probabilities. The maximum posterior probability is typically used to assign an individual to a given group.

The GBME and the mixture model extension of the GBME are estimated using Bayesian Markov Chain Monte Carlo (MCMC) algorithms. To keep the focus on applied versions of such methods, the full description of each model along with the Bayesian prior specifications are omitted from this chapter. Instead, the reader is referred to Hoff (2005) and Handcock et al. (2005) where a full description of each algorithm can be found. For both the GBME and the mixture extension, estimation software is freely available in contributed packages for the R statistical analysis program (R Development Core Team,

2005). Both algorithms can be found in the *latentnet* package (Handcock, Hunter, Butts, Goodreau, & Morris, 2003), which also bundles the *sna* package (Butts, 2006), containing numerous helpful algorithms and functions for general social network analysis.

Application of the Stochastic Model for Group Detection in Social Networks

The mixture model extension of the GBME was used to assess the number of and composition of groups in our example data set. Using the *latentnet* package in R, a series of algorithm runs were conducted, each with a differing number of groups extracted (ranging from two through seven groups). Because the algorithm used to estimate the model was an MCMC algorithm, careful examination of the algorithm output to determine convergence must be conducted before reporting and interpreting any results. Therefore, following the termination of each algorithm run, the time series plot of the parameter estimates was examined for convergence (roughly speaking, a check to see if each parameter converged to a stable location, a steady state). Because a detailed examination of MCMC output is beyond the scope of this chapter, the reader is referred to sources such as Raftery and Lewis (1995) for more information. For each algorithm run, chain convergence was assessed, and each was considered to be converged.

The first question to be addressed is of how many groups should be extracted. Because model-based clustering algorithms use statistical likelihoods, a set of criteria based on the statistical information of the model can be used to assess which solution provided the best "fit" with the most parsimonious set of parameter values. Information criteria such as the AIC (Akaike's Information Criterion; Akaike, 1974) and the BIC (Bayesian Information Criterion, also known as Schwarz's Criterion, Schwarz, 1976) are often-used criteria that are also output from the *latentnet* package. With either criterion, the lowest value is an indicator that a specific model should be chosen. Figure 13.5 displays the AIC and BIC for the differing group number algorithm runs. Based on the AIC, the model that should be selected is the model without any groups, the one-class model. Based on the BIC, the model that should be selected is the model with three groups. The discrepant results allows us the opportunity to suggest that selection of a model based only on information criteria is tenuous at best, and in mixture model assessment, can lead to results that are spurious in nature. Because a little about the grouping structure of our data set is already known, in that there are three classrooms of sixth graders, the three-class model will be chosen as the "best fitting,"

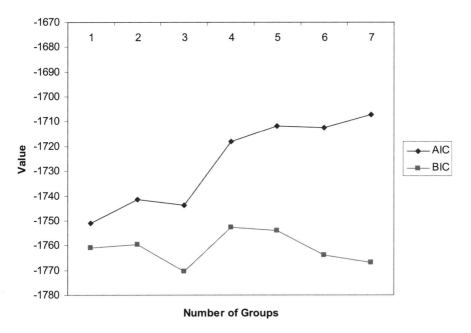

Figure 13.5. Estimated stochastic model AIC and BIC values.

and will thus be used for analysis and interpretation of the results for this model.

The first part of the three-class model to be interpreted is the set of model parameter estimates. Table 13.2 displays the parameter estimates for the model parameters of the three-class model. The parameter estimate shown is the Expected A Posteriori (EAP), or posterior mean, found by taking the mean value of the parameters from the (assumed) converged section of the MCMC chain. The first two model parameters to interpret are the regression weights, $\hat{\beta}_0$, and $\hat{\beta}_1$. The parameter $\hat{\beta}_0$ is the estimate of the overall tendency for a tie to be present between any two individuals in the network, essentially the intercept of the logistic regression model. By the estimated value being less than zero (at -0.72), this indicates that in general, there is less than a 50% chance any two individuals have ties across the network. $\hat{\beta}_1$ is the regression weight corresponding to the Euclidean distance between individuals in the latent social space. The estimated parameter value, 1.40, is significantly different from zero, indicating that the larger (Euclidean) distance between any two individuals in the latent social space makes the chance of a tie between the two individuals significantly smaller. Another interpretation for $\hat{\beta}_1$ is that network characteristics such as reciprocity and transitivity play a role in helping to determine if a relational tie exists between two individuals.

TABLE 13.2
Stochastic Model Parameter Estimates

Parameter	Estimate (Posterior Mean)	Standard Error
$\hat{\beta}_0$ (Intercept—overall tendency to have a tie)	-0.72	0.23
$\hat{\beta}_1$ (Euclidean distance weight)	1.40	0.17
$\hat{\mu}_1$	(-0.08, -0.05)	(0.52, 0.43)
$\hat{\mu}_2$	(0.25, -0.32)	(0.66, 0.61)
$\hat{\mu}_3$	(-0.33, 0.27)	(0.57, 0.57)
$\hat{\sigma}_1^2$	0.93	0.36
$\hat{\sigma}_2^2$	0.65	0.38
$\hat{\sigma}_3^2$	0.38	0.17

The next set of parameters to be interpreted are those associated with the latent social space. Recall that the latent social space is where the mixture model is implemented (via a mixture of multivariate normal distributions). With three groups, there are three sets of parameters to interpret: the mean vector for each group and the variance parameter for each group. The actual location of the mean vectors is relatively meaningless, but rather the proximity to the other mean vectors is important. The mean vector and variance parameter estimates can be found in the bottom part of Table 13.2. From each of these, a picture of the extent to which groups overlap can be built. Furthermore, a network diagram of individuals partitioned according to the latent social space is provided in Figure 13.6. The shading of the individuals indicates the group to which each is most likely to belong. This plot, along with the mean vector parameters, helps describe the latent social space in terms of the group configuration. What can be seen is that Groups 2 and 3 are fairly widely separated, with Group 1 existing between them. Whether this result is meaningful can only be found by external validation: examining the composition of the groups, a step which is conducted next.

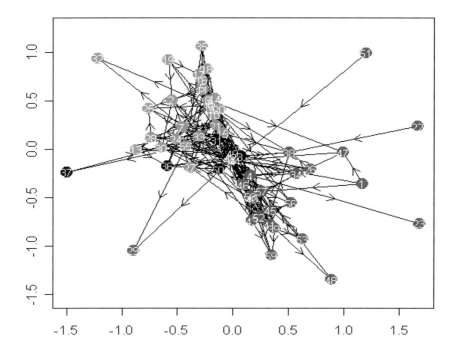

Figure 13.6. Latent social space diagram: three-group solution.

To inspect the composition and nature of each group, each individual is
assigned to the group to which they are most likely to belong (the group
with the highest posterior probability). Table 13.3 portrays the descriptive
statistics for gender, classroom affiliation, and between/within group density
values. Upon initial inspection, the number of students in each group is
skewed, with 8 students in Group 1, 24 students in Group 2, and 27 students
in Group 3. Furthermore, unlike the non-stochastic clustering solution, the
composition of groups does not correspond largely to classroom affiliation.
The closest comparison to classroom affiliation comes from Groups 2 (with
15 students from Classroom 3) and 3 (with 15 students from Classroom 1
and 11 students from Classroom 2). Group 1, in contrast, has about an equal
number of students from Classrooms 2 (three students) and 3 (four students).
It appears that the students who comprise Group 1 are those who do not select
many other classmates, regardless of which classroom they are part of, which
may be why the group was extracted. Or perhaps there are other affiliations
not apparent in the data set which provides more reasoning for such student
group structure (perhaps students in Group 1 are part of similar clubs or play
sports together). In any event, validation of a grouping algorithm result is a
vital step which must be conducted prior to using such a result for further

TABLE 13.3
Descriptive Statistics From Stochastic Grouping Algorithm

Measure	Group 1	Group 2	Group 3
N (Most Likely Class)	8	24	27
Gender (M/F)	1 / 7	12 / 12	12 / 15
Classroom (1/2/3)	1 / 3 / 4	2 / 7 / 15	15 / 11 / 1

Density	Group 1	Group 2	Group 3
Group 1	0.20	0.03	0.07
Group 2	0.13	0.09	0.02
Group 3	0.09	0.02	0.13

analysis or interpretation. Our (brief) exercise of attempting to validate a grouping result with classroom affiliation information is only one step which could be conducted, with many further steps needed before confidence in the result can be obtained.

CONCLUSION

The search for groups in social network data is a complicated task, with many options for users to consider. This chapter sought to highlight several types of methods for determining groups in social networks with the hope to help the user choose a method which was most appropriate for their analysis. Because of the interdependency of the relations present in a graph, social network data presents many challenges in applying statistical analyses. Statistical models with distributional assumptions must incorporate some modeling apparatus to handle the tendency of network characteristics to influence the likelihood of a tie being present (or the magnitude of a tie). In all, the user is faced with many choices of algorithms, methods, and routines which will help provide grouping information about the individuals in a network. It is expected that the choice of a routine will be driven largely by the research question and goals of the study at hand.

In clustering research, a vital step often overlooked is that of validating the result. In this chapter, I attempted to provide a brief method of validation by comparing our group results to that of the classroom structure present in the example network data set. Methods for validation are numerous, and many do not involve complicated steps. The main goal of validation is verifying that the grouping structure is truly that, and not some artifact of the algorithm (or of the statistical criteria upon which the number of groups was based). It may be the case that groups do not exist in a data set, a result which may be more common than researchers expect. If it seems groups do not exist (or if the result is tenuous at best), then perhaps such research is best left with not trying to split a nongrouped structure because such results can be misleading and damaging to research in a field. If groups do exist, understanding why actors/individuals/subjects form groups is a difficult task, yet one which will no doubt lead to larger discovery of the nature of the phenomena under study. It is extremely important to be sure of the groups being indicated by an algorithm prior to seeking the answer for why groups exist.

In all, this chapter attempted to provide a survey of existing methods for determining groups of individuals in social network data. The goal of the chapter was to provide the user with an overview of such methods, along with the benefits and deficiencies of using such approaches. Furthermore, it is important to emphasize that results from any of the procedures presented here are not necessarily meaningful in and of themselves – that validation is as important (if not more so) than selection and proper application of a grouping algorithm. Social network grouping algorithms are numerous, and the user may be overwhelmed by the choices at hand. It is my hope that this chapter provides the user with a bit more information to make a better informed choice of an algorithm, one which suits the purposes they are seeking.

REFERENCES

Akaike, H. (1974). A new look at the statistical identification model. *IEEE Transactions on Automated Control*, *19*, 716-723.

Alba, R. D. (1973). A graph-theoretic definition of a sociometric clique. *Journal of Mathematical Sociology*, *3*, 113-126.

Barnes, J. A. (1954). Class and communities in a Norwegian island parish. *Human Relations*, *7*, 39-58.

Borgatti, S., Everett, M., & Freeman, L. (2002a). *UCINET 6 for Windows*. Harvard: Analytic Technologies.

Borgatti, S., Everett, M., & Freeman, L. (2002b). *UCINET for Windows: Software for social network analysis*. Harvard: Analytic Technologies.

Borgotti, S. P. (2002). *Netdraw*. Harvard: Analytic Technologies.

Breiger, R., Boorman, S., & Arabie, P. (1975). An algorithm for clustering relational data, with applications to social network analysis and comparison with multidimensional scaling. *Journal of Mathematical Psychology*, *12*, 328-383.

Butts, C. T. (2006). *sna: Tools for social network analysis. R-package version 1.1.* (URL: http://erzuli.ss.uci.edu/R.stuff)

Card, N. A., Little, T. D., & Selig, J. P. (chapter 11). Using the bivariate Social Relations Model to study dyadic relationships: Early adolescents' perceptions of friends' aggression and prosocial behavior. In N. A. Card, J. P. Selig, & T. D. Little (Eds.), *Modeling dyadic and interdependent data in the developmental and behavioral sciences*. New York, NY: Routledge/Taylor & Francis Group.

Criswell, J. H. (1939). A sociometric study of race cleavage in the classroom. *Archives of Psychology*, *33*, 1-82.

Evans-Pritchard, E. E. (1929). The study of kinship in primitive societies. *Man*, *29*, 190-194.

Fienberg, S. E., & Wasserman, S. (1981). Categorical data analysis of single sociometric relations. *Sociological Methodology*, *11*, 156-192.

Finin, T., Ding, L., Zhou, L., & Joshi, A. (2005). Social networking on the semantic web. *The Learning Organization*, *12*, 418-435.

Frank, O., & Strauss, D. (1986). Markov graphs. *Journal of the American Statistical Association*, *81*, 832-842.

Handcock, M. S., Hunter, D., Butts, C. T., Goodreau, S. M., & Morris, M. (2003). *statnet: An R package for the statistical modeling of social networks*. (URL: http://www.csde.washington.edu/statnet)

Handcock, M. S., Raftery, A. E., & Tantrum, J. M. (2005). Model-based clustering for social networks. (Center for Statistics and the Social Sciences, University of Washington. Working paper.)

Hoff, P. D. (2005). Bilinear mixed-effects models for dyadic data. *Journal of the American Statistical Association*, *100*, 286-295.

Lazarsfeld, P. F., & Henry, N. W. (1968). *Latent structure analysis*. Boston, MA: Houghton Mifflin Company.

Moreno, J. L. (1934). *Who shall survive? Foundations of sociometry, group psychotherapy and sociodrama.* New York: Beacon House.

Padgett, J. F., & Ansell, C. K. (1993). Robust action and the rise of the Medici, 1400-1434. *American Journal of Sociology, 98,* 1259-1319.

R Development Core Team. (2005). R: A language and environment for statistical computing. R Foundation for Statistical Computing, Vienna, Austria. http://www.r-project.org.

Raftery, A. E., & Lewis, S. M. (1995). The number of iterations, convergence diagnostics, and generic metropolis algorithms. In W. R. Gilks, D. J. Spiegelhalter, & S. Richardson (Eds.), *Practical Markov chain Monte Carlo* (p. 115-130). London: Chapman and Hall.

Schwarz, G. (1976). Estimating the dimension of a model. *Annals of Statistics, 6,* 461-464.

Snijders, T. A. B., & Nowicki, K. (1997). Estimation and prediction for stochastic block models for graphs with latent block structures. *Journal of Classification, 14,* 75-100.

Snijders, T. A. B., Pattison, P. E., Robins, G. L., & Handcock, M. S. (2006). New specifications for exponential random graph models. *Sociological Methodology, 36,* 99-153.

Van Duijn, M. A. J., Snijders, T. A. B., & Zijlstra, B. J. H. (2004). p_2: A random effects model with covariates for directed graphs. *Statistica Neerlandica, 58,* 234-254.

Wasserman, S., & Anderson, C. (1987). Stochastic a posteriori blockmodels: Construction and assessment. *Social Networks, 9,* 1-36.

Wasserman, S., & Faust, K. (1994). *Social network analysis: Methods and applications.* Cambridge, UK: Cambridge University Press.

Wasserman, S., & Pattison, P. E. (1996). Logit models and logistic regressions for social networks I: An introduction to Markov random graphs and p*. *Psychometrika, 60,* 401-425.

Zijlstra, B. J. H., Veenstra, R., & Van Duijn, M. A. J. (chapter 15). A multilevel p_2 model for the analysis of binary bully-victim network data in multiple classrooms. In N. A. Card, J. P. Selig, & T. D. Little (Eds.), *Modeling dyadic and interdependent data in the developmental and behavioral sciences.* New York, NY: Routledge/Taylor & Francis Group.

CHAPTER FOURTEEN

Can We Make Causal Inferences About the Influence of Children's Naturally Existing Social Networks on Their School Motivation?

Thomas A. Kindermann

Portland State University

When researchers try to characterize the role of peer influences in child development, they find themselves caught between two extremes. Five decades ago, the dominant position was that the role of peers was almost negligible. The important influences that shaped children's development were all considered to come from adults, and mainly from parents and teachers. There was little empirical research on the developmental impact of peers. For the most part, children's relationships with other children were considered to be outcomes of healthy development and diagnostic indicators of their social functioning.

This position has been almost completely reversed in recent years. Today, parents and teachers seem to be convinced that peer relationships exert strong effects on children's academic motivation, their behavior in the classroom, and their academic success. Researchers have rediscovered theorists' claims that relationships with age-mates constitute important socialization influences (e.g., Baldwin, Piaget, Vygotski), and have come to re-appreciate the corresponding empirical contributions from the 1930s (e.g., Sherif, Parten, Moreno; see Renshaw, 1981). Today, some theorists even insist that the most important bonds shaping children's development are with peers and that influences from adults are comparably small (e.g., Harris, 1998). Consistent with such claims, studies continue to reveal strong correlations between children and their peers, and experimental studies document the potential causal influences from peers.

Amid these extremes, some researchers point out the need for a more balanced position (e.g., Berndt & Murphy, 2002; Jaccard, Blanton, & Dodge, 2005; Kindermann, 2003; Rubin, Bukowski, & Parker, 2006). On the one hand, they agree with the Zeitgeist that peer relationships are ubiquitous in children's lives and play an important role in their development. On the other hand, they are skeptical about the extent to which most empirical studies actually support these claims. Serious questions exist about what correlations between children and their peer groups mean. Although, without exception, studies show that children with high quality peer relationships tend to do better in school, is this because peers support school performance? Or is it because children who do well at school tend to affiliate with peers who are highly functioning? Or, is it possible that quality of peers and school performance are not causally related at all because they are both caused by some third variable, such as high quality parenting or teaching?

Rather than making specific claims, these researchers have concentrated their efforts on identifying the most valid analytical procedures for examining them. They point out that empirical studies are faced with *four critical challenges* (e.g., Berndt & Murphy, 2002; Jaccard et al., 2005; Kindermann, 1996; 2003): Who among a child's peers is most important? How can the relevant characteristics of peer affiliations be specified and measured? How should processes of influence be conceptualized and tracked empirically? How can studies be conducted so that we can be relatively certain that correlational findings indicate actual peer influences?

The contention is that when careful procedures are used so that the interdependencies between the characteristics of individuals and those of the members of their peer groups are taken into account, a more accurate picture of peer influences will emerge. A tacit assumption is that peer effects identified in such studies will not be as large as suggested by experimental studies in which peers are randomly assigned to children. Nevertheless, as this chapter aims to show, there is reason to believe that they will be present and that they will hold up against the simultaneously competing effects of member selection processes and of influences from other sources.

This chapter is organized in four parts that follow the four key questions. In each section, empirical examples of specific strategies will be based on two previous studies (Kindermann, 1993; Kindermann, 2007); the specifics are outlined in Table 14.1. The first part addresses questions of network identification. A review of the correlational evidence for peer influences on children's motivation and behavior in school is followed by a discussion of the major ways that peer network information can be collected, with a specific focus on Robert Cairns' strategy of *Socio-Cognitive Mapping*. The second part outlines how the psychologically relevant characteristics of peer networks

TABLE 14.1
Design Characteristics of Two Studies That Used Socio-Cognitive Mapping to Examine Peer
Group Influences on Children's Engagement in the Classroom

Study	Kindermann, 1993	Kindermann, 2007
Sample	109 children: two 4th and two 5th grade classrooms	366 children: entire cohort of 6th graders in a town
Design	Fall/spring student self-report measures	Fall/spring teacher-report measures; fall student measures
Measures	**SCM Interviews:** 57 children (52% of four classrooms) Peer networks in classrooms, $\kappa = .70$	**SCM questionnaires:** 280 children (76% of the grade cohort) Peer networks in 6th grade, $\kappa = .88$
		Nominations of group "names"
		Friendship nominations
	Student Self-Report of Behavior Engagement	**Teacher-Report of Student Behavioral and Emotional Engagement**
		Student-Report on Teacher and Parent Involvement
		Mathematics Grades in 5th and 6th grades

can be captured once networks have been identified. The third part addresses how peer group influences can be conceptualized in longitudinal designs that focus on children's own change as an outcome of influences from their groups. The final part introduces additional safeguards to make sure that the correlational findings can be interpreted as peer influences.

How Can Naturally Existing Peer Groups in School Be Identified?

Naturally existing peer groups are a ubiquitous part of children's lives. They are usually self-organized, "fuzzy," overlapping, and highly fluid. Unlike work groups or clubs that have specific purposes, they are more informal and "circumstantial" in nature, and are formed for a variety of reasons (Arrow, McGrath, & Berdahl, 2000). Ever since Moreno's ((1934)) pioneering efforts to define sociometric groups, it has been assumed that knowledge about a person's affiliations with a group has diagnostic value for assessing his or her functioning, and that group membership leads to social interactions that exert socialization influences. Several approaches have provided evidence that characteristics of such affiliations predict positive and negative aspects of children's social and academic development. For example, characteristics of children's friends have been shown to predict academic performance as well as problem behavior (e.g., Altermatt & Pomerantz, 2003; Berndt, Hawkins, & Jiao, 1999; Poulin, Dishion, & Haas, 1999; Urberg, Değirmencioğlu, & Pilgrim, 1997; Wentzel, McNamara-Barry, & Caldwell, 2004). Similarly, membership in sociometric "groups" has been linked to adjustment in school (e.g., Bukowski & Cillessen, 1998; Chen, Chang, & He, 2003; Guay, Boivin, & Hodges, 1999), and so has membership in social crowds and groups of children who typically just "hang out" together (e.g., Brown, 1999; Cairns, Cairns, & Neckerman, 1989; Kindermann, 1993).

Access To Relationships: Self-Reports, Partner-Reports, and Observer-Reports

To identify peer groups, researchers have traditionally focused on *self-reports*. However, skepticism has been voiced about whether self-reports of affiliations are always accurate (e.g., Cairns & Cairns, 1994) because children tend to exaggerate their associations with popular peers (Leung, 1996). Thus, alternative strategies have been developed to define peer groups more objectively. Friendship researchers have dealt with this by focusing on *reciprocity* between self- and partner-reports; friendships are assumed to exist when both friends agree. However, participation rates can create problems because a friendship can only be identified if both friends participate in a study. This reduces the information available in a data set; analyses are usually restricted to a child's three best friends, and across time, often to just one stable best friend.

Because reciprocal dyads tend to form interconnections, researchers have expanded their focus to *friendship groups*, defined as groups of reciprocal self-reported dyads (e.g., Urberg et al., 1997). Such groups are often very complex, and graph-theoretical reduction techniques are used in common identification programs (e.g., NEGOPY, Richards, 1995; UCINET, Borgatti, Everett, & Freeman, 1999). Typically, three conditions are invoked: First, a child is considered to be a member of a group when he or she can be reached from every other member directly or via an intermediary connection; individuals further removed away are excluded. Second, a group is accepted to exist when removal of any single individual within the group would not make it fall apart. Third, a friend of a specific child's friend is also assumed to be affiliated with that child, even if he or she does not share a direct reciprocal connection.

When the goal is to identify overall group structures parsimoniously, topological assumptions are plausible. However, they may not be optimal for studies that aim to detect socialization influences. For example, a child who is connected to just one or two members of a larger group will likely be excluded and potential influences can only be detected among the well-connected members. Similarly, when a child is a member of multiple groups at the same time, decisions are required to assign this child to his or her most cohesive group and to disregard the other connections. This is justified when the goal is to describe overall structures, but, when social influences are of concern, exclusion of partners can lead to exclusion of influences.

Social consensus. Because robust techniques to make sense of the "abstract art" of Moreno-type sociograms do not exist (Cairns, 1983, p. 432), many researchers have shifted their focus towards *social consensus*. Contemporary sociometric researchers use shared opinions (votes) of all of the children in a setting (i.e., whether a classmate is overall liked or disliked, or both, or neither) to determine the "group" to which a specific child belongs (e.g., Asher & Coie, 1990). Some network researchers have adopted similar strategies. Social crowds, for example, "brains," "nerds," or "popular kids" (Brown, 1999) have similarly been defined as groups of people for whom social consensus exists with regard to key characteristics. Although use of social verdicts minimizes problems with reliability and participation rates, it can also change the definition of a group. "Groups" that represent social categories (e.g., of rejected children) differ from groups defined by social interactions among members. Many members of sociometric "groups" may not share affiliations and may have few, if any, social interactions. Processes of influence are likely to differ as well. In the current chapter, the terms *peer group* and *social network* will be reserved for groups of children whose members share frequent contact and interactions.

Observer-reports and Socio-Cognitive Maps. Cairns, Perrin, and Cairns (1985) have developed an approach called *Socio-Cognitive Mapping* (SCM) that also relies on assumptions of social consensus but follows the example of observational research. Observations of interactions have long been favored for identifying natural affiliations (e.g., Gest, Farmer, Cairns, & Xie, 2003; Strayer & Santos, 1996), but they are costly and have design problems of their own (e.g., representativeness across situations). SCM employs children themselves as *expert observers* because children have access to information about natural affiliations in a way that cannot be easily matched by trained observers. Multiple children in a classroom are asked to report about classmates whom they see to frequently "hang around" with one another. From these reports, composite maps are formed of the networks on which reporters agree (see Figure 14.1). One strength of the approach is that observers' level of agreement can be determined; SCM Maps have been shown to be consistent with independent observations (e.g., Gest et al., 2003). A second strength is that if public consensus exists, not every student in a classroom needs to participate. When the sample of reporters is fairly representative for a setting, reports from slightly more than half of its members seem to be sufficient (Cairns & Cairns, 1994).

Empirical Examples

Results from two studies will demonstrate how SCM strategies can be used to identify natural peer networks (see Table 14.1). Study 1 focuses on four classrooms of fourth and fifth graders (Kindermann, 1993). Students were from a lower-middle to middle class economic background, almost equally divided by grade, classroom, and sex. Study 2 focuses on an entire cohort of sixth graders in a rural/suburban town during their first year of middle school (Kindermann, 2007). This school was the town's only public school for this age range.

Peer networks. Networks were assessed via Socio-Cognitive Mapping (Cairns et al., 1985). Study 1 used individual interviews (following Cairns, Gariépy, & Kindermann, 1990; Kindermann, 1996); Study 2 used questionnaires in which children listed groups of students in their grade whom they knew to "hang out" with one another. Students were asked to list as many groups and members as they knew, to include dyads, to include themselves, and to include the same children as members of different groups if appropriate. A typical report denotes, for example, children A, B, and C to form one group, and D and E to form another.

At the beginning of fourth and fifth grades (Study 1), 57 students were interviewed (52% of the sample, equally divided across gender and classrooms); at the end of the school year, 25 children from one fourth-grade class were re-interviewed. At the beginning of sixth grade (Study 2), 280 students (76% of the population in the town; 56% were girls) provided information about networks in their grade, and 219 students participated at the end of the school year. For descriptive purposes, these students were also asked to give nominated peer groups *names* that characterized "what the group was about" and "made" the people a group. In addition, they were asked about their *three best friends* in class, in school, and outside of school. The goal was to capture peer relationships of students who would not be members of peer networks because they were not known well enough or only shared relationships that were not publicly known.

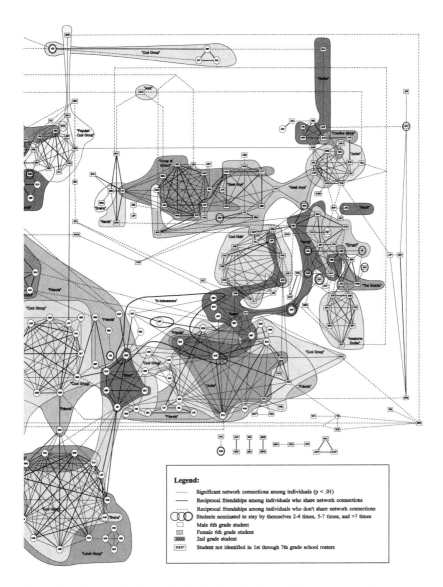

Figure 14.1. Subset of a Composite Socio-Cognitive Map of 6th graders' social networks in a small town.

Note. The entire map can be viewed at www.psy.pdx.edu/~thomas/Research

Network identification. To identify groups, the nominations were arranged in a *co-occurrence matrix* containing the frequencies with which each child was nominated to belong to the same group as any other child. A portion of the matrix from Study 2 is presented in Table 14.2. Binomial z-tests examined whether each child was more likely to be nominated as being in a group with any other candidate than could be expected by chance (NETWORKS, Kindermann & Kwee, 1995). For example, across all 36 reports in which student KER was nominated to have a group, student RYB was noted 28 times in the same group (78%). Overall, RYB was nominated in 32 of the 694 reported groups. The conditional probability of finding RYB in KER's network, given that KER had a group ($28/36 = .78$), was compared with the unconditional probability with which RYB was found in any group at all ($32/694 = .05$). The significant z-score of 21.47 identifies RYB as a member of KER's group. Because of many cases with low expected cell frequencies, Fisher's exact test was used in addition (see Kindermann, 1993). Only connections were accepted that were significant ($p < .01$) when using both strategies. Significant connections based on single co-nominations were not accepted; in most cases, these were children's self-nominations.

Results

The resulting composite social maps depict all significant network connections; Figure 14.1 shows a portion of the resulting sixth grade map; individual placements are arbitrary and based on drawing convenience only. As a criterion of accurateness, kappa indices (Gest et al., 2003) showed that individuals' reports were consistent with the composite map (average *kappa* was .88 in sixth grade and .70 in fourth grade; the lower consistency in the earlier study may have been due to the smaller number of participants). Only errors of commission were considered. Errors of omission were excluded because it is unrealistic to expect that all students would know the same amount about all networks (e.g., girls may know less about boys' groups). As expected, the map of the entire cohort of sixth graders was quite complex; many networks bridge across classrooms. At the beginning of sixth grade, 80% (293) of the students were identified as members of social networks and a typical student was connected to 4.9 others (ranging from 0 to 17 members, 73% had networks larger than dyads). In Study 1 on fourth and fifth graders, 88% were members of networks and a student had 2.2 other members in his or her group; the smaller group size is likely a result of the fact that this study was classroom-based and did not include affiliations with children from other classrooms.

TABLE 14.2
Co-Occurrence Matrix Among (a Subset of) Girls in a Cohort of Sixth Graders.

	KER	RYB	DAL	COD	SUO	ROM	STQ	CHR	KAA	KAW	ELT	JEP	LIP	...	Total Nominations
KER	-	28	23	12	10	3	3	0	0	0	0	0	0		36
RYB	28	-	20	11	12	3	4	0	0	0	0	0	0		32
DAL	23	20	-	10	9	4	2	0	0	0	0	0	0		28
COD	12	11	10	-	19	8	13	0	0	0	0	0	0		29
SUO	10	12	9	19	-	9	10	0	0	0	0	0	0		29
ROM	3	3	4	8	9	-	4	0	0	0	0	0	0		11
STQ	3	4	2	13	10	4	-	0	0	0	0	0	0		17
CHR	0	0	0	0	0	0	0	-	10	10	9	10	0		14
KAA	0	0	0	0	0	0	0	10	-	13	13	12	0		16
KAW	0	0	0	0	0	0	0	10	13	-	13	10	0		17
ELT	0	0	0	0	0	0	0	9	13	13	-	10	0		18
JEP	0	0	0	0	0	0	0	10	12	10	10	-	0		13
LIP	0	0	0	0	0	0	0	0	0	0	0	0	-		24
...															...
N Informants															260
Total Nominations															3047
N of Groups Generated															694

Note. Total nominations are smaller than the sums of co-nominations. Boldfaced cells denote significant co-nominations ($p < .01$).

For illustration, Figure 14.1 includes children's reciprocal friendships (bold-faced ties denote friendships matched by SCM affiliations, dashed lines denote friendships outside of peer groups; the entire map can be viewed at www.psy.pdx.edu/~thomas/Research), as well as the names that children gave to nominated groups (with frequencies > 2). Students with large networks were typically simultaneous members of several crowds. For example, KER, RYB, and COD (lower right corner) were members of a "cool" crowd; the male student RYB was also a member of a group of a female group of "jocks," and COD was also a member of groups of "nerds" and "in-betweeners." (All three were additionally members of a large crowd of "friends".) Large crowds of "cool" students or "nerds" tended to bridge between otherwise separate groups. For example, among the six separate crowds of "nerds" and "geeks" in the cohort, two provided the main connection between the otherwise separate male and female crowds of "popular" students.

Summary

SCM strategies can be used in small studies of selected classrooms as well as in studies of social systems. Cohort-based studies can yield maps that are complex, with groups that are highly interconnected and overlapping. Nevertheless, SCM networks may not always capture all of a child's peer relationships. Because SCM networks focus on public knowledge, such networks tend to not include reciprocal friendships that are more private in nature.

How Can the Characteristics of Children's Peer Groups Be Captured?

The second challenge to studying peer group influences is to specify and assess the peers' potentially influential features. This involves two questions: First, how should groups be defined in complex composite maps and which key characteristics need to be assessed? Second, after decisions have been made about which kinds of groups can be identified: How should their psychologically relevant attributes be measured?

Individuals and their groups. Because natural peer groups are (largely) self-selected, they tend to be fuzzy and overlapping, and a child can be a member of several different subgroups at the same time. In Figure 14.1, student KER (lower right corner) has eight members in her peer network, while COD has 14; many members are shared but many others are not. For examinations of social influences from such groups, it will make a difference how social networks are defined.

Decisions about "group-ness." Assumptions about the kinds of groups that exist influence the groups that will be identified. Two general strategies can be followed: One follows the premise that groups should be distinct whereas the other assumes that separate groups exist only in exceptional cases. Likely, the best guide in the search for group structures is the nature of the phenomenon under study. When research questions require the identification of distinct groups that do not overlap, the main goal is to reduce overall complexity and to define boundaries in parsimonious ways (e.g., in sociological studies; Bearman, Moody, & Stovel, 2004). Typically, such decisions are based on graph-theoretical considerations (e.g., when using NE-

GOPY or UCINET) or on decision rules for group inclusiveness (Cairns et al., 1990). However, increased clarity may come at a cost. Decisions to reduce complexity affect the nature of the groups: Some affiliations are considered to be more important while others are ignored. When questions are about group socialization processes, decisions may exaggerate differences between groups (because only individuals are included who are well embedded in groups), and may also lead to underestimations of group influences (because only the most homogeneous and cohesive subunits are considered). Excluding partners excludes their potential influences. For example, in Figure 14.1, COD is a member of several "groups" at the same time. Graph-theoretical decisions would likely exclude MEK and COR (and probably also KER), because they do not share most of their connections with the other members of COD's group.

When socialization influences are concerned, it seems preferable to consider *all affiliates* (unless theoretical expectations suggest that specific members be excluded). One option is to define a "group" *individually*, with respect to each specific individual, so that socialization processes are assumed to take place between each individual and all of the others who are identified as his or her frequent interaction partners. Figure 14.2 shows an example. Student COD is assumed to have her individual network, consisting of all the others with whom she shares a connection. This has one advantage. Traditionally, groups are assumed to exist on a conceptual level above individuals, on a higher level of organization, and the group context is assumed to be the same for each member. Researchers have become skeptical of such assumptions in the family literature (e.g., the family environment may not be the same for every child; see Harris, 1998), and skepticism may also be helpful with regard to peer groups. Instead of assuming that socialization contexts are the same for all group members, each member can be seen as having his or her own unique network. Thus, if a girl is in a group with two boys, she will be influenced by children of the other sex, while the boys share mixed-sex interactions. Then, socialization influences can differ even among members of the same group.

Group profiles. The traditional method for forming accounts of groups' psychological characteristics has been to ask children themselves about their groups. However, individuals and their descriptions of affiliates are not independent of each other. Not surprisingly, children's self-reports about peer contexts are typically closely related to reports about their own characteristics, and inferring influences from such similarities is problematic. Correlations may indicate influences, but they may also indicate the reverse, namely, that children's own characteristics shape their perceptions of affiliates. In contrast, when groups are defined independently of people's own perceptions,

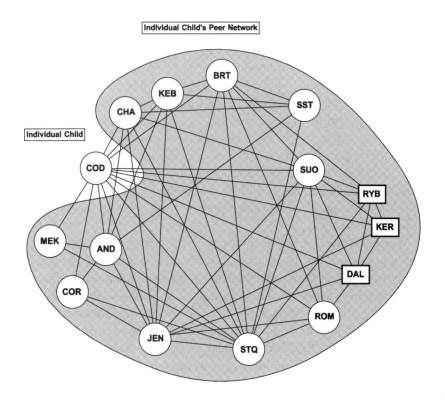

Figure 14.2. Individual peer group engagement profile.

the psychological characteristics of groups can be assessed independently as well. In the example of Figure 14.2, peers can describe their own characteristics (or other reporters, like teachers, can give descriptions), and the descriptions can be aggregated across each child's network to form composite group profiles. Typically, researchers have used *group averages* (e.g., Kindermann, 1993; Kurdek & Sinclair, 2000). When groups are fairly homogeneous, averages across members can be assumed to capture their central characteristics.

Assortativeness: Selection processes and group homogeneity. Peer groups are typically not formed at random. Children seem to have assortative preferences with regard to a variety of individual characteristics, and school motivation seems to be one of these (e.g., Epstein, 1983; Kindermann, 2003). Preferences can also extend to a variety of other characteristics (e.g., gender, IQ, achievement, grades; e.g., Hamm, 2000). For example, girls mainly form groups with other girls during most of their school years (and boys with boys), and girls tend to be more motivated and to often show higher achievement (e.g., Eccles, Wigfield, & Schiefele, 1998). When girls generally perform better in school over time, only part of this should be due to their peer groups. Assortativeness also has implications beyond individuals. Selection preferences may extend to characteristics of groups (group size, homogeneity), and when children affiliate with others who share similar experiences, members of a group may also be similar with regard to influences from outside the groups. Thus, members of a group may experience similar levels of stimulation and parental involvement at home (e.g., Fletcher, Darling, Steinberg, & Dornbusch, 1995), and similarity in home environments, at least for some children, may be a selection criterion. Such assumptions also pertain to teachers; children may form groups with others who are perceived similarly by teachers or who share similarities in their own perceptions. When indicators of the central characteristics of groups are formed, it is important to examine group homogeneity in these features because selection preferences may overshadow actual influences from the groups.

Empirical Examples

In Study 1, 109 children from two 4th grade and two 5th grade classrooms participated in questionnaire assessments (96% of students in the classes). In Study 2, 340 sixth grade students participated (93% of students in the town), as well as their 13 homeroom teachers. As a measure of school motivation, student and teacher reports of students' *classroom engagement* were obtained at two time points within the first three months of the school year and within three months of its end. The focus was on engagement because it is a characteristic that is highly valued in this setting and openly observable by students and classmates (Fredricks, Blumenfeld, & Paris, 2004; Skinner, Zimmer-Gembeck, & Connell, 1998). The construct consists of the two components of behavioral and emotional engagement; parallel forms exist for assessments via self- or teacher-reports (e.g., "I try as hard as I can in school"; "In my class, this student tries hard"). Study 1 used the 10-item *self-report* measure of behavioral engagement; Study 2 used the parallel 14-item scale tapping *teachers'* perceptions of students' engagement (Wellborn, 1991).

In addition, students reported on the extent to which they experienced differential levels of *teacher* and *parent involvement* at the beginning of the school year. The teacher measure consists of eight items tapping perceptions of availability, caring, warmth and affection (e.g., "My teacher knows me well"; Skinner & Belmont, 1993). The parent measure consists of 16 items tapping perceptions of warmth (e.g., "My parents understand me very well") and rejection (e.g., "Sometimes I wonder whether my parents like me"). In previous studies, the measures showed moderate correlations with student engagement, academic competence, and achievement (Skinner, Wellborn, & Connell, 1990; Skinner, Johnson, & Snyder, 2005). Finally, students' mathematics grades were obtained from the end of fifth and sixth grades (both grades were averaged) as a measure of *academic achievement*. Mathematics grades were used because they were assumed to be a close approximation of students' ability, and, compared to other grades, less directly affected by levels of classroom engagement.

Descriptors of network characteristics. Composite *group profiles* were formed as markers of the motivational characteristics of peer groups. Scores were calculated by averaging the individual engagement scores across the members of each child's group. Because of the large sample in Study 2, it was also possible to examine details in the networks' composition. The number of members in a student's group was used to indicate *network size*. To indicate group homogeneity, the percentage of group members who were students of the *same gender,* in the *same homeroom,* and the *same grade* was computed. The (absolute) difference between a child's own engagement score and his or her group's composite was taken as an indicator of *within-group homogeneity* in engagement. Finally, the number of students with whom a student maintained group ties across the school year was taken as an indicator of *network stability*.

Results

The description of the relations between children's own characteristics and those of their peer networks will mostly be based on Study 2; interrelations are more reliable with the larger sample. For the correlational analyses, SEM (AMOS 5, Arbuckle, 2003) was used and missing values were estimated using Full Information Maximum Likelihood estimation (FIML). Thus, the overall N is 366 for the cohort; exceptions will be noted. In both studies, students were highly motivated ($M = 2.9$ and 3.3 on the four-point scales), and motivation remained stable across the school years (.74 and .75, $p < .001$). In both studies, girls were more motivated than boys, but did not change differentially. There were no differences in engagement between (consenting) students who participated in the network assessments and students who did not.

Member selection preferences. Students were expected to be similar to the members of their groups. It was not expected that children would directly seek out candidates according to their motivation, but rather, that selection processes would target similarities in a wide range of characteristics that would be differentially compatible with a focus on academic work. Thus, group homogeneity was assumed to be a by-product of selection processes that followed interindividually different criteria. At the beginning of the school year, students were found to be moderately similar to the members of their groups; highly engaged students were members of groups that had similarly high engagement profiles (Study 1: $r = .28$, $p < .01$, Study 2: $r = .44$, $p < .001$). The large sample in Study 2 made it possible to examine assortative preferences. Within-group similarities in age, gender, and classroom location were pronounced; on average, 98% of a child's group members were also sixth graders, 94% were of the same gender (80% of networks were gender-homogenous), and 60% were classmates from the same homeroom.

Students' own levels of motivation were related to several properties of their networks, suggesting that differently engaged students had differing member preferences: highly engaged children tended to affiliate with networks that were larger ($r = .22$, $p < .001$) and gender-homogeneous ($r = .22$, $p < .001$), and with networks that remained more stable across time ($r = .16$, $p < .05$). In addition, selection preferences were also suggested by relations between network profiles and children's own characteristics: members of highly engaged networks tended to be higher achieving ($r = .36$, $p < .001$), were more likely girls ($r = .22$, $p < .001$), and tended to perceive their teachers ($r = .23$, $p < .001$) and parents ($r = .15$, $p < .05$) as more involved. Finally, group homogeneity in terms of engagement (absolute differences between individuals' own scores and their groups' scores) was also related to members' characteristics: students who were more similar to their group were more engaged ($r = .22$, $p < .001$), higher achieving ($r = .21$, $p < .01$), and perceived teachers (but not parents) to be more involved ($r = .20$, $p < .01$).

Member selection across time. Following Kandel (1978), it is wise to assume that most of the similarity between children and the members of their networks is not the result of social influence, but rather due to member selection processes. Thus, the similarity between individuals and the members of their peer groups should mainly be taken as an outcome of peer selection. When selection processes continue across time, children's selection criteria can change based on experiences within and outside of groups, but it is also possible that some selection criteria remain the same. Continuity would be indicated if the motivational composition of children's networks remained consistent over time and if children's group characteristics continued to be related to their own classroom engagement at both times.

Stability of network memberships was moderate in both studies. An average fourth or fifth grade child maintained ties with 50% of his or her (2.2) initial peer group members. An average sixth grader maintained ties with three (61%) of his or her five initial group members (range 0 to 11); 25% of the children lost network connections to all of their earlier affiliates, and 50%

lost connections to at least half of their members (conversely, 50% of the students without a fall network had formed new affiliations in spring.) Only 19% of the sixth graders remained in entirely stable networks. Nevertheless, group homogeneity persisted over time in both studies, as indicated by significant continuity of the motivational composition of the networks (fourth grade $r = .47$, $p < .05$, $n = 25$; sixth grade: $r = .42$, $p < .001$). Thus, member turnover occurred in a way that did not affect much of the groups' motivational characteristics, and one can expect that influences from peer groups may also be somewhat consistent across time.

Study 1 also examined a specific model of member selection. Patterson, Littman, and Bricker (1967) have suggested a "shopping" model of how adolescents search for candidates for relationships. The model was adapted with the assumption that over time, children would tend to optimize their peer group membership. It was expected that children's own levels of engagement at the beginning of the school year would predict how their groups' engagement profiles changed across the year. Two indices were used: a *selection index* denoted the number of newly gained peer group members at the end of the school year; an *elimination index* denoted the number of group members lost over time. In the one classroom examined ($n = 25$), students' own initial engagement was related to changes in their groups' motivational composition when children's scores were weighted with the number of peers newly gained across time ($\beta = .37$, $t = 2.42$, $p < .05$). This indicates that highly motivated children, especially when they acquired many new ties, were affiliated with peer networks that changed in a positive direction over time (and vice versa).

Gauging the potential for peer network influences. Person-to-group similarity can be an outcome of three processes: Member selection (e.g., according to similarity), social influences from group members, and influences from outside of a child's group. The time-lagged assessments in Study 2 make it possible to assess the extent to which the peer processes uniquely contributed to children's engagement scores at the end of the school year. Figure 14.3 shows the respective model. The engagement levels of children's group members in fall were predictive of their engagement in spring, even when competing processes were controlled. The first set of assortativeness controls focused on individual characteristics, namely, children's *sex* (because of gender differences in motivation), and academic *achievement* (because students with higher academic ability had more engaged networks). Both variables were significant predictors of engagement. The second set of controls addressed group characteristics, namely, the *size* of peer networks (because larger groups consisted of more motivated members), their *stability* (because stable networks were typically more engaged), homogeneity in the groups' *gender-composition* (because of preferences for same-sex affiliates) and *similarity in engagement*

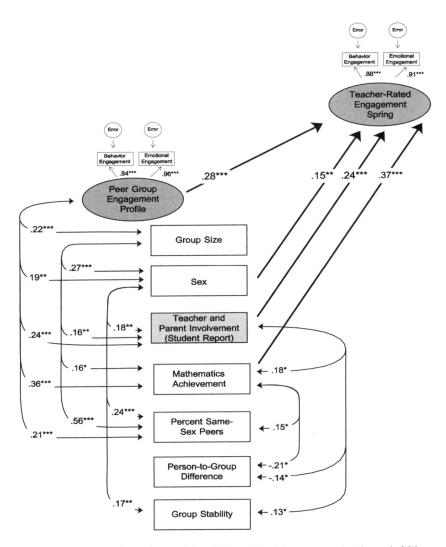

Figure 14.3. Structural equation model predicting students' engagement at the end of 6th grade (Kindermann, 2007).

between children and the members of their groups (because children who were more similar to their group tended to be more engaged). These variables did not contribute significantly.

A third set of controls addressed the extent to which the engagement outcomes can be results of influences of involvement from *teachers and parents*. Separate regressions showed that teacher and parent involvement were both predictors of child engagement at the end of the school year ($\beta = .37$, $t =$

5.95, $p < .001$; and $\beta = .30$, $t = 4.66$, $p < .001$). When teacher and parent scores were combined, teacher involvement continued to be a predictor, but at the expense of parent involvement. Thus, both scores were summed as an indicator of *adult involvement*, which showed a strong contribution to spring engagement.

Overall, children's group profiles remained significant predictors of their own resulting classroom engagement over and above the contributions of the controls. The entire variable set explained about half (47%) of the variance in children's spring engagement; the data fit the model very well (X^2 (15) = 19.005, $p = .214$; CMIN/DF = 1.267, CFI = .996, RMSEA = .027; 90% confidence interval .000 to .059), and nested comparisons showed that all network variables together explained about 24% of the variance in spring engagement, and that fall peer group profiles accounted for slightly more than half of this percentage. On the one hand, this confirms expectations that about half of the similarity between children and their groups is an outcome of selection processes (e.g., Hamm, 2000; Kandel, 1978). On the other hand, the cross-lagged analysis focuses on engagement outcomes, not individual change, and identifies similarities between earlier network profiles and children's own later engagement. Some of this similarity denotes socialization influences, but some should be due to the fact that children change in a way that is consistent with their past behavior. When groups are expected to *influence* children's behavior, estimates of peer group influence need to examine group effects on children's change.

Summary

The findings are consistent with those of other studies (e.g., Epstein, 1983, Hamm, 2000; Kandel, 1978) and suggest that about half of the similarity between children and their group affiliates was due to peer selection processes. There were many indications for interindividual differences in selection processes, and there were some indications that selection processes lead to moderate motivational continuity in peer networks. Despite the fact that half or more of the members of a child's peer network were exchanged across the school year, there was moderate stability in the motivational make-up of the groups. Overall, it seems unlikely that peer socialization processes are able to account for more than 15% of the variance in children's resulting engagement scores. When peer socialization processes are examined, analyses need to include children's earlier (fall) engagement as a control, and when children serve as their own controls, their own past behavior will be most predictive of their later behavior. Thus, actual socialization effects will likely be smaller than suggested by the cross-lagged effects.

How Should Peer Influences Be Conceptualized and Examined?

The third challenge is how influences from children's peer networks should be conceptualized. Historically, such influences have been conceived of as *socialization processes*, and they are indicated when the characteristics of a child's peer group at one point in time influence this child's development across time. The concept dominated the psychology literature between the late 1940s and 1970s (Bronfenbrenner, 1994), but since then has almost "gone out of fashion" (p. xi). Traditionally, the concept implied that influence was unidirectional, from a socialization agent to a child, and that influences would "make" a child similar to a socialization ideal, the socialization agent, or to a group of others who are influenced by the same socialization agents. With peer relationships, socialization agents are other children who have the same characteristics as target children under study, and influences can occur simultaneously from each member of a group to any other member. There is typically not much of a socialization ideal or socialization goal, and similarity may be primarily what leads children to select peers as members of their peer groups. It seems advantageous to use the term socialization to refer to processes by which social interactions are *actively changing* something about a person, and to processes that can produce change in multiple directions. This perspective leads to three implications.

Natural peer groups are characterized by assortativeness. Traditionally, peer *selection* has been seen as a "problem" for socialization studies (e.g., Kandel, 1978) and as a threat to interpretations of correlations in terms of social influence. However, selection processes are what constitutes social networks. Peer groups tend to be formed in such a way that children are similar to their affiliates, a characteristic also described as assortativeness. Over time, members of a group may follow similar developmental pathways just because they have something in common. Correlation patterns that look like peer "influences" may actually be outcomes of the fact that similar children have congregated. For example, children who are more accepted by their peers tend to adapt more favorably to school (e.g., Chen et al., 2003). Popular children may have larger peer networks, and although their changes could be outcomes of peer influences, it is also possible that well-adjusted students have joined with similar students who all show positive change. To indicate socialization, predictions of children's change need to remain robust when selection preferences are controlled.

Assortativeness can exist with regard to third-party influences. Because children in a group tend to share similar experiences, assortativeness can extend to external characteristics. *Teacher involvement* may be the most powerful determinant of children's classroom behavior (e.g., Skinner & Belmont, 1993). When teachers are effective in promoting "good" students' development, and those students form groups with other "good" students, students' change over time may be a result of peer influence, but it may also be an outcome of teachers' efforts. Similarly, *parent involvement* has also been implicated as a determinant of school success (e.g., Grolnick & Slowiaczek, 1994). It is possible that children's home environments are primarily responsible for their change across time, while peer influences would add only little.

Because individuals and the members of their peer groups are interdependent, alternative processes need to be eliminated that can produce patterns of change that only resemble peer socialization. Because genuine peer group influences may exist in addition to these alternative pathways, it needs to be determined whether peer influences make independent contributions over and above teachers' and parents' involvement. If they do, that does not necessarily mean that influences from adults were not important, but rather, that peer influences add something in addition. If they do not, that would not mean that peer influences were not important; they can be moderators of parental influences (e.g., Chen, Chang, He, & Liu, 2005). It would mean, though, that adult influences would be stronger than direct influences from peers.

Peer influences do not necessarily produce similarities. Traditionally, studies of group socialization have taken similarity (conformity) among group members as their primary target in experimental as well as naturalistic studies (e.g., Asch, 1955; Sherif et al., 1961). Although convergence can be an indicator of group influence, it may be just one of several possible outcomes. For example, even Asch himself regarded his experimental findings as examples of the extent to which individuals show self-reliance and resistance to group pressures (Friend, Rafferty, & Bramel, 1990). It may be that researchers have too easily extended models of task groups towards natural groups that function differently (e.g., Levine & Moreland, 1998).

In fact, a focus on convergence interferes with the study of natural groups in three ways. First, homogeneity is *not a clear indicator* of influence; it indicates influence only when people are randomly assigned to a group and cannot escape. Natural groups tend to show moderate homogeneity when they are formed and similarity may be the basis for their formation (e.g., Hamm, 2000; Kandel, 1978). Since natural groups tend to be fluid, it becomes hard if not impossible to distinguish group changes that are due to member turnover from changes due to member convergence, and analyses need to be restricted to stable members (i.e., "after selection has occurred," Urberg et al., 1997, p. 835). Likely, stable peer groups differ from groups that are not stable. Second, group convergence is hard to distinguish from *regression to the mean* when members with scores in the tail of the distribution become more similar to their groups' average. The remedy is to include more than two measurement points, which exacerbates problems of participation rates because stable subgroups will be small. Third, the focus on group convergence has led researchers to "reify" groups and to assume that they are *discrete units of analysis*. This is warranted in cases of assigned groups, but since natural groups tend to be self-selected and fuzzy, a child can be a member of many groups at the same time (see Figure 14.1).

One can assume that the main outcome of peer affiliations is *change*, and change in different directions among the individuals who are members of a group (see also Mounts & Steinberg, 1995). Then, the question is whether changes in individuals can be predicted from the earlier characteristics of their group members. A specific model has been suggested for the study of motivation in school (Kindermann, 1993; 1996): Children who are initially "rich" (in terms of their own motivation as well as in terms of their affiliates) may become "richer" across the time they spend with their groups, whereas initially "poor" children would decline. This expectation does not imply that group influences would lead to uniform trends, but implies that group affiliations produce changes that can make children *increasingly different* from one another.

To extend socialization hypotheses beyond group convergence has several advantages. First, intraindividual change in the members of a group can be examined as an outcome of the characteristics of the group; selection influences are not confounded with socialization because group homogeneity is not expected. Second, changes can still be expected to contribute to convergence, but within-group similarity is only one possible outcome and interpretations are not jeopardized (as much) by regression to the mean. Third, hypotheses can focus on differential change; influences from peer affiliates, at least in some circumstances, at some times, and for some children, may lead children to become different from one another. Theoretically, it appears hard to reconcile beliefs that intimate relationships provide nurturance and mutual support, with the expectation that they would produce uniform results in the form of a "social mold" (Cairns & Cairns, 1994). Favorable peer contexts may not just foster individual adjustment, they may also encourage increasing autonomy and differentiation (e.g., Deci & Ryan, 1985).

Empirical Examples

The studies were guided by an interactional perspective on development (e.g., Baltes, 1996; Bronfenbrenner & Morris, 1998), and by the assumption that those peers would have most influence on development with whom a child spends most time interacting. Peer influences were examined in terms of the extent to which the motivational composition of a child's group of peers allowed predictions of that child's own change in motivation across the school year. Longitudinal designs were used to separate processes of peer influences from peer selection and from simultaneous influences from other socialization agents outside children's peer groups.

Results

A first set of analyses used multiple regressions to examine whether change in children's own engagement across the school year can be predicted from the characteristics of their earlier peer groups. The results converged across the two age ranges (Study 1: $\beta = .15$, $p < .01$, $n = 96$; Study 2: $\beta = .10$, $p < .01$, $n = 263$), across the group assessment formats (interviews versus questionnaires), and across engagement measures (self- versus teacher-reports). Because Study 2 included an entire cohort of students in a town, its results should be most representative. Children who, at the beginning of the school year, were members of networks that had a higher than average level of motivation (who also tended to be more motivated themselves) remained themselves stable across time (3.30 and 3.29), whereas children who were with less motivated groups decreased in motivation (from 2.96 to 2.90, about 2% on the 4-point scale). Although the partial correlations were relatively small and matched by relatively small average changes, this does not mean that peer effects were negligible. Given the high stability of motivation, it is unlikely that changes would be large. Most children are "average," have average peer groups and change only little across a year. There were, however, subsets of children in Study 2 for whom peer influences appeared more powerful: Peer groups explained 3% of the variance in engagement change when only students below the median were considered, and 13% when only the 41 students were considered who changed more than one standard deviation on the scale.

Controls for assortativeness: Member selection and third-party influences. Study 2 included additional analyses of the extent to which predictions of change remained robust when the assortativeness controls were included. When children select group members, it is possible that their own characteristics and the criteria they use to select members are better indicators of their developmental pathways than the engagement characteristics of their groups. Thus, the goal was to show that changes in children's motivation can be predicted from the characteristics of their peer groups, over and above the contributions of the selection controls, and over and above the simultaneously competing influences from teachers and parents.

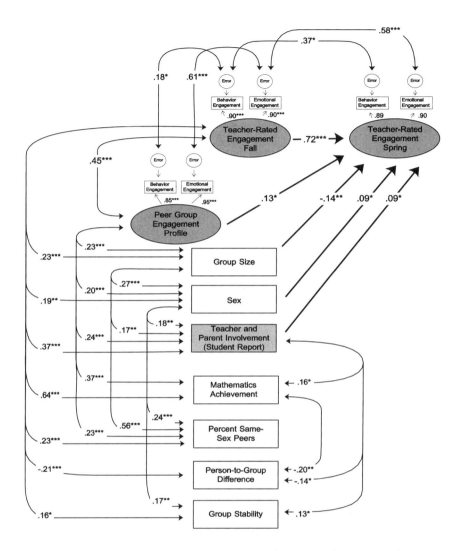

Figure 14.4. Structural equation model of peer group influences on changes in students'
engagement during 6th grade (Kindermann, 2007).

Structural equation modeling (AMOS 5, Arbuckle, 2003) was used to determine whether children's peer network characteristics predicted their own
change in engagement over and above controls; missing values were estimated
using FIML. Figure 14.4 shows the results. The data fit the model very well
(X^2 (23) = 22.660, p = .481; CMIN/DF = .985, CFI = 1.00, RMSEA = .000,
90% confidence interval from .000 to .042), and peer group engagement profiles continued to be significant predictors of individuals' change across time.

In addition, sex was also a predictor of engagement change (girls showed more positive change when their groups' engagement levels were held constant). Adult involvement and network size were also significant predictors. The other control variables were correlated with individual and group scores but not related to children's changes in engagement.

Summary

Although the cross-lagged predictions (Figure 14.3) suggested effects that were relatively large and comparable to those found in traditional studies, peer group influences appeared to be smaller when the contributions of selection variables and influences from adults were included. In fact, compared to traditional analyses of peer socialization, the current analysis strategy has four features that make the results more conservative. First, because the target outcome is intraindividual change and not group homogeneity, effects of group selection are not confounded with estimates of socialization effects. Second, because children's initial motivation is included as a control, relative person-to-group similarity is held constant. Third, the inclusion of the assortativeness variables makes the analysis quite robust against rival interpretations. Finally, because the expectation is that children with highly motivated groups would increase (and vice versa) the analyses are fairly safe against the effects of regression to the mean.

How Sure Can We Be That Predictions of Change Indicate Causality?

The studies suggest that children's frequent interactions with peer groups in school have a small amount of influence on changes in their own classroom engagement over a school year. While this is encouraging, two further questions need to be addressed: First, is it really the engagement level of a child's frequent interaction partners that is predictive of engagement change, or is it some other feature of this child's relationships (e.g., friendships) that is only correlated with peer networks? Second, is it possible that peer affiliations are just diagnostically predictive of children's path of development, but not causal antecedents? To use an analogy, the weather report may be the single best predictor of the weather, but it is not at all a causal antecedent. A child's peer affiliations may tell us what a child "is about" at a specific time, but predictive power does not necessarily imply causality.

Peer Networks Versus Friendships

The studies were based on the premise that *frequency of interaction* would be the active ingredient of developmentally influential peer contexts. Although interaction frequency is considered a key force of development in many classical theories (e.g., attachment theories), it may not be all that matters. In his editorial for a special issue of the *International Journal of Behavior Development,* Laursen (2005) describes *close relationships* as the "building blocks of human culture" (p. 97), and friendship researchers assert that close relationships are most important to consider for developmental influences (e.g., Altermatt & Pomerantz, 2003; Berndt & Murphy, 2002; Gest, Graham-Berman, & Hartup, 2001; Ladd, Birch, & Buhs, 1999). It is possible that peer networks only appear influential because they contain many of a child's close friends. Figure 14.1 (see the dashed lines) shows that many friendships in Study 2 were included among children's groups of frequent interaction partners, while many others were not. Slightly more than half of a child's reciprocal friends were members of his or her social network, but 70% of a child's group members were not reciprocal friends. In short, relationship quality may boost the influence of peer groups, and the most important influences may be from those peers who are close to a child and who, at the same time, interact frequently with him or her.

One may see this as low "concordance" between different assessments of children's peers. However, there may be more than one valid representation of a child's social world, and children may have groups of frequent interaction partners while at the same time having friends who are not publicly known. To make sure that the focus on frequent interaction partners was appropriate, an additional model in Study 2 included the engagement profiles of those students who were reciprocal friends of a child *but not* members of his or her peer group. The results showed that these friendship profiles did not contribute to changes in engagement, and that their inclusion had no effect on the fit of the model (X^2 (26) = 23.947, p = .579, CMIN/DF = .921, CFI = 1.0, RMSEA = .000; X^2 (1) difference = 1.347). This suggests that groups of frequent interaction partners were most predictive of children's change in engagement.

Mechanisms of Social Influences Within Peer Networks

Even in longitudinal designs, the question of whether peers are a causal antecedent for children's change cannot be decided solely based on correlational evidence. Following Donald Baer's suggestion for strategies of *convergent operations* (1973; Baltes, 1996), one can argue that experimental evidence clearly suggests that peer group contexts *can influence* children's behavior in controlled conditions (e.g., Sherif et al., 1961), but that it is unclear whether they normally do so in the classroom. Experimental analogies cannot easily show that natural affiliations (in which children select their partners) necessarily have the same effects. Conversely, the current correlational findings support notions that group influences may exist in the real world, but it is unclear whether group interactions are really *causal* antecedents or just diagnostic indicators of school motivation. In a third step, one needs to examine whether the same *mechanisms* can be identified in children's natural interactions with peer groups that have been experimentally identified as producers of change. If such mechanisms can be found and if they are able to produce change over time that converges with the observed patterns of correlations, this would be supportive of a causal relationship. The weather report predicts well but has no such mechanisms.

To study mechanisms requires observations in natural environments. Several studies have documented that a variety of interactions (e.g., discussions, evaluative discourse, prosocial interchanges, learning contingencies) can be mechanisms of social influence in groups (e.g., Berndt, Laychak, & Park, 1990; Dishion, Andrews, & Crosby, 1995; Hawley, Little, & Pasupathi, 2002; Wentzel et al., 2004). One such study (Sage & Kindermann, 1999) focused on learning contingencies in fifth graders' classroom interactions. Across 10 days, 22 students in a classroom were observed by five trained observers. Children's interactions were coded in the natural sequence of their occurrence by trained observers (*kappa* = .71), after students participated in an SCM assessment and the teacher provided ratings of their classroom engagement.

Sequential analyses (Bakeman & Quera, 1995) examined whether children's on- and off-task behaviors in the classroom had different consequences when children were members of different networks. Results showed that the more engaged students were, the more likely they experienced contingent support for their (frequent) on-task behavior from the members of their (similarly engaged) peer groups ($\beta = .63$, $t(24) = 2.24$, $p < .05$), while nonmembers responded at random. Low-motivated students had only the teacher as a source of support for their (less frequent) on-task behavior, and positive responses from their (low engaged) group members were rare and almost significantly inhibited. This indicates that contingency learning can be one mechanism of social influence that emanates from peer group interactions. The contingency patterns are consistent with the engagement changes found in the correlational studies. Over time, children who receive contingent support from the members of their networks will be likely to maintain their on-task behavior, and likely, this will lead them to maintain their overall engagement in the classroom.

CONCLUSION

This chapter tried to carve out some territory between two extreme positions: one holding that the influence of peers is negligible and one arguing that peers are more influential than parents or teachers. Within this territory, a high priority is identifying the design features that allow studies to achieve accurate estimates of the extent to which naturally existing peer groups influence individual children's development. Four design features were suggested: reliable and exhaustive identification of groups, longitudinal assessments, separation of selection and socialization analyses, and controls for the interdependent effects of individual, group-based, and group-external processes. These strategies should improve the ecological validity of the kinds of peer networks that are considered, as well as the precision with which potential socialization influences can be identified, thereby increasing the level of confidence with which we can infer social influences from correlational results. Taken together, these features can lend support to the contention that findings from such studies can safely be interpreted as *socialization influences*.

Group identification. Socio-Cognitive Mapping is a promising method for capturing naturally occurring peer groups in real-life settings. By focusing on public consensus about affiliations, peer groups can be identified objectively and reliably; 80% or more of the children under study were identified as members of social networks. SCM also makes it possible to overcome some of the problems with participation rates that occur with other strategies (e.g., Newcomb & Bagwell, 1995). However, researchers using SCM need to be aware of the fact that the method focuses on public consensus; students without social networks are not necessarily isolated at school. For example, although in the cohort of sixth graders, 20% of the children were found without a social network at school, many of them nevertheless had friends (and vice versa). SCM tends to underestimate connections that are private and not publicly known (e.g., in sixth grade, many of the private friendships may denote emerging romantic relationships). Conversely, friendship assessments can underestimate the extent to which children without friends are nevertheless well-embedded in interaction networks. Similarly to other studies using SCM techniques, the majority of participants in Study 2 who were without reciprocal friends were nevertheless identified as members of peer networks.

Socialization effects and their magnitude. In addition to reliable and exhaustive identification of groups, the studies suggest three further design features that make it likely that findings accurately reflect social influences from peer groups. Students' intra-individual change was the target outcome, peer group selection processes were disentangled from group influences, and controls were included for simultaneous influences from teachers and parents.

What can be concluded from the studies about the effects of peer groups on children's engagement in school?

On the one hand, the studies show that group influences on motivation exist over and above selection effects and over and above simultaneous influences from teachers and parents. Moreover, the findings appear to be robust across different populations. The current effects found in a rural town appear to converge well with those found in studies in a suburban school (Sage & Kindermann, 1999; average engagement level was 3.2) and in an inner-city school (Kindermann, McCollam, & Gibson, 1996; average engagement level was 2.60).

On the other hand, when assortativeness controls were included, the magnitude of peer group effects was modest. Perhaps, this should not be too surprising. Several factors place constraints on the effects of peers. First, children with an average level of motivation tend to select average peers. Only children whose own levels of engagement deviate markedly from those of their peers should be influenced more. Second, peer influences contribute about 2% to the variance in changes in children's motivation, whereas teachers and parents combined contribute about 4% more. It may be wise not to overestimate the extent to which any specific context agent can affect children's change. Unless student subgroups are identified who are particularly susceptible to peer influences, the strongest predictor of children's engagement will always be their prior engagement, which includes the cumulative effects of a history of selection and socialization. Finally, there seems to be a pattern of continuous decline in children's motivation across the years they spend in school (e.g., Fredricks et al., 2004). Most studies trace the path of only one school year. It is possible that peer group influences are small in any given year but accumulate across a child's entire school career.

Future Research on Mechanisms of Group Influences: Studies of Interacting Systems

The focus of current studies converges with many theories in postulating that those social partners who interact most frequently with a child should be most influential, and it follows a perspective that social interactions are the "engine" of development (Bronfenbrenner & Morris, 1998). However, frequency of interaction may be just one of the determinants. Children's close friendships may also contribute to changes in motivation. In the current analyses they did not, and this may be an outcome of the fact that most of a child's friends were also among his or her frequent interaction partners. Nevertheless, researchers need to remain open to the possibility that different kinds of peer relationships may be differentially predictive of children's development. Closeness and frequency of interaction may both need to be studied in combination, which would require the separation of SCM and friendship group profiles. In addition, these two kinds of affiliations may not be the only peer relationships that matter. For example, victimization researchers (e.g., Snyder et al., 2003) and antipathy researchers (Hodges & Card, 2003) point out that peers with whom a child has comparably little desire to spend time or form a relationship may nevertheless have profound influences on his or her experiences in school. The same may apply to admired fellow students, even if there is not much interaction. If studies attempt to examine *overall peer influences*, relationships with other kinds of peers will need to be included.

Overall, research may move away from studies that show a net effect of peers, teachers, or parents on children's development in school, and more in the direction of studies examining how all three kinds of partners form systems of influence for a specific child. The study of conjoint systems of influence and how these systems work in the real world is a relatively new field; guiding models still need to be developed (but see Fletcher et al., 1995; Hoglund & Leadbeater, 2004; Wentzel, 1998), but researchers should be encouraged to examine the interplay among simultaneous influences from peers, teachers, and parents. The current studies focused only on controls for potential simultaneous influences; future studies will want to focus on interconnected processes themselves. Such studies may be less concerned with the unique effects from peers or other partners, and more with questions about how influences from peers can work synergistically or antagonistically with influences that emerge from other partners.

Some recent studies show that the field is moving in this direction. Studies have begun to explore specific hypotheses about combinations of effects from multiple partners. For example, Chen and colleagues (2005), and Goldstein, Davis-Kean, and Eccles (2005) showed that peer affiliations can moderate how characteristics of parenting at home shape children's social and academic pathways in school. Conversely, studies by Mounts and Steinberg (1995) and Pettit, Bates, Dodge, and Meece (1999) indicate that parenting practices can moderate influences from peers. Moreover, investigations have begun to move one step further and to examine influences from teachers in combination with those from parents and peers (e.g., Ladd et al., 1999; Wentzel, 1998). For future studies incorporating the effects of children's affiliations with peers on their development in school, this chapter aims to raise optimism about the importance of peers. At the same time, it highlights some strategies for tackling the complex conceptual and empirical issues of how to detect their effects in naturalistic studies.

REFERENCES

Altermatt, E. R., & Pomerantz, E. M. (2003). The development of competence-related and motivational beliefs: An investigation of similarity and influence among friends. *Journal of Educational Psychology, 95,* 111-123.

Arbuckle, J. L. (2003). *Amos 5.* Chicago, IL: SmallWaters Corp.

Arrow, H., McGrath, J. E., & Berdahl, J. L. (2000). *Small groups as complex systems: Formation, coordination, development, and adaptation.* Thousand Oaks, CA: Sage.

Asch, S. E. (1955). Opinions and social pressure. *Scientific American, 193,* 31-55.

Asher, S. R., & Coie, J. D. (Eds.). (1990). *Peer rejection in childhood.* New York: Cambridge University Press.

Baer, D. J. (1973). The control of developmental processes: Why wait? In J. R. Nesselroade & H. W. Reese (Eds.), *Life-span developmental psychology: Methodological issues* (pp. 187-193). New York: Academic Press.

Bakeman, R., & Quera, V. (1995). *Analyzing interaction: Sequential analysis with SDIS and GSEQ.* New York: Cambridge University Press.

Baltes, M. M. (1996). *The many faces of dependency.* New York: Cambridge University Press.

Bearman, P. S., Moody, J., & Stovel, K. (2004). Chains of affection: The structure of adolescent romantic and sexual networks. *American Journal of Sociology, 110,* 44-91.

Berndt, T. J., Hawkins, J. A., & Jiao, Z. (1999). Influences of friends and friendships on adjustment to junior high school. *Merrill-Palmer Quarterly, 45,* 13-41.

Berndt, T. J., Laychak, A. E., & Park, K. (1990). Friends' influence on adolescents' academic achievement motivation: An experimental study. *Journal of Educational Psychology, 82,* 664-670.

Berndt, T. J., & Murphy, L. M. (2002). Influences from friends and friendships: Myths, truths, and research recommendations. *Advances in Child Development and Behavior, 30,* 275-310.

Borgatti, S. P., Everett, M. G., & Freeman, L. C. (1999). *UCINET V for Windows: Software for social network analysis. Version 5.2.0.1.* Natick, MA: Analytic Technologies.

Bronfenbrenner, U. (1994). Foreword. In R. A. LeVine et al. (Eds.), *Child care and culture: Lessons from Africa* (pp. xi-xvii). New York: Cambridge University Press.

Bronfenbrenner, U., & Morris, P. A. (1998). The ecology of developmental processes. In W. Damon (Series Ed.) & R. M. Lerner (Vol. Ed.), *Handbook of child psychology: Vol. 1. theoretical models of human development* (5th ed., pp. 993-1028). New York: John Wiley & Sons.

Brown, B. B. (1999). Measuring the peer environment of American adolescents. In S. L. Friedman & T. D. Wachs (Eds.), *Measuring the environment across the life span: Emerging methods and concepts* (pp. 59-90). Washington, DC: American Psychological Association.

Bukowski, W. M., & Cillessen, A. H. N. (Eds.). (1998). Sociometry then and now: Building on six decades of measuring children's experiences with the peer group. *New Directions for Child Development, Vol. 80.* San Francisco: Jossey-Bass.

Cairns, R. B. (1983). Sociometry, psychometry, and social structure: A commentary on six recent studies of popular, rejected and neglected children. *Merrill-Palmer Quarterly, 29,* 429-438.

Cairns, R. B., & Cairns, B. D. (1994). *Lifelines and risks: Pathways of youth in our time.* New York: Cambridge University Press.

Cairns, R. B., Cairns, B. D., & Neckerman, J. (1989). Early school dropout: Configurations and determinants. *Child Development, 60,* 1437-1452.

Cairns, R. B., Gariépy, J.-L., & Kindermann, T. A. (1990). Identifying social clusters in natural settings. Unpublished manuscript, University of North Carolina at Chapel Hill, Social Development Laboratory.

Cairns, R. B., Perrin, J. E., & Cairns, B. D. (1985). Social structure and social cognition in early adolescence: Affiliative patterns. *Journal of Early Adolescence, 5,* 339-355.

Chen, X., Chang, L., & He, Y. (2003). The peer group as a context: Mediating and moderating effects on relations between academic achievement and social functioning in Chinese children. *Child Development, 74,* 710-727.

Chen, X., Chang, L., He, Y., & Liu, H. (2005). The peer group as a context: Mediating and moderating effects on relations between academic achievement and social functioning in Chinese children. *Child Development, 76,* 417-434.

Deci, E. L., & Ryan, R. M. (1985). *Intrinsic motivation and self-determination in human behavior.* New York: Plenum Press.

Dishion, T. J., Andrews, J. D. W., & Crosby, L. (1995). Antisocial boys and their friends in early adolescence. *Child Development, 66,* 139-151.

Eccles, J. S., Wigfield, A., & Schiefele, U. (1998). Motivation to succeed. In W. Damon (Series Ed.) and N. Eisenberg (Vol. Ed.), *Handbook of child psychology: Vol. 3. Social, emotional, and personality development* (5th ed., pp. 1017-1095). New York: John Wiley & Sons.

Epstein, J. L. (1983). The influence of friends on achievement and affective outcomes. In J. L. Epstein & N. Karweit (Eds.), *Friends in school: Patterns of selection and influence in secondary schools* (pp. 177-200). New York: Academic Press.

Fletcher, A. C., Darling, N. E., Steinberg, L., & Dornbusch, S. M. (1995). The company they keep: Relation of adolescents' adjustment and behavior to their friends' perceptions of authoritative parenting in the social network. *Developmental Psychology, 31,* 300-310.

Fredricks, J. A., Blumenfeld, P. C., & Paris, A. H. (2004). School engagement: Potential of the concept, state of the evidence. *Review of Educational Research, 74,* 59-109.

Friend, R., Rafferty, Y., & Bramel, D. (1990). A puzzling misinterpretation of the Asch 'conformity' study. *European Journal of Social Psychology, 20,* 29-44.

Gest, S. D., Farmer, T. W., Cairns, B. D., & Xie, H.-L. (2003). Identifying children's peer social networks in school classrooms: Links between peer reports and observed interactions. *Social Development, 12,* 513-529.

Gest, S. D., Graham-Berman, S., & Hartup, W. W. (2001). Peer experience: Common and unique features of the number of friendships, social network centrality, and sociometric status. *Social Development, 10,* 23-40.

Goldstein, S. E., Davis-Kean, P. E., & Eccles, J. S. (2005). Parents, peers, and problem behavior: A longitudinal investigation of the impact of relationship perceptions and characteristics on the development of adolescent problem behavior. *Developmental Psychology, 41,* 401-413.

Grolnick, W. S., & Slowiaczek, J. L. (1994). Parental involvement in children's schooling: A multidimensional conceptualization and motivational model. *Child Development, 65,* 237-252.

Guay, F., Boivin, M., & Hodges, E. V. E. (1999). Predicting change in academic achievement: A model of peer experiences and self-system processes. *Journal of Educational Psychology, 91,* 105-115.

Hamm, J. V. (2000). Do birds of a feather flock together? The variable bases for African American, Asian American, and European American adolescents' selection of similar friends. *Developmental Psychology, 36,* 209-219.

Harris, J. R. (1998). *The nurture assumption.* New York: Free Press.

Hawley, P. H., Little, T. D., & Pasupathi, M. (2002). Winning friends and influencing peers: Strategies of peer influence in late childhood. *International Journal of Behavioral Development, 26,* 466-474.

Hodges, E. V. E., & Card, N. A. (Eds.). (2003). *Enemies and the darker side of peer relations.* San Francisco, CA: Jossey-Bass.

Hoglund, W. L., & Leadbeater, B. J. (2004). The effects of family, school, and classroom ecologies on changes in children's social competence and emotional and behavioral problems in first grade. *Developmental Psychology, 40,* 533-544.

Jaccard, J., Blanton, H., & Dodge, T. (2005). Peer influences on risk behavior: An analysis of the effects of a close friend. *Developmental Psychology, 41,* 135-147.

Kandel, D. B. (1978). Homophily, selection, and socialization in adolescent friendships. *American Journal of Sociology, 84,* 427-436.

Kindermann, T. A. (1993). Natural peer groups as contexts for individual development: The case of children's motivation in school. *Developmental Psychology, 29,* 970-977.

Kindermann, T. A. (1996). Strategies for the study of individual development within naturally existing peer groups. *Social Development, 5,* 158-173.

Kindermann, T. A. (2003). Development of children's social relationships. In J. Valsiner & K. Connolly (Eds.), *Handbook of developmental psychology* (pp. 407-430). Thousand Oaks, CA: Sage.

Kindermann, T. A. (2007). Effects of naturally-existing peer groups on changes in academic engagement in a cohort of sixth graders. *Child Development, 78,* 1186-1203.

Kindermann, T. A., & Kwee, R. (1995). Networks (version 35.01) [computer program]. Portland State University, Department of Psychology.

Kindermann, T. A., McCollam, T. L., & Gibson, E. (1996). Peer group influences on children's developing school motivation. In K. Wentzel & J. Juvonen (Eds.),(pp. 297-312) *Social motivation: Understanding children's school adjustment* . Newbury Park, CA: Sage.

Kurdek, L. A., & Sinclair, R. J. (2000). Psychological, family, and peer predictors of academic outcomes in first through fifth grade children. *Journal of Educational Psychology, 92,* 449-457.

Ladd, G. W., Birch, S. H., & Buhs, E. S. (1999). Children's social and scholastic lives in kindergarten: Related spheres or influence? *Child Development, 70,* 1373-1400.

Laursen, B. (Ed.). (2005). Dyadic and group perspectives on close relationships. Special Issue. *International Journal of Behavioral Development, 29,* 97-100.

Leung, M. C. (1996). Social networks and self enhancement in Chinese children: A comparison of self reports and peer reports of group memberships. *Social Development, 5,* 146-157.

Levine, J. M., & Moreland, R. L. (1998). Small groups. In D. Gilbert, S. T. Fiske, & G. Lindzey (Series Eds.), *Handbook of social psychology:* Vol. 2. (4th ed., pp. 415-469). New York: John Wiley & Sons.

Moreno, J. L. (Ed.). (1934). *Who shall survive? A new approach to the problem of human interrelations.* Washington, DC: Nervous and Mental Disease Publishing.

Mounts, N. S., & Steinberg, L. (1995). An ecological analysis of peer influence on adolescent grade point average and drug use. *Developmental Psychology, 31,* 915-922.

Newcomb, A. F., & Bagwell, C. L. (1995). Children's friendship relations: A meta-analytic review. *Psychological Bulletin, 117,* 306-347.

Patterson, G. R., Littman, R. A., & Bricker, W. (1967). Assertive behavior in children: A step towards a theory of aggression. *Monographs of the Society for Research in Child Development, 32,* no. 5 (serial No. 113).

Pettit, G. S., Bates, J. E., Dodge, K. A., & Meece, D. W. (1999). The impact of after-school peer contact on early adolescent externalizing problems is moderated by parental monitoring, perceived neighborhood safety, and prior adjustment. *Child Development, 70,* 768-778.

Poulin, F., Dishion, T. J., & Haas, E. (1999). The peer influence paradox: Friendship quality and deviancy training within male adolescent friendship. *Merrill-Palmer Quarterly, 45,* 42-61.

Renshaw, P. D. (1981). The roots of peer interaction research: A historical analysis of the 1930s. In S. R. Asher & J. M. Gottman (Eds.), *The development of children's friendships* (pp. 1-25). New York: Cambridge University Press.

Richards, W. D. (Ed.). (1995). *Negopy 4.30*. Brunaby, BC, Canada: Simon Fraser University.

Rubin, K. H., Bukowski, W. M., & Parker, J. G. (2006). Peer interactions, relationships, and groups. In W. Damon, R. M. Lerner (Series Eds.), & N. Eisenberg (Vol. Ed.), *Handbook of child psychology: Vol. 3. Social, emotional, and personality development* (6th ed., pp. 571-645). New York: John Wiley & Sons.

Sage, N. A., & Kindermann, T. A. (1999). Peer networks, behavior contingencies, and children's engagement in the classroom. *Merrill-Palmer Quarterly, 45*, 143-171.

Sherif, M., Harvey, O. J., White, B. J., Hood, W. E., & Sherif, C. W. (Eds.). (1961). *Intergroup conflict and cooperation: The robber's cave experiment.* Norman, OK: University of Oklahoma Book Exchange.

Skinner, E. A., & Belmont, M. J. (1993). Motivation in the classroom: Reciprocal effects of teacher behavior and student engagement across the school year. *Journal of Educational Psychology, 85*, 571-581.

Skinner, E. A., Johnson, S., & Snyder, T. (2005). Six dimensions of parenting: A motivational model. *Parenting: Science and Practice, 5*, 175-236.

Skinner, E. A., Wellborn, J. G., & Connell, J. P. (1990). What it takes to do well in school and whether I've got it: A process model of perceived control and children's engagement and achievement in school. *Journal of Educational Psychology, 82*, 22-32.

Skinner, E. A., Zimmer-Gembeck, M. J., & Connell, J. P. (1998). Individual differences and the development of perceived control. *Monographs of the Society for Research in Child Development, 63 (Serial No. 245).*

Snyder, B. M. J., Patrick, M. R., Snyder, A., Schrepferman, L., & Stoolmiller, M. (2003). Observed peer victimization during early elementary school: Continuity, growth, and relation to risk for child antisocial and depressive behavior. *Child Development, 74*, 1881-1898.

Strayer, F. F., & Santos, A. J. (1996). Affiliative structures in preschool peer groups. *Social Development, 5*, 117-130.

Urberg, K. A., Değirmencioğlu, S. M., & Pilgrim, C. (1997). Close friend and group influence on adolescent cigarette smoking and alcohol use. *Developmental Psychology, 33*, 834-844.

Wellborn, J. G. (1991). *Engaged vs. disaffected action: Conceptualization and measurement of motivation in the academic domain.* Unpublished Dissertation. Graduate School of Human Development and Education, University of Rochester, Rochester, NY.

Wentzel, K. R. (1998). Social relationships and motivation in middle school: The role of parents, teachers, and peers. *Journal of Educational Psychology, 2*, 202-209.

Wentzel, K. R., McNamara-Barry, C., & Caldwell, K. A. (2004). Friendships in middle school: Influences on motivation and school adjustment. *Journal of Educational Psychology, 96*, 195-203.

CHAPTER FIFTEEN

A Multilevel p_2 Model With Covariates for the Analysis of Binary Bully–Victim Network Data in Multiple Classrooms

Bonne J.H. Zijlstra

University of Amsterdam, The Netherlands

René Veenstra

Marijtje A.J. van Duijn

University of Groningen, The Netherlands

INTRODUCTION

Many studies have been aimed at defining the exact nature of bullying, identifying bullies and their victims in school classes, investigating the personal and developmental characteristics of bullies and victims, and evaluating intervention programs to prevent bullying (see, e.g. Espelage & Swearer, 2003). Children have different roles in bullying (Schwartz, 2000), and some pairs of children lead to more bullying than others (Coie et al., 1999). Relatively little is known about the dyadic properties of bullies and victims (Rodkin & Berger, in press). Recently, a dual perspective theory of bullying was proposed, focusing on the dyadic nature of the bully–victim relationship (Veenstra et al., 2007).

This theory is tested on preadolescent data from TRAILS (Tracking Adolescents' Individual Lives Survey). TRAILS is designed to chart and explain the development of mental health and social development from preadolescence into adulthood (De Winter et al., 2005; Oldehinkel, Hartman, De Winter, Veenstra, & Ormel, 2004). Students were asked to report about several of their ties with classmates. This round robin design yields in principle two observations for each relationship between two children A and B, one from the perspective of child A (the nominator or "sender"), reporting whether or not he or she bullies child B (the target or "receiver"), and vice versa. These two reports may not always coincide and are less likely to be in agreement for a bullying tie than for a friendship tie. The set of dyadic data collected in a closed group forms a social network. Many methods and models have been proposed for social network analysis (see Wasserman & Faust, 1994). For a review on the intricacies of dyadic designs and dyadic data analysis, see Kenny, Kashy, and Cook (2006).

We use a multilevel p_2 model (Zijlstra, Van Duijn, & Snijders, 2006) to analyze bully network data from 54 classes collected in the TRAILS study. This model takes into account the dependent nature of the data and employs the characteristics of sender and receiver individually and as a dyad. Moreover, class characteristics can be used to explain differences per classroom; for instance, between prevalence rates of bullying in school classes. We follow the dual perspective theory as laid out by Veenstra et al. (2007) but slightly modify the covariates used in the analysis. In the next section we start with the definition and interpretation of the simple p_2 model, followed by the multilevel p_2 model, and its relation to other models for social network data. In the third section, we present the data and theory to be tested. After a section introducing the interpretation of p_2 model results, we present the results obtained for the dual perspective theory. The final section summarizes and discusses the findings.

The (Multilevel) p_2 Model

The p_2 model (Lazega & Van Duijn, 1997, Van Duijn, Snijders, & Zijlstra, 2004) analyzes a single binary network Y of size n, modeling the probability of the four possible dyadic tie outcomes (Y_{ij}, Y_{ji}), where Y_{ij} denotes the presence (1) or absence (0) of a tie (i.e. nomination) between sender (nominator) i and receiver (target) j for all n actors in the network. In the p_2 model, Y represents the bully network in a classroom of n students (i.e. the actors in the network). Although the p_2 model is aimed at the analysis of complete networks where all actors report their ties with all others in the network, the model does not require all observations of the network to be present, and thus only analyzes the available dyads.

The p_2 model builds on the p_1 model (Holland & Leinhardt, 1981), which characterizes the dyadic outcome probability by four important parameters: μ (density), ρ (reciprocity), α (sender) and β (receiver). In the p_1 model, given in equation (1), the probability that child i bullies child j is determined by i's sender parameter α_i, j's receiver parameter β_j, overall density μ, and if j also bullies i, overall reciprocity ρ. Likewise, the probability that child j bullies child i is determined by j's sender parameter, i's receiver parameter, overall density μ, and if i also bullies j, overall reciprocity ρ.

$$P(Y_{ij} = y_1, Y_{ji} = y_2) = \tag{1}$$

$$\frac{\exp\{y_1(\mu + \alpha_i + \beta_j) + y_2(\mu + \alpha_j + \beta_i) + y_1 y_2 \rho\}}{1 + \exp\{\mu + \alpha_i + \beta_j\} + \exp\{\mu + \alpha_j + \beta_i\} + \exp\{2\mu + \alpha_i + \alpha_j + \beta_i + \beta_j + \rho\}}$$

where $y_1, y_2 \in \{0, 1\}, i \neq j$.

The interesting part of the p_1 formula is the numerator. The denominator is needed to ensure that the four outcome probabilities sum to 1. It is informative because it contains the four possible numerator outcomes. Ignoring the first term in the denominator (i.e. the 1), the second term in the denominator contains the parameters in the numerator involved in modeling the asymmetric (1,0) dyadic outcome. This unreciprocated tie from i to j where child i bullies child j, but j does not bully i, corresponds to the values $y_1 = 1$ and $y_2 = 0$. The probability of this tie depends on i's sender parameter α_i, j's receiver parameter β_j, and the network density μ. The third term in the denominator, obtained for the opposite asymmetric (0,1) dyad, includes μ, α_j, and β_i, and therefore depends on j as a sender and i as a receiver. For the case where both ties are reported, (1,1), corresponding to the fourth term in the denominator, the reciprocity parameter ρ is present in addition to the parameters involved in the single asymmetric dyadic outcomes. Thus, the density parameter is included twice (2μ). In friendship networks the concept of reciprocity reflects the increased probability of reciprocal ties. In bullying networks, we expect an absence of reciprocity or possibly even a reversed reciprocity. Finally, the first term in the denominator (1) corresponds to the (0,0) outcome, the null tie, which serves as a reference category, against which the probabilities of the other outcomes are compared. The dyadic outcome probabilities according to the p_1 model are summarized in Table 15.1.

   Through the use of the exponential function in numerator and denominator, the p_1 model is reminiscent of a logistic regression model, and the interpretation of the parameters are indeed similar. For instance, the higher the sender and receiver parameters, the higher the probability of the presence of a (sent and/or received) tie. Holland and Leinhardt (1981) define log-odds ratios for the interpretation of the density and reciprocity parameters. The density parameter, μ, represents the log-odds of a tie (i.e., an asymmetric

TABLE 15.1
Dyadic Outcome Probabilities in the p_1 Model

Dyad (y_{ij}, y_{ji})		Observed Tie From j to i, y_{ji}	
		0	1
Observed Tie	0	1	$\exp(\mu + \alpha_j + \beta_i)$
From i to j, y_{ij}	1	$\exp(\mu + \alpha_i + \beta_j)$	$\exp(\mu + \alpha_i + \beta_j) \exp(\mu + \alpha_j + \beta_i)\exp(\rho)$

Note. All entries are to be divided by the sum of the four elements in the table;
$(1 + \exp(\mu + \alpha_i + \beta_j) + \exp(\mu + \alpha_j + \beta_i) + \exp(2\mu + \alpha_i + \alpha_j + \beta_i + \beta_j + \rho)$

dyad $(1,0)$ or $(0,1)$ vs. $(0,0)$, the reference outcome). This value is equal to the log ratio of the off-diagonal elements and the top-left element in Table 15.1. The reciprocity parameter, ρ, represents the log-odds of a symmetric dyad $(0,0)$ and $(1,1)$, vs. an asymmetric dyad, $(1,0)$ and $(0,1)$, which is equal to the log ratio of the diagonal elements and the off-diagonal elements in Table 15.1. If there is no reciprocity (ρ equal to zero), the two ties (from i to j and from j to i) are independent in the p_1 model and become a simple product of two logistic regression models. When applied to bullying networks, the log-odds of an asymmetric tie from child i to child j vs. the reverse asymmetric tie is an informative measure which we will call the asymmetric log-odds. This log ratio of the bottom left element and the top right element in Table 15.1 is equal to $(\alpha_i + \beta_j)$-$(\alpha_j + \beta_i)$, the difference in sender parameters minus the difference in receiver parameters.

The p_1 model can be regarded as a (saturated) loglinear model for a cross-table representing the n x n adjacency matrix Y (Fienberg & Wasserman, 1981). For identification purposes, the p_1 model needs a restriction on the sender and receiver parameters, for instance $\Sigma_i \alpha_i = \Sigma_i \beta_i = 0$. When further restrictions are put on the sender and receiver parameters (e.g., distinguishing several categories of senders and receivers), the loglinear model can be viewed as a multinomial logistic regression model for four possible outcomes (see also Agresti, 2002). Another way to classify the p_1 model is as a fixed effects version of the Social Relations Model (SRM; Kenny & La Voie, 1984) for binary network data (Kenny et al., 2006).

The desire to use additional (covariate) information about the actors in a network (e.g., the child's sex) and the undesirable statistical properties of a saturated model (see Van Duijn et al., 2004) led to the development of the p_2 model. In this model individual sender and receiver parameters are replaced by regression equations:

$$\alpha_i = X_{1i}\gamma_1 + A_i, \tag{2}$$
$$\beta_i = X_{2i}\gamma_2 + B_i.$$

Actor covariates, X_1 and X_2, can thus be used to predict individual sender and receiver effects. Either categorical or continuous covariates can be used, which may or may not be the same for explaining sender and receiver parameters. The residuals in the regression equations represent unexplained differences among the actors in the network. These residuals can also be viewed as latent variables or random effects and interpreted as individual tendencies to send or receive ties. A bivariate normal distribution is assumed for the pairs of random sender and receiver effects (A_i, B_i), with zero mean and common covariance matrix with three distinct elements: sender variance, receiver variance, and sender–receiver covariance. The bivariate distribution reflects the association between the tendencies to bully and to being bullied. The sender and receiver variances are fairly interpretable. For instance, if the sender variance is larger than the receiver variance, then the variation between actors as senders is much larger (which makes the tendency to send ties less predictable) than the variation between actors as receivers.

Where the p_1 model has $2n$ parameters (an individual sender and receiver effect for each actor in the network), the p_2 model has fewer parameters in addition to the density and reciprocity parameter, equal to the number of regression parameters $\dim(\gamma_1)+\dim(\gamma_2)$ plus the three elements of the covariance matrix of the random sender and receiver effects. Due to this reduction in the number of parameters to be estimated, dyad specific density and reciprocity parameters are regressed on dyadic covariates Z_1 and Z_2 in the p_2 model:

$$\mu_{ij} = \mu + Z_{1ij}\delta_1, \tag{3}$$
$$\rho_{ij} = \rho + Z_{2ij}\delta_2.$$

Parameters μ and ρ now denote the mean density and reciprocity when the values of the dyadic covariates are zero. The dyadic covariates can be derived from actor specific covariates, indicating, for example, whether both children have the same sex. In that case the covariate matrix Z is symmetric. Z may also be asymmetric, such as when the difference between actor covariates are used or when a network of different tie relations (e.g., friendship) is used to predict the density. Due to the inherent symmetry of reciprocity and its definition as an interaction effect in the p_2 model, the choice of Z_2 is restricted to the subset of symmetric dyadic covariates used as Z_1. In the present application, we will not model reciprocity with covariates.

The multilevel p_2 model (Zijlstra, Van Duijn, & Snijders, 2006) is a straightforward extension of the p_2 model for the analysis of multiple networks. It assumes the same p_2 model for a sample of networks of possibly different size. Similar to sample size considerations in normal multilevel analysis, a reasonable number of classes, say at least 15 but preferably more, is required to apply the multilevel p_2 model meaningfully.

Similar to the simplest normal multilevel model with two levels, the intercept varies over the higher level. In the multilevel p_2 model the mean density parameter μ is normally distributed over the networks (expressed by the random effect M_k) and possibly related to network characteristics (through Z_{1ijk} with constant values for each dyad in network k):

$$\mu_{ijk} = \mu + M_k + Z_{1ijk}(\delta_1 + D_{1k}). \tag{4}$$

Note that in (4) the effect of dyad characteristics is also allowed to vary, by including random effects D_{1k}, comparable to the random slope model. The estimated mean μ can be viewed as the grand mean density (over all networks) when all covariate values equal zero. The estimated variance of the mean density indicates how much the mean density varies over networks. More generally, the multilevel p_2 model may include random effects for μ, ρ, γ_1, γ_2, δ_1, and δ_2. We will only apply a random effect for μ. The p_2 model and the multilevel p_2 model can be viewed as the binary counterparts of the SRM expressed as random effects (i.e., as a multilevel model; Snijders & Kenny, 1999).

The parameters of the p_2 model and the multilevel p_2 model are estimated using Markov Chain Monte Carlo (MCMC) algorithms implemented in specialized software for social network analysis (StOCNET; Boer et al., 2006). In addition to the MCMC specifications (we used the standard option of 4,000 burn-in iterations and a sample size of 8,000), the estimation time depends on the number of networks to be analyzed and their size. On the present data set (54 networks, with a median of 15 students in roughly 7,500 dyads) it took approximately 12 hours on a standard PC to run an analysis. The estimation results in estimated posterior means and posterior standard deviations of the p_2 model parameters. The p-values of covariate effect parameters are derived from approximate t-ratios. Bayesian credibility intervals are available as approximate confidence intervals. The software is freely available for download at http://stat.gamma.rug.nl/stocnet, with manuals for both StOCNET and for the p_2 model. Details of the estimation procedures can be found in Zijlstra, Van Duijn, Snijders (in press) for the p_2 model, and in Zijlstra et al. (2006) for the multilevel p_2 model.

Bullying Networks—Theory and Data

The bullying network data were collected as part of TRAILS, a large longitudinal study among (pre)adolescents in the Netherlands. Due to the set-up of the study, in each participating classroom some but not all of the students provided information on several aspects of their dyadic relations with classmates. Thus, a not necessarily complete subnetwork of each classroom with varying size is available. Due to incomplete data the sample size varies from 7 to 33 students per class.

The dyadic nature of the bullying network data was theoretically investigated in Veenstra et al. (2007). They used a dual goal-framing approach to highlight the opposite perspectives of bullies and victims and the inherent asymmetric or hierarchical nature of bullying. For self-proclaimed bullying it was hypothesized that bullies are likely to be dominantly aggressive boys whose victims are vulnerable, rejected, and not aggressive. Additional hypotheses were formulated about the positive effect of disliking on bullying. The influence of same-sex or mixed-sex bullying was not quite clear a priori. Boy–boy bullying ties might be more likely, because boys are more aggressive and because they may achieve more prestige by bullying boys instead of girls. On the other hand, girls, being less aggressive and more vulnerable may be more likely to be victimized. Before we set up the p_2 model to investigate (several) operationalizations of the expectations based on the dual perspective theory, the available network, dyadic and individual data are described in more detail.

Individual (Actor) Covariates

Teachers were asked to rate each pupil on aggressiveness and vulnerability, using an adapted version of the Revised Class Play instrument (Masten, Morison, & Pellegrini, 1985, see also Veenstra et al., 2007). We constructed 6 ordinal categories of approximately equal size from the skewed distributions (within and over all classes) to enhance comparability between classrooms and prevent too much influence of the relatively few aggressive pupils. In addition, sex was used as an actor covariate.

Network Variables and Dyadic Covariates

The dependent variable Y is the network on self-reported bullying based on the question "Who do you bully?" The network with dislike relations ("Who do you not like at all?") is used as a dyadic covariate. The asymmetric dyadic variable rejection R was derived for each dyad from the dislike relation D by computing the percentage of classmates other than the nominator who dislike the target: $R_{ij} = \Sigma_{k \neq i} D_{kj}/(n-1)$. Thus this variable separates the effects of child i's dislike D_{ij} from dislike by fellow classmates.

From the child's sex, two symmetric dyadic covariates were constructed, the first to indicate mixed-sex (boy–girl and girl–boy) dyads and the second to indicate only boy–boy dyads (girl–girl dyads are the reference group), thereby distinguishing the two kinds of same-sex dyads. The first type of dyadic covariate is a standard dyadic similarity variable, generated in the p_2 model software by obtaining the absolute difference of the binary sex indicator variable and takes on the value 1 for mixed-sex dyads and 0 for same-sex dyads. Thus a negative parameter estimate indicates a preference for same-sex bully ties. The second dyadic variable expresses the difference between boy–boy dyads and girl–girl dyads, the latter being the reference dyad if the mixed-sex dyadic variable is included.

From the individual aggression scores of nominator and target, a dyadic variable is obtained by taking the difference score, also a standard option in the p_2 model software. The derived dyadic variable is always asymmetric: $Z_{ij} = X_i - X_j$, and thus $Z_{ji} = -Z_{ij}$. A positive parameter estimate indicates a dominance effect where larger (i-j) differences increase the probability of i being the bully and j the victim in the (i,j) dyad. In this case, the (1,0) dyad is more likely than the (0,1) outcome.

ILLUSTRATION

We start with three simple models presented in Table 15.2 to illustrate the interpretation of p_2 model results. The first model is without covariates (an "empty" or "basic" model), and the other two models investigate the effect of sex. For the "basic" p_2 model parameters, no significance level is indicated. The density parameter estimate is highly negative, indicating that the probability of a bully tie is much smaller than 0.50, making the null (0,0) dyadic outcome most likely. This is a phenomenon often observed in the analysis of social network data, even when the outcome variable is a positive relationship. Especially in larger networks, it is quite improbable that an actor would choose half of the other actors in the network. Thus, density is related to network size, which is also indicated by the rather large class density variance. As expected for bullying, the estimated reciprocity parameter is low. This low estimate facilitates the interpretation of the other covariate parameters because both ties in the dyad are approximately independent from a statistical point of view. The large sender variance indicates that the tendency to report bullying is highly variable over children.

TABLE 15.2
Parameter Estimates of Multilevel p_2 Models Investigating the Effect of Sex on Bullying in 54 Classes

Effect	Model 0: No Effects Posterior Mean (Posterior *S.D.*)		Model 1A: Individual and Dyadic Effects Posterior Mean (Posterior *S.D.*)		Model 1B: + Class Effects Posterior Mean (Posterior *S.D.*)	
Density	-6.02	(0.20)	-7.00	(0.32)	-5.12	(0.55)
Reciprocity	0.55	(0.37)	0.58	(0.31)	0.57	(0.34)
Sender Covariates						
Being a boy			0.93	(0.20) *	0.91	(0.28) *
Receiver Covariates						
Dyadic Covariates						
Mixed-sex			0.98	(0.20) *	1.02	(0.19) *
Boy–boy			0.75	(0.29) *	0.81	(0.30) *
Class Covariates						
Percentage boys					-4.10	(1.49) *
Random Effects						
Class density variance	1.41	(0.52)	1.58	(0.62)	1.79	(0.49)
Sender variance	5.51	(0.65)	5.07	(0.66)	5.24	(0.70)
Receiver variance	1.68	(0.25)	1.55	(0.23)	1.56	(0.25)
Sender–receiver covariance	0.47	(0.34)	0.29	(0.27)	0.29	(0.29)
Number of Dyads	7668		7668		7668	

*$p < 0.05$.

Note. * $p < 0.05$.

The expected probabilities of the four dyadic outcomes can be derived from the model parameter estimates using (1). They are equal to 99.5% for the null dyad, and slightly lower than 0.25% for the two asymmetric dyads. The probability of a mutual dyad is negligible (approximately 0.25 * 0.25 = 0.0625%). Note that in calculating these expected probabilities the sender and receiver variance values are disregarded. Thus, the probabilities concern dyads consisting of the "average" nominator and target (i.e., with zero sender and receiver random effects) and for the "average" network (with zero density random effect). Just for illustration, we can also compute the expected probabilities for child A with a large sender random effect (equal to 3) and an average receiver effect, and child B with an average sender effect and a small negative receiver effect (equal to --0.5) in a network with an above-average density (random effect equal to 1). This parameter configuration changes the estimated probabilities to 92% for a null dyad, 0.085% for the mutual dyad, 7.4% for the asymmetric tie from child A to child B, and 0.61% for the reverse asymmetric tie. Approximately, the odds of an asymmetric tie (compared to "average" children) from child A to child B have increased with a factor 12 (this can also be determined without computing the probabilities first, by taking the exponent of 2.5, i.e., the sum of sender and receiver effects). The odds of the reverse tie have not changed. The asymmetric log-odds of A bullying B instead of B bullying A is also equal to 2.5 (the sum of A's sender and B's receiver effect minus the sum of A's receiver and B's sender effect, where the latter two terms are equal to zero, hence the correspondence with the odds of an asymmetric tie).

The second model (model 1A in Table 15.2) has a sender effect for boys and the mixed-sex and boy–boy dyadic covariates defined previously. Note that we choose three parameters to contrast the four possible dyadic sex combinations with the girl–girl dyad as the reference group. Significant covariate parameter estimates, based on a t-ratio larger than 2, are indicated with an asterisk. Slight changes in the basic p_2 model parameters with respect to Model 0 are observed. The sender effect of being a boy is positive and significant, in line with the expectation that boys report more bullying ties than girls. The two dyadic sex covariates are also positive and significant, indicating that both mixed-sex and boy–boy ties are more likely than girl–girl bully ties. Disregarding the most common null dyad, the asymmetric boy–girl bully tie is slightly more likely than the asymmetric boy–boy bully tie, yet only low probabilities of 0.6% vs. 0.5%, for "average" children in an "average" network. The numerators are essential for the computations and comparisons of these probabilities. The numerator of the (1,0) boy–boy dyad is equal to the exponent of the sum of the density effect (−7.00), the sender effect of being a boy (0.93) and the boy–boy dyadic effect (0.75), exp(--5.32) =

0.0049. In the numerator of the (1,0) boy–girl dyad, the dyadic boy–boy effect is replaced by the mixed-sex effect of 0.98, and therefore slightly larger: exp(–5.09)=0.0062. The estimated asymmetric girl–boy and girl–girl bully tie probabilities are 0.24% and 0.1%, respectively. The null dyad probabilities for all sex-combinations are larger than 99% and the mutual dyad probabilities smaller than 0.01%. The asymmetric log-odds ratio is equal to the sender effect of being a boy: 0.93. This (possibly too) simple model would support the hypothesis that boys bully more than girls, and also that boys bully each other more than girls bully each other. However, no support is found for the hypothesis that boys bully boys more than they bully girls. Note that all probabilities of dyads with at least one bully tie reported are extremely low, making it difficult to predict the outcome on the basis of sex alone.

Mainly for illustrative purposes, a class covariate related to sex (i.e., percentage of boys) is added in model 1B. It assesses whether the varying tendency to report bullying can be explained by the sex composition of the classes. The percentage of boys in each class is found to have a negative effect (see Table 15.2), implying that a higher percentage of boys in a class leads to a lower propensity to bully. The variability of the density parameter is not reduced but increased, suggesting that in spite of the relationship between sex composition and general tendency to report bullying in a classroom, many deviations are found in the sampled classes. The posterior standard deviation of the density parameter is increased compared to model 1B. This type of result likely indicates that the parameter estimates are not stable yet due to nonconvergence of the MCMC estimation procedure. In such situations, a possible solution is to run the model again with more iterations (more details can be found in the p_2 manual). Therefore, the interpretation of this model is explicitly preliminary.

RESULTS

The hypotheses generated by the dual perspective theory are tested stepwise, in three models, presented in Table 15.3. In Model 2 we investigate the effects of aggressiveness and vulnerability, without sex effects (as they may be related to these individual characteristics). On the basis of the theory, we expect a sender effect of aggressiveness and a receiver effect of vulnerability. We first investigated in some preliminary model specifications (not reported) the linearity of the 6 categories of aggressiveness and vulnerability which turned out to be tenable. Although the expected nonaggressiveness of the target could be defined as a receiver effect, we chose a model with a dyadic difference effect of nominator and target aggressiveness. As expected, the sender effect of aggressiveness and the receiver effect of vulnerability are

TABLE 15.3
Parameter Estimates of Several Multilevel p_2 Models Testing the Dual Perspective Theory of Bullying in 54 Classes

Effect	Model 2: Aggression and Vulnerability Effects		Model 3: + Rejection		Model 4: + Sex + Dislike	
	Posterior Mean (Posterior *S.D.*)		Posterior Mean (Posterior *S.D.*)		Posterior Mean (Posterior *S.D.*)	
Density	-9.96	(0.53)	-9.37	(0.44)	-10.3	(0.50)
Reciprocity	0.46	(0.31)	0.56	(0.31)	0.53	(0.32)
Sender Covariates						
Being a boy					1.07	(0.26) *
Aggressiveness	0.76	(0.09) *	0.68	(0.09) *	0.62	(0.08) *
Receiver Covariates						
Vulnerability	0.37	(0.06) *	0.23	(0.06) *	0.18	(0.06) *
Dyadic Covariates						
Mixed-sex					0.48	(0.20) *
Boy-boy					-0.05	(0.29)
Diff. aggressiveness	-0.21	(0.05) *	-0.12	(0.05) *	-0.08	(0.05)
Rejection			4.06	(0.58) *	4.00	(0.68) *
Dislike					1.98	(0.16) *
Random Effects						
Class density variance	1.55	(0.55)	1.19	(0.46)	1.28	(0.49)
Sender variance	4.75	(0.66)	4.48	(0.59)	4.69	(0.68)
Receiver variance	1.32	(0.22)	0.76	(0.19)	0.89	(0.20)
Sender-receiver covariance	0.23	(0.26)	0.10	(0.24)	0.12	(0.27)
Number of Dyads	6841		6838		6838	

Note. $^*p < 0.05$.

positive. The effect of the difference in aggressiveness is negative, which can be interpreted as reducing the effect of aggressiveness for highly aggressive nominators vs. less aggressive targets. This effect is illustrated in the asymmetric log-odds where the effect of the dyadic difference in aggressiveness counts twice. Because the sender effect of aggression (0.76) is more than twice as large as the minus dyadic difference effect of aggressiveness (-0.21), the log-odds are equal to 0.34 times the difference in aggressiveness minus 0.37 times the difference in vulnerability. The largest asymmetric log odds, 35, is obtained for maximally aggressive and minimally vulnerable bullies and minimally aggressive, but maximally vulnerable targets. This dyadic combination does not lead to an extremely large probability of an asymmetric bully tie: 1.4%. Due to the strong sender effect of aggressiveness, the maximum probability of an asymmetric bully tie is from a nominator with maximum score (6) on aggression and minimum score (1) on vulnerability to a target with the maximum score on vulnerability and aggression: 4.0%. This probability is still as large as 3.8% for nominators who are maximally vulnerable themselves. On the opposite of the scale for minimally aggressive and vulnerable nominators and targets, the probability of a mutual or asymmetric bully tie is negligible (less than 0.1%). Although the probabilities are still rather small, they are much larger than the predicted probabilities from model 1A. We can interpret this difference as the increased predictive power of model 2.

Thus, model 2, although incomplete, supplies support for the dual perspective theory in the sense that bullies are likely to be aggressive boys and their victims vulnerable. The hypothesis about bullies seeking less aggressive victims, is not quite supported in the sense that the model predicts bullying between aggressive children as much (or even a little more) than between aggressive and less aggressive children. On the other hand, given a dyad with one more aggressive and one less aggressive child, it is more likely to observe that the aggressive child bullies the less aggressive child than the opposite.

In model 3, reported in Table 15.3, we add the effect of rejection of the target. It is positive, supporting the hypothesis that the more children are rejected by others, the more they are prone to being bullied. All other effects are slightly smaller, but still significant. Calculating the probabilities of a bullying tie between a maximally aggressive and vulnerable nominator and a target where neither are rejected gives only a 2.0% probability of an asymmetric bullying tie, most likely because the value of 0 for rejection is unrealistic. It is now somewhat more difficult to find meaningful combinations of characteristics for nominators and targets. The negative effects of the difference in aggression level and of the level of vulnerability and the positive effect of percentage of rejection offset each other. Aggression, vulnerability, and rejection are all moderately positively correlated with each other (see

Veenstra et al., 2007). If we choose child A with aggression level 6, vulnerability level 2, and rejection level 0.1 (i.e. disliked by 10% of the class mates) and child B with aggression level 6, vulnerability level 3, and rejection level 0.3, the probability that child A reports a bully tie with child B is 3.0%, that child B reports a bully tie with child A is 1.0%, and that they both report bullying each other is 0.05%.

In the final model (model 4 in Table 15.3), sex effects are added according to model 1A as well as the effect of dyadic dislike. Not surprisingly, dislike turns out to be an important dyadic covariate. The strength of the effect is comparable to a rejection value of 0.50, but it is clearly separate, given that the estimate for the effect of rejection was unchanged. A comparison of models 1A and 3 indicates subtle changes in the parameter estimates, where especially the reduced effects of the mixed-sex and boy–boy dyads are of interest. These changes can be interpreted as a form of (partial) mediation. Recomputing the probabilities for the dyad with the same configuration as in model 3, rather large differences are found between the different sex combinations. Focusing on the two asymmetric bully ties $(1,0)$ and $(0,1)$—3% and 1% in model 2—and assuming that the children do not like each other, we find the probabilities to be equal to 12.7% and 4.8% for boy-boy dyads, 20.1% and 2.6% for boy-girl dyads, 7.6% and 8.2% for girl-boy dyads, and 5.2% and 2.0% for girl-girl dyads. These probabilities are all rather high, and we might question whether the configuration of a girl with aggression level 6, and vulnerability level 1 or 3 is realistic. Therefore, interpretation of p_2 model results requires a lot of careful assumptions and considerations. In summarizing and further interpreting the results in the next section we avoid the complex language involved in discussing odds and probabilities, and highlight the support found for the dual perspective theory in model 4.

CONCLUSION

In this chapter the multilevel p_2 model was used to test several hypotheses coming from the dual perspective theory of bullying put forward by Veenstra et al. (2007) on self-proclaimed bullying data in 54 Dutch school classes. The multilevel p_2 model is a good choice for the analysis of this large number of dyadic ties in multiple social networks because it distinguishes the roles of sender and receiver in a dyadic link, and their individual characteristics, while at the same time taking into account the dependence between the two ties within the dyad and between the ties to and from the same actors. The multilevel p_2 model also incorporates dyadic and network information and, just like any regression model, gives estimates of the effects of several covariates simultaneously. Complete network data is not required for a p_2 model analysis, but the usual concerns about missing data do apply (see, e.g., Little & Rubin, 2002).

Testing the significance of effects is straightforward, whereas interpretation of p_2 model results is more difficult, because they have to be translated into four dyadic outcome probabilities. This translation process is similar to, but a bit more complex than in logistic regression, due to the interdependence of the dyadic outcomes and sensitivity to the dyadic covariate configuration. The random effects of senders and receivers (and potentially more parameters in the multilevel p_2 model) adds another level of complexity. This complexity can be overcome, as long as one keeps in mind that the results are about "average" children (in an "average" classroom).

We found that bullies have an advantage over the children they victimize by being more dominantly aggressive than their victims. These results are consistent with earlier results at the individual (see also Vaillancourt, Hymel, & McDougall, 2003) and at the dyadic level (Dodge, Price, Coie, & Christopoulos, 1990). As we expected, bullies pick on targets that they do not like and who are vulnerable (i.e. fearful/isolated) and rejected by others. This last point is also consistent with earlier findings at the individual level (Boivin, Hymel, & Bukowski, 1995; Hodges, Boivin, Vitaro, & Bukowski, 1999; Hodges & Perry, 1999). We also found that boys tend to bully more than girls. Moreover, controlling for aggression, vulnerability, rejection, and dislike, a bully tie is most likely from a boy to a girl. The analyses with the p_2 model also revealed that the dual perspective theory explained some of the highly variable tendency to report bullying as well as part of the much lower target variance.

ACKNOWLEDGMENTS

Bonne J.H. Zijlstra, Department of Educational Sciences; René Veenstra and Marijtje A.J. van Duijn, Department of Sociology and Interuniversity Center for Social Science Theory and Methodology (ICS). Zijlstra and Van Duijn belong to the Interuniversity Graduate School for Psychometrics and Sociometrics (IOPS).

This research is part of the TRacking Adolescents' Individual Lives Survey (TRAILS). Participating centers of TRAILS include various Departments of the University of Groningen, the Erasmus Medical Center of Rotterdam, the Radboud University of Nijmegen, University of Utrecht, and the Trimbos Institute the Netherlands. TRAILS is financially supported by grants from the Netherlands Organization for Scientific Research (GB-MW 940-38-011, GB-MAGW 480-01-006, GB-MAGW 457-03-018, NWO 175.010.2003.005, ZonMw

100-001-001, ZonMw 60-60600-98-018), the Ministry of Justice (WODC), and by the participating centers.

REFERENCES

Agresti, A. (2002). *Categorical data analysis* (2nd ed.). New York: John Wiley & Sons.

Boer, P., Huisman, M., Snijders, T. A. B., Steglich, C. E. G., Wichers, L. H. Y., & Zeggelink, E. P. H. (2006). *StOCNET: An open software system for the advanced statistical analysis of social networks (Version 1.7)*[Computer software]. Groningen: ICS/SciencePlus.

Boivin, M., Hymel, S., & Bukowski, W. M. (1995). The roles of social withdrawal, peer rejection, and victimization by peers in predicting loneliness and depressed mood in children. *Development and Psychopathology, 7*, 765-785.

Coie, J. D., Cillessen, A. H. N., Dodge, K. A., Hubbard, J. A., Schwartz, D., Lemerise, E. A., et al. (1999). It takes two to fight: A test of relational factors and a method for assessing aggressive dyads. *Developmental Psychology, 35*, 1179-1188.

De Winter, A. F., Oldehinkel, A. J., Veenstra, R., Brunnekreef, J. A., Verhulst, F. C., & Ormel, J. (2005). Evaluation of non-response bias in mental health determinants and outcomes in a large sample of pre-adolescents. *European Journal of Epidemiology, 20*, 173-181.

Dodge, K. A., Price, J. M., Coie, J. D., & Christopoulos, C. (1990). On the development of aggressive dyadic relationships in boys' peer groups. *Human Development, 33*, 260-270.

Espelage, D. L., & Swearer, S. M. (2003). *Bullying in American schools: A social-ecological perspective on prevention and intervention.* Mahwah, NJ: Lawrence Erlbaum.

Fienberg, S. E., & Wasserman, S. (1981). Categorical data analysis of single sociometric relations. In S. Leinhardt (Ed.), *Sociological methodology* (pp. 156-192). San Fransisco: Jossey-Bass.

Hodges, E. V. E., Boivin, M., Vitaro, F., & Bukowski, W. M. (1999). The power of friendship: Protection against an escalating cycle of peer victimization. *Developmental Psychology, 35*, 94-101.

Hodges, E. V. E., & Perry, D. G. (1999). Personal and interpersonal antecedents and consequences of victimization by peers. *Journal of Personality and Social Psychology, 76*, 677-685.

Holland, P. W., & Leinhardt, S. (1981). An exponential family of probability distributions for directed graphs. *Journal of the American Statistical Association, 77*, 33-50.

Kenny, D. A., Kashy, D. A., & Cook, W. L. (2006). *Dyadic data analysis.* New York: Guilford Press.

Kenny, D. A., & La Voie, L. (1984). The Social Relations Model. *Advances in Experimental Social Psychology, 18*, 141-182.

Lazega, E., & Van Duijn, M. A. J. (1997). Formal structure and exchanges of advice in a lawfirm: A random effects model. *Social Networks, 19*, 375-397.

Little, R. J. A., & Rubin, D. B. (2002). *Statistical analysis with missing data* (2nd ed.). New York: John Wiley & Sons.

Masten, A. S., Morison, P., & Pellegrini, D. S. (1985). A revised class play method of peer assessment. *Developmental Psychology, 21*, 523-533.

Oldehinkel, A. J., Hartman, C. A., De Winter, A. F., Veenstra, R., & Ormel, J. (2004). Temperament profiles associated with internalizing and externalizing problems in preadolescence. *Development and Psychopathology, 16*, 421-440.

Rodkin, P. C., & Berger, C. (in press). Who bullies whom? Social status asymmetries by victim gender. *International Journal of Behavioral Development*.

Schwartz, D. (2000). Subtypes of victims and aggressors in children's peer groups. *Journal of Abnormal Child Psychology, 28*, 181-192.

Snijders, T. A. B., & Kenny, D. A. (1999). The Social Relations Models for family data: A multilevel approach. *Personal Relationships, 6*, 471-486.

Vaillancourt, T., Hymel, S., & McDougall, P. (2003). Bullying is power: Implications for school-based intervention strategies. *Journal of Applied School Psychology, 19*, 157-176.

Van Duijn, M. A. J., Snijders, T. A. B., & Zijlstra, B. J. H. (2004). p_2: A random effects model with covariates for directed graphs. *Statistica Neerlandica, 58*, 234-254.

Veenstra, R., Lindenberg, S., Oldehinkel, A. J., De Winter, A. F., Verhulst, F. C., & Ormel, J. (2005). Bullying and victimization in elementary schools: A comparison of bullies, victims, bully/victims, and uninvolved preadolescents. *Developmental Psychology, 41*, 672-682.

Veenstra, R., Lindenberg, S., Zijlstra, B. J. H., De Winter, A., Verhulst, F. C., & Ormel, J. (2007). The dyadic nature of bullying and victimization: Testing a dual perspective theory. *Child Development, 78*, 1843-1854.

Wasserman, S., & Faust, K. (1994). *Social network analysis: Methods and applications*. Cambridge: Cambridge University Press.

Zijlstra, B. J. H., Van Duijn, M. A. J., & Snijders, T. A. B. (2006). The multilevel p_2 model: A random effects model for the analysis of multiple social networks. *Methodology, 2*, 42-47.

Zijlstra, B. J. H., Van Duijn, M. A. J., & Snijders, T. A. B. (in press). MCMC estimation of the p_2 model for directed graphs with covariates. *British Journal of Mathematical and Statistical Psychology*.

CHAPTER SIXTEEN

Beyond the Dyad:
Prospects for Social Development

Charles F. Bond, Jr.
David Cross
Texas Christian University

Developmental researchers are interested in a variety of interactions that involve children. One way they pursue this interest is by studying children's play groups. Suppose that a researcher arranges for three children to enter a playroom and notes the amount of time the children play before they leave the room. Perhaps the children would play for half an hour before leaving; perhaps they would play for two hours. Of course, the researcher would want to study more than one play group. Perhaps the mean duration of play across many groups would depend on the age of the children involved, their level of acquaintanceship, time of day, and features of the play environment.

In conducting statistical analyses of their data, many developmental researchers are interested in means—like the mean duration of play across a number of play groups. Our focus is elsewhere. We are interested in differences, not means. We seek to model differences among three-person groups in terms of the people who comprise the group. Here we would want to understand why some groups of three children play longer than others.

Warner, Kenny, and Stoto (1979) pioneered methods for studying groups of size 2. These led to a Social Relations Model (Kenny & La Voie, 1984). It partitions variance among dyadic data points into components that reflect the people comprising the dyads. When Cindy chooses Suzy as a friend, when Buster bullies Alphonzo, developmental psychologists would be well advised to exploit these dyadic methods.

Cook and Dreyer (1984) adapted the Social Relations Model to describe families. They focused on families that consist of a mother, a father, and two children. With Kashy and Kenny (1990), Cook and Dreyer seek to attribute variance in four-person family data to differences among the people who occupy various family roles—differences among women in their role as mother, differences among men in their role as father, differences among children in their roles as older sister and younger brother. For understanding perceptions within the family, for dissecting family interaction patterns, scholars would be wise to draw on these methods.

In the present chapter we present methods for analyzing data from groups of size 3. We partition variance among triadic data points into components that reflect the people constituting those triads. We begin with a simple model for triads, then introduce a series of models of increasing complexity. We can use these models to analyze a number of phenomena in social development—including group play.

An Individualistic Model

Suppose that we have observed a large number of triadic play groups and discovered that the groups vary widely in play duration. Some of the groups play for many hours; others stop playing after barely a minute.

For an initial explanation of these differences, let us note that play groups consist of different individuals. Perhaps groups that include certain individuals play for a long time, and groups that include other individuals do not. Having described this individualistic model in words, let us also offer a statistical description.

For the latter, let

$$X_{ijk} = \mu_X + A_i + A_j + A_k + e_{ijk} \tag{1}$$

where X_{ijk} measures duration of play in a particular group
  (say, a group consisting of Irv, Jane, and Kathy),
μ_X is a population mean,
A_i is Irv's effect on duration of group play,
A_j is Jane's effect,
A_k is Kathy's effect, and
e_{ijk} is a residual term.

This model assumes that when Irv and two other children have the chance to play together, Irv has a certain effect on how long they play. Perhaps Irv's effect is to prolong group play by half an hour; perhaps his effect is to reduce play duration by 10 minutes. The model makes no a priori assumption about whether Irv's membership in a group tends to increase play duration or decrease it, and it says nothing about why this effect occurs. It does, however, presuppose that Irv would have the same effect on duration of play for any three-person play group to which he belonged. Here Jane and Kathy happen to be Irv's play partners; however, that fact is incidental to Irv's effect. More generally, individualistic models assume that the impact of a person on a phenomenon does not depend on the other people in the group.

Here we have been discussing Irv, as well as Jane and Kathy. However, as students of three-person groups our focus is not on these particular children. In fact, we will not be trying to estimate the effect of play duration of any particular child. Rather, we are interested in the determinants of social play—especially the impact on triadic play duration of individuals, as opposed to other factors. We assess the impact of individuals with a variance-partitioning procedure. Our goal is determine the proportion of variance in a three-person phenomenon that is due to variance among individuals. For this purpose, it is insufficient to study a number of independent groups or to study a single group on a number of different occasions. Rather we must configure children into triads, watch the triads play, then reconfigure the same children into different triads (Bond & Kenny, 2002). If we are to assess the impact of individual children on group play, each child must play in more than one group.

In the current chapter, we propose some triadic research designs. These will allow us to quantify the determinants of triadic phenomena. Each design requires us to begin with a certain number of individuals. The number will always be greater than three, and for our purposes it will be a multiple of three. The design will tell us how to configure and reconfigure individuals into three-person groups. We make observations on the resulting triads and analyze those observations to illuminate the variance among triadic data points. The design we use to study a triadic phenomenon will depend on our model for the phenomenon. Among various designs that could be envisioned, we focus on those that require the least time commitment from the individual research participant.

Let us begin with a design that is appropriate for our individualistic model of triadic play duration. We call it the two-trial design. We begin with a set of nine children and (at random) designate each of the nine with a number. We divide these nine children into three triads and measure the duration of play in each triad. We then divide the nine children into three other triads and measure play duration in these latter triads too. The layout of this two-trial design is as follows:

Trial 1:	123	456	789
Trial 2:	147	258	369

Note that each child plays in two triads—once with two children and once with two other children. No pair of children plays together twice. Here we present a statistical procedure for decomposing the variance among triads in the two-trial design into variance due to individuals and other variance.

Let X_{ijk} be duration of play in a triad consisting of child i, child j, and child k. Let M_i be the mean play duration for the two triads that include person i. Let $M_{\bullet\bullet\bullet}$ be mean duration of play across all six triads.

$$\text{Define} \quad SS_1 = \sum (X_{ijk} - M_{\bullet\bullet\bullet})^2$$
$$SS_2 = \sum (M_i - M_{\bullet\bullet\bullet})^2 \quad (2)$$

Let σ_A^2 denote variance due to individuals and σ_e^2 denote other variance.

We are assuming that these variances are related to the effects in equation (1) above. In particular, we make the following assumptions about the expected values of these effects.

$$E(A_i) = E(A_j) = E(A_k) = 0 \qquad E(e_{ijk}) = 0$$
$$E(A_i^2) = E(A_j^2) = E(A_k^2) = \sigma_A^2 \qquad E(e_{ijk}^2) = \sigma_e^2 \quad (3)$$

Given these assumptions, we can use a traditional procedure to yield unbiased estimates of the variances in question. We begin by expressing the expected value of each of the sum of squares in (2) in terms of the variances in (3), solve for the variances, then substitute the observed value of each sum of squares for its expectation. Doing so, we find that

$$E(SS_1) = E(\sum X_{ijk}^2) - 6E(M_{\bullet\bullet\bullet}^2) \qquad (4)$$
$$= (18\sigma_A^2 + 6\sigma_e^2) - 6(\sigma_A^2 + \sigma_e^2/6) = 12\sigma_A^2 + 5\sigma_e^2$$
$$E(SS_2) = E(\sum M_i^2) - 9E(M_{\bullet\bullet\bullet}^2)$$
$$= (18\sigma_A^2 + 4.5\sigma_e^2) - 9(\sigma_A^2 + \sigma_e^2/6) = 9\sigma_A^2 + 3\sigma_e^2$$

Solving these two equations in two unknowns and substituting observed for expected sums of squares, we get unbiased estimates for the variance due to individuals and other variance, respectively, of

$$\hat{\sigma}_A^2 = \frac{5}{9}SS_2 - \frac{1}{3}SS_1 \quad \text{and} \quad \hat{\sigma}_e^2 = SS_1 - \frac{4}{3}SS_2 \qquad (5)$$

The ratio of the first estimate over the second indicates the proportion of variance due to individuals. Note that in the equations above, the order of subscripts on a triadic data point is arbitrary, in that the subscripts can be permuted. Like X_{ijk}, X_{kij} refers to the duration of play in the triad consisting of child i, child j, and child k. Except when noted otherwise, this will be true for all subscripts in the equations below.

Ideally, our developmental researcher would have many independent sets of nine children. If so, he or she could implement the two-trial design with each set, estimate variances from each set, and pool the estimates.

There are other designs for fitting individualistic models to triadic data. The best known is a classical rotation design (Kenny, Hallmark, Sullivan, & Kashy, 1993). It requires each person to participate in four triads, rather than two. Although variance estimates from the classical rotation design may be more precise than variance estimates from our two-trial design, our design requires only half as much time from the individual research participant. For research on children, this time advantage may be crucial.

Suppose that with many replications of the two-trial design, our developmental researcher discovers that 40% of the variance in triadic play duration is due to variance among individuals. This result is suggestive and may tempt the researcher to look to psychological characteristics of individual children as the antecedents of play duration. Before searching for individual differences, the researcher would be wise, though, to recognize a limitation in her two-trial results. Although the two-trial design allows the researcher to isolate variance among individual children in their contribution to play duration, it does not allow her to quantify the impact on play duration of groups of children. Having given each group only one chance to play, the researcher may wish to know whether the group-to-group differences observed would resurface on another occasion. To assess the stability of group differences, our developmental researcher could extend her two-trial design to four trials as follows:

123	456	789	X (Free Play)
123	456	789	Y (Pretend Play)
147	258	369	X (Free Play)
147	258	369	Y (Pretend Play)

Now each of the earlier triads is given two opportunities to play—once in a room that accommodates general free play and once in a room that encourages social pretend play. One wonders if group-to-group differences in play duration will generalize across the two play settings. One also wonders if individuals have similar effects on the duration of these two types of play. As Kenny (1994) notes, sources of interpersonal variance can be stable or unstable. The stable variance in a construct like play duration generalizes across multiple measures of that construct. The unstable variance does not.

Let us now use the equations developed above to estimate the stable variance in play duration due to individuals and due to groups. The approach is simple. We use the equations above three times. First we apply those equations to data on X. Next we apply the equations to data on Y. Finally, we apply the equations to data that represents each triad's total duration of play - that is, the sum of X+Y. From each of the analyses, we extract an estimate of variance due to individuals and other variance. Stable variance can be inferred from inter-relationships for play duration across the two types of play. We would infer perfectly stable group variance if group-level effects on free play were perfectly correlated with group-level effects on pretend play. To the extent that these effects are not perfectly correlated, the variance is unstable.

As Kenny (1994) notes, one can estimate the stable variance for an effect from the following equation:

$$\hat{\sigma}_{X,Y} = 0.5(\hat{\sigma}^2_{X+Y} - \hat{\sigma}^2_X - \hat{\sigma}^2_Y) \tag{6}$$

where $\hat{\sigma}_{X,Y}$ is the stable variance of a particular effect,
$\hat{\sigma}^2_X$ is a variance estimate for the effect from the analysis of X,
$\hat{\sigma}^2_Y$ is a variance estimate for that effect from the analysis of Y, and
$\hat{\sigma}^2_{X+Y}$ is the corresponding variance estimate from the analysis of $X + Y$.

Note that the stable variance of an effect is simply the covariance of that effect in X with the corresponding effect in Y. The unstable variance of the effect is simply that covariance minus the average of the variances of the two measures:

$$\hat{\sigma}_{X,Y} = 0.5(\hat{\sigma}_X^2 + \hat{\sigma}_Y^2) \tag{7}$$

Armed with these new equations, our developmental psychologist runs the four-trial study just described with a new set of nine research participants. Each participant is given four opportunities to play—twice in general free play and twice in pretend play. Analyzing data from this study, the psychologist could draw some conclusions about the impact of individuals on play duration. Suppose results show that (as before) individuals account for roughly 40% of the variance in play duration. From this new study the psychologist discovers, however, that only 10% of the variance in individuals' effects on play duration is stable, the other 90% being specific to one type of play or the other.

From the four-trial study, the developmentalist could also reach conclusions about the impact of groups on play duration. Groups constitute the other source of variance in equation (2). Examining that other variance, our researcher learns that groups account for some 60% of the variance in play duration, that three-fourths of this variance is stable and only one-fourth is unstable. This pattern of results would encourage the researcher to focus on groups as a determinant of play duration. Relative to individuals' effects, group effects on play duration are stronger and more stable.

Each group here consists of three people. However, group-level variance that is extracted from the four-trial design need not be triadic. In fact, variance could be introduced by a combination of two children, and this dyadic variance would show up as variance across groups. This should be apparent. Suppose persons 1 and 2 have a huge positive dyadic effect, while persons 7 and 8 have a huge negative dyadic effect. Then 123 will be displaced upward and 789 will be displaced downward—adding to group-level variance.

A Three-Level Model

Having discovered from a four-trial study large stable variance across triadic play groups that cannot be accounted for by the individuals in the group, our researcher would wish to know if this variance results from the fact that dyads within certain groups have synergistic effects or if the variance emerges from configurations of three children. To extract individual-level variance, dyadic variance, and other variance in play duration from three-person groups, a number of designs could be used. The most comprehensive would be a generalized round-robin design, in which the researcher configured a group of children into every possible triad that could be formed from the group. For the smallest case of $N = 6$, this would require the researcher to observe 20 play triads. A given child would need to play in 10 different groups. For an introduction to the generalized round-robin design, see Bond, Horn, and Kenny (1997). Much simpler than the generalized round-robin is the following three-trial design:

123	456
126	453
134	256

Here each child plays with four of the five other children. Each plays with two of their peers twice and the other two once.

Here equation (1) would not provide an appropriate model for the data, because it does not allow for the possibility of dyadic-level effects. A more appropriate model would be the following

$$X_{ijk} = \mu_X + A_i + A_j + A_k + D_{ij} + D_{ik} + D_{jk} + e_{ijk} \qquad (8)$$

As in equation (1), X_{ijk} measures duration of play in a particular group
   (say, a group consisting of Irv, Jane, and Kathy),
   μ_X is a population mean,
   A_i, A_j, A_k represent effects of Irv, Jane, and Kathy as individuals,
   e_{ijk} is a residual term.

In addition, there is a dyadic-level effect for each pair of individuals in the triad D_{ij}, D_{ik}, and D_{jk} are the effects for dyads consisting of Irv and Jane, Irv and Kathy, and Jane and Kathy, respectively. Again, we assume that the expected value of each effect is 0 and that the expected value of each effect squared is equal to a variance. Variance due to individuals and other variance have been defined above. Now we also have variance due to dyads.

$$E(D_{ij}^2) = E(D_{ik}^2) = E(D_{jk}^2) = \sigma_D^2 \qquad (9)$$

To analyze data from this three-trial design, let X_{ijk}, M_i , and $M_{\bullet\bullet\bullet}$ be defined as above. Let M_{ij} be the mean of the triads involving persons i and j.

Define:

$$
\begin{aligned}
SS_1 &= \sum (X_{ijk} - M_{\bullet\bullet\bullet})^2 \\
SS_2 &= \sum (M_i - M_{\bullet\bullet\bullet})^2 \\
SS_3 &= \sum (X_{ijk} - M_i)^2
\end{aligned}
\tag{10}
$$

Following the ANOVA procedure outlined above, we can express the expected value of each of these three sums of squares in terms of the three population variances (due to individuals, dyads, and other variance). We solve the resulting system of three equations in three unknowns and substitute observed values of the sums of squares for the expected values. What results are unbiased estimates for variance due to individuals, variance due to dyads, and other variance. These are, respectively,

$$
\begin{aligned}
\hat{\sigma}_A^2 &= -\frac{7}{38}SS_1 - \frac{9}{38}SS_2 + \frac{31}{114}SS_3 \\
\hat{\sigma}_D^2 &= \frac{23}{76}SS_1 - \frac{3}{76}SS_2 + \frac{53}{228}SS_3 \\
\hat{\sigma}_e^2 &= -\frac{4}{19}SS_1 - \frac{3}{19}SS_2 + \frac{41}{114}SS_3
\end{aligned}
\tag{11}
$$

Again, our researcher would be wise to double the three-trial design and observe each triad twice under different play conditions. From the resulting six trials, we could estimate the variance of an effect from the duration of general free play (X), the variance of that effect from the duration of social pretend play (Y), and the corresponding variance from X+Y. Then the stable variance of that effect could again be estimated from equation (6) above. Equation (7) would again estimate the unstable variance. Equations (6) and (7) will be applicable anytime we get two measures of the same construct from the same set of research participants and are extracting the same variance components from each measure. For an explanation, see Searle, Casella, and McCullagh (1992, p. 379).

A Copartner Model

There are different ways to assess group play. Each time a group of children play, one might get a single measure of play for the group as a whole—say, the amount of time that elapses before everyone in the group stops playing. Another possibility is to measure some aspect of play for each member of the group individually. Individual-level measures have an advantage over group-level measures, as we now explain.

From group-level measures, one can conduct the analyses outlined above. These allow us to partition differences among triadic play groups into differences among individuals, differences among dyads, and differences among triads. They also allow us to assess the stability of these differences. However, group-level measures obscure an important distinction. Children serve two functions in social play. At a given moment, each child is or is not engaged in play. At that same moment, each child may or may not be stimulating other children to play. From analyses of a group-level measure, our developmental research has drawn conclusions about group play—in particular, the extent to which play duration depends on children as individuals, as dyads, and as triads. However the group-level measures do not allow the researcher to distinguish between differences among children as actors (who at any given moment are more or less likely to be playing) and differences among children as partners (who facilitate or inhibit peer play).

To capture this functional distinction, our researcher must get individual-level measures of play. She arranges new triadic play sessions and notes the duration of each child's play. As before, she seeks to partition variance in the resulting data into different levels (at the individual level vs. the dyadic level, for example). However, the researcher also has a more ambitious goal: to extract components of the data that reflect the two functions each child serves—as an enactor of play and as play partner.

Although we are interested in the statistical analysis of play that involves three children, it will be helpful if we begin by considering a simpler case. Suppose that our developmentalist was studying play that involved only two children, rather than three; and that she wished to describe how long Irv played when Jane was his partner. To do so, she could use the Social Relations Model (or SRM: Kenny & La Voie, 1984; Card, Little, & Selig, chapter 11; Malloy & Cillessen, chapter 10). The SRM would describe how long Irv played with Jane as the sum of four components: a mean, Irv's actor effect, Jane's partner effect, and a relationship effect for Irv and Jane as an actor–partner dyad. Symbolically, this dyadic description is

$$X_{ij} = \mu + A_i + B_j + AB_{ij} \qquad (12)$$

where μ represents mean play duration in a population of dyads,
A_i represents Irv's actor effect (his tendency to play),
B_j represents Jane's partner effect
(her tendency to stimulate peer play),
AB_{ij} represents an emergent actor–partner relationship effect
(for Jane to stimulate Irv).

Applying appropriate statistical procedures to a suitable database (Kenny, 1994), the researcher could partition variance among dyadic observations into variance from actor to actor in the tendency to play, variance from partner to partner in the tendency to stimulate play, and variance from dyad to dyad in the special tendency for one child to stimulate another to play.

Having measured how long Irv played when Jane was his partner, a researcher would also want to measure how long Jane played when partnered with Irv. Let us offer some comments about these reciprocal observations. First, it is important to recognize that the two observations need not be equal. In principle, it would be possible for Irv to play for three hours while Jane stood motionless beside him. Symbolically, this implies that we must distinguish X_{ij} from X_{ji}. The first subscript indexes the actor whose play duration is being measured; the second indexes the partner. Although Irv and Jane would rarely play for exactly the same amount of time when they were in a room together, in playing the two children would be likely to influence one another, and their play times would be interdependent. The SRM assesses interdependence with covariances.

Perhaps a researcher would find that the longer one child plays when in the presence of a second child, the longer the second child plays. The dyadic SRM would partition the resulting covariance into two components—one at the individual level and one at the dyadic level. At the individual level, there is the covariance between an individual's actor effect and his or her partner effect. This actor–partner covariance would be positive if children who generally play for a long time stimulate their partners to play for a long time. At the dyadic level, there is the covariance between one child's special effect on a second child and the second child's special effect on the first. Traditionally, this has been called the dyadic covariance, but here we call it the covariance between actor × partner and partner × actor. Suppose that it was true that if one child had a special tendency to stimulate another child to play, the second child had a special tendency to stimulate the first. This would produce a positive covariance at the level of the dyad between actor × partner and partner × actor.

Although the Social Relations Model would offer an appropriate framework for understanding dyadic play, our developmental psychologist is interested in play that involves three children—not two. Thus, she will assess how long Irv plays when he is in a room with Jane and Kate. To analyze the resulting data, our psychologist might be tempted to treat each triadic observation as though it were two dyadic data points. Having measured how long Irv plays when partnered with Jane and Kate, the researcher would (under this plan) enter Irv's play duration into a two-way actor × partner matrix. In fact, she would enter this play duration twice—once with Irv as actor and Jane as partner and a second time with Irv as actor and Kate as partner. Having entered a number of triadic observations into a two-way actor × partner matrix in this fashion, the psychologist might then consider it appropriate to analyze her data with the dyadic Social Relations Model. We cannot endorse this practice. Models of a social phenomenon should reflect all of the people who contribute to the phenomenon and all of the influences those people may have.

For a description of how long Irv plays when partnered with Jane *and* Kate, we favor a three-person copartner model (Bond & Kenny, 2002).

$$X_{ijk} = \mu + A_i + B_j + B_k + AB_{ij} + AB_{ik} + BB_{jk} + ABB_{ijk} \qquad (13)$$

Here μ represents mean play duration in a population of triads
   A_i represents Irv's actor effect (his tendency to play),
   B_j represents a partner effect (for Jane),
   B_k represents a second partner effect (for Kate),
   AB_{ij} represents an actor × partner effect (for Irv and Jane),
   AB_{ik} represents a second actor × partner effect (for Irv and Kate),
   BB_{jk} represents a dyadic partner × partner effect
      (for Jane and Kate),
   ABB_{ijk} represents a triadic actor × partner × partner effect
      (for Irv, Jane, and Kate).

For analyzing Irv's duration of play on this occasion, we have no a priori reason to distinguish between Jane and Kate as play partners. Thus, equation (4) designates these two play partners by the same letter (B). Although we have listed the two play partners in a certain order (first Jane, then Kate), it would have been equally appropriate to list them in the reverse order (first Kate, then Jane). Thus, Irv's play when partnered with Jane and Kate is identical to Irv's play when partnered with Kate and Jane. More generally, the copartner model requires that $X_{ijk} = X_{ikj}$. The first subscript designates the actor. Its position is fixed. Because the second and third subscripts designate copartners, they can be transposed.

Let us note some differences between the SRM and the copartner model. The SRM accommodates two-way actor × partner data. As a two-way ANOVA model, the SRM describes these data with a mean and three effects— a main effect for actor, a main effect for partner, and an actor × partner interaction. The copartner model describes three-way actor × partner × partner data. It does so with a mean and seven effects—a main effect for the actor, a main effect for each of the two partners, two actor × partner interaction effects, a partner × partner interaction effect, and a three-way actor × partner × partner interaction effect.

Like the SRM, the copartner model is a random-effects ANOVA. It partitions variance in three-way actor × partner × partner data into components. Like the SRM, it estimates a variance from actor to actor in the tendency to play, a variance from partner to partner in the tendency to stimulate peer play, and a variance across actor–partner dyads in the actor's special tendency to be stimulated by the play partner. In addition, the copartner model extracts two other sources of variance—partner × partner variance and actor × partner × partner variance. Like actor/partner dyads, partner/partner dyads may have synergistic effects. Jane and Kate would have a positive partner × partner effect if when serving as copartners they stimulated peer play beyond what would be predicted from the sum of their individual partner effects. Jane and Larry would have a negative effect if as copartners they inhibit peer play more than would be expected from the sum of their partner effects. Statistically, partner × partner effects represent departures from additivity, and partner × partner variance reflects differences across dyads in these two-way interaction effects.

Actor × partner × partner effects receive input from three individuals, one functioning as an actor and two as partners. The effect represents any special impact the copartners have on this particular actor. Jane and Kate's actor × partner × partner effect on Irv would be positive if (as copartners) Jane and Kate stimulated Irv's play more than they stimulated the average child's play. Jane and Irv's actor × partner × partner effect on Kate would be negative if (as copartners) they inhibited Kate's play more than they inhibited the play of the other children. Statistically, actor × partner × partner effects represent three-way interaction effects, and differences among the effects produce actor × partner × partner variance. To disentangle this variance from error, a researcher would need to measure each triad with more than one indicator or on more than one occasion.

Like the dyadic SRM, the copartner model can handle interdependencies in data. It assesses interdependencies with four covariances: one at the individual level, two at the dyadic level, and one at the triadic level. These are the covariance between actor effects and partner effects, the covariance between reciprocal actor × partner effects, the covariance between actor × partner effects with partner × partner effects, and the covariance between reciprocal actor × partner × partner effects. Let us explain each of these forms of interdependence.

Like the dyadic SRM, the copartner model recognizes that actor effects may be related to partner effects—Irv's tendency to stimulate peer play may depend on Irv's own tendency to play. Like the dyadic SRM, the copartner model also acknowledges that Jane's special effect on Irv's tendency to play may be related to Irv's special effect on Jane. Statistically, this would produce a covariance between two actor × partner effects. In the first effect, Irv is the actor and Jane is the partner; in the second, the two individuals swap functions, so that Jane becomes the actor and Irv becomes the partner. To denote the function swapping, we call this an interdependence between actor × partner and partner × actor.

Another interdependence in the copartner model has no counterpart in the SRM. Suppose that Jane has a special tendency to stimulate Irv's play. Perhaps this is associated with a special synergistic influence Jane and Irv have when the two are paired as partners. If so, Kate and Larry and Melanie (indeed all actors) would have a special tendency to play when placed in a room with Irv and Jane. Statistically, this would contribute to a positive dyadic covariance between actor × partner effects and partner × partner effects. Here we are acknowledging the possibility of a covariance between one type of dyadic effect (actor × partner) and another type (partner × partner), so long as the two effects involve the same pair of individuals. In this way, the interdependence between actor × partner and partner × partner differs from the form of dyadic interdependence familiar to students of the SRM—between an effect involving two functions and a reciprocal effect involving those same functions.

Finally, the copartner model allows for a triadic interdependence. Suppose that Irv plays for a longer time when partnered with Jane and Kate than one would expect based on all relevant individual-level and dyadic-level effects. Perhaps Jane would also play for a longer time than expected on these occasions. This would produce a positive covariance between two actor × partner × partner effects. In the first effect, Irv is the actor and Jane is one of the partners (along with Kate). For the second effect, Irv and Jane swap functions so that Jane becomes the actor and Irv becomes Kate's copartner. Again, we wish to denote the swapping of functions, so we call this a triadic covariance between actor × partner × partner and partner × actor × partner.

Triadic Relations Model

Having analyzed individual-level measures of play duration with the copartner model, our psychologist draws some conclusions. Most of the variance in triadic play duration is stable, and most of it derives from three sources: partner variance, partner × partner variance, and actor × partner variance. Studying videotapes of play interactions, the psychologist forms a hypothesis about these results. She focuses on instances when two of the children in a triad are playing with one another and the third child seeks to join them in play. Sometimes, the third child begins playing with the other two, and the three proceed to interact cooperatively. On other occasions, one of the two playmates rejects the third child's overture, excluding her from play. These social exclusions may underlie differences in play duration and are of interest in their own right (Feshbach & Sones, 1971; Williams, 2001).

To understand social rejection, the psychologist studies the tapes more closely, coding the number of exclusion episodes. These episodes arise when two children are playing and the third tries to join them in play. Each child serves a different function in social exclusion. One child functions as an actor—rejecting the play overture. One is the actor's play partner. And the third child becomes an outcast, having had her play overture rebuffed. Reviewing her videotapes, our psychologist codes each instance of social exclusion, noting the children who serve each of the three functions. On one occasion, for example, she notes that Irv rejects Kate to play exclusively with Jane. Thus, Irv is the actor; Jane is the partner; and Kate is the outcast.

For analyzing such instances, we would use the following model:

$$X_{ijk} = \mu + A_i + B_j + C_k + AB_{ij} + AC_{ik} + BC_{jk} + ABC_{ijk} \qquad (14)$$

Here X_{ijk} represents the number of times Irv rejects Kate
     to play with Jane,
    A_i represents Irv's actor effect (his tendency to exclude peers),
    B_j represents Jane's partner effect (to inspire social exclusion),
    C_k represents Kate's outcast effect (to initiate overtures that
     are rejected),
    AB_{ij} represents an actor × partner effect (for Irv and Jane),
    AC_{ik} represents an actor × outcast effect (for Irv and Kate),
    BC_{jk} represents a partner × outcast effect (for Jane and Kate),
    ABC_{ijk} represents a triadic actor × partner × outcast effect
     (for Irv, Jane, and Kate).

This Triadic Relations Model (Bond, Horn, & Kenny, 1997) offers an appropriate description for phenomena that involve three individuals serving three distinct functions. Here the functions are actor, partner, and outcast. Measures that are appropriate for this model must distinguish among the individuals who serve each function. Symbolically, this implies that Triadic Relations measures must have three subscripts, with the position of each subscript fixed. X_{ijk}, for example, refers to Irv's rejections of Kate when Irv is playing with Jane. X_{ikj} would refer to something different—Irv's rejections of Jane when he was playing with Kate.

Let us introduce the Triadic Relations Model by comparison to the co-partner model. Like the copartner model, the Triadic Relations Model (or TRM) describes a triadic data point as the sum of seven effects: three at the individual level, three at the dyadic level, and one at the triadic level. Like the copartner model, the TRM attributes variance among triadic data points to variance in these effects. Our psychologist will find actor variance in social exclusion data if some children typically exclude peers from play dyads, while others do not. The psychologist will find partner variance if (as dyadic play partners) some children inspire social exclusion, while others do not. The psychologist will find outcast variance if some children initiate many failed play overtures, while others do not. She may also find dyadic variance in her data—actor × partner variance if there are more rejected attempts to join certain actor/partner dyads than others, actor × outcast variance if certain children are especially likely (and others are unlikely) to be rejected by a particular peer, and partner × outcast variance if certain children are likely (and others are unlikely) to be rejected by those who are playing with a particular peer. Triadic variance would be evident if certain actors had a special tendency to outcast certain peers when playing with certain partners. Again, triadic variance could be distinguished from error variance by assessing social exclusions on more than one occasion.

In decomposing variance, the TRM resembles a standard three-way random-effects ANOVA model. As usual, there are seven effects in the model and seven corresponding sources of variance. The TRM becomes more intricate when it allows for interdependencies among data points. It allows for an interdependency between any effect of an individual (or combination of individuals) with any other effect of that individual (or combination of individuals). This yields 16 covariances: three at the individual level, nine at the dyadic level, and four at the triadic level. Some of these interdependencies may be of a priori interest to the TRM researcher; others may not. In any case, the researcher would be wise to look for all of 16 forms of interdependence, if only to discover that many of them are negligible in the data set at hand.

At the individual level, the TRM considers interdependencies between actor and partner, between actor and outcast, and between partner and outcast. Our researcher would find a negative covariance between actor and partner if children who often reject peers preempt the need for their playmates to reject them; she would find a positive covariance between actor and outcast if children who are often rejected when they try to join a play dyad show a generalized retaliation by rejecting peers who wish to join their play dyads.

At the dyadic level, there are nine interdependencies. There can be an independency between any dyadic effect involving two particular children with any other dyadic effect involving those same children. Thus, an actor × partner effect (of Irv rejecting those who would intrude when he was playing with Jane) might be related to the reciprocal actor × partner effect (of Jane rejecting those who would intrude when she was playing with Irv). Here an effect involving two functions is related to an effect involving those same functions, when two individuals reverse the functions they enact. As before, we designate this function reversal in our notation. Thus, we label three forms of dyadic interdependence as actor × partner with partner × actor, actor × outcast with outcast × actor, and partner × outcast with outcast × partner. These should be accessible to readers who are familiar with the dyadic Social Relations Model.

Like the copartner model, the Triadic Relations Model also allows for a different form of dyadic interdependence—between two distinct types of dyadic effect, so long as the individuals who contribute to the first type also contribute to the second. Suppose Irv has a special tendency to reject peers who want to intrude when he is playing with Jane. Perhaps Irv would show a special tendency not to reject Jane's efforts to join Irv when he was playing with someone else. If so, this would contribute to a negative covariance between actor × partner effects and actor × outcast effects. Similarly, actor × partner effects might be related to outcast × partner effects, and actor × outcast effects might be related to partner × outcast effects. There would be a positive covariance between an actor × partner effect and outcast × partner effect if Irv's rejection of peers when he was playing with Jane inspired peers to reject Irv when they had the chance to play with Jane. In this example, Jane serves as the partner in both the actor × partner and outcast × partner effect. Indeed, the same individual serves a common function in all three forms of dyadic interdependence we have mentioned: actor × partner with actor × outcast, actor × outcast with partner × outcast, as well as actor × partner with outcast × partner.

The remaining dyadic interdependencies in the TRM are complementary to these three. We designate the remaining interdependencies as: actor × partner with outcast × actor, actor × partner with partner × outcast, and actor × outcast with outcast × partner. Assume that Irv has a special tendency to reject peers when playing with Jane. Perhaps this would motivate children to exclude Jane when they were playing with Irv. This would contribute to a positive covariance between actor × partner and partner × outcast. Note that Jane serves as the partner in the first effect and Irv serves this function in the second.

The TRM allows for covariances between any effect of a particular triad and any other effect of that triad. Thus if Irv rejects Jane when playing with Kate, several related effects might be observed. Kate might be preempted from rejecting Jane by Irv's rejection of her; Jane might retaliate by rejecting Irv when she plays with Kate; Irv might invite Kate to join when he is playing with Jane; or Jane might reject Kate when playing with Irv. These would contribute to four distinct triadic covariances: a negative covariance of actor × partner × outcast with partner × actor × outcast, a positive covariance of actor × partner × outcast with outcast × partner × actor, a negative covariance of actor × partner × outcast with actor × outcast × partner, and a positive covariance of actor × partner × outcast with partner × outcast × actor.

To understand these triadic interdependencies, it is helpful to associate them with interdependencies at the dyadic level. In fact, each triadic interdependence in our example serves to qualify one of the dyadic interdependencies we have described. One example should suffice to illustrate this point. In general, actor–partner dyads may introduce an interdependence into data when they swap functions—if the actor's rejection of peer overtures to join a play dyad preempts the partner from the need to reject such overtures. The resulting dyadic covariance is between actor × partner and partner × actor. Suppose, though, that the preemption is specific to one outcast. If the actor's rejection of a particular peer (more than others) preempts the partner's rejection of that peer (more than others), we are led to a triadic interdependence between actor × partner × outcast with partner × actor × outcast.

Generalized Block Design

Like the other triadic models we have been discussing, the Triadic Relations Model requires data from a reconfiguration design (Bond & Kenny, 2002). It cannot be fit to data from disjoint triads or a single triad measured on numerous occasions. It requires individuals to be configured into triads and then reconfigured into other triads. Unlike the simpler models, it requires each individual to fulfill three different functions within the triad.

Warner, Kenny, and Stoto (1979) described a round-robin design for dyadic models. It requires each individual in a group to interact as part of a dyad with each of the other individuals in the group. Each member of the dyad serves two different functions—as actor and partner, for instance. The smallest round-robin design for fitting the dyadic Social Relations Model consists of 12 data points—each of the individuals in a group of four forms a dyad with every other individual in that group, and the dyad produces two data points (as dyad members swap functions). In this minimal round-robin design, each research participant contributes to six data points—three as an actor and three as a partner.

Bond, Horn, and Kenny (1997) proposed an analogous design for the Triadic Relations Model. Theirs is a generalized round-robin. It requires each subset of three individuals in a group to interact as a triad. Each member of the triad serves three different functions—as actor, partner, and outcast, for example. The smallest generalized round-robin design for fitting the Triadic Relations Model consists of 120 data points. From a group of six individuals, all 20 possible triads are formed, and each of these produces six data points (as the researcher observes every possible assignment of the three triad members to three functions). In this minimal generalized round-robin, each research participant contributes to 60 data points—20 when serving one function, 20 when serving a second function, and 20 when serving a third function. For some research questions, contribution to a given data point requires the individual to invest some substantial amount of time—10 minutes, 20 minutes, or even an hour. For those questions, the generalized round-robin is impractical. It would be especially impractical in studies of young children.

Here we present another triadic design—the generalized block design. From this design, one can estimate the seven variances and sixteen covariances in the Triadic Relations Model. Relative to the generalized round-robin, this design requires substantially less time from the individual. We hope that it will encourage use of the TRM to address a broader range of research questions.

The number of individuals in a triadic block design is $3N$—where N is a number greater than 1. These individuals are assigned to three equal-sized groups of size N. Let us call each such group a block. Individuals participate in the research in groups of size 3. The generalized block design consists of all such groups that can be formed such that all three of the members of the group belong to different blocks. Suppose, for example, that $N=2$. Then six individuals would participate, and we could assign individuals 1 and 2 to one block, 3 and 4 to a second block, and 5 and 6 to a third block. Individual 1 would participate in the following triads: 135, 136, 145, and 146. The number of triads would equal $2 \times 2 \times 2$—or 8. More generally, the triadic block design yields $N \times N \times N$ triads—where N is the size of each block.

This design could be used with several of the models we have discussed. It could be used to analyze a single datum produced by each group—say, the duration of play for the group as a whole. Then the total number of data points in the $2 \times 2 \times 2$ design would be 8—one for each group. The design could also be used to fit the copartner model. There, two of the members of the group serve one function (B), while the third serves a distinct function (A). Then each group yields three data points (with the first member of the group, then the second, and finally the third serving the A function). So the total number of copartner data points for the $2 \times 2 \times 2$ design would be 24. Each child participates in four distinct groups, and those groups contribute 12 data points to the results.

Our current interest is in fitting the Triadic Relations Model to block data. Here the three members of a triad serve three distinct functions. To rotate each individual through each function, the analyst will need data from the $3 \times 2 \times 1$ (=6) permutations of a given group. Thus, individual 1 (and every other individual in this generalized block) would contribute data to 24 triads. For fully triadic data, the number of data points in the $2 \times 2 \times 2$ generalized block design is 48, with each individual contributing data to four groups (and 24 data points). More generally, the $N \times N \times N$ generalized block design produces $6 \times N \times N \times N$ triadic data points, each individual contributing to $6 \times N \times N$ data points.

Having collected data from a triadic block design, the researcher will need to conduct an appropriate analysis. Here we offer a traditional analytic procedure, three-block design. For a block study of social exclusion with N individuals per block, seven triadic relations variances can be estimated: actor variance (σ_A^2), partner variance (σ_B^2), outcast variance (σ_C^2), actor $\times$ partner variance ($\sigma_{A \times B}^2$), actor $\times$ outcast variance ($\sigma_{A \times C}^2$), partner $\times$ outcast variance ($\sigma_{B \times C}^2$), and triadic variance ($\sigma_{A \times B \times C}^2$). To estimate these variances from one of the six blocks (say, people from block 1 functioning as actors, people from block 2 functioning as partners, and block 3 functioning as outcasts), one would begin by computing the following sums of squares:

$$S_A = \sum_{i=1}^{N} (M_{i\bullet\bullet} - M_{\bullet\bullet\bullet})^2$$

$$S_B = \sum_{j=1}^{N} (M_{\bullet j\bullet} - M_{\bullet\bullet\bullet})^2$$

$$S_C = \sum_{k=1}^{N} (M_{\bullet\bullet k} - M_{\bullet\bullet\bullet})^2$$

$$S_{A \times B} = \sum_{i=1}^{N} \sum_{j=1}^{N} (M_{ij\bullet} - M_{i\bullet\bullet} - M_{\bullet j\bullet} + M_{\bullet\bullet\bullet})^2$$

$$\boldsymbol{S}_{A\times C} = \sum_{i=1}^{N}\sum_{j=1}^{N}(\boldsymbol{M}_{i\bullet k} - \boldsymbol{M}_{i\bullet\bullet} - \boldsymbol{M}_{\bullet\bullet k} + \boldsymbol{M}_{\bullet\bullet\bullet})^2$$

$$\boldsymbol{S}_{B\times C} = \sum_{i=1}^{N}\sum_{j=1}^{N}(\boldsymbol{M}_{\bullet jk} - \boldsymbol{M}_{\bullet j\bullet} - \boldsymbol{M}_{\bullet\bullet k} + \boldsymbol{M}_{\bullet\bullet\bullet})^2$$

$$\boldsymbol{S}_{A\times B\times C} = \sum_{i=1}^{N}\sum_{j=1}^{N}\sum_{k=1}^{N}$$
$$(\boldsymbol{X}_{ijk} - \boldsymbol{M}_{ij\bullet} - \boldsymbol{M}_{i\bullet k} - \boldsymbol{M}_{\bullet jk} + \boldsymbol{M}_{i\bullet\bullet} + \boldsymbol{M}_{\bullet j\bullet} + \boldsymbol{M}_{\bullet\bullet k} - \boldsymbol{M}_{\bullet\bullet\bullet})^2$$

A complete triadic relations analysis would also require computation of 19 sums of cross products. Here we illustrate how they would be computed, by computing three: (1) the sum of cross products for the covariance between the actor effect and the partner effect, (2) the sum of cross products for the covariance between the actor × partner effect and the outcast × partner effect, and (3) the sum of cross products for the covariance between the actor × partner × outcast effect and the partner × actor × outcast effect.

$$(1)\ \boldsymbol{S}_{A,B} = \sum_{i=1}^{N}(\boldsymbol{M}_{i\bullet\bullet} - \boldsymbol{M}_{\bullet\bullet\bullet})(\boldsymbol{M}_{\bullet i\bullet} - \boldsymbol{M}_{\bullet\bullet\bullet})$$

$$(2)\ \boldsymbol{S}_{A\times B,C\times B} = \sum_{i=1}^{N}\sum_{j=1}^{N}$$
$$(\boldsymbol{M}_{ij\bullet} - \boldsymbol{M}_{i\bullet\bullet} - \boldsymbol{M}_{\bullet j\bullet} + \boldsymbol{M}_{\bullet\bullet\bullet})(\boldsymbol{M}_{\bullet ji} - \boldsymbol{M}_{\bullet j\bullet} - \boldsymbol{M}_{\bullet\bullet i} + \boldsymbol{M}_{\bullet\bullet\bullet})$$

$$(3)\ \boldsymbol{S}_{A\times B\times C,B\times A\times C} = \sum_{i=1}^{N}\sum_{j=1}^{N}\sum_{k=1}^{N}$$
$$(\boldsymbol{X}_{ijk} - \boldsymbol{M}_{ij\bullet} - \boldsymbol{M}_{i\bullet k} - \boldsymbol{M}_{\bullet jk} + \boldsymbol{M}_{i\bullet\bullet} + \boldsymbol{M}_{\bullet j\bullet} + \boldsymbol{M}_{\bullet\bullet k} - \boldsymbol{M}_{\bullet\bullet\bullet})$$
$$(\boldsymbol{X}_{jik} - \boldsymbol{M}_{ji\bullet} - \boldsymbol{M}_{j\bullet k} - \boldsymbol{M}_{\bullet ik} + \boldsymbol{M}_{j\bullet\bullet} + \boldsymbol{M}_{\bullet i\bullet} + \boldsymbol{M}_{\bullet\bullet k} - \boldsymbol{M}_{\bullet\bullet\bullet})$$

Having computed these quantities and given $N > 1$, we can get standard ANOVA estimates for the variance components in a nonreplicated three-way random-effects design. See Searle, Casella, and McCulloch (1992, chapter 4). We estimate the actor variance from

$$\hat{\sigma}_A^2 = \frac{[\boldsymbol{S}_A - \boldsymbol{S}_{A\times B}/(\boldsymbol{N}-1) - \boldsymbol{S}_{A\times C}/(\boldsymbol{N}-1) + \boldsymbol{S}_{A\times B\times C}/(\boldsymbol{N}-1)^2]}{[\boldsymbol{N}^2(\boldsymbol{N}-1)]} \quad (15)$$

and all of the other individual-level variances and covariance from analogous equations. We estimate the actor × partner variance from

$$\hat{\sigma}^2_{A \times B} = \frac{(S_{A \times B} - S_{A \times B \times C})}{[N(N-1)^2]} \tag{16}$$

and all of the other dyadic-level variances and covariances from analogous equations. We estimate the actor × partner × outcast variance from

$$\hat{\sigma}^2_{A \times B \times C} = \frac{S_{A \times B \times C}}{(N-1)^3} \tag{17}$$

and all of the triadic-level covariances from analogous equations.

Having estimated all of the triadic relations variances and covariances within each of our six blocks, we average those estimates across blocks. The resulting estimators are unbiased, minimum-variance, and translation-invariant (Searle, Casella, & McCulloch, 1992).

CONCLUSION

Life becomes more complicated for developmental psychologists when they look beyond the dyad. Special research designs are required, and special analytic techniques must be used. These are extensions of dyadic designs and techniques (Kenny, Kashy, & Cook, 2006). Phenomena that involve three people can be considered at various levels of complexity. The simplest model is individualistic and the most complex assesses all possible triadic relations. Some triads consist of an actor and two copartners; others yield only group-level data. These don't require analysts to fathom all of the intricacies of triadic relations. We invite researchers to incorporate these insights into their understanding of social development.

REFERENCES

Bond, C. F., Jr., Horn, E. M., & Kenny, D. A. (1997). A model for triadic relations. *Psychological Methods, 2*, 79-94.

Bond, C. F., Jr., & Kenny, D. A. (2002). The triangle of interpersonal models. *Journal of Personality and Social Psychology, 83*, 355-366.

Bond, C. F., Jr., Kenny, D. A., Broome, E. H., Stokes-Zoota, J. J., & Richard, F. D. (2000). Multivariate analysis of triadic relations. *Multivariate Behavioral Research, 35*, 397-426.

Card, N., Little, T. D., & Selig, J. P. (chapter 11). Using the bivariate Social Relations Model to study dyadic relationships: Early adolescents' perceptions of friends' aggression and prosocial behavior. In N. A. Card, J. P. Selig, & T. D. Little (Eds.), *Modeling dyadic and interdependent data in the developmental and behavioral sciences.* New York, NY: Routledge/Taylor & Francis Group.

Cook, W. L., & Dreyer, A. S. (1984). The social relations model: A new approach to the analysis of family-dyadic interactions. *Journal of Marriage and the Family, 46*, 679-687.

Feshbach, N., & Sones, G. (1971). Sex differences in adolescent reactions to a newcomer. *Developmental Psychology, 4*, 381-386.

Kashy, D. A., & Kenny, D. A. (1990). Analysis of family research designs: A model of interdependence. *Communication Research, 17*, 462-482.

Kenny, D. A. (1994). Using the Social Relations Model to understand relationships. In R. Erber & R. Gilmour (Eds.), *Theoretical frameworks for personal relationships.* Mahwah, NJ: Lawrence Erlbaum.

Kenny, D. A., Hallmark, B. W., Sullivan, P., & Kashy, D. A. (1993). The analysis of designs in which individuals are in more than one group. *British Journal of Social Psychology, 32*, 173-190.

Kenny, D. A., Kashy, D. A., & Cook, W. L. (2006). *Dyadic data analysis.* New York: Guilford Press.

Kenny, D. A., & La Voie, L. (1984). The Social Relations Model. In L. Berkowitz (Ed.), *Advances in experimental social psychology* (Vol. 14, pp. 141-182). New York: Academic Press.

Malloy, T. E., & Cillessen, A. H. N. (chapter 10). Variance component analysis of generalized and dyadic peer perceptions in adolescence. In N. A. Card, J. P. Selig, & T. D. Little (Eds.), *Modeling dyadic and interdependent data in the developmental and behavioral sciences.* New York, NY: Routledge/Taylor & Francis Group.

Searle, S. R., Casella, G., & McCulloch, C. E. (1992). *Variance components.* New York: John Wiley & Sons.

Warner, R. M., Kenny, D., & Stoto, M. (1979). A new round robin analysis of variance for social interaction data. *Journal of Personality and Social Psychology, 37*, 1742-1757.

Williams, K. (2001). *Ostracism: The power of silence.* New York: Guilford Press.

CHAPTER SEVENTEEN

Thinking About the Developmental Course of Relationships

David A. Kenny

University of Connecticut

This book focuses on the intersection of two incredibly challenging topics: relationships and development. By itself each topic is daunting, and any integration of the two topics becomes an almost impossible challenge. That said, the two topics need to be integrated. To discuss relationships without discussing change is not to understand relationships and to discuss change without understanding how change is embedded in relationships is not to understand change. Thus, if we are to understand each topic, we need to understand the other, and we are forced to face the challenge of a combined understanding of both change and relationships. Moreover, in recent years considerable progress has been made in both of these areas, and they have begun to communicate to one another. This book continues that dialogue.

Time and relationships are similar in the sense that both create similarity between a pair of scores. With time, the similarity is called *stability* or *autocorrelation*, and with relationships, the similarity is usually called *nonindependence*. Combining these two difficult problems presents us with a most challenging opportunity.

In this chapter, I first attempt to provide a systematic overview of each topic. I then attempt to integrate them. Throughout, I use the various chapters in the book to illustrate that integration. In a single chapter, I cannot provide all the details and formulas, but I do provide citations to more detailed sources. Moreover, in some cases, I am not aware of statistical or computational solutions to the questions raised. In some ways, the chapter represents an agenda for future work. The chapter then has three major sections: relationships, change, and an initial integration of the two.

This chapter begins with an examination of relationships. There the focus is on three questions. The first is the linkage structure or who has links to whom. I then consider the measurement of variables and next causal effects in relationships.

STUDYING RELATIONSHIPS

The Linkage Structure: Who Is Linked to Whom?

Usually not all of the people in our studies have relationships with one another. If there are n people in the study, the set of possible linkages can be represented as an n by n matrix commonly denoted as W (Cliff & Ord, 1973). An entry of w_{ij} denotes that person i has a relational tie with person j. Although it is possible that w_{ij} may not be symmetric (i.e., $w_{ij} \neq w_{ji}$), the chapter limits itself to the simpler symmetric case.

There are important specialized linkage structures. In a *standard dyad* structure, each person linked to one and only one person. For this structure, there is one link in each row and column of W. For instance, Kashy and Donnellan (chapter 8) studied 450 child–adolescent dyads. An adolescent is linked to his or her mother, but not linked to any other adolescent or mother. The standard dyad structure is commonly called a *dyadic* structure.

A second common linkage structure is a *group* structure. The persons are divided into groups and each member of the group is linked to every other member of the group. Families are an example of this. For instance, in Branje, Finkenauer, and Meeus's study (chapter 12), there are 323 four-person families. All persons in the same family are linked to each other. The size of the groups need not be equal. For instance, several chapters (Card, Little, & Selig, chapter 11 ; Cillessen & Borch , chapter 4; Malloy & Cillessen, chapter 10; Zijlstra, Veenstra & van Duijn, chapter 15) studied groups of varying size. In particular, Zijlstra et al. (chapter 15; reported more fully in Veenstra et al., 2007) studied 122 schools of varying size.

In a group structure, each person is a member of one and only one group. When the groups are overlapping, as in the study by Cillessen and Borch (chapter 4), persons are members of multiple groups, often referred to as *cliques*.

For both the dyad and group linkage structure, there is an important consideration of distinguishability. Consider the study by Kashy and Donnellan (chapter 8) where the two people who are linked are mother and child. The two members of the dyad are distinguished by family role and the dyad is said to be *distinguishable*. A similar distinction can be made for group members. In studies of Branje et al. (chapter 12) and Cook (chapter 3), members of groups are distinguished by their family role. Note, however, for the Card et al. study (chapter 11), the students in the classroom are indistinguishable: There is no reasonable way to order children in the classroom.

The final possibility considered is a network structure. There is a group a people and some of the persons, but not all, are linked to one another. In fact, one person may not be linked to any of the other members in the group. Such a structure is found in Kindermann (chapter 14).

A given group may have multiple linkage structures. For instance, there might be in a network some choices that are reciprocal, designated as W_1, and others nonreciprocal, designated as W_2. Alternatively in a network, it might be asked with whom the person works or W_1 and with whom the person parties or W_2. Change in the linkage structure can be represented as different W matrices.

A fundamental question is how to determine W. The experimental design sometimes specifies the linkage structure. Researchers bring into the laboratory individuals who then interact with one another. Consider the study by Latané and L'Herrou (1996) in which there were 25 persons each of whom is linked to four different others, but the linkage structures were quite different.

Alternatively, the sampling unit defines W. Researchers often sample couples or families and either a dyad or group W is assumed. For example, it is assumed that four family members in Branje et al. (chapter 12) are all linked to each other and to no one else in the study.

Finally, W can be empirically derived. Normally, this is what is done when W has a network structure. Group members state who in the group is their friend. The chapter by Kindermann (chapter 14) describes the Social Cognitive Mapping technique for obtaining W using a method developed by Cairns, Perrin, and Cairns (1985). Cillessen and Borch (chapter 4) use an algorithm to determine cliques. Finally, Templin (chapter 13) proposes an innovative use of mixture modeling to estimate groups of persons.

It can happen in relationship research that it is known that a person has a link or tie to another person, but that other person is not measured. Consider a study that compares people who are married versus those who are not. For the married couples, only one of the two members of the marriage is measured. In this case, there is a W matrix and each person may or may not have a link to another person, but for people with a link, their partner would not be measured.

MEASUREMENT OF VARIABLES

Special attention needs to be given to the specific types of variables in the study. There are several key issues in the measurement of variables. They are the measurement scale, the unit of measurement, and types of variables.

The issue of unit of measurement is particularly relevant for the study of relationships.

Measurement Scale

Generally today, variables are considered to be one of three types: quantities, counts, and categories. More conventionally, quantities are said to be measured at the interval level of measurement and categories are measured at the nominal level. Counts are assumed to have a Poisson distribution. In this chapter, the focus is on quantities, as it is the structure most commonly assumed. Also considered are categorical variables as is appropriate for nomination data (Card, Little, & Selig, chapter 11; Zijlstra et al., chapter 15).

Unit of Measurement

For relationships, the unit of measurement of the variables is an important consideration. As an example, take the case of families. Some measures can be called *monadic* or *individual*. For such a measure, there is one score for each member of the family. An example of such a measure would be the age of the person in the family. Other measurements are called *dyadic*. Each person has a score to every one person to whom he or she is linked. In this case, the father's affection toward his wife and each of his children would be measured. By definition in dyadic measurement, there are two people: the person who provides the data point and the person's partner. A third type of measure is a group measurement. Family size would be a group measure. Although the vast majority of measurements in the study of relationships are either monadic, dyadic or group, other types of measurements are possible (Bond & Kenny, 2002). For instance, as discussed by Bond and Cross (chapter 16), there is triadic measurement. There is a score for person i who is linked to person j who is linked to person k. For instance, the father might be asked to report on the mother's affection toward each of her children.

Types of Variables

The third issue refers to the associations between variables in a model. Classically, some variables are viewed as independent variables and others as dependent variables. In this chapter, variables are denoted as either *fixed* or *random* variables. A random variable is an outcome variable and the major interest is how it is affected by other variables in the model. Note, however, one random variable might cause another random variable. A fixed variable is a variable all of whose levels are sampled. For instance, gender would be considered a fixed variable. Normally, fixed variables are treated as causal variables.

MEASUREMENT OF THE STRENGTH OF LINKAGE

Earlier the concept of a linkage structure was introduced and symbolized by the matrix W. When a person has a relationship with another person, there is a linkage. That linkage can be viewed as a correlation between observations. That is, two people who are linked are more similar (or different) than two people who are not linked. In this section, it is described how that correlation can be measured for different linkage structures.

Measuring strength of linkage is important for several reasons. First, it is a measure of nonindependence. If persons who are linked have similar responses, then the two people cannot be considered as independent replications and should not be used as the unit of analysis. Second, strength of linkage measures the degree to which two persons are tied together. That strength can be interpreted as similarity, reciprocity, compensation, homophily, synchrony, or mutual influence, depending on design and theoretical concerns.

Standard Dyad

In this case, each person is linked to one and only one other person. When members are distinguishable, e.g., mother and child, the correlation between those two scores is a measure of the strength of linkage. When dyad members are indistinguishable, the measure of the strength of nonindependence for quantities is the intraclass correlation (Kenny, Kashy, & Cook, 2006). When members are distinguishable, the standard Pearson product-moment correlations can be used for quantities. As discussed in Selig, McNamara, Card, and Little (chapter 9), pairwise or double entry measures of nonindependence are also possible.

The theoretical meaning of that linkage measure depends very much on the variables measured. It might measure reciprocity, similarity, complementarity, or a measure of rapport.

Group

With group data, the measurements can be at different levels. Considered in this section are individual, dyadic, and triadic measures in groups.

Individual. An example of this case is the gender of children in a classroom (Card, Hodges, Little, & Hawley, 2005). The measurement of strength of linkage in this case would be measured in much the same way as that for the standard dyadic design. When members are distinguishable, as in the case of family of mother, father, and child, and the measure is a quantity, the covariances between the three scores would be computed. When members are indistinguishable, some form of the intraclass correlation can be used. Pairwise measures are also possible (Gonzalez & Griffin, 2001).

Cillessen and Borch (chapter 4) studied cliques which are groups that are overlapping. So far as I know, there is no way to measure linkage for this case. The measure developed by Kenny and Judd (1996) can be used, but it is less than optimal because it is likely not statistically optimal. Moreover, probably it should be allowed for the fact that two persons who are in two cliques together are more similar than two persons who are in just one clique together.

Dyad. If measurement is at the dyad level, then a person would rate or interact with each other person in the group. Many of the papers in this volume (Branje et al., chapter 12; Cook, chapter 3; Malloy and Cillessen, chapter 10; Card, Little, & Selig, chapter 11; Zijlstra et al., chapter 15) have this structure. Note that when unit of measurement is not the individual, the linkage structure becomes complex.

For such data, the Social Relations Model (Kenny & La Voie, 1984) can be used for such data. As an example if there was a measure of the wife's commitment to her husband, within the Social Relations Model, the wife would be called an actor and the husband the partner. There are potentially five types of linkage: two scores from the same group, two from the same actor, two with the same partner, actor–partner covariance, and one from the same interaction (e.g., mother with father and father with mother) dyadic covariance.

Triad. Bond and Cross (chapter 16) have considered the issue of measurement of linkage for triadic data. There are 30 different types of linkage for this type of design. I refer the reader to Bond, Horn, and Kenny (1997) for a discussion of these different types of linkage.

Network

For network linkage there is a group of persons, some of whom are linked and some are not. Somewhat surprisingly, there has not been much consideration of the measurement of this correlation. There has been concern for what has been called *network autocorrelation*. Kenny and Judd (1996) did develop a very general method to estimate the strength of linkage, or what they call nonindependence. However, that approach does not provide statistical optimal estimates. The measurement of strength of linkage for networks is an important problem that requires serious attention. Leenders (1997) suggested embedding the estimation within an approach for the estimation of spatial autocorrelation models. Another idea would be to use Generalized Estimation Equations or GEE (Liang & Zeger, 1986) to measure network autocorrelation.

Within a network, two members may be indirectly linked. For instance, person i and k need not be linked, but i is linked to j and j is linked to k. Perhaps linkage should not be conceptualized as a correlation, but rather as a feedback loop, which has been labeled as a model of endogenous feedback (Erbring & Young, 1979).

One strategy for measuring linkage is to change W into a structure for which there are conventional structures to study linkage. Sometimes investigators treat members of a network as pairs of dyads (Kenny & Kashy, 1994) which is essentially the strategy used by Laursen, Popp, Burk, Kerr, and Stattin (chapter 2). Much more commonly, they are divided into subgroups (Templin, chapter 13).

A General Solution

It would be desirable if there was a computer program that would do the following: It would prompt the user for the linkage structure. Then the program would provide the strength of those linkages. Either the program would develop specialized measures of strength of linkage for certain designs (e.g., the intraclass for the standard dyad designs with indistinguishable members) or even more desirable some general all-purpose algorithm could be developed. Ideally, linkage could be treated either as a correlation or as a causal path.

MEASUREMENT OF CAUSAL EFFECTS IN RELATIONSHIPS

Here I consider measuring the effect of a fixed variable or random variable on another random variable with relationship data. The causal variable is denoted as X and the outcome as Y. Considered first is the causal effect of linkage: Are there differences between linked and unlinked persons? I then consider the measurement of causal relationships for a standard dyadic and group designs. Discussion of networks is considered when I consider over-time data.

Linkage as the Cause

In essence for this case, the cause or X is W, the linkage structure. It may be the case that some of the partners are not measured. I consider two aspects of this design: individual and network.

Individual. Consider the question of whether married people are happier than unmarried people. For such a study, both marriage partners need not be measured. Only one needs to be measured, as long as that one is sampled randomly. If married are compared to unmarried, it can be seen if linked partners have a different score from unlinked partners.

Network. Here I treat as the causal variable some measure of the linkage structure and determine if this variable relates to outcome variables. Among the possible network variables are: Persons who have no links, commonly called *isolates*, are compared to those who have more links; persons with more links are compared to those with no links. As discussed by Cillessen and Borch (chapter 4), there are other ways to measure the importance of a person in a network, i.e., centrality, besides the number of links. It should be noted that the construct of social support essentially compares those who have more links to those who have fewer ties.

In this volume, there are two chapters that perform such an analysis. Kindermann (chapter 14) examines those who have more links in their social groups versus those who have fewer links. Additionally, Cillessen and Borch (chapter 4) examine those who are in cliques and those who are not.

Standard Dyad

Most of the work on examining causal effects and relationships has focused on this design. Three major models have been proposed: Actor–Partner Interdependence Model, the Mutual Influence Model, and the Common Fate Model. In terms of the published literature, the most popular model is the Actor–Partner Interdependence Model, the model that is first considered here.

Actor–Partner Interdependence Model (APIM). A basic model for this case where there is a fixed variable X and a random variable Y is the Actor–Partner Interdependence Model or APIM. This model is presented by Sadler and Woody (chapter 7), Selig et al. (chapter 9), and Laursen et al. (chapter 2) and is described in more detail in Kenny et al. (2006). In this model, a person's score is influenced by not only his or her X, but by his partner's X. The fact that one's Y is influenced by partner's X is a key idea in the study of relationships. When dyad members are distinguishable, there are two partner effects; for heterosexual married couples, there is one from the wife to the husband and from the wife to the partner. A partner effect can be viewed as a measure of influence, but it should be realized that influence might sometimes not mean that the person is being controlled by the partner but rather the person is being responsive to his or her partner. If the mother's happiness is affected by her child's academic performance, it might be argued that the mother is not so much controlled by the child but rather the mother allows herself to respond to her child.

Mutual influence model. Sadler and Woody (chapter 7) also consider the mutual influence model. In this model, there are no partner effects, but rather each person's Y influences the other's Y. Sadler and Woody discuss what they consider the situations in which this model and the APIM are relatively more plausible. It would appear that this model is currently underutilized in the study of dyads.

Common fate model. This is one of the oldest models of dyadic and group data, being proposed as early as 1985 by Kenny and La Voie, and has been elaborated extensively by Gonzalez and Griffin (2001). In this model, the two scores of members of the dyad load on a latent variable and this latent variable causes Y_1 and Y_2. This model has not been used very much in the study of dyads.

Group

A key consideration in studying relationships in groups is the level of measurement of the variables. Considered are the individual and the dyad levels of measurement. Not considered is the triad level, as it is used rather infrequently.

Individual. With group data for which there is one measure per person, the current conventional approach is multilevel modeling. Within such an approach, X is treated as a fixed level-one variable. To measure group effects, the mean of X in the model is a level-two or group-level factor. The level-one X variable can either be grand mean centered or centered using the group mean.

An alternative model is the APIM. For group data, the partner effect would be defined as the mean of all others in the group besides the participant. For more details, the reader can consult Kenny, Mannetti, Pierro, Livi, and Kashy (2002).

The common fate model has also been proposed for group data (Gonzalez & Griffin, 2001). In this model, there is a random group-level variable for X that causes a random group-level variable for Y. Both standard multilevel and the APIM treat the group or partner effect as fixed.

Dyad. With a dyad-level group variable, each person rates or interacts each other person in the group. The causal variable X can be treated as either fixed or random. If treated as fixed, X is added to the model which includes group, actor, partner, and relationship effects (Snijders & Kenny, 1999). As in any multilevel model, there would be two pieces, fixed and random. In this case the random piece is very complicated.

If X is treated as a random variable, then there are four components for X: group, actor, partner, and relationship. Seven different Social Relations Model bivariate relationships can be computed: group–group, actor–actor, actor–partner, partner–actor, partner–partner, relationship intrapersonal and relationship interpersonal (Kenny et al., 2006). It is this potential plethora of possible relationships that concerns Cook (chapter 3).

MODELS OF CHANGE

Change is a topic that fills entire books and its study requires not a few sentences but a whole lifetime of study. One way of conceptualizing change is to separate models that emphasize randomness, what are called *stochastic models*, and models that emphasize change that is systematic with respect to time or what are called *deterministic models*. Although any reasonable model contains both deterministic and stochastic processes, it nonetheless helps to consider whether the major emphasis of the model is deterministic or stochastic.

Regardless of whether the model is stochastic or deterministic, over-time models contain assumptions that certain parameters do not change over time. These assumptions, often called *stationarity assumptions*, require close attention.

Stochastic Models

In a stochastic model, as a variable moves through time it has added to it a random component. The classic stochastic model is a first-order autoregressive model, a model that is used in Ferrer and Widaman (chapter 6). Basically, in this model the current value equals the past value times a coefficient, called an *autoregressive* or *stability coefficient*, plus a random error. The covariance resulting from such a structure is called a *simplex* (Humphreys, 1960) and it has the structure that covariances between adjacent time points tend to be larger than covariances between time points separated farther in time. Returning to the simplex model, one can also allow for error variance at each time and the resulting covariance matrix is called a *quasisimplex* (Humphreys, 1960). Second-order models in which the current value is determined by the previous two values are discussed in Ferrer and Widaman (chapter 6).

A special case of the simplex model is a model in which the autoregressive coefficient is one and the amount of error variance that is added at each time is the same. The resulting covariance structure is one in which all of the lagged covariances are the same value and all the variances are the same, a structure called *compound symmetry*. Such a structure is consistent with the view that the construct is a trait and it is the structure presumed by a repeated measures analysis of variance. While theoretically plausible, such structures are rarely encountered with real data.

The trait model and the quasi-simplex model can be combined in a trait-state-error model or what has been called the STARTS model (Kenny & Zautra, 2001). For such a model, correlations get weaker as the lag length increases. However, at long lags the correlations asymptote above zero which reflects trait variance. For instance, in Cillessen and Borch (chapter 4), the correlations in Table 4.1 exhibit this structure. However, successfully fitting these models can be quite difficult (Cole, Martin, & Steiger, 2005).

Popular in time-series modeling are moving average models. In this model, the current score can be viewed as the sum of random time series. When researchers compute differences (time t minus time $t - 1$) in a time-series analysis, a moving average structure usually results.

Deterministic Models

Before beginning a discussion of these models, an issue raised by Kashy and Donnellan (chapter 8) requires some discussion: the measurement of time. Typically, in developmental research the time measured is defined by the clock at the time of measurement. So if, as in Cillessen and Borch (chapter 4), children at schools are measured each year, then the different times might be denoted as one, two, three, and so on. There are, however, alternatives in the measurement of time. The clock can be set differently for each individual. One obvious choice is to measure time for each person from the time of birth and so time becomes age. Alternatively, time could start when the child entered school or entered college.

Even when chronological time is used, there is a choice as to how to define time zero. Very often the convention is to set the first point of measurement at time zero. However, there are alternatives. One idea is to set the middle time point as time zero and in that way, the intercept approximates the mean of the sample. Alternatively for studies of interventions, time zero might be better defined as the last point in time.

Finally, time need not be linear. Following work by Fraley and Roberts (2005) time goes slowly for the young and speeds up for older people in the sense that there is more change when people are younger than when they are older. A measure of exponential time (Kenny et al., 2004) or some alternative function is possible.

In this section, I discuss only growth-curve models which are the most popular form of deterministic model. I defer to a later section the discussion of other deterministic models.

By far the most common deterministic model is what has come to be called a *growth-curve model*. There is a rather extensive discussion of such models in Kashy and Donnellan (chapter 8) and in Cillessen and Borch (chapter 4). In its simplest form, a growth-curve model postulates a linear relationship between time, however scaled, and the outcome variable. For each person, a slope and intercept parameter can be estimated. At a bare minimum three waves of measurement are needed and more waves are desirable. These parameters are both latent variables which have both a mean and covariance. It is possible to also estimate the correlation between the slope and the intercept. If there are causal variables (e.g., gender), the effect of these variables on both the slope and intercept parameters can be estimated.

I should note that the trait model, discussed in the prior section on stochastic models, can be viewed as special case of a growth-curve model. It is a model in which there is variance in the intercept parameter, but no variance in the slope parameter.

As is nicely shown in Kashy and Donnellan (chapter 8), growth-curve models can be estimated by structural equation modeling and multilevel modeling. Moreover, it is possible to blend autoregressive and growth-curve models (Curran & Bollen, 2001). A generalization of the growth-curve model is the Latent Difference Score model or LDS model which is reviewed by Ram and Pederson (chapter 5). The linear growth-curve model is a special case of the LDS model.

Summary

In this brief section, we divided over-time models into two types. Historically, the older type of model is a stochastic model, the first-order autoregressive being the most common. Of late, there is much more interest in deterministic models, most notably growth-curve models.

For each type of model there are many variants. Moreover, for each type of model, we can consider the variable that is changing to be a latent, not measured variable. Once latent variables are introduced, we need to then model the structure of change in the errors of measurement.

THE INTEGRATION OF RELATIONSHIP
AND CHANGE MODELS

We have finally come to the defining topic of this volume: the combining of relationship and over-time models. Consider first the case of the unchanging W and then a changing W. In both cases, what is presented is more an outline of possibilities and an agenda for future research. So far as I know, definitive and general solutions are not available for all of these questions.

Unchanging W

Most of the chapters in this book consider models of change, but no change in W. For family relationships, such an assumption makes sense. However, for voluntary relationships like friendship, it does not. I first consider chapters that examine the standard dyadic design and then consider groups (i.e., families).

Standard dyadic design. As examples, Kashy and Donnellan (chapter 8) examine changes in conflict in the mother–adolescent dyads, and Ferrer and Widaman (chapter 6) examine changes in negative affect in heterosexual couples.

A key feature, emphasized in several papers, is the need to model cross-person change. That is, the changes in one person are a function of not only that person, but a function of characteristics of the other person. For instance, in Ferrer and Widaman (chapter 6), there is some indication that prior negative affect determines one's own current negative affect as well as the current negative affect of one's partner. These cross-person effects have been called *partner effects*.

In other models, dyadic effects are modeled by correlations between the two persons' change parameters. For instance, Kashy and Donnellan (chapter 8) find a correlation of .39 between mother's and adolescent's growth curves and so if the mother is experiencing diminishing conflict in her relationship with the child, a negative growth curve, her child might also be experiencing the same.

Ram and Pederson (chapter 5) discuss three over-time data analytic methods for the standard dyadic design. These methods are LDS analysis, coupled linear oscillators, and dynamic factor analysis, the latter technique is extensively reviewed by Ferrer and Widaman (chapter 6). All of these techniques allow for the alteration of one person's trajectory to mirror the other person's trajectory. For instance, coupled linear oscillators can be viewed as springs that are attached. Other techniques that are possible are APIM extended to longitudinal data, crossspectral analysis, and dynamic systems (Kenny et al., 2006). For the longitudinal APIM, it is possible to measure individual differences in actor and partner effects and determine their correlation across the two dyad members.

One potential advantage of over-time analyses is the possibility of both an ideographic analysis and a nomothetic analysis. That is, the analysis can be conducted separately for each dyad (an ideographic analysis), and then results can be combined across the different dyads (a nomothetic analysis).

Group design with dyadic data. Both Branje et al. (chapter 12) and Cook (chapter 3) consider the difficult problem of examining data from family members in which there are multiple components of change. If a Social Relations Model decomposition is performed and relationships over time are measured, there are a total of seven covariances: group–group, actor–actor, actor–partner, partner–actor, partner–partner, relationship–relationship, and relationship–relationship'. (The symbol ' means the transpose and so for mother–child, the effect would be how the mother sees the child at time 1 with how the child sees the mother at time 2.) The group–group, actor–actor, partner–partner, and relationship–relationship can be viewed as standard stabilities (the relationship of a variable with itself) whereas actor–partner, partner–actor, and relationship–relationship' can be viewed as cross-person stabilities (the relationship across time and person). Note that it might be possible for some effects to change in one way and other effects to change in a different way. For instance, the mean might show a correlational structure that is more trait-like (i.e., very high stabilities) and the relationship may act more state-like (i.e., low stabilities).

Branje et al. (chapter 12) consider the complicated question of testing the potential association between variables measured for four different components: group, actor, partner, and relationship.

Changing *W*

Models of relationships become much more interesting, but much more complicated, when *W* changes over time. Unfortunately, very little is currently known about this most important case. Considered in this section are experimental changes in *W*, changes in dyad linkages, and changes in network linkages.

Experimental changes in W. An experimental researcher can vary group composition over time. If *W* is changed by the experimenter, then it is known that neither *X* or *Y* caused the change in *W*. The two most common types of planned changes in groups are the generations design and the rotation design. In a rotation design, persons are placed in different groups with different people. For instance, the design has been used to study whether someone is a leader in one group, or if he or she is a leader in another group (Zaccaro, Foti, & Kenny, 1991). Rotation designs are useful if there is interest in testing the stability of individual differences and relationship across groups. The co-actor model discussed in Bond and Cross (chapter 16) can be viewed as version of a rotation design. Imagine that a researcher observes children interacting in groups, whose composition is continually changing. However, if children form groups in nonrandom ways, then it cannot be safely assumed that changes in W are independent of Y.

In the generations design, members enter and leave groups (e.g, Jacobs & Campbell, 1961). Such a design would be useful in the study of the socialization of newcomers into the group. The design can be used to track changes in the group effect.

Dyads. In this case at time 1, all persons are in a relationship and at time 2 some of the people remain in the relationship and others are no longer in that relationship. The prototypical study is longitudinal study of marriage in which at the second wave, some of the couples have broken up. Ideally, there would be measurements Y at time 2 for those people who are no longer in the relationship. However, some variables may no longer be meaningful if the dyad relationship no longer exists.

One analysis to consider is to use the time 1 data to predict the dissolution of the relationship. The data from both persons in the dyad should be used to predict breakup. For distinguishable dyads (e.g., husbands and wives), one strategy is to use the average and the difference as predictors. If the difference is needed in the prediction equation, then that would imply that one of the persons is more influential in determining the breakup. Either a logistic analysis or some sort of event history analysis can be performed if there is a measurement of how long they had been in their relationship at time 1.

Another analysis to consider is to perform an APIM and treat breakup as a moderator. Presumably partner effects would be larger for those who remained in a relationship than for those whose relationship ended.

Network. If members of a social network are measured at two time points, there is a linkage structure at time one or W_1 and at time two or W_2. There will be an issue that some members of the network are not measured at each time and that some people are no longer a member of the network. Considered is an individual-level variable (e.g., smoking behavior), denoted as Y. Following the chapters by Kindermann (chapter 14) and Laursen et al. (chapter 2), three types of effects can be distinguished: Selection: If persons A and B are not linked at time 1, they are much more likely to become linked at time 2, if they are similar on X or Y. Socialization: If persons A and B are linked at time 1, person A's score on Y affects person B's score on Y

and vice versa. Alternatively, socialization can be measured as cross-variable influence: X_1 affects Y_2 and perhaps Y_1 affects X_2. Buffering: If persons A and B are linked at time 1 and are very similar on X or Y, then they are more likely to stay linked at time 2 than if they were different on X or Y. Note the fact that the two linked persons are more similar on Y at time 1 reflects all three of these processes. It is only by having over-time data that the three effects can be disentangled.

Complicating the measurement of the three effects is that when a relationship changes, the time when that link changes is unknown; ideally it would be desirable to know when the changes took place. Consider the influence parameter. If the relationship between A and B ends very near time 2, then there was considerable time for the two to influence one another; however, if the relationship ended very near time 1, then there was little or no time for the two people to influence one another. One reasonable plan would be to presume that if the relationship changes, it changes at the midpoint of the interval. Another idea would be to randomly assign people points of break up, redo the analysis several times, and then pool these different analyses. It should also be noted that both selection and buffering concern the effect of similarity on either obtaining a new link or retaining an old link. Perhaps the two can be combined into a single parameter.

Both Kindermann (chapter 14) and Laursen et al. (chapter 2) grappled valiantly with these difficult issues and developed strategies to measure these different effects. However, I am unaware of any strong consensus currently on exactly how to approach this problem. This would seem to be an important problem for methodologists to solve. Certainly the study of social influence in social networks requires such a breakthrough.

Summary

I have only sketched an outline of possibilities for the study of change in relationships. Complicating the problem is that relationships facilitate change, but also change alters relationships and may even end them.

CONCLUSION

This chapter, like the book, has a very ambitious goal: to outline general issues in the study of relationships and change. What I have done is a start and quite clearly there is much more to do. Although currently there is a pretty good understanding of how to handle dyad and group designs, network structures are not well understood.

One clear limitation of this chapter, but not so much the book, is that I focused on variables that are measured at the interval-level measurement.

Many important outcomes are measured at the nominal level of measurement, e.g., the perception of another person as a bully (Zijlstra et al., chapter 15). Fortunately, many computer programs no longer require that the outcome variable be at the interval level of measurement, making it easier to analyze nominal and ordinal outcomes.

One complicating issue deserves mention. Especially for network linkages, there might well be measurement error in the measurement of W. Most likely, there may be a tie between two people but that tie is not observed. Ideally, analytic techniques would take into account such measurement error, but doing so would not likely be easy.

I would hope that there would be a computer program that would prompt the user about the W matrix and how it changes over time. It would then ask about the variables in the data, their unit and level of measurement, whether they are fixed or random, and causal structure. Given this information, the program would ask about assumptions about change over time. With this information and perhaps other information, the computer program would estimate all of the effects of interest. It would seem that such a program is not too far over the horizon.

Methods for the analysis of group and dyad data are fairly well developed. However, the analysis of social network data, particularly when the outcomes are at the interval level of measurement appear not to be well developed. I echo the call of Kanfer and Tanaka (1993), who argued that they are needed to advance the understanding of network methods.

Additionally, I note the innovative use of mixture analysis to study subgroups, introduced by Templin (chapter 13). Mixture analysis might well be applied in other domains of relationships. For instance, mixture analysis might be used to separate couples in two groups, one in which the APIM partner effect is stronger from husband to wife than from wife to husband and the other for whom the partner effect is stronger from wife to husband.

I have a suggestion for those who are studying change in relationships. Typically, we think of variables as belonging to one person or the other in relationships. For instance, there is measure of the husband's marital satisfaction. It is a mistake to think of the variable as just the husband's. After all it is a measure of the husband's satisfaction with his marriage to his wife. Researchers who think relationships and groups are important need to stop thinking of variables in terms of people, but rather in terms of relationships (Bond & Kenny, 2002). Paradoxically, researchers need to realize that so-called "relational" measures may not be relational. For instance, a measure of "family functioning" that is made up of the sum of the perceptions of the family member may not reflect the functioning of the family, but rather the biases of individual family members.

Although I sincerely hope that readers will find this framework helpful, I would strongly discourage researchers from thinking that there is only one way to think about relationships and change. Having labored in both of these areas now for over 40 years, I have seen fads come and go in both of these areas. Researchers need to search for the method that best fits the question which they are asking. One size definitely will not fit all. However, the methods discussed in this book provide us with an opportunity to advance the understanding of change in relationships. I strongly urge researchers to try out these methods and if necessary extend them. If social and behavioral scientists are to understand how relationships change, they will need to apply the methods described in this volume.

If I could, I would like to conclude on a personal note. I have been studying these two topics for over 40 years. When my study began, there were not any multilevel or structural equation modeling computer programs. For dyads about the most complicated analysis was a repeated measures analysis of variance. Growth curve modeling as we now know it did not exist, although we had fitting of orthogonal polynomials. We had little or no idea how to analyze social network data. Thus, although the challenge that we face of combining the study of change with the study of relationship seems daunting, we have now a vast array of tools that are available and it is reasonable to expect that methodological and statistical tools will become even better. If researchers accept this challenge, we are likely to see a burst of energy and excitement in this area.

REFERENCES

Bond, C. F., Jr., Horn, E. M., & Kenny, D. A. (1997). A model for triadic relations. *Psychological Methods, 2*, 79-94.

Bond, C. F., Jr., & Kenny, D. A. (2002). The triangle of interpersonal models. *Journal of Personality and Social Psychology, 83*, 355-366.

Cairns, R. B., Perrin, J. E., & Cairns, B. D. (1985). Social structure and social cognition in early adolescence: Affiliative patterns. *Journal of Early Adolescence, 5*, 339-355.

Card, N. A., Hodges, E. V. E., Little, T. D., & Hawley, P. H. (2005). Gender effects in peer nominations for aggression and social status. *International Journal of Behavioral Development, 29*, 146-155.

Cliff, A. D., & Ord, J. K. (1973). *Spatial autocorrelation*. London: Pion Press.

Cole, D. S., Martin, N. M., & Steiger, J. H. (2005). Empirical and conceptual problems with longitudinal trait-state models: Support for a trait-state-occasion model. *Psychological Methods, 10*, 3-20.

Curran, P. J., & Bollen, K. A. (2001). The best of both worlds: Combining autoregressive and latent curve models. In A. Sayer & L. M. Collins (Eds.), *New methods for the analysis of change* (pp. 107-135). Washington, DC: American Psychological Association.

Erbring, L., & Young, A. (1979). Social structure: Contextual effects as endogenous feedback. *Sociological Methods and Research, 7*, 396-430.

Fraley, R. C., & Roberts, B. W. (2005). Patterns of continuity: A dynamic model for conceptualizing the stability of individual differences in psychological constructs across the life course. *Psychological Review, 112*, 60-74.

Gonzalez, R., & Griffin, D. W. (2001). A statistical framework for modeling homogeneity and interdependence in groups. In G. J. O. Fletcher & M. S. Clark (Eds.), *Blackwell handbook of social psychology: Interpersonal processes* (pp. 505-534). Malden, MA: Blackwell.

Humphreys, L. G. (1960). Investigations of the simplex. *Psychometrika, 25*, 313-323.

Jacobs, R. C., & Campbell, D. T. (1961). The perpetuation of an arbitrary tradition through several generations of a laboratory microculture. *Journal of Abnormal and Social Psychology, 62*, 649-658.

Kanfer, A., & Tanaka, J. S. (1993). Unraveling the web of personality judgments: The influence of social networks on personality assessment. *Journal of Personality, 61*, 711-738.

Kenny, D. A., Calsyn, R. J., Morse, G. A., Klinkenberg, W. D., Winter, J. P., & Trusty, M. L. (2004). Evaluation of treatment programs for persons with severe mental illness: Moderator and mediator effects. *Evaluation Review, 28*, 294-324.

Kenny, D. A., & Judd, C. M. (1996). A general procedure for the estimation of interdependence. *Psychological Bulletin, 119*, 138-148.

Kenny, D. A., & Kashy, D. A. (1994). Enhanced co-orientation in the perception of friends: A social relations analysis. *Journal of Personality and Social Psychology, 67*, 1024-1033.

Kenny, D. A., Kashy, D. A., & Cook, W. L. (2006). *The analysis of dyadic data.* New York: Guilford Press.

Kenny, D. A., & La Voie, L. (1984). Separating individual and group effects. *Journal of Personality and Social Psychology, 48*, 339-348.

Kenny, D. A., Mannetti, L., Pierro, A., Livi, S., & Kashy, D. A. (2002). The statistical analysis of data from small groups. *Journal of Personality and Social Psychology, 83*, 126-137.

Kenny, D. A., & Zautra, A. (2001). Trait-state models for longitudinal data. In A. Sayer & L. M. Collins (Eds.), *New methods for the analysis of change* (pp. 243-263). Washington, DC: American Psychological Association.

Latané, B., & L'Herrou, T. (1996). Spatial clustering in the conformity game: Dynamic social impact in electronic group. *Journal of Personality and Social Psychology, 70*, 1218-1230.

Leenders, R. Th. A. J. (1997). Longitudinal behavior of network structure and actor attributes, network structure, and their interdependence. In P. Doreian & F. N. Stockman (Eds.), *Evolution of social networks* (pp. 165-184). New York: Gordon and Breach.

Liang, K. Y., & Zeger, S. (1986). Longitudinal analysis using generalized linear models. *Biometrika, 73*, 13-22.

Snijders, T. A. B., & Kenny, D. A. (1999). The Social Relations Model for family data: A multilevel approach. *Personal Relationships, 6*, 471-486.

Veenstra, R., Lindenberg, S., Zijlstra, B. J. H., De Winter, A., Verhulst, F. C., & Ormel, J. (2007). The dyadic nature of bullying and victimization: Testing a dual perspective theory. *Child Development, 78*, 1843-1854.

Zaccaro, S. J., Foti, R. J., & Kenny, D. A. (1991). Self-monitoring and trait-based variance in leadership: An investigation of leader flexibility across multiple group situations. *Journal of Applied Psychology, 76*, 308-315.

Author Index

Price, J. M., 216, 240, 383, 385

Q

Quera, V., 360, 364

R

Rabiner, D. L., 245, 274
Rafaeli, E., 92, 103
Rafferty, Y., 354, 365
Raftery, A. E., 311, 322, 326, 332, 333
Rajaratnam, N., 238, 240
Ram, N., 5, 6, 8, 87–102, 105, 422, 423
Rawlins, W. K., 237, 243
Reese, H. W., 87, 103
Reis, H. T., 12, 36, 277, 308
Reise, S. P., 130, 137
Renshaw, P. D., 335, 367
Rhymer, R. M., 107, 135
Rice, R. E., 27, 36
Richard, F. D., 409
Richards, W. D., 27, 36, 338, 368
Richardson, S. A., 213, 214, 241
Riddle, M., 67, 83
Roach, M. A., 253, 276
Roberts, B. W., 139, 161, 421, 429
Robins, G. L., 13, 27, 37, 311, 333
Rodkin, P. C., 62, 63, 67, 83, 84, 369, 386
Rogosch, F. A., 238, 243
Romero, P. A., 254, 273
Rosenberg, A., 220, 237, 241
Ross, H., 275
Ross, H. S., 15, 36, 40, 60, 144, 162, 236, 243, 253, 275
Ross, L., 141, 162, 218, 234, 243
Ross, M., 40, 60, 144, 162, 253, 275
Rothbart, M., 218, 243

Rubin, D. B., 383, 385
Rubin, K. H., 61, 85, 256, 275, 336, 368
Rusbult, C. E., 278, 279, 284, 296, 304, 308
Rushton, J. P., 141, 162
Russell, A., 279, 308
Ryan, R. M., 355, 365

S

Sack, A., 74, 84
Sadalla, E. K., 280, 307
Sadler, P., 5, 6, 8, 22, 37, 139–160, 162, 163, 192, 206, 212, 255, 257, 275, 276, 418, 419
Sage, N. A., 360, 362, 368
Salovey, P., 218, 242
Sameroff, A. J., 60, 87, 105
Santos, A. J., 339, 368
Sarason, B. R., 302, 308
Sarason, I. G., 302, 308
Sarigiani, P. A., 236, 238, 240
Savitsky, K., 219, 220, 236, 241, 243
Sawalani, G. M., 199, 211, 260, 273
Sayer, A., 93, 103
Saylor, C. F., 285, 307
Sbarra, D.A., 108, 136
Scarlett, H. H., 238, 243
Scarpatti, S., 215, 242
Scheier, I. H., 97, 103
Schiefele, U., 346, 365
Schiff, H. M., 235, 240
Schmidt, J. A., 160, 163
Schmitz, B., 136
Schofield, J. W., 74, 85
Scholte, R. H. J., 40, 42, 45, 60, 274
Schrepferman, L., 368

Z

Subject Index

A

Actor effect
  Actor–Partner Interdependence
    Model, 20–24, 147, 206,
    208
  Mutual Influence Model, 151,
    153-156
  Social Relations Model, 41–43,
    45–57, 246–252, 254, 257,
    258, 261, 264–266, 268, 269,
    280–283, 285, 287–289, 292,
    293, 296, 301, 303, 396–
    401, 403, 407
Actor–Partner Interdependence Model,
  5, 13, 15, 20–25, 32, 39,
  49–52, 55, 147, 149, 158,
  159, 193, 198, 204–208, 210,
  255, 418, 419, 423–425, 427
Affiliation, 16, 31, 64, 153, 154,
  158, 320, 329, 330, 336,
  338, 339, 342, 345, 350,
  355, 358, 360, 361, 363
Antipathetic relationships, 2, 3, 271,
  363
APIM *see Actor–Partner*
  Interdependence Model
Assimilation, 217, 218, 223, 224,
  226, 233, 235, 236, 250,
  264, 288, 303
Assumed similarity, 218, 222, 226,
  228, 234, 235, 305
Asymmetric block design, 216, 221–
  223, 233
Attachment theory, 55, 58, 359

B

Biases in social perception, 141, 144,
  154, 159
Bidirectional feedback loop, 148, 152,
  158
Block design, 216, 221–223, 233,
  404–406
Blockmodel, 311, 312, 322

C

Clans, 67, 312, 314–318
Clique, 16, 18, 19, 61, 62, 64, 65,
  67, 68, 70, 72–81, 312, 314–
  318, 412, 413, 416, 418
Co-occurrence matrix, 342, 343
Common fate, 418, 419
Confirmatory factor analysis, 45,
  51, 56, 285–287, 324
Consensus, 63, 217, 223, 224, 226,
  233, 234, 236, 250, 254,
  264, 288, 293, 303, 339,
  340, 361, 426
Correlated measurement errors, 14,
  53, 144, 153, 288, 295, 296,
  298

D

Developmental contextualism, 88,
  90, 93, 102
Differential equations, 89, 90, 92–
  94, 96, 97, 101
Distinguishability, 13–15, 21–24, 27,
  140, 157, 158, 160, 166,
  167, 171–173, 187, 192, 193,
  257, 271, 412, 413, 415–
  418, 425